REPRESENTING THE WOMAN

Representing the Woman

Cinema and Psychoanalysis

Elizabeth Cowie

University of Minnesota Press
Minneapolis

First published 1997 by
MACMILLAN PRESS LTD

Published simultaneously in the United States 1997
by the University of Minnesota Press
111 Third Avenue South, Suite 290
Minneapolis, MN 55401-2520

Printed in Great Britain

Library of Congress Cataloging-in-Publication Data

A catalog record for this book is available from the Library of Congress

ISBN 0–8166–2912–9 (hc)
ISBN 0–8166–2913–7 (pb)

The University of Minnesota is an
equal-opportunity educator and employer

Contents

List of Plates

Fury
Katherine has just arrived to find Joe trapped in the burning jail.
Her horrifed gaze is alternated with low-angle shots of Joe at the
barred window, seen here in frame-stills from shots 1, 2, 3, 8 and 12
from the sequence. The sequence is discussed on page 110.

Plate 3

The Reckless Moment
Stills 1 and 2: Lucia goes downstairs after her row with Bea over
Ted Darby to take Tom's call from Germany. High and low-angle
travelling shots of the staircase recur in the film, as the camera penetrates the house and draws the characters through encounters of
crisis and conflict and apparent reconciliation. The second still
marks the absence of the father as it brings together in very deep
focus the family – Grandfather, son David, shirtless, Sybil the maid
in the far background, and Bea in foreground receiving the phone
from Lucia who has not told her husband about their row or its
cause.

In still 3 Donnelly is about to explain his blackmail demand to
Lucia. Still 4 shows the end of a complex travelling shot which
tracks back and around as Lucia leaves Bea in the scullery having
learnt that the letters could be harmful to her, passes Sybil in the
kitchen – who asks whether Mr Donnelly will stay to dinner – and
arrives back in the living room to find Donnelly chatting with her
father, looming large in foreground as the camera tracks back past
him. Donnelly here has been narrated into the family mise en scène
through the camera-movement.

Stills 5 and 6: While Lucia contrasts Donnelly's venal criminality
with her own family's values these shots set the scene for his transformation into husband, father and lover. At the drugstore Lucia
needs more change and runs to Donnelly for it, producing this
husband-and-wife scene in still 5. The following shot, still 6, shows
a pensive Donnelly just before he turns to buy a cigarette filter for
Lucia, whose heavy smoking he has already disapprovingly remarked upon. Stills 7 and 8: Lucia, crying, tends Donnelly's injuries
from the car crash and his struggle with his partner Nagle whom
he has killed to protect her. Donnelly, however, returning Bea's
letters to Lucia, urges her to go before the police arrive or else 'it
will all have been for nothing'.

Stills 9 and 10 are from the end of the film. As Lucia, still crying, comes downstairs to speak to Tom on the phone she learns from Bea that Donnelly, found, dying, has confessed to killing both Darby and Nagle. Lucia then tells Tom how much she loves him.

Plates 4 and 5

Morocco

Discussed in Chapter 7; the image in the frame-stills has been left at the slightly squarer aspect ratio of the original 35 mm print. In the stills from shots 8, 9, 13, 14, Tom Brown finds himself the object of a look. The two dolls in Amy's dressing-room are shown in shot 49, followed in shots 50–52 by a typically Sternbergian mise en scène in which Amy's studied masculinity contrasts with Lo Tinto's sexually ambiguous appearance in shot 62. The contrast is reversed is shot 90. Where Amy appears exquisitely feminine.

Stills from shots 83–87 show Amy taking the flower from the woman after she has kissed her, and turning and throwing it to Tom. The still from shot 101 shows Tom with the flower behind his ear as he enjoys her second song. Stills from shots 118–123 show the exchange of apples and money between Amy and Tom, overlooked by La Bessiere. The sequence ends with Tom's appreciation of the apple as well as the key he has received from Amy.

Plate 6 and 7

Blue Steel

Discussed on pp. 312–13. Stills 1–6 are from the opening credits-sequence, showing the homage to the hand-gun (stills 1 and 2), which is packed into a holster (still 3), worn, we learn, by Megan. Stills 3–6, showing Megan dressing for her graduation ceremony, continue the visual style of big close-ups on part-objects, now her body rather than a Smith & Wesson. Megan's satisfaction with her image in still 6 is given affirmation in still 7 when, returning home after graduation, two women turn to look back at her appreciatively. Stills 8–10 again show Megan dressing, matched shot for shot but now different: the uniform – stolen from her male colleague as she escapes from the hospital to hunt down Eugene – does not fit her, and the trainers contrast with her polished shoes in still 5.

Stills 11–15 are from a sequence of 25 shots in which Megan challenges the gunman in the supermarket. He treats her challenge as a joke, then turns to shoot her, but Megan fires first. Thrown back by the force of the bullet, his gun flies up out of his hand (still 14) and falls beside Eugene who slides it underneath him (still 16).

The stills from *Blue Steel* are reproduced here by courtesy of Vestron Pictures, Inc. The stills are reproduced in the aspect ratio of the 35 mm print, and correspond approximately to the image seen on video or television. The film was photographed for both theatrical and video release. For theatrical release the film would normally be projected in a wide-screen ratio, reducing the height of image and thereby cutting out about one-third of the visual information at the top and bottom of of the frame

Plate 8

Smooth Talk
Discussed on pp. 304–6. In still 1 Connie, just returned home, watches her parents and sister June playing a game of cards together. This contrasts with the preceding scene of Connie and Laura enviously watching the local youth meeting at a diner. Still 2 shows Connie and Laura at the diner; Connie is dancing, watched by a man we later learn is Arnold Friend. In still 3 Connie is being chatted-up by a boy, leaving Laura temporarily out in the cold. As Connie leaves with the boy, in still 4, she passes Arnold who says, 'I'm watching you'.

Stills 5–9 are taken from the final shots of the scene of Arnold's 'seduction' of Connie. Connie, terrified, has withdrawn into her home. The reverse-field shots through the door mark it as a threshold rather than a barrier, for Arnold uses verbal threats rather than physical violence to draw her out to him.

In still 10 mother and daughter are reconciled, but while they close the gap opened by the harsh words of their earlier row, Connie's tears of relief at being back with her family also mark her new and different separation from them.

The stills from *Smooth Talk* are reproduced with permission.

Acknowledgements

This book arises from work over a number of years during which I have benefitted from the help, encouragement and intellectual support of a large number of friends and colleagues, not all of whom I am able to mention here. An important catalyst for this book has been my work on the feminist journal *m/f*, which I co-founded with Parveen Adams and Rosalind Coward and later co-edited with Beverley Brown and Parveen Adams. Chapter 1 draws upon an essay 'Woman as Sign' which appeared in *m/f*, no. 1, 1978. Chapter 2 is a revised and abbreviated version of 'The Popular Film as a Progressive Text – a discussion of *Coma*' published in *m/f*, no. 3, 1979 and no. 4, 1980. Chapter 4 is a revised version of 'Fantasia' published in *m/f*, no. 9, 1984. These articles were all helped enormously by my co-editors. Part of the discussion of *Gertrud* in Chapter 6 was published in *The Oxford Literature Review*, vol. 8, nos 1–2, 1986. A version of the discussion of the drive in Chapter 5 appeared in *Jean Laplanche: Seduction, Translation and the Drives*, edited by John Fletcher and Martin Stanton, ICA, 1992.

The work of Stephen Heath has been a formative influence for this book, and I am also indebted to him for his warm support and meticulous editing in bringing it to publication. Its errors and inelegancies remain my own. I would also like to thank Ben Brewster, whose intellectual generosity has been invaluable. I have benefitted, too, from the work and friendship of Constance Penley, Jacqueline Rose, Slavoj Žižek and Joan Copjec. My thanks also go to Glenn Bowman, Celia Cowie, Anne Bloom, Anne Cottringer, Nancy Wood, Claire Buck, Laura Marcus, Steve Neale, John Fletcher, Caroline Rooney, and Julia Borossa. I should also like to thank Howard Booth for his research, Luke Thurston for his helpful insights and his invaluable work on the index, and the secretaries at Rutherford College, University of Kent, for their help in typing the manuscript. My thanks as well to Jim Styles and Spencer Scott at the Templeman Library, University of Kent, for their work in producing prints of the stills, and to Ken Giber printing the cover still from *Gertrud*.

ELIZABETH COWIE

Introduction: The Woman's Image – A Woman's Imaging

When Gertrud, suddenly noticing the picture behind her, exclaims, 'That's…that dream I had', her nightmare finds its echo in a vision both conventional and publically sanctioned. This scene from Carl Theodor Dreyer's *Gertrud* (1964) brings into focus the central concerns of this book: the representation of women and the figuring of feminine desire. At the same time *Gertrud* poses questions about film form and its theorisation which will also be addressed. The scene, shown in two frame-stills in plate 1, presents a series of references producing a complex montage within the frame. Earlier, Gertrud, when meeting with Erland in a park before going to his apartment to make love for the first time, had described to him her dream the night before in which '….I ran naked through the streets, pursued by hounds. I woke up when they caught me.' The next evening Gertrud is taken ill during her husband's speech at a banquet in celebration of the poet Lidman, Gertrud's former lover, which Erland is also attending. Gertrud is escorted to a nearby room where she is seated in front of a large picture before being joined by an old friend, Axel Nygren, who has come from Paris. They talk of the book on free will which Axel is writing. Gertrud refers to her father as 'a mournful fatalist. He taught us that everything in life was predestined. I remember you once said: to want is to choose.' And she affirms that she has sought to choose rather than believe in fate. Axel describes his studies in Paris, involving hypnosis, and work on 'psychosis, neurosis, dreams and symbols'. Gertrud says 'How I envy you', to which Axel replies 'Come and join us in Paris. You'll enjoy it.' 'I'm sure I would' she answers and looks towards Axel, and only now does she catch sight of the picture behind them. She turns and rises slightly in order to view it fully, while Axel turns and stands up so that he too can see this scene which the spectator has had cognisance of all along. The pose is held for a few seconds, as Gertrud says 'That's…that dream I had'.

The scene depicted in the picture appears to be a rendering of an oft-used theme from a story in Boccaccio's *The Decameron*, in which

1

a young man, scorned by the lady he loves, goes walking in some woods and sees a vision of a naked woman chased by hounds who is then slain by a horseman and devoured by his dogs. He learns from the horseman that her death is punishment for her cruelty in rejecting the love of the young rider, and that they are both condemned to eternally re-enact this punishment. The young man then arranges a magnificent banquet for his family and his loved one in the woods, so that they might also witness the vision, whereupon the lady, fearing a like fate, agrees to take the young man as her husband.[1]

The picture is therefore itself a quotation, a visual realisation of a scene from a story which also reiterates a classic paradigm of the conventions of representing women – naked and subject to, indeed here victim to, masculine desire. It figures Gertrud's dream but in a repetition that is now visual in contrast to her earlier words, while the themes of the tapestry are also the themes of Gertrud's own life and thus of the film which narrates her story. For Gertrud, too, is pursued and, despite their pleadings, will reject each of the three men she has loved. She does so not out of feminine capriciousness (an implicit motivation in Boccaccio's story) but because in their love there is no room for her as subject rather than simply object of desire. The film then sets aside the classic paradigm of representing the woman which the picture depicts; Gertrud suffers no fateful punishment. Instead, insisting on her demand for complete love, she will go to Paris to study, joining Axel in his work. The themes of fate and free will which she and Axel discuss are sharply contrasted to the picture's very different view of the fate of the wilful woman, while the role of symbols and dreams – later to be the object of her studies in Paris – is given uncanny emphasis by Gertrud's startled recognition of her own dream in the scene depicted.

It is of course a common practice and respectable literary convention to preface or introduce a book with a quotation. This rhetorical gesture may be apposite, or playfully ironic, it may be used to make a combative and oppositional point, or simply be illustrative. In any case the quotation will have at least a twofold role, on the one hand as a signifying statement in itself, and on the other hand as a referent, both to the larger text from which it is extracted, and to the author of that text and hence to a literary and intellectual tradition with which the text and author is associated or which it opposes or is excluded from. Frame-stills, however, can never play the same role as the literary quotation. This is not merely because they are pictorial rather than linguistic, for the visual representation which the film quotes here – the vivid picture portraying a naked woman in a wood, surrounded by baying hounds – is clearly a statement. Rather, a frame-still is excerpted from a series of images to which it relates and in relation to which it derives its signification. This series of images, furthermore, is only ever realised as a series when projected as moving images, constituting a movement in time and space which frame-stills can never figure. Moreover, a frame-still is partial, it presents only one level of filmic signification – the visual – whereas a film is composed of multiple levels – of sounds, music, dialogue and even written statements. Thus frame-stills must be accompanied – as here – by a description of what happens in the scene. Finally, film presents – if not uniquely, at least in an extreme form – the problem of the source of enunciation, of the subject of the statement, and hence the point of address of the spectator. For, lacking a grammatically marked narrating voice, the question arises of who and where the author of a film is. As a result, neither a film and its author nor an intellectual tradition are easily summoned by visually quoting from a film. It is this complexity of filmic representation which I will be addressing in this book.

Discussions of the representation of women in film have centred on the image of the woman as it is visually and narratively constructed, and there are, I suggest, three interrelated issues here. First, there is the issue, and political stake, of the images of women which arise from the social definition of women, that is from the way in which social discourses constitute the category of woman through which woman is then defined and hence recognised or interpellated. Second, there is the issue of the image as identity; this is twofold, on the one hand it can be seen as an external imposition, so that these social definitions penetrate or interpellate the woman as an image of her identity, socially defined – and which, recognised by the woman as other and as imposed, is also resisted. On the other hand there is the image as identity which is possessed and appropriated by the woman as social agent and psychical subject. But insofar as one is an image for oneself, one is also a divided subject, constituted, Lacan says, in that splitting which arises when the subject identifies with its image as other, taking that image as its own. As a result our image of ourselves always comes to us from outside ourselves, from the place of the other. The story of our identities is the negotiation of this otherness of ourselves. The construction of identity, of the subject, is not the effect of a set of contents of identification but of the process of identification as such. Nevertheless as a result particular contents become invested as material supports for this identity. The corollary of this is that the definitions and meanings produced by forms of representation are not simply external and objective, and thus available to rational reform. Social definitions are contingent – they can be changed and they have changed – but a change in the images alone may not change the form of psychical investment involved. The structural role of imaging for the subject must also be addressed.

Thirdly, there is the *desire* for the image. It is perhaps already clear that psychoanalysis has been central for the discussions which will be presented here; moreover, I will argue, it is through psychoanalysis that we can begin to understand our pleasure in and our desire for the image. The pleasure of representation lies not only in what is signified – a meaning – in the traditional, realist, sense, that is, a coming to know; it also lies in a coming to desire made possible by the scenario of desire which I come to participate in as I watch a film, view an image, or read a text. It is psychoanalysis which addresses the subject as the one who knows very well that the image is only an image, but who all the same takes it for real. This is the subject who misrecognises in Lacan's mirror phase as well as the subject who disavows.

Desire for the image is therefore always potentially double, it is both a desire for the image – to be or to have the image – which is a desire for oneself or for the other as image, as an imagined entity, and perhaps a coherent whole, but certainly a knowable and possessable self, or other. And it is a desire for imaging itself, not as simple visual stimulus to biological sensory motors, but as the desire for the process which constitutes the self. Visual and acoustic pleasure is thus closely bound to the pleasures of repetition, exemplified for both Freud and Lacan in the *fort-da* game played by Freud's grandson.[2] Hence what is also produced in representations is the very position of desire for the spectator. Here too is the pleasure of images as fantasy. In cinema, then, the availability of social definitions enables its narrative figures to be readable by a social group, while at the same time film offers up the pleasures and pains of identifications and perhaps attendent identities in so far as it founds itself on scopophilic, epistemophilic and auditory pleasures in its presentation of figures of desire.

All this is to say that there is a certain power in the image which exceeds its function as the mere construction of a definition. Whether they are images of motherhood or of pornography or whatever, we cannot necessarily accept or reject them simply through an act of conscious will. We will be moved by images in ways which we neither expect nor seek nor want. And it is through the images and narratives of representation that we can find ourselves spoken in a way which we take to be real, or wish to be true. However the demand by feminists – or by other groups – for images which are felt to be real and true can never be met in any absolute sense. For images are not already 'truthful', they become so only at the point at which they produce identification in the spectator-subject, when she or he 'finds' them true. The demand and desire for identity in the image as the right image at the same time raises the difficulties of difference, and especially the difference of the other's desire, and some of the fiercest debates within feminism have involved the issue of identity, its definition and its images, giving rise to disputes over lesbian versus heterosexual desire, the use of pornography, and the pleasures of sexual fantasy.

Understanding the role of recognition and identification is central to understanding the role and power of images. Identification does not involve a simple matching of self and image. What we are dealing with here is the desire for such images, so that through these images, narratives, etc. we come to know ourselves as we truly are, truly know ourselves to be, at the same time only discovering all this in the moment of reading, in the act of watching, the novel or film. Here again is the misrecognition of Lacan's mirror phase in which the child joyfully seizes its image as itself, and identifies with it, thus coming to exist as a subject but one which is thereby already a split subject, divided between the ideal mirror image which is at the same moment lost forever, the self who identifies with it, and the image, the ego-ideal, by which it might regain its identity as perfect and perfectly lovable. In this sense, therefore, we are our images.

It is here that the desire for realism arises, for that verisimilitude in our representations which Lyotard, following amongst others Brecht, so roundly condemns for what he calls its mission to address the subject as a unified centre of consciousness and knowledge and thereby to affirm the subject as a knowing subject.[3] The issue is not, however, to condemn realism as a system of deception, but to acknowledge its role in the construction of identity as

unified, and to recognise our relation to realism as a relation of
desire, a desire for that unified identity. Rachel M. Brownstein in
her book *Becoming a Heroine* pointed to the pleasure of literature for
women as offering just that, a unified identity and one which was
also idealised so that the 'heroine' is someone important and
special:

> What the female protagonist of a traditional novel seeks – what
> the plot moves her toward – is an achieved, finished identity, re-
> alised in conclusive union with herself-as-heroine. Her marriage
> or death at the end of the narrative signifies this union. When he
> continued *Pamela* past the wedding, Samuel Richardson made
> the point that the aim of the female protagonist of a novel is not a
> husband but a realised identity, which is only real, for Pamela,
> when all the neighbors and their servants acknowledge her as
> her husband's wife.[4]

What this example from Richardson also shows is that this identity
is not an essential and timeless feminine identity, but one which is
historically-specific and discursively constructed – the identity here
is Pamela's position as her husband's wife, a position in society –
and this is achieved not when she marries but when the status of
her marriage is recognised by others. Brownstein, however, is critical of the role of popular romance fiction for women for what she
sees as the 'misleading illusion of the self perfected through a resolution of the female destiny – by the idea of becoming a heroine'[5]
while at the same time she acknowledges her own pleasure in and
voracious consumption of such stories. Here again is the dilemma
of feminism as it is caught between the politics and pleasures of
positive, women-centred stories, and the difficulties of fantasy.
Brownstein's solution is the heroine-centred novel 'which proposes
a sophisticated version of the ideal of romance as the heroine comes
to transcendent closure, but that ideal is undercut as transcendence
and closure are characterised as romantic, proper to Art, not Life'.[6]
This solution is no solution at all, for it involves simply re-erecting
the reality principle against fantasy. A more complex view of
fantasy emerges in Lacan's recasting of Freud's reality principle as
the real. What is needed is not the re-assertion of the primacy of
reality but an exploration of the junctures and disjunctures between
fantasy and reality and the way in which our identity is constructed
– or broken – on the contradictions and difficulties of being desiring

subjects within the discourses of social relations. It is in our public, published forms of fantasy – of which cinema is one – that we play out, in the sense Freud gave to children's play, our relations of self and other, of desire and its repression, as well as the impossibility of desire.

This book explores these positions of pleasure and identity for both the feminine and masculine spectator in relation to the demands of feminist critiques and the desires of feminist theory. It begins with the debates in feminism concerning the politics of women's oppression and the role of images within this, which were my own starting point in the study of cinema. Two issues which emerged from these debates are the focus for this book. The first concerns the way in which we theorise representation, including filmic representation, in order to pose questions and demands in relation to the representation of women. The second concerns the theorisation of the subject as a subject of sexual difference and as the addressee and subject for these representations – the spectator in fact.

The 1960s and 1970s had seen the introduction to the English-speaking world of a number of new theories from France which transformed the theoretical basis for our understanding of representation. First and foremost was the role of structuralism and structural linguistics. The structural understanding of language proposed in the work Ferdinand de Saussure and Charles Sanders Pierce opened up the study of signs in general, and not only linguistic signs, as the study of semiotics or semiology. The anthropologist Claude Lévi-Strauss drew upon Saussure's theories to develop a structural study of kinship relations and of myth. Roland Barthes set out the beginnings of a visual semiotics as well as a structural study of narrative. A new attention to psychoanalysis emerged as the result of the radical re-thinking and re-presentation of Freud's theories by Jacques Lacan.[7] The figure of Louis Althusser stood over much of this work, as the major re-interpreter not only of Marx's economic theory, but also of his theory of ideology which Althusser, using both the work of Gramsci and Lacan, transformed with his notion of the interpellation of the subject in ideology. This work was taken up by a new generation of writers on film in the French journals *Cahiers du Cinéma* and *Cinéthique* and translated into English by the British journal *Screen*, where these ideas were developed and extended. At the centre of many of these debates was the issue of the theory of the subject. For Lacan the subject is constituted through language, it is the subject of speech and subject to that order, but Lacan, drawing upon Saussure's concept of the arbitrary nature of the linguistic sign, also argues that there can be no final securing of language and hence no securing of the subject.

It is because psychoanalysis places sexual difference as a central mechanism – as well as problem – in the construction of the human subject that feminists in Britain first turned to it for a theoretical understanding of femininity. However, for psychoanalysis the difference of sexuality is produced through our relation to ourselves and to others as having or not having a penis. The phallus, as the symbol of the penis, is the signifier of lack, of difference. Moreover for Lacan, accession to the symbolic is through the acceptance of the law prohibiting incest, the Name-of-the-Father as Lacan designates it, a law of the fathers, a patriarchal law. Psychoanalysis seemed, therefore, to be a theory of the dominant culture and it now became a means to demonstrate the way in which cinema, too, is patriarchal, and hence it became a basis for a theorising of cinema's oppressive representation of women. This approach assumes that through psychoanalysis we can understand the construction of the subject in patriarchy, and hence be in a position to change it. But, at its most radical, this implies the abolition of the function of the phallus as privileged signifier in the construction of the subject and hence also the overthrow of the unconscious of our time – which is difficult to imagine. Or, less radically, it seemed that it might be possible to discover an alternative understanding from within psychoanalytic theory of the construction of sexual difference and thereby to displace the phallus as the privileged signifier.

Juliet Mitchell's conclusion in her important study *Psychoanalysis and Feminism* opened this debate.[8] However, notwithstanding the tremendous political importance of her arguments that women's position, our oppression, is not immutable, Mitchell's suggestion – that change may be wrought 'through some other expression of the entry into culture' than the phallus and the exchange of women as formulated by Lévi-Strauss – has not been productive. Indeed, it has led to attempts to find a substitute on the body of the woman which can stand instead of the phallus as guarantor of culture, or at least of the woman's sexuality, in a way that has mirrored the debates within psychoanalysis in the 1920s and 1930s on the nature of femininity.[9]

While psychoanalysis is seen as patriarchal in its theory of the phallus as the privileged signifier it is also this very psychoanalysis which is used to deconstruct, to expose, the workings of patriarchy. Psychoanalysis has had a two-fold role: on the one hand feminists have excoriated it as a theory of the institution of patriarchy at the level of the psychical, and on the other hand it has been used critically to question those psychical structures. Psychoanalysis is here both a normative system involved in discursively constructing subjects *and* a metatheory which explains this normative system. The result has been for many of us a highly ambivalent relation to psychoanlysis. Mary Ann Doane, for example, has commented that her own relation to psychoanalysis

> might be described as one of attraction-repulsion. Psychoanalysis is clearly the most powerful theory of the psyche and subjectivity we have and it is impossible to ignore its influence. On the other hand, its epistemological quandaries are frequently linked with a problematic inscription of sexual difference which makes psychoanalysis one of the most blatantly symptomatic of cultural productions.[10]

Psychoanalysis has given us the most cogent and compelling description and theory of women's sexuality and desire only in order, it often seems, to enclose these in normative definitions of a proper femininity which is the other to a prior masculine. More precisely, it is often assumed that within psychoanalysis masculinity has been fully described while femininity has been an also-ran, its theorisation incomplete. That this crisis or gap in psychoanalysis parallels the cultural challenge of feminism in the twentieth century is not a coincidence, for psychoanalysis came into existence because of the ills of women, the women hysterics of Freud's early work. The new discourses of medicine and of health together with the scientific optimism about the curability of disease which arose during the nineteenth century meant that these women's ills were allowed a hearing and, with Freud, were finally heard. At the same time the discourses of democracy and egalitarianism and of individual rights, which were coming to hold sway in the world of politics, the world of men, came into conflict with the assumptions of feminine inferiority, and with the maintenance of women's social and legal and political status as that of virtual slave without effective rights. Psychoanalysis undertook not the shoring-up of patriarchy, but the treatment of its victims, both men and women. Nevertheless, despite its origins, it has often seemed that it has been the clamorous voices of men and the dilemmas of masculinity which found the most sustained understanding. The institution of positions of sexual difference was shown to be fundamental for the construction of the human subject, but normative assumptions continued to obscure the processes of this, for the biology of motherhood seemed incontrovertible, and hence it was assumed that it must have a complementary psychology in the woman.[11] The relativising of this biological essence – for example through the use of contraception which has meant that for the most part women's lives can be lived without reference to the biological consequences of sexual relations – has enabled us to see as normative the assumptions of a psychological destiny of femininity as motherhood.

For Freud, however, as Mitchell emphasised in an interview in 1982, the psyche never directly reflected either the biological or the social. Nevertheless the nature of the relationship between the biological, the social and the psychical remains a problem, nowhere more so than in relation to Freud's theory of the castration complex where, as Mitchell goes on to note:

> In this instance we are talking about the relationship father, Name-of-the-father; penis, phallus. It is one thing to say the one does not reflect the other – with that I completely agree – it is another to say that there is no relationship between them, and that I doubt.[12]

One view of this relationship is suggested by Mitchell in her introduction to the collection of essays by Lacan and other members of the *École Freudienne* where she describes the founding role of castration insofar as it is understood that

> The phallus – with its status as potentially absent – comes to stand in for the necessarily *missing* object of desire at the level of sexual division. If this is so, the Oedipus complex can no longer be a static myth that reflects the real situation of father, mother and child, it becomes a structure revolving around the question of where a person can be placed in relation to his or her desire. That 'where' is determined by the castration complex.[13]

If this is the case then, too, a restructuring of the entry into human subjectivity is no longer necessary in as much as the specific conditions of the social oppression of women are not instituted psychically – lack and its concomitant splitting of the subject define the human condition as such and as a result being a man, having 'the phallus', will help not a whit. Instead, Mitchell concludes, for Lacan,

> To be human is to be subjected to a law which decentres and divides: sexuality is created in a division, the subject is split; but an ideological world conceals this from the conscious subject who is supposed to feel whole and certain of a sexual identity. Psychoanalysis should aim at a destruction of this concealment and at a reconstruction of the subject's construction in all its splits. This may be an accurate theory, it is certainly a precarious project.[14]

A new problem arises here, however, insofar as psychoanalysis is placed outside ideology, and thus marshalled as a weapon against ideology. Moreover the very way in which psychoanalysis shows how the subject is fundamentally split in its emergence as a subject also shows why the ideal of unity, of wholeness, is equally fundamental. This is not an ideologically imposed fiction, but the inevitable corollary of splitting. Nor can it be replaced by another ideal, of the precariously split subject. Nevertheless the forms in which this appears socially are not essential or immutable but on the contrary demand analysis and political intervention.

In truth, therefore, it is not possible to produce a singular theory of femininity and masculinity; psychoanalysis cannot provide a metatheory of human sexuality as a fixed relation – Lacan's important insight is that there is no sexual relation. What passes for such a relation is the symptom, *la femme*, and correlatively, *l'homme*. This is not imprinted genetically, but constructed anew although no doubt constructed upon historical – and familial – legacies; the issue is not a 'truth' of sexual difference but the 'clothing' given to it within human social relations. The material of this 'clothing' is fantasy.

This book presents a deconstruction of certain arguments within psychoanalytic film theory and within feminism and it challenges the assumption that the construction of woman, of her image, of her desire, is always for the masculine spectator. This cannot, however, lead to discovering or erecting the woman as subject for herself, for this reintroduces the essentialist subject so effectively and necessarily ejected by structuralist and post-structuralist theory. Chapter 1 reviews the role of structuralist theories of language and the work of Lévi-Strauss on kinship for feminist arguments in order to show that the importance of Lévi-Strauss's thesis is not, primarily, as a theory of patriarchy, but as a way of understanding the institution and construction of social definitions – in social practices such as kinship and in representation. Drawing upon his related arguments concerning myth, the issues of exchange and the representation of women are explored through the example of the films of Howard Hawks in order to show the ways in which the filmic processes of representation produce meanings.

The discussion in Chapter 2 of *Coma* (Michael Crichton, 1978) takes up the view of filmic representation developed in Chapter 1 in order to address the issue of 'positive' images of women, and specifically the notion of a positive woman protagonist. The demand for such positive images, both to challenge existing, negative definitions and as progressive figures for identification, has been a central element in feminism. In *Coma*, however, the narration on the one hand constructs Susan Wheeler as the film's central actant and active protagonist in relation to the film's events, while on the other hand she is also the object of strategies of narrative suspense within the film which undermine her position as active. As a result not only is identification with the narrative position of Susan shown to arise across gender definitions, but also Susan is shown to be not always or only an active protagonist.

Identification is not, however, a mere narrative device which positions the spectator in relation to the unfolding of knowledge with regard to the story's enigma. It is also part of the pleasure of cinema, and of the way in which we are moved by films. Consequently, as suggested earlier in this introduction, the issues of identity and identification are not so straightforward. The interrelationship of the institution of identity in and for the human subject as it is understood by psychoanalysis, as well as the production of systems – and pleasures – of identification in filmic representations, is the concern of Chapter 3. Psychoanalysis cannot, however, offer cinema a ready-made theory of its identifications, and here the book takes issue with Christian Metz's claim that the cinema is an 'imaginary signifier'.[15] 'Identification' in fact implies several distinct psychical and cinematic processes but in each case, it is argued, what is involved is the taking up of a position by the subject who is also a subject of desire. It is, therefore, also closely bound up with fantasy, with that mise en scène of desire whereby the subject imagines a scenario through which he or she represents a wish, and hence which also represents a place for the subject in which his or her wish is obtained so that the subject identifies with this place. Drawing upon Freud's discussion of public forms of fantasy in 'Creative Writers and Daydreaming', Chapter 4 argues that fantasy can be seen to be involved in both narrative structures and aesthetic devices in films, as well as being a scene of conscious and unconscious desires. This approach, moreover, introduces the woman's desire into the picture, and the issue of the sexual difference of desire is posed.

Fantasy is also closely involved with the work of disavowal, while disavowal, as the process giving rise to fetishism, has been a central term for theories of representation as both ideological – in Barthes's terms – and as the psychical mechanism in the service of the masculine subject who seeks to deny the reality of the difference of the woman, namely, her 'castration'. These issues are the concern of Chapter 5 which examines the place of scopophilia, voyeurism and fetishism in Freud's theory of the drives and seeks to place both fantasy and Lacan's concept of the *objet petit a* in relation to the concept of disavowal developed in Freud's later texts. Drawing upon the work of Jean Laplanche, the nature of the binary couple active/passive in the drives, and the career of the drive in the woman are addressed in order to question how, if at all, a woman's passivity is feminine. The disavowal of fetishism – apparently exclusively masculine – is shown to involve a double disavowal, for the 'theory' of the mother's 'castration' is already a disavowal of her difference since it 'solves' the mystery of the mother's 'lack' of a penis by seeing it as having been taken away. In Chapter 6 the implications of this revised view of castration and disavowal are considered in relation to the institution of femininity for the girl, and from this a new way to understand the asymmetry of masculinity and femininity is proposed which does not assume a necessary subordination of feminine to masculine. The social subordination of women, therefore, can no longer be seen as just a reflection of or as the effect of a psychical construction which privileges the masculine as defined against what is its other, its negative, the feminine. Nevertheless that it is not guaranteed at a general psychical level does not make the social subordination and inequality of women any less a reality, nor are the psychical structures irrelevant to the social. But the nature of both, and of their interdetermination, cannot be understood as given by a general theory – and certainly not by psychoanalysis, whatever our recent hopes have led us to expect. Instead, what emerges is a complex web of interrelationship between the subject and the other of desire organised not only around having or being the phallus, but also between active or passive forms of the drive in relation to the other of desire. The necessity of sexual difference is not dissolved however, but rather affirmed, and this whether desire is heterosexual or homosexual. The analysis of *Gertrud,* with which Chapter 6 concludes, explores the relations of desire and positions of identification constituted for its characters and for the spectator by the film and its authorial narration.

The fetishism of representation and the role – and pleasure – of disavowal, including the masquerade and the disavowal of sexual difference, are examined in Chapter 7 through a consideration of Joseph von Sternberg's *Morocco* (1930). The final chapter addresses the concept of fetishism in theories of ideology and discusses the possibilities for a politics of representation in relation to the view of fetishism, fantasy and sexual difference presented in the book. The question of a specifically feminine cinema is explored in two films, *Smooth Talk* (Joyce Chopra, 1985) and *Blue Steel* (Katherine Bigelow, 1990), both of which centre a woman protagonist but in each film a different problem of the woman as a subject of desire and as subject to social discourses is presented. What emerges is not a prescription or formula for women's film-making but a re-posing of the contradictions of sexual difference in representation. It is through such a re-posing – rather than in the delivery of the new or the proper place of identity and identification in film – that our difficulties as subjects of desire within sexual difference can be re-figured in different fantasy formations, and through changed social relations. There is no utopia of representation, of images and stories which will fully speak our desires, nor can we rely on a utopian role for representation, as that through which our relation to ourselves and our desire for the other can be reformed and remodelled. This is not to say that the new will not arise, but we cannot hope to be able to simply imagine the new in advance. Jean Laplanche has commented that the new is not the message which is hitherto unknown to the receiver, but is that which is enigmatic to the producer of the message. The message need not, of course, be itself new. We need, perhaps, to hear anew as enigmas the signs of our cultural production.

1

Feminist Arguments

The issue of representation has been fundamental for the modern feminist movement. While equality, especially in relation to equal pay and equal opportunity, continued to be a fundamental objective of women activists, what marked the re-emergence of feminism as a political and social movement from the late 1960s was a new articulation of the contradictions of 'femininity', of motherhood and gender for women in the industrial West, together with a new analysis of the conditions – social as well as economic – producing these contradictions. The conditions which made possible this new articulation were the series of conjunctural changes in the decade 1960–1970. The 'sexual revolution' of the 1960s refers to the tumultuous personal experience of a generation for whom sex and sexual pleasure came out of the bedroom and the closet, off the back seat of cars and cinemas, and into the public sphere. Sexuality and its pleasures were asserted as an affirmation of identity and as a human right. But the 'sexual revolution' also refers to the gradual development of a broad acceptance in western societies of new norms of sexual activity involving non-marital sexuality both heterosexual and, with its decriminalisation, of homosexuality (in Britain, for those over 21 years of age).[1] The decade also saw the introduction of new norms of state intervention, including the liberalising of the provision of abortion and the emergence of state-funded birth control clinics which served unmarried as well as married women. Access to forms of birth control and especially the availability of the pill as a (comparatively) safe and reliable form of contraceptive freed women to engage in heterosexual relations on the same basis as men; the 'double-standard' which condoned men's pre-marital sexual activity but condemned it on the part of women began to crumble. What arose in its place was not the hoped-for sexual freedom of both men and women, but a new tyranny as a result of an emphasis on sexual activity and sexual relationships defined in terms of a freedom from responsibility. For the women who came together in consciousness-raising groups to

15

form the new Women's Movement, this freedom was a male-defined and male-serving sexual freedom which ignored and denied the difference of women's sexuality and needs, as well as finding no place for the sexual and social position of motherhood. The high expectations nurtured by the expansion of higher education in which women participated, and by a decade of full-employment, were dashed as the reality of unequal pay, unequal opportunity, and unequal responsibility for domestic and family life became apparent to women.

In this new analysis the role of the production and circulation of images of women came to be of central importance, and feminists began to address the issue of ideology. For images, it was argued, not only exploited women – for example the use of a woman and her usually unclothed body to sell cars, etc. – but, and more importantly, they produced definitions of women and femininity that were presented as true, timeless, and hence 'natural'. Such representations presented not woman, but mother, virgin, whore, or just image. She was a sign of everything and anything but herself. The debate was therefore framed in terms of women's oppression by male-serving, male-produced images within male-dominated image industries – those of the press, television and cinema, as well as the pictorial arts. The call for equality alone, as a demand for as much as and hence the same as men, could not challenge or change the kinds of images of women circulated. Instead, the rhetoric of the liberation movements was adopted, producing a feminist discourse of oppression and exploitation in which it was men who imposed, maintained, and benefitted from women's oppression. At its most radical this produced a view of men as the enemy, a force which aimed to dominate women and to use women for its own purposes – purposes antithetical and opposed to the aims and desires of women; this was a model based on the Marxist opposition between owners of capital and workers. And, insofar as it was not every individual man who was involved in this oppression, the term 'patriarchy' – drawn from Engels's work on the family – was adopted to refer to the general system of women's oppression even where this was not supported by or directly in the interests of individual men.[2]

This form of argument has had serious implications for feminist theory and analysis for it has locked many debates into a finally fruitless search for the source, means and agents of our oppression so as to dispose of them. At the same time this form of argument

assumes a unified subject, 'woman', who is the recipient of this oppression but who pre-exists it. While the reductiveness of this approach was soon recognised, the implications for feminist theory
and argument have often been ignored. For there is no such pre-
given subject, rather the category 'woman' is the product of specific
discursive practices, that is, of the legal, medical and political discourses of an historical moment which each construct definitions of
'woman' which may not be, and often have not been the same. As a
result, what we have called 'patriarchy' can only be an effect of a
particular arrangement of competing discourses, not an expressive
totality which guarantees its own self-interests.[3] Moreover there is
also the 'woman' constructed by feminist discourse; the woman
who is the victim of patriarchal oppression, whose voice is sup-
pressed, whose body as image is dispossessed by the male gaze,
the woman who functions as a sign in exchange between men.
Feminism, too, has produced competing discourses and definitions
of woman, and these are no more essentially true than those of
patriarchy are false. We need to look at the effectiveness of our arguments, and the effects of our discourses.

SUBJECT TO REPRESENTATION

At the same time as feminists were challenging particular images of
women, new theoretical work emerged that undermined the very
notion of representation on which much of the feminist critique had
been based. The structural linguistics which developed from the
work of the Swiss linguist Saussure[4] showed that the ability of the
sign to be meaningful, to function as representation, depends not
on its definition in some absolute dictionary or its relation to a real
referent, but on its production within the system of language, *la
langue*. Signification is produced not as the effect of a unique
essence of the sign, a meaning given once and for all, but as a result
of its functioning within a chain of signs; a sign's meaning is conditional upon its difference from other signs within that particular
language system. Language signifies because it is a system of differential oppositions. Meaning is thus not some substance contained
within the sign which might be examined independently of the
signs in which it takes part. However, for Saussure the sign remained pre-eminently tied to the articulation of a mental concept in
language – a concept *for* someone – which is to assume a concept or

image which pre-exists the sign and is awaiting, ready to be united with it. Thus a psychologism marks his theory of language – as well as the semiological project which has emerged from it – for it involves a concept of communication which, Jacques Derrida states, 'in effect implies a transmission charged with making pass, from one subject to another, the identity of a signified object, of a meaning or of a concept rightfully separable from the process of passage and from the signifying operation.'[5] This arises from the 'original' separation of signifier and signified by Saussure when he proposed the division of the sign into two parts, distinguishing between the sensible and the intelligible, and as a result implying that the intelligibility of the signified existed '*before* its "fall", before any expulsion into the exteriority of the sensible below'.[6] But this is to presuppose, as support for the operation of signification, subjects or psyches whose identity and consciousness are fully present and which are constituted prior to and outside of the process of signification. Further, it requires that the identity of that which is signified is established outside the act of signification and remains unsullied by the actions of the means of signification.[7] Meaning once again transcends form.

But there is no 'gold standard' for the sign, no guarantee of its truth or reality by virtue of the referent that lies behind the represented. Representation is not a system of signs referring to reality and therefore there can be no recourse to an original essence against which the achievement or shortcomings of images produced by cinema, television, literature etc. can be measured. The corollary of this is that it is no longer possible to argue that woman as signifier of woman is absent or distorted in representation, for here again the signified, woman, is held to be a referent fully present to itself outside of the representation, and with reference to which the representation can be judged as inadequate. Of course there are real women, but there is no essence 'woman'; rather we are constructed as agents within the social by legal and economic discourses. Sexual difference may or may not be constituted as an aspect of that agency.[8]

Unlike spoken and written language, however, cinema and the still photographic image appear to be truly analogical and to present a literal mimesis of the world in which we can see people, objects, and the natural world just as in reality. But images are not transparent and do not reflect a reality prior to and other than them, on the contrary images are polysemic and without fixed meaning until organised as a statement. Meaning only arises in the construction and circulation of the representation. It is not 'added on to' the image, and, contrary to Barthes's early claims, there is no moment of pure denotation for the image prior to connotation.[9] It is not therefore a question of simply unmasking the constructedness of representations, for this still implies a pure form of representation in which meaning exists unmediated by any such construction. The new developments in film theory in the 1970s drew upon the work in semiology and structural linguistics to show that film is a system of meaning involving the articulation, the combination, of signifying elements. This, not only in the more obvious sense in terms of film as a series of shots, but also as a combination within the shot of sound, image, music, dialogue and even writing, organised together in space and time, a mise en scène of events. The meaning emerges in the particular articulation of the specific filmic system. The work of a film is not, then, the simple representation of an already constituted meaning or content. As a consequence, therefore, it must be involved in producing meanings, and hence in producing specific definitions of women.

Nevertheless when the political project of feminism is posed in relation to the semiological analysis of film, the object – woman – is again assumed to have a definition, a meaning, which exists already and outside the system of representation of the film, and which the film denies or denigrates. A new form of the argument that the filmic representation is inadequate to the real woman is produced in the claim that woman as signifier of woman is absent or excluded. The image of the woman refers not to the referent woman, existing in the real world outside of representation, but to a meaning produced by and for men. Patriarchy controls the image of woman, assigning it a function and value determined by and for men, and in the service of the construction of definitions of the male and more especially of masculine desire. Patriarchy and the interests of men become a unified field which is able to determine meanings outside of the process of signification. The challenge of structural and post-structural linguistics and semiotics is sidestepped in a return to an essentialist realism even while the terms of that project are adopted.

These arguments drew upon the work of the anthropologist Claude Lévi-Strauss on kinship structures (work also used by Jacques Lacan in elaborating his concept of the Law of the Father).

Kinship structures, Lévi-Strauss says, are based on the exchange of women between family groups, an exchange which makes of the woman a sign. Juliet Mitchell took up this thesis in *Psychoanalysis and Feminism,* a book whose significance for feminist theory has already been noted.[10] Using Lévi-Strauss's description of kinship structures, she argued that the exchange of women as signs fixes our positions as women in patriarchy as signs exchanged by men. While this offered feminism a theory of women's subordination it was still within essentialist terms, for it presumed a woman, already present and waiting, who is then appropriated (oppressed) in her exchange in kinship. Woman as sign in exchange is the communication which appropriates one signified – a woman – as the signifier for another signified, kinship. In Barthes's sense of connotation, woman, instead of denoting herself, connotes kinship.[11] The image/meaning of woman in social discourse, in representation, is explained by reference to a structure – here exchange in kinship – which is itself dependent on appropriating pre-given terms, woman, as a value already recognised in the society. This original 'valuing' has, however, remained unexamined. This contradiction is at the heart of Lévi-Strauss's own arguments, for he assumes woman as the valuable available and waiting in kinship exchange while at the same time he argues that kinship structures *inaugurate* social relations, in which case there can be no prior *social* valuing of women. The contradiction arises from the way Lévi-Strauss uses the notion of 'sign' which he draws from structural linguistics.

Lévi-Strauss's work on kinship, which inaugurated the approach he termed structural anthropology, was based on Saussure's theory of language as a system of arbitrary signs which Lévi-Strauss discovered through the linguistic theories of Roman Jakobson.[12] As a result he conceived of a radically new approach both to the understanding of kinship patterns and to what appears to be the decisive moment for the institution of patriarchy, namely, the emergence of the *family*. He writes:

> the meaning of marriage rules, which is incomprehensible when they are investigated in isolation, can only emerge by seeing them as mutual oppositions, in the same way that the true nature of the phoneme does not lie in its phonic individuality but in the oppositive and negative relations in which phonemes stand to one another.[13]

Lévi-Strauss shows that it is the rule of exogamy, that is, the requirement to marry outside the family, which founds kinship structures and thus secures the group *as* a social group via the series of affiliations which marriage ties produce. The rules of kinship *are* the society. These are organised, he argues, in a series of structural oppositions in the same way Saussure describes in language. It is a system of rules of combination, of who can marry who, which gives rise to certain meanings for the members of the group for, depending upon the kinship tie, each member of the group acquires duties and reciprocal obligations as a result of the placing – as father, son, husband and brother or uncle, and as mother, daughter, wife, sister or aunt – which kinship as a structure effects. Kinship rules are a kind of language, therefore, 'a set of processes permitting the establishment, between individuals and groups, of a certain type of communication.'[14] Lévi-Strauss does not see exogamy as a system of communication of the same order as language, but sees them both as two solutions to the same fundamental requirement, namely, the necessity for the resolution of the opposition between the self and others in order to make possible social intercourse. It is the rule of reciprocity which ensures this through the exchange of valuables between individuals. In other words, the agreement to give a present right (to this woman) for a future right (access to other women, or another woman in a certain group) is, Lévi-Strauss argues, the fundamental principle of culture and founds the possibility of culture as a social structure. But he also says that kinship is a system of communication involving the production of meaning between members of the system; it is a signifying system in which women are produced as a sign which is circulated in an identical way to words. The exchange of women between marriage groups, which is the positive form of the prohibition of incest,[15] thus makes of women a sign, signifying the 'social contract' of the group. Kinship, like language, communicates in so far as it exchanges. And women, like words, are the signs which are exchanged.

Communication, however, is never simply an exchange between the speaker and receiver, as if an object – a word or a woman – is passed from hand to hand, mouth to ear. It is also a construction of the receiver and sender as 'I' or 'You', and this is necessary for any communication to take place at all. Thus communication, or signification, also involves the very constitution of the speaking subject, of the social subject, in its relation to the other. It is the 'exchange' which constitutes the subjects, and not the subjects who constitute the exchange. The notion of sign which Lévi-Strauss employs, moreover, reproduces the psychologism of Saussure in seeing it as a link between the concept and the image or object, thus assuming a meaning already there, awaiting a signifier.[16] At the same time he also asserts that 'as producers of signs, women can never be reduced to the status of symbols or tokens'.[17] Here again his argument produces a confusion between the woman who has value, who is a user of signs, and the woman-as-sign in the exchange of women in marriage. It is this confusion which has opened the way to the feminist argument that woman-as-sign is a function of and a cultural reflection of male power which denies her subjectivity and makes of her a sign.[18]

The sign 'woman', however, is produced within a specific signifying system – kinship structures – and hence while the form or rather signifier of the sign (which in language would be the sounds making up the word) is the physical female person, the meaning of the sign, its signified, is *not* the concept woman, but 'woman-as-sign in exchange' (hence the kinship relations of wife, father etc.). 'Woman-as-sign' is not exchanged as a symbolic expression of the two kinship groups' relations to each other, rather it *is* the expression, and it is also a positioning, so that it is through the exchange in which she is a sign of the kinship relationship that a daughter will be constructed as a wife. Exchange is not just a series of acts but a structure which makes possible all particular acts of exchange within a group. This structure and its rules prescribes the kinships relations of a group, producing the positions of men and women in the group in terms of their marriage relations:

> from a social viewpoint, these terms cannot be regarded as defining isolated individuals, but relationships between these individuals and everyone else.... Every family relationship defines a certain group of rights and duties, while the lack of family relationship does not define anything; it defines enmity.[19]

In traditional societies, kinship is *the* structure which defines relationships; exogamy as a practice signifies men and women as mother, sister, brother, son etc. To have no such relations is to be an enemy and thus one to whom the group has no obligations.[20] It is not that a pre-existing category, women, is situated in a family; rather, it is in the family – as the effect of kinship structures – that those members who are biologically female are produced, are defined, by the group, first as daughters and sisters, later as wives and mothers. Moreover the categories 'men' and 'women' may not be produced at all – as Lévi-Strauss points out, some human groups have no general term for either 'man', or the human, in which case it is not 'woman' that is exchanged, but an unmarried daughter. The incest taboo itself involves not so much women, as mothers, sisters and daughters etc., while the particular kinship relations which are made taboo are not the same from society to society.

It is this production of persons as social subjects, as daughters to be married, as nieces and nephews, with corresponding obligations, duties and privileges, which is a key contribution in Lévi-Strauss's work on kinship, and which must be retained by feminist theory. Nevertheless while both men and women are positioned in exchange – as husbands or wives etc. – only women are exchanged, Lévi-Strauss says, and hence only women are produced as signs. Firstly, in so far as this is the case, it does not require that there is a prior established difference which determines that women are signs for, as Saussure emphasised in relation to language 'there are only differences without positive terms'.[21] Secondly, that women are always the element of exchange is a simplification of the complex and highly variable phenomenon of kinship relations and marriage structures in which the biblical account – patrilineal and patrilocal – is given precedence: 'Then we will give our daughters unto you, and we will take your daughters to us, and we will dwell with you, and we will become one people' (Genesis 34:16). It is not men who exchange women but kinship groups, and although it is usually men who represent the group in kinship exchange, nevertheless the widespread use of matrilineal kinship groups as well as, although less commonly, matrilocal marriage indicates that the exchange of women is a complex social practice.[22] In matrilineal descent lineage is from uncle to nephew through the sister and hence sisters must not be lost to the group; rather husbands must be acquired through whom the nephews can be obtained. Matrilocal marriage in which the husband goes to live in the wife's village or house, although comparatively rare, gives further support to the view of kinship as the exchange of daughters *and* sons, since it is the sons who circulate.[23] Thirdly, whatever the cultural value woman – or rather wives, daughters etc. – may have for a social group, this cannot have been determining in the institution of the group as a sociality for Lévi-Strauss argues that it is through exogamy that culture, and hence the social group, is possible.

If exogamy is characterised by an exclusive term of exchange – women – because of an already existing value of women for the group, then the group must have already entered culture to the extent of recognising women as socially valuable, and a social sexual division is already in place for the group. The institution of a social rule in kinship exchange which secures the group as a group has become confusingly identified with men's control of women in exchange. Lévi-Strauss asserts that 'political authority, or simply social authority, always belongs to men'.[24] The social and psychical function of reciprocity, of exchange, for which kinship is the pre-eminent form, is therefore conducted for and by men. Hence the negotiation of the opposition between self and other is undertaken by men alone. Women, Lévi-Strauss says, are placed outside the structure of reciprocal gifts, and hence outside that which is defined as the condition for the group as a social group. What then enables women to be social participants of the group, to be social subjects? The problem posed by this question arises because of the way in which Lévi-Strauss shifts between a discussion of the social group implying both men and women, and a homogenised category 'men'. But what defines the groups involved in kinship exchange is not the biological sexual distinction, but a consanguinal relation; it is 'fathers' as a category (who may not be biologically fathers) who arrange marriages for sons and daughters, or nieces and nephews. There is no such homogenised category of 'men' for whom the social and psychical construction of identity through reciprocal exchange is reserved.[25] Through kinship structures the social group is constituted in a series of definitions which produce social rather than reproduce biological relations. Nevertheless, while this no doubt produces a series categories of persons all of whom who may also be biologically female, we cannot assume as well that this constitutes the subordination of women in general. Much of the anthropological material in the literature on kinship has been produced in the context of modern Western discourses about what constitutes the political and political power, as well as in relation to contemporary concepts of oppression and subordination, but it cannot be assumed that these same meanings of power and oppression functioned for the group in question.[26]   .

Lévi-Strauss's thesis on the circulation of goods and women was taken up by Jacques Lacan in his concept of the Symbolic Law:

The primordial Law is therefore that which in regulating marriage ties superimposes the kingdom of culture on that of a nature abandoned to the law of mating. The prohibition of incest is merely its subjective pivot...This law, then, is revealed clearly enough as identical with an order of language.[27]

Moreover, he says 'It is in the *name-of-the-father* that we must recognise the support of the symbolic function which, from the dawn of history, has identified his person with the figure of the law'.[28] Lacan thus reproduces Freud's gesture in appealing to and allying his theory with an anthropological thesis of man's, and society's, origin, and it is here that psychoanalysis appears most cogently as a patriarchal theory of the human psyche. The exchange of women – exogamy – and the rule of reciprocity enable and ensure the institution of culture, while its obverse, the incest taboo and its unconscious counterpart, castration, produce the social/symbolic inscription of sexual difference. However, this law of the Father is never a law imposed or wielded by fathers, and no man may occupy the place of the Name-of-the-Father, though a father – or a mother – may assume its authority. Rather, Lacan argues that this law requires that each human subject submits to the law of castration, that is, to a limiting of the subject's desire and its access to *jouissance* – its 'enjoyment'.[29] This constitutes a very different law of the father from the patriarchy of the feminist critique whereby the exchange of women ensures male control and power over women and goods, and thus which ensures – feminists might say – precisely man's full enjoyment, his *jouissance*.[30]

In drawing upon the prestige of Lévi-Strauss's account of kinship to support his concept of the symbolic law Lacan has also introduced the contradictions of Lévi-Strauss's theory of woman as sign. The argument presented here, however, has been that 'Woman' is not given, biologically or psychologically, but is a category produced in signifying practices. These practices, whether kinship structures, or the processes of signification in the unconscious, or the signifying systems of public and published forms of representation, do not produce a unified identity equivalent to biological women. On the contrary, biological women may not be mothers or sisters, or wives, and, in some communities, they may be legal 'fathers' of children whose mother they have taken as a 'wife'. We must therefore keep separate the question of the representation of women and woman as a sign, in order to avoid any simple denunciation of the sign as inadequate representation/signification of the 'real' object woman. Moreover the visual image is never always already a sign of a woman which may then be appropriated as a signifier in the construction of another, oppressing, meaning. There is no pure denotation which can be recovered, no essential, sovereign meaning. Yet the demand for the 'true' image that arises in the face of the often violent sense of alienation which a spectator can experience as she confronts what is offered as an image of herself attests to the power of images. Of course, the very alienation which the image can give rise to bears testimony to the failure of the ideology to impose its definitions. The power of images is not that they 'dupe' us, but that they are encountered at both a cognitive level as significations and at the level of identification in all its complex forms.

SIGNS AND CODES, HEROINES AND HEROES IN HOWARD HAWKS'S FILMS

How then is 'woman' produced as a category in film? Cinema is not simply filmed reality; it frames the world in order to picture it on celluloid, hence it selects and excludes. It is therefore, even without the spoken or written word, an utterance or enunciation, an *organised* presentation of reality which presupposes an intelligibility of the utterance; it is organised for understanding. The image is coded, or rather – since what is involved is not something like morse code where a message is transposed into another form – it produces meaning in so far as it is structured in a series of codes. Some of these codes are specific to cinema – such as editing, or camera movements, which have no fixed meaning until their organisation in a particular film – while other codes are more general and are found in a variety of media, such as conventions of dress or speech by which we recognise the 'worker' or the 'London cockney' and by which the image 'connotes'. However the specifically cinematic codes are not neutral forms for the expression of these general codes – a low angle or high angle shot, a close-up or long shot will each give a slightly different 'worker'. And there are other non-cinematic codes such as narrative which similarly have no inherent meaning but which organise the reader's or spectator's expectations and thus produce meaning in relation to the events presented. In addition there are the codes constituted by the film itself which we 'read' in terms of the motivations produced within the film – notably for example through repetition.[31] The articulation of these codes constitutes the filmic system. Analysis then involves not a de-coding, as if one were translating the film 'back' from another code, but the discovery of the various codes in play in the film and the structure of meaning produced by their combination in that specific film.[32]

This approach to a semiology of film draws upon a different aspect of Lévi-Strauss's use of structural linguistics arising in his study of myths and totemic structures, where he argues that there is no intrinsic meaning in the elements of the system until they are articulated as structure:

> Now, the question can be raised as to whether all the characters of the phoneme do not reappear in those entities which we have called 'mythemes': these are the elements from which mythic discourse is constructed, and they also are entities which are at one and the same time oppositive, relative and negative; they are, to use the formula applied by Jakobson to phonemes, 'purely differential contentless signs'. For we must always distinguish the meaning or meanings which a word has in the language from the mytheme which this word can denote in whole or in part. In everyday language the sun is a heavenly body which appears in the daytime; but the mytheme 'sun' does not, taken in and for itself, have any meaning. Depending on the particular myths under consideration it can range over a whole variety of different ideal contents. In fact nobody coming across 'sun' in a myth, would be able to say in advance just what specific content, nature or functions were in that myth. Its meaning could only be identified from the relations of correlation and opposition in which it stands to other mythemes within this myth. The meaning does not, properly speaking, belong to any individual mytheme: it is a consequence of their combination.[33]

The films of Howard Hawks present a particularly interesting example through which to explore Lévi-Strauss's proposition regarding myth and the production of filmic codes, for it was through a comparison of Hawks's films and those of John Ford that Peter Wollen elaborated his structural analysis of authorship in *Signs and Meaning in the Cinema*. The representation of women, and of men's relation to women, in his films was seen by Wollen as a central aspect of Hawks's authorship, while it was this aspect of his films which has also been critically addressed by feminists; for example Molly Haskell has suggested that 'The charge levelled by feminists that Hawks's women must model themselves after men to get their attention is largely true.'[34]

Wollen adopts the 'structural approach' to authorship study suggested by Geofrey Nowell-Smith in his book on Visconti – an approach drawn from the work of Lévi-Strauss – which proposes 'the definition of a core of repeated motifs' in the work of a director as the criteria for 'authorship'.[35] Wollen, however, argues that 'Structuralist criticism cannot rest at the perception of resemblances or repetitions (redundancies, in fact), but must also comprehend a system of differences and oppositions.'[36] Applying this to Hawks's films he argues that 'a systematic series of oppositions can be seen very near the surface, in the contrast between the adventure dramas and the crazy comedies. If we take the adventure dramas alone it would seem that Hawks's work is flaccid, lacking in dynamism; it is only when we consider the crazy comedies that it becomes rich, begins to ferment: alongside every dramatic hero we are aware of a phantom, stripped of mastery, humiliated, inverted.'[37] For Wollen, however, Hawks's films lack the complexity he ascribes to those of John Ford, a complexity which he sees as arising as a result of the production of bundles of differential elements and pairs of opposites, seen for example in the related but variously recombined sets of oppositions which define the Fordian heroes of his films. Yet Hawks's films are similarly complex, and this is most apparent precisely in relation to the representation of men and women in his work. There is not, as Wollen claims, a simple pairing of oppositions inverted between the comedy and the adventure film, but a series of elements complexly re-worked across both genres.

Hawks's adventure films are characterised by their celebration of male camaraderie and their emphasis on an all-male group engaged in typically masculine pursuits – big-game hunting, flying, etc. – in which danger is encountered, testing the heros as men and as professionals. Within this world, Wollen argues, women are always a threat, a potential danger:

> Man is woman's 'prey'. Women are admitted to the male group only after much disquiet and a long ritual courtship, phased round the offering, lighting and exchange of cigarettes, during

which they prove themselves worthy of entry. Often they perform minor feats of valour. Even then they are never really full members.[38]

Once she has become 'one of the boys' she is no longer a threat. The woman's love is often paralleled by that of a male character who also 'loves' the hero, and it is that kind of love which she must learn. A typical dialogue, Wollen suggests, sums up their position: 'Woman: "You love him don't you?" Man (embarrassed): "Yes...I guess so..." Woman: "How can I love him like you?" Man: "Just stick around".'[39] As a result Wollen concludes that there is an undercurrent of homosexuality in Hawks's films which, although it is never explicit, runs very close to the surface. This is seen most clearly in *The Big Sky* (1952), while Hawks himself has described *A Girl in Every Port* (1928) as 'really a love story between two men'.[40] Claire Johnston, taking up Wollen's structural account, goes further and argues that 'For Hawks, there is only the male and the non-male.'[41] Robin Wood rejects this view, arguing that sexual difference remains much more of an issue in Hawks's films. In his postscript to the second edition of his book on Hawks, written after he had come out as gay, he says 'There lies the enormous interest of Hawks's women: they are anomalous and threatening, but *there*. The much-noted attempt to turn them into men never quite works: they remain obstinately, men/women, demanding a recognition somewhat different from that exchanged between males; they are a permanent problem as they scarcely are in Ford.'[42]

The heroine in Hawks's films is certainly not a conventional image of femininity, and it is this which has given rise to the notion of Hawks's women as positive heroines, as well as to the charge that they are just like men. They are active, in charge of their lives, streetwise, they talk back to their men – especially the hero – challenging him sexually; they know what they want and will go out and get it including, invariably, the hero. Molly Haskell, writing of Lauren Bacall's roles, puts it well:

This is not to say that Bacall somehow escapes being a male fantasy, but she pulls her weight – verbally, professionally, sexually – to a much greater degree than most heroines. She's tough, smart, feminine, neither virgin nor whore, and if she makes no bones about loving Bogey, she somehow gains the upper hand by having the confidence to be open and funny and honest. She not only isn't a threat to male supremacy but, in *To Have and Have Not* (1944) she represents the alternative – heterosexual pairing of equals – that is, finally and unequivocally, both adult and *fun*.[43]

There is in fact in Hawks's films a number of different representations and hence definitions of women, only some of which are valorised. One is the woman who is 'trouble'. In *To Have and To Have Not* (1944) she is the kind of woman which Harry Morgan (Humphrey Bogart) at first thinks Slim (Lauren Bacall) will be, and the kind of trouble that the resistance leader's wife will turn out to be, and that Rita Hayworth as Judith was to Cary Grant's Jeff Carter in *Only Angels Have Wings* (1939), the kind of woman whose fears and dependency emasculate the man. Another kind of trouble/woman is Dude's (Dean Martin) fancy lady in *Rio Bravo* (1959) who, we learn, came in on the stagecoach, and which Sheriff John T. Chance (John Wayne) thinks Feathers (Angie Dickinson) will be – a betraying femme fatale. In the adventure films such a woman is normally an absent figure of the past, or is attached to another man. She is always in striking contrast to the heroine who will finally get the hero. A series of definitions by opposition is set up, but this is not simply or primarily between a femme fatale-type 'bad' girl and the heroine, but is more usually – as in *To Have and Have Not* and *Only Angels Have Wings*, between the woman with guts and the wimp. In *Rio Bravo*, while Feathers has some of the characteristics of a femme fatale – she is a girl off the stagecoach like Dude's fated love, she is sexually provocative and a professional gambler – she will subsequently 'prove' herself and be vindicated as a positive figure.

It is, of course, in becoming active that the Hawks heroine also appears to be more like a man, but this is true only in terms of what is conventionally understood as attributes of the masculine. What is striking about Hawks's films is the lack of fixity of the conventional characteristics of masculine and feminine; not only do women act like men, but men act like women, and this is true of the adventure films as well as the comedies.[44] Thus within the male group there is a hierarchy which closely resembles that of generations in a family, and in which certain characters take the role of mother and father to the sons. In *Rio Bravo* for example it is Chance's deputy Stumpy (Walter Brennan) who is the housewife/mother fussing over Dude and Chance (John Wayne), as is made explicit when Chance kisses the horrified Stumpy in response to the latter's demand for some appreciation. At the same time Chance acts as mother to Dude – as well as father; Chance has kept Dude's clothes, clean and ironed, as well as buying back his guns.

There is a play of reversals and inversions in relation to sexual difference within and between individual films which is not fixed with regard to any particular gender. This very play is the plot itself of *I Was A Male War Bride* (1949). *His Girl Friday* (1940) has the form of an adventure film but with a reversal of gender and role, so that Hildy (Rosalind Russell), in a part which was a man's in the original stage play of *The Front Page* and in Lewis Milestone's earlier screen version (1931), is indeed the 'male' Hawks character, beset by ex-husband Walter as the 'female' who is messing her life up; she is a professional who proves herself the best in the (male) group of journalists but has to be rescued from her wimp fiancé by Walter (Cary Grant). *Bringing Up Baby* (1938) has a similar plot but with a reversal of gender – Cary Grant must be rescued from his wimp fiancée. In *Ball of Fire* (1941), on the other hand, there is a different shuffling of elements: instead of the disruptive element (Barbara Stanwyck as Sugar Puss) winning out over the staid and stuffy element (Gary Cooper as Bertram Potts), she is won over to his world and style of life. This includes a male group but one whose values are distinctly not 'macho' – they are a group of professors who have been working for the past twenty years or more on a new world encyclopedia.

Hawks does not have, as Wollen argued, a general system of sexual difference, of either man in control of nature and woman in his adventure films, or woman as nature in control of man in the comedies. The binary oppositions Hawks sets in play are not a fixed structure which is then inverted, rather each film works a set of distinctions around sexual difference producing definitions of masculinity and feminity. Woman, no more than man, is not a singular category in Hawks's films, but nevertheless his films, especially those termed the adventure-dramas, undoubtedly centre on the issue of masculine identity. As Jacques Rivette noted, 'By proving themselves, by achieving their ends they [Hawks's heroes] win the right to be free and the honour of calling themselves men.'[45] Yet it is never enough for the Hawksian hero to have made it as a man with his male comrades: there is always and in addition the necessity to recognise and accept a relationship with a woman. In the adventure films the narrative drive and action involves not only challenges and dangers for the hero which are external and social – flying, racing, hunting, facing cattle rustlers and Indians – but also internal and emotional, namely the requirement to come to terms with loving a woman.

It is also precisely here that Hawks's 'positive' heroines are deemed ultimately to fail, in that they are seen to submit to the sexual relation, that is, to the man. For example Feathers in *Rio Bravo* is active and sexual, yet she is ready to lay these aside or rather to put these in the service of one man. And indeed in the adventure films it is always the woman who 'stays', implying that she gives up her independent existence – including perhaps her work – which she had prior to meeting him. Moreover these films clearly privilege their male characters in that they centre on the work of men, as flyers, ranchers, law officers etc., whereas while the female character is always shown to be self-supporting or independent in some way, her work itself is a matter of narrative indifference.

Nevertheless staying with the hero is not shown to be in conflict with her independence of mind, and her active traits are not replaced by passive characteristics. The simplistic representation of the sexual relation as one of domination/submission is one which Hawks's films tend to oppose, instead they assert the figure of a woman who is an equal to the man.[46] At the end of *Rio Bravo* it is Feathers who does all the talking, in relation to whom John T. Chance appears passive. In any case, committing oneself to a sexual relation, to loving another person, is precisely a situation in which each person has to give up a certain independence, a certain freedom. More specifically, it is in the sexual relation that one must confront castration, difference, and this equally for the man as well as the woman. To love, to accede to sexual desire as love, is also to accede to a recognition of a lack-in-being, in so far as the other becomes the necessary supplement (which Lacan's refers to as the fantasy of the sexual relation). To desire is therefore also to lack, to be incomplete. As a result it is also rather 'unmasculine', though men as well as women have to place themselves thus. Desire appears, conventionally, to unman a man. It isn't only for laughs, therefore, that John Wayne's 'macho' style as Chance in *Rio Bravo* receives a series of sexual humiliations from Feathers from their very first meeting over a pair of red frilly bloomers.

In Hawks's films this placing of the man and woman within a couple is played out in a rite of initiation in which each participant learns or comes to accept what is necessary in love. This is signalled and symbolised in some sort of exchange, gesture or act which signifies 'I love you'. It is as if a form of symbolisation must be interposed to signify the relation. This binds the two in relation to that symbolic act as an external and third term, which thereby mediates the relation of the couple. Such a symbolisation is used over and over again by Hawks, in both his comedies and his adventure films, and the signifier may pass from the woman to the man, as with the ring in *Ball of Fire* or the whisky bottle in *To Have and Have Not*, the leopard in *Bringing Up Baby* or the black tights in *Rio Bravo*. Or it may pass from the man to the woman, as with the coin in *Only Angels Have Wings*, the elephant in *Hatari* (1962), or the watch in *His Girl Friday*.

In *Only Angels Have Wings* the symbolisation and exchange involves a series of elements: a joke, a negation and an affirmation. In response to Bonny's (Jean Arthur) challenge to Jeff that she won't stay around unless he asks her to, Jeff mockingly agrees, saying he'll settle it by the toss of a coin and, taking one from his pocket, he proceeds to throw it, naming heads for Bonny staying. Furious at being treated so casually, she stops him. Jeff then goes out, and as Bonnie prepares to leave she idly plays with the coin until she suddenly realises that it is doubleheaded. The game of chance Jeff was acting out was only an act, for there was no chance at all. The coin is thus a token of love which Bonny has to 'read'. The coin, however, has already been in circulation within the film in an earlier series of exchanges – again, though, not as money or even as fate. It was this coin which Jeff's best friend, Kid Dabb, used to try and fool Jeff into letting him fly a mission, and later it passes to Jeff as one of the few possessions he leaves behind after his death. On the one hand it would therefore appear that Bonnie now occupies the place of Kid's love for Jeff through the circulation of the coin; on the other hand it is Jeff who uses the coin in relation to Bonnie, thus occupying the place of Kid in the earlier scene in relation to himself.[47]

In *Rio Bravo* the use of a pair of black tights as the signifier is also an example of Hawks's ironic treatment of the fetishisation of femininity, seen as well in *Gentlemen Prefer Blondes* (1953) and *Monkey Business* (1952). In the penultimate scene of the film, Chance has gone over to see Feathers, his intentions remaining ambiguous although his very actions – and Stumpy's prior urging – imply that he wants to ask her to stay. She receives him in her room, dressed as a showgirl in readiness to entertain in the saloon down below. She is wearing sheer black tights with a figure-hugging bodice. As usual, Feathers does the talking, which amounts to a challenge to Chance: if he loves her he'll refuse to let her be seen by any other men dressed that way. As she goes to leave, Chance does indeed stop her, threatening her with jail if she goes downstairs dressed in this way. Taking this as a declaration of love, she changes behind a screen, promising him that he will be the only one to see her in the tights, which she then passes to him. However the tights, which stand metonymically for Feathers as a 'fetishised' sexual object, are rejected by Chance when he throws them out of the nearby open window. The fetishised image of woman is rejected and instead a different displacement and substitution occurs in Chance's declaration that he'll 'put her in jail'. This is only apparently the strong arm of the law appropriating the woman's body. Chance does not speak as the bearer of the law but as a subject of desire. In the next shot the tights are seen landing on Stumpy as he and Dude walk past outside, and Stumpy then ties them round his neck like a scarf. The comic image produced reiterates the rejection of the tights and, by extension, of Feathers as fetish, while its humour, arising in the inappropriate juxtaposition of elements – the black tights around not a show-girl's legs but Stumpy's neck – also displays the very process of substitution and displacement of signifiers and signifieds in Hawks's films. It is a process of production of meaning through a system of signifying oppositions which are specific to the filmic system formed by the corpus of Hawks's films. This certainly confirms the intuition of a Hawksian 'author'. What is also confirmed is the centrality within this system of the Hawksian heterosexual couple, while at the same time what is shown is that the two readings of Hawks's films – of either a latent homosexuality or on the contrary of a reinstatement of heterosexuality – are not exclusive and opposed accounts. *Rio Bravo*'s closing image, after all, restates – even if comically – the dilemma of masculinity penetrated by or excluding the feminine. The joke at fetishism's expense is only possible because of the role fetishism has in sexual relations.

Hawks's films demonstrate the ways in which the meanings, the definitions, of masculinity and femininity are determined through the textual system – of a single film or, as here, across an author's work, or across a genre. Woman and man are both categories of the social world whose meaning within a film is produced by the operation of the film's textual system. The definitions arising in Hawks's films are complex and it is this complexity in his representation of men and women, rather than any image alone, which makes his films so interesting for contemporary sexual politics. The issue of how far, if at all, films can be seen as progressive in their representation of men and women is explored further in the following chapter on *Coma*, which investigates whether and in what ways the film's woman protagonist is a positive image for feminism, drawing on the semiological approach outlined here in order to examine the narrative form and structure of *Coma* as a suspense thriller and detective story.

2

Narrative Positions and the Placing of the Woman Protagonist in *Coma*

THE PROGRESSIVE WOMAN'S FILM

> parts of it are very plausible and very frightening…[but] I was so busy applauding Genevieve Bujold I forgot to be cowardly. She storms through the film, undaunted and unstoppable, at last providing me with the heroine for which I've been searching. …Most of all she *does* things. [John] Berger's remark that 'men act – women appear' doesn't apply to Bujold. She chucks fire extinguishers about, overturns security guards and escapes from the house of horrors without hanging around a man's neck. … But the film isn't a simple role-reversal… Enjoy *Coma* for Bujold's acting and the stupefied silence in the audience when they realise she's going it alone.[1]

This comment by Penny Hallow in her review of *Coma*, a mainstream Hollywood film directed by Michael Crichton and released in 1978,[2] makes it clear that for her the film is progressive for women, and she enthusiastically welcomes Genevieve Bujold's role as Dr Susan Wheeler as a positive heroine with whom to identify. Marjorie Bilbow, writing for the British trade journal *Screen International* similarly draws attention to the film's woman protagonist:[3]

> The rarity of having a woman as the plucky investigator makes a welcome change of identification for female viewers; what men lose from the absence of punch-ups they gain from coming over all-protective.[4]

Bilbow's point of a 'welcome change of identification' seems to suggest, however, that while she assumes women normally identify with the male hero, she has no such reverse expectation of men, offering instead an alternative structure of pleasure and identification for them – 'coming over-all protective'. At the same time Bilbow emphasises the kind of character and role of Susan Wheeler:

> Genevieve Bujold's Susan is a well-rounded characterisation, intelligent, courageous but never unfeminine in the butch superwoman or invincible sexpot styles of telly heroines. Her vulnerability is played down by director Michael Crichton; it is all the more telling when he reminds us that tights and shoes with heels are not the best thing to wear when scrambling about on ladders.[5]

Coma was not made as a feminist film, however, and although it can be seen as part of a new Hollywood cycle of 'independent women' films, it is not about the lives of women or women's issues or the position of women in society.[6] Instead it presents a thriller, exploiting aspects of sci-fi as well as the horror film in its futuristic image of care for irreversible coma cases, while at the same time presenting the gory reality of medical practice, and thereby evoking our fears of the lethal power of medicine to kill and to cure, as well as our worries over the ethical control of organ transplant.

The progressive elements are seen exclusively in the role and character of Dr Susan Wheeler as a 'strong woman', based first and foremost on the fact that she is the protagonist of the film, not only because the action centres on her, but also as a result of the way the action is initiated and carried out by her. She is the active agent, instigating the investigation and its consequent events in the film, presenting a clear contrast to the usual secondary or passive roles of women, even to the point of physical danger which she nevertheless successfully overcomes through her own resourcefulness and cunning. The film carefully constructs for us the character of Susan: she is intelligent, successful (viz her job as resident surgeon), tough, capable (as when treating her patients, or in her investigation), caring (in her affection for best friend Nancy, and her kindness to a small boy patient), warm and loving (seen in her weekend away with fellow-surgeon and boyfriend Mark), but also independent and self-respecting, demanding equality (for example, her row with Mark over who gets the dinner) and human in her self-questioning (shown in the scene with the psychiatrist). She is presented visually as quite ordinary, with her unelaborate and slightly unkempt hairstyle, lack of make-up, and a 'low-key' style of dress – white hospital skirt and coat, casual slacks and shirts, etc. There is also the element of moral rectitude in Susan – her role is one of searching after the truth, and she rejects the power-politics engaged in by Mark and the hospital director, Dr Harris.

The emphasis on these elements, however, and on the character and role of Susan Wheeler, obscures the way in which otherwise, through choosing another list of elements, the film can be shown to be totally conventional in its representation of women. First of all, Susan Wheeler is the only example in the film of a 'positive' image of women; there are very few other female characters, all her colleagues are male, and her investigations lead her exclusively to encounters with other men – the pathologists, the anaesthetists, the computer operator, the maintenance man – until she arrives at the Jefferson Institute and meets a woman who, it will emerge, is a key villain. And while Susan is presented as an 'ordinary' though attractive woman, her friend Nancy is, in contrast, glamorously beautiful. We are first introduced to Nancy in a medium close-up as the camera picks her and Susan out from amongst an exercise class, thus affording a titillating and voyeuristic display of women's bodies. An alternative might have been to show a game of squash, while the narrative function of the meeting of Susan and Nancy – to inform us of Nancy's forthcoming abortion – could have been fulfilled by their meeting in a bar, as male characters might have done. What this scene does afford, however, is the spectacle of the woman's body, just as the earlier scene of Susan showering at Mark's flat had done.[7]

As a result, while *Coma* was seen by audiences as well as reviewers as progressive for women because of the active and positive woman protagonist it presents, it was also held to be an example of how such progressive representations are recuperated in dominant cinema, most damningly because the film ends with Susan, helpless and prostrate, being rescued by her lover Mark. Yet what such discussions ignore in centering on Susan's role and image in order to assess *Coma* as progressive is the work of the film as a signifying system and the effects of its narrative production. Instead particular elements in the film are selected and evaluated in relation to the cultural values of feminism, being seen as progressive or negative, true or false.[8] As a result these elements are also assumed to have already fixed and determinate meanings outside of the film – and indeed outside of the discourse of feminism. But signifying systems such as films do not simply reproduce given definitions, they are the specific sites of a circulation which is also a (re)constitution of definitions in the particular process and play of narration and image. A film is itself a discursive practice, constituting 'images' of women as definitions in circulation which are also *narrative* images, and hence determining of as well as determined by other discursive practices in the social formation.

There can be, therefore, too, no simple 'recuperation' of something progressive in a film. For this would be to suppose that the image is in some sense an object, *a* content, which can be held by either camp, but whose specific use by one will have opposing effects on the other. 'Recuperation' is then that process by which a progressive content or meaning has been appropriated and inserted into another context where it 'loses' that meaning.[9] And, given the current position of women, it is assumed that the images produced by women on behalf of feminism will always be appropriated by dominant interests and turned against us; they will always be recuperated. But images are not 'things' outside of particular signifying systems or structures whose meaning can be fixed prior to their circulation. There is no 'true' image before its capture and manipulation by a dominant or false ideology. Thus, while this use of the concept of recuperation correctly emphasises the circulation of images and meanings, it at the same time denies the moments of productivity in that circulation, and of possible redefinition – by feminism as well as by the image industry in general. That images produced by feminists will enter circulation as 'quotable' is inevitable, but the problem of recuperation is a red herring. The issue of images should be one of production, not hoarding.

The image of Susan Wheeler as a 'strong woman' is in fact not straightforward. Susan's independence is seen as a problem by the other characters in the film and she is viewed, variously, as neurotic, as irrational and hysterical, as unreasonable – as well as unreasonably rational, and as just a trouble-maker. Nevertheless her suspicions of murder prove all too well-founded and she is vindicated. The film also shows Susan as conventionally feminine and weak, as when she breaks down in tears during the second interview with Dr Harris, and when her car fails to start she responds with helpless frustration, futilely beating the roof of the car. Later in the film she collapses in hysterical crying when she arrives at Mark's flat after having escaped from the hired killer. Yet she has just ingeniously and courageously dealt with her would-be assassin by covering him with frozen cadavers, while earlier, following her discovery of the horribly burnt body of the maintenance man in the hospital basement, she calmly set about finding for herself the carbon monoxide gas lines to the operating rooms he had told her of, before obtaining obtained illegal access to Dr George's records. In contrast, the idyllic weekend away with Mark after her second interview with Dr Harris not only offers conventional romantic images of a couple in love, but also also portrays Mark as – equally conventionally – active and Susan as passive as he chases her on the beach and catches her in his arms. As a result Susan is presented by the narration as alternately strong and weak, producing a contradictory character whose actions we cannot necessarily anticipate in the light of what we already know of her, and who may seem therefore either complex and realistic or inconsistent and unverisimilitudinous.

This split in the figure of Susan does, however, motivate what is perhaps the most important problem for a progressive reading based on 'elements', namely that, although Susan is the investigator, she doesn't discover 'the answer' in time; she fails to realise, or even consider, Dr *George* Harris as the chief villain rather than Dr *George* (Head of Anaesthesia) until her third and final discussion with him in his office, after he has spiked her drink. Thus though she is in a position of knowledge in the film normally denied women she still doesn't 'know', to her cost. As a result her rescue must be effected by Mark, albeit at Susan's instigation. It is the narrative function of the figure of Susan Wheeler, and the relations of identification *Coma*'s narration constructs, which the following analysis will explore.

THE STORY AND ITS NARRATION

A story, or history, presents a series of events and actions in an order of time and in a relation of cause and effect. What distinguishes stories or histories from chronicles, which also record events, is the employment of a narrative form to account for the events so that these become consequential, and not merely sequential.[10] In this way from a seamless actuality certain events and persons are selected to become fixed and focused as history in a relation of cause and effect. When imaginary persons and events are presented – as in fiction and the novel – the relation of cause and effect is no longer given by or deduced from the selected facts, but is constructed, invented, for the events and actions. Nevertheless in each case it is the telling of the tale, the production of the story as a statement, which produces the events as a relation of cause and effect.

A story tells us 'what happened' but to do so it must have already posited a something that has happened and given sense to the events. Contradictorily, while storytelling produces the story it tells, in that process it also makes itself secondary and subordinate to the story which it must posit as already having happened in order that it may tell it. There are then two forms and orders of time and event, the story itself and its time and order of happening, and the telling of the story with both its time of telling and the order of time it tells the events in. The Russian Formalist Viktor Shklovsky distinguished these two orders as *fabula* and *syuzhet*, or story and plot. The *fabula* is the order of events and their causal logic referred to by the narrative, so that the story is 'the action itself' while the *syuzhet* or plot is 'how the reader learns of the action'.[11] The term 'plot' in English has however a certain ambiguity when used with reference to literary works. It is often used to refer to the story outline, in the sense of a 'ground plan', or basic scheme, hence referring to the major events and actions of the story. Here the term is a figure of speech drawing on its meaning in English as a map or plan of a space which itself is derived from the separate meaning of the term as a plot of ground, or a building-plot, the spatial reference being transposed into or conjoined with a temporal reference in the sense of the plan or order of events. There is, however, another sense of plot, namely the use of the term to refer to the devising of a fiction, here the meaning lying in the sense of the *contrivance* necessary to bring about the connections between events in the story, though this would also include the sense of an order, since the devising involves a temporal aspect.

The notion of plot as a contrivance or fashioning is the sense I understand from the translation of the Russian Formalist term *syuzhet*.[12] The *fabula* is a construct of the narration, the *syuzhet*; it is the logical structure of a sequence of events and their causes and effects which the narration enables us to infer. The *syuzhet* is the narrative material as it is presented to the viewer or reader; as a result the order of events presented in the narrative discourse may be different from the *fabula*. For example, a film might present narrative information through a visual flashback which the spectator must then re-order into the 'proper' time of the *fabula*. Our sense of this 'proper' time of the story is so strong, however, that summaries of films often omit such narrative or plot devices. Nevertheless, as Peter Brooks emphasises, 'the apparent priority of *fabula* to *syuzhet* is in the nature of a mimetic illusion', in that the *fabula* – 'what really happened' – is simply a mental construction that is derived from the *syuzhet*, which is all that is directly known.[13] As Boris Tomashevsky points out, the *syuzhet* not only establishes the 'relevance and order' of the story information but it also determines 'the place in the work in which the reader learns of an event, whether the information is given by the author, or by a character, or by a series of indirect hints'. And while 'all this is irrelevant to the story', nevertheless 'the aesthetic function of the plot is precisely this bringing of an arrangement of motifs [functional elements in the narrative] to the attention of the reader'.[14] The plot involves a structure of arranging through which the reader or spectator learns of the event, a *narrating*.[15]

The narration, as a process of narrating, opens us to knowledge of events – not only knowledge of what happened but also, and for some narratives more importantly, why the events occur – that is, we come to understand what motivated characters to act as they do, and this motivation, rather than the actions themselves, may become what the fictional work as a whole is 'about'. Knowledge of the story-events and their motivation is revealed to us by the narration, and this may be straightforward and open, emerging concurrently with the action or event, or the narration may inhibit our coming to know through tactics of delay. The narration may offer us knowledge directly, so that we see the event in a film or are told of it by impersonal narration. Or we may receive information through a character. This is variously referred to by the term 'narrative perspective' or 'point-of-view', or 'focalisation', but in film the representation of a character's mental point-of-view or subjective experience is comparatively rare, although the camera will take up a character's optical point-of-view.[16] Or we may come to understand the events indirectly as a result of inferences made possible by the narration. The process of narrating therefore implies an enunciating subject, an intentional force which is guiding our understanding, a storyteller who unfolds the tale for us. This, too, however, is an effect of the text.[17]

The distinction *fabula/syuzhet* was used by the Russian Formalists to challenge the division between form and content whereby the form is held to be a neutral or transparent medium for conveying the content.[18] Instead it was emphasised that the 'content' of the narrative is dependent on the form through which it is constructed. There is no story without the telling, for the story cannot be separated from its forms of representation, as though the story might be told in any number of ways while remaining the same story.[19] Rather 'story', as the *fabula* – the actions and events and characters – marks the possibility of a tale which is only produced in its telling. As a result, if asked what a story was about, most people, rather than outlining the *fabula*, the events and actions as such, will attempt to sum up the themes of the film, producing an interpretation or summary of the enounced, of the meaning of the telling. The story here is the totality of signifieds, it is what the film was 'about' as a human experience for the characters and the spectator, the 'real' story lying in the transformation in the characters and the understanding given to the spectator as a result of the events and actions, and not these events and actions alone. The plot here is not merely a means to enable us to know the events which have already happened, although, as noted earlier, the effect of narration is to produce this mimetic illusion. Reading the story becomes an act of making sense not of the 'story' but of the 'storytelling', the *syuzhet*. Considered in this way the traditional distinction between form and content must disappear in favour of analytic categories through which a narrative can be understood to come into being in its process of narration.

Peter Brooks has argued for the need for a third term to refer to this process of 'sense-making', which he sees as arising in 'the interpretive activity elicited by the distinction between *syuzhet* and *fabula*, the way we *use* the one against the other'.[20] This third term, for which nevertheless Brooks proposes to use the English word 'plot',[21] becomes necessary because Brooks limits the *syuzhet* to the work of the narration in the ordering and revealing or retarding of narrative information. Plot now designates for Brooks the 'dynamic shaping force of the narrative discourse', 'the organising line and intention of narrative' but this is 'a structuring operation elicited in the reader trying to make sense of those meanings' and hence it 'belongs to the reader's competence'.[22] It is unclear, however, whether this is a force in the reader as the subject of the interpretive activity or, whether – as for the Formalists – it is an effect of the *syuzhet*.[23]

David Bordwell similarly introduces a third term – narration – but whereas for him the *syuzhet*, as the ordering of the narrative information, carries out the function of 'sense-making', he separates out the role of form and style, and the term 'narration' designates for him the combined process 'whereby the film's *syuzhet* and style interact in the course of cueing and channelling the spectator's construction of the *fabula*'.[24] The terms 'style' and 'technique' – which Bordwell uses interchangeably – refer to a 'film's systematic use of cinematic devices' – mise en scène, cinematography, editing, sound which are 'customarily used to perform *syuzhet* tasks – providing information, cueing hypotheses, and so forth'.[25] While style in the classical narrative film is typically subordinate to the *syuzhet*, it can also be foregrounded as such, he argues, 'deforming' through an excess of signifying without signifieds the *syuzhet*'s work of enabling sense-making.[26]

The separation of style from plot reproduces in a new manner the split between form and content, where content now has two aspects – the *fabula* as the signified and the *syuzhet* which sets in play sense-making through motivating the signifiers, and form again becomes a means of expression for the content, fulfilling – or not – the *syuzhet*'s tasks. For Shklovsky, however, aspects of *syuzhet* such as retardation and digression are themselves stylistic or formal devices and, as he showed in his analysis of Laurence Sterne's *Tristram Shandy*,[27] plot devices such as time shifts can be used excessively, that is, without sufficient narrative purpose or motivation, resulting in a laying bare of technique as such to produce what he termed a defamiliarisation.[28] Such a laying bare the devices of plot implies a dynamic engagement and problematisation of sense-making in the text, not a relation of displacement or subordination. Stylistic devices must, therefore, be understood as an aspect of the plot, but in becoming apparent as such, that is, in becoming noticeable as devices, they appear distinct from the 'story' being told, and thus to exceed what is needed for the narration of the *fabula*. This effect must, of course, itself be the result of the plot narration.[29]

'Plot', in this larger sense, involves a series of levels which intersect, reverberating so that 'content' and 'meaning' are no longer solely related to the inferring of a *fabula*. Signification occurs across the work as a process of production, not relay. Rather than part of the means of articulation of meaning, literally its representation, narration can be seen as involved in the constitution of meaning, its coming into being, and is an effect, a production of the text. Roland Barthes argues that 'meaning is not "at the end" of the narrative, it runs across it; just as conspicuous as the purloined letter, meaning eludes all unilateral investigation'. Thus 'To understand a narrative is not merely to follow the unfolding of the story, it is also to recognise its construction in "storeys", to project the horizontal concatenations of the narrative "thread" on to an implicitly vertical axis; to read (to listen to) [to watch] a narrative is not merely to move from one word to the next, it is also to move from one level to the next.'[30] As a result *what* we come to learn, the 'story', may not be straightforward.

Reading or viewing is not only a matter of cognition, of recognising and evaluating information, it is also a relation of desire, which is, at the very least, the wish to know. The corollary of this wish is that the spectator is a subject of lack – we lack the knowledge of what will happen in the narrative, and the narration will feed or tease us until it draws us to its already determined conclusion. *How* the story is told – for example through which characters do we learn of events (through which characters is it focalised), how does the film place us visually in relation to characters and events (visual point-of-view), how much the narration communicates – all this moulds and manipulates our understanding and our desire in relation to the narrative – the story we infer – and in relation to the characters. As a result, what comes to be narrated by the *syuzhet*, that is, how we learn of the events, may also encompass an affective component so that the structure of suspense in a melodrama or a thriller may give rise to emotions of anxiety or compassion as well as enabling us to cognitively anticipate the narrative outcome or to evaluate the position of characters.

Narrative is, therefore, a form of representation which provides its own determining conditions of reading, of meaningfulness. To this extent all forms of social discourse involve a certain narrativity. Nevertheless it is necessary to retain a more specific notion of narrative in order to differentiate the statement whose meaning exists in its narrative operations of motivation, for example the detective story, from one which while having the form of narrative, has its meaning constituted in its insertion within a series of further discourses – as is the case with a police statement to a court of law. The distinction is not, however, between 'true' stories and 'untrue' stories or fiction. Rather it lies in the different constitution of the relationship of the 'reader' to the knowledge of the discourse. In this more limited sense, narration is the representation of a relationship to knowledge where the problem of knowledge in relation to events is set up wholly by and within the text, and thus the *text* will resolve the problem – only it can give the answer (though it may desist from doing so). It does not matter whether the knowledge is 'real' or not, past or present. A documentary film will be narrative not only because, as in the classic documentary, it is heavily 'recounted' with a voice-over telling the story of coal, or the story of truants, etc., but because the film has established its own terms for the knowledge it will convey, the story it will construct. Its status as a discourse is constituted not as part of negotiations between union and management in the coal industry, nor between school and parents over truancy, but within cinema and television as discursive institutions.

As spectators or readers we recognise the different forms of narrative in social discourse as distinct from fictional genres, so that while a Western film can be understood as an allegory of American politics and of the American way of life, it is still read as a Western (albeit allegorical) and not as politics. Often a film or novel makes reference, is situated within, significant political or social events, but in narrativising these within its own system it separates them from the discursive practice – the political or social determinants – which constituted their meaning as political or social. They may connote politics within the film, but this does not constitute the film as political. In the same way *Coma*'s use of the connotations of feminist politics in its portrayal of Susan Wheeler does not make it political, let alone progressive, for this depends on the narration's articulation of these elements, and this makes very different reading.

THE POSSIBILITY OF KNOWLEDGE AND THE DETERMINATION OF THE ENIGMA

In *Coma* the figure of Susan Wheeler as a 'progressive protagonist', a positive image of a woman, needs to be considered in relation not to the *fabula*, a supposed narrative reality, or to the knowledge of what she did and who she is – powerful or weak – but in relation to how the film tells its story, the *relations of knowledge* it sets out for Susan within the plot, and for us as spectators in relation to her and to other characters. We must understand Susan Wheeler as a construct of the plot, so that she is strong or weak, active or passive, to the extent that the plot requires her to be. She isn't anything before the narration makes her something. To put it another way, Susan's strength is a character function narrated by the plot situations presented in the film. For this the narration draws on contemporary cultural references and connotations to motivate verisimilitudinously its image of Susan – and it is here that the possibility of Susan as a positive image for women begins to take shape in so far as the film draws on new, feminist, images of the active woman professional – but to assess this image we must return to the film's narration.

The narration always offers the spectator a position in relation to the narrative, it constitutes how we come to know, and while knowledge may well also be provided it is never the heart of the matter, for what is important is not so much 'what' happened, but 'how' will I learn of events. The narration therefore not only constitutes the knowledge, the *fabula*, it also organises how the spectator comes to know. The narration may be open, revealing events fully, or it may be very uncommunicative, omitting information crucial to understanding character relationships – for example, the information that two characters are blood relations. Narrative information is also communicated through characters, and again the spectator may be given the same knowledge as a character, or more knowledge, or less knowledge, or we may share knowledge with one character but which is withheld from another, as in Minnelli's *Home from the Hill* (1960) in which the audience is told early on that Rafe is Theron's half-brother, but Theron remains ignorant of the relationship until more than half-way through the film. The extent to which sympathy for characters is elicited or solicited by the narration is a further way in which the spectator is positioned by the narration.

At the same time the narration places the spectator as more or less active in as much as the spectator is by definition ignorant of what the film will reveal. Hence our position is characterised by lack of knowledge, and we take up a passive position in the sense of being recipients of the knowledge the narration will convey. The spectator must 'wait to know'. But, to work as narrative, a desire to know must also be set in motion in the spectator, and this is fuelled by the plot's formulation of an enigma, of a problem or conflict. As a result the spectator becomes an active pursuer of the knowledge about the enigma, trying to piece together the information afforded by the narration, and to anticipate what will happen next and how characters will respond on the basis of knowledge already acquired in the narrative. Narrative is a contract where the spectator demands to be put in a position of lack of knowledge but on condition that the narration will engage the spectator in a sense-making which can be experienced as an active process of discovery, or even a battle of wits, as with the detective story.[31] False information – as in Hitchcock's *Stagefright* (1950) with its lying flashback – or crucial information suddenly introduced to resolve the situation, makes apparent the narration's controlling role, breaking the contract. Obvious narrative manipulation can however be a source of pleasure, as in *Basic Instinct* (Paul Verhoeven, 1992) where the duplicitous and unknowable woman and her possible dangers is paralleled by the narration's patent manipulations of our expectatations so that our narrative desire as spectators has the same structure as that of the police detective who is investigating the woman – a wish to be deceived as well as to know.[32]

The spectator's 'passivity' may be made relative in so far as the narration is open or concealing relative to the knowledge of characters within the plot, so that if we know more than a character we are less in thrall to the narration, less a victim to its surprises. But since the spectator cannot act in the narrative, she or he cannot do anything with this knowledge, and is made into a helpless bystander, a passive position arising as much in suspense thrillers as in romantic melodrama. We may, of course, take up an active or passive position in so far as we take up the position in the narrative of a character who is an active or passive protagonist. We commonly call this an identification with a character; in *Coma* the active protagonist is a woman, raising the question of whether we identify with her as a character and hence as a woman, or with her narrative position as active protagonist.

Coma draws on two different though related narrative strategies: the detective story (the 'whodunnit') and the suspense thriller, each of which posits quite different relations of knowledge for the spectator. In the classical detective narrative the story of the crime is unfolded by the investigations of a character through whom we discover both what happened and why.[33] The detective will not only know more about the enigma or crime than any other character, but also, at times, more than the spectator or reader. In *The Big Sleep* (Howard Hawks, 1946), for example, Humphrey Bogart's Marlowe always seems to know already what has happened or is

going to happen. The enigma of the crime is thus paralleled or displaced by the enigma of the detection, of how the detective will
come to know who perpetrated the criminal act or acts. As a result,
while a whodunnit is predicated on a question and its answer, its
story lies in the telling of the tale, the 150 or so pages or 80 minutes
which recount the detection and not the crime so that the spectator
is engaged in coming to know how, as well as what, the detective
knows. This telling is also a process of *delay*, of withholding the
answer, which must therefore be effaced for if 'seen' it will expose
the contrivance of the narration and hence disrupt that 'suspension
of disbelief in favour of coming to know' which is central to narrative.[34] It is this function of delay which, Barthes has argued, is
central to all narratives. In *S/Z*, Barthes designated the operations of
the unfolding of the enigma as the hermeneutic code – the 'Voice of
Truth' – because it is the code through which we will know, but
whose operations within the text must always be a putting off of
knowledge, else the story will end. It has a contradictory role therefore; it is the mode by which the answers will be given, and it is the
mode whereby an answer is withheld in favour of continued narration. The story is the period of delay between the setting of the
enigma and the solution. Thus the hermeneutic code structures the
enigma according to the expectation and desire for its resolution in
terms of both enabling and delaying the solution.[35] Barthes has described this function of delay as a distortion or distending whereby
the narration holds apart or suspends the elements which will give
the solution, and the space thus created is then 'filled up' with the
narrating. Instead of a chronological or natural time, another –
'logical' – time is created with very little connection with real time
but which is held together in the logic of narrating.[36] For example,
in a novel a character might hold out his hand to shake that of
another character and between the beginning of the gesture and its
completion there may be inserted paragraphs of description, responses, thoughts on the context of the handshake, on the appearance of the other character, the position of the character in relation
to others in the narrative etc. In film, the camera might cut between
a shot over the shoulder of the first character, to a reverse shot of
that character, (shot-reverse-shot), or to another character, or a cutaway could be made to a photograph or some object, or to other
events elsewhere (cross-cutting or parallel editing).

The suspense thriller, while equally involving a problem of
knowledge and its delay, produces very different relations of

knowledge and hence of identification, so that the audience is implicated within the film quite differently and, perhaps, more extremely. First, where the detective or mystery story is an unravelling of the enigma through clues and deduction in relation to which the reader/viewer is less knowledgeable than the narrative actants, in the suspense thriller there is on the contrary a continual holding back of information about, and interruptions in the pursuit of, the resolution of the enigma by the characters, while the audience will tend to have *greater* knowlege than any of the characters. Secondly, while the suspense thriller, too, is predicated on a crime or criminal activities which are being investigated, it involves a different structure of time for, as Todorov, says 'We are no longer told about a crime anterior to the moment of the narrative; the narrative coincides with the action', and the investigator, too, is embroiled in the action.[37] As a result interest shifts from wanting to know what *has* happened and how the detective finds out, to wanting to know what *will* happen. Barthes argues that

> 'suspense' is clearly only a privileged – or 'exacerbated' – form of distortion: on the one hand, by keeping a sequence open (through emphatic procedures of delay and renewal), it reinforces the contact with the reader [viewer], has a manifestly phatic function; while on the other, it offers the threat of an uncompleted sequence, of an open paradigm (if, as we believe, every sequence has two poles), that is to say, of a logical disturbance, it being this disturbance which is consumed with anxiety and pleasure (all the more so because it is always made right in the end). 'Suspense', therefore, is a game with structure, designed to endanger and glorify it, constituting a veritable 'thrilling' of intelligibility: by representing order (and no longer series) in its fragility, 'suspense' accomplishes the very idea of language: what seems most pathetic is also the most intellectual – 'suspense' grips you in the 'mind', not in the 'guts'.[38]

Barthes connects the process of narrative-as-delay with the structure of language itself: 'To narrate (in the classic fashion) is to raise the question as if it were a subject which one delays predicating; and when the predicate (truth) arrives, the sentence, the narrative, are over, the world is adjectivised (after we had feared it would not be).'[39] Narrating redoubles the structure of language, rather than merely using it as means to express its content. But in addition, and again like language, narrative-as-delay creates a structure which, in putting off the answer, produces the expectation and demand for an answer and thus opens onto desire.

Narrative-as-delay is always a question of a position in relation to a knowledge (the answer, the 'truth'). In suspense this delaying of the answer is not simply more extreme but rather arises because some, but not all or enough, knowledge has been given to the spectator, as a result a different form of relation to knowledge is brought about. The reader/viewer, placed in a privileged position of knowledge in comparison to the protagonist, is made aware of the actions of other characters and the risks this poses to the protagonist – whether in certain sequences or across the whole film – and thus is made anxious on behalf of the protagonist. Alfred Hitchcock has pointed to the way that suspense is not produced through a simple 'not knowing' – it is not just a delay in coming to know, but always depends on the fact that *something* is known – and it is the form of this lack of full knowledge which is the basis of suspense. His example of the contrast between surprise and suspense is the bomb beneath the table seen by the audience so that the audience is offered a partial knowledge, that there is a bomb, but the suspense is the delay in knowing whether it will explode, whether the characters will gain knowledge of it and be able to prevent the explosion, or not, so that 'the public is participating in the scene. The audience is longing to warn the characters on the screen.'[40] Our knowledge is effectively 'useless' for though we know something may happen, we can neither act to prevent its occurrence, nor find out the answer sooner than the film narrates it to us. Our place and relationship is literally constructed by the narrating. The delay itself is effected by the narration, the cutaway shots to the bomb beneath the table, the innocuous clock, the innocent conversation presented as shot-reverse-shot, 'the logical disturbance' which Barthes speaks of. The difference, the dissonance, thus created has the effect of redoubling anxiety, since not only is there a threat, but it is unknown to the characters. And the audience is impelled into the scene in its concern on behalf of the characters, yet the spectator's point of view is never only that of the characters – we see the bomb beneath the table and thus also occupy the camera's omniscient place of view.

The audience sees the 'full' scene whose 'meaning' emotionally implicates them, but precisely whose seeing places them outside the film. Thus it is not simply that the viewer knows more than the characters – it is not a twist on the detective story in which, for once, the viewer has more clues than the detective – but rather our relation to this knowledge is different. We don't necessarily know the whole of the enigma but we are already given what the character must find out, indeed often 'endure', and the form of the gap between the two knowledges produces suspense. Moreover, Hitchcock argues, the form of this knowledge-structure produces an emotional response:

> To my way of thinking, mystery is seldom suspenseful. In a who-dunnit, for instance, there is no suspense, but a sort of intellectual puzzle. The whodunnit generates the kind of curiosity that is void of emotion, and emotion is an essential ingredient of suspense... In the classical situation of a bombing, it's fear for someone's safety. And that fear depends upon the intensity of the public identification with the person who is in danger... A curious person goes into somebody else's room and begins to search through the drawers. Now, you show the person who lives in that room coming up the stairs. Then you go back to the person who is searching, and the public feels like warning him, 'Be careful, watch out. Someone is coming up the stairs'. Therefore, even if the snooper is not a likeable character, the audience will still feel anxiety for him.[41]

Suspense or narrative delay is typically a *local* operation of the narrative system, existing within a sequence or segment of narration. In many of his films, however, Hitchcock seems to create whole series of scenes structured in terms of this sense of suspense so that it thereby constitutes the overall narrative form in the film, rather than being just one element. This has important consequences. As already noted, the 'hero' is displaced as site of knowledge though he or she never ceases to be the protagonist – provoking and taking action within the narrative. However a different structure of identification/implication within the narrative is established with the abandonment of the illusion that we are finding out along with/in competition with the detective and we are thrust into the insecurity of not yet knowing all but worse off than the character since we know something. As a result 'having knowledge' in the suspense film is not simply part of the pleasure of 'finding out', indeed it is associated with the thrill of unpleasure, and hence the relation of 'coming to know' is not commensurable across different types of narrative. This marks the radical divergence possible within a general strategy of delay, and shows the importance of the narrative's construction of the positions of protagonist and viewer/reader vis-a-vis the knowledge itself. The character or protagonist in suspense becomes, in a way, the victim of the narrative – acting blindly in comparison with the audience's knowledge.

It is in terms of these two forms – the detective narrative and suspense thriller – that I want to consider *Coma*.

THE DETECTIVE

Marjorie Bilbow in her review of *Coma* says, 'It is not the who and the why that makes the story an entertaining mixture of suspense and black humour but the macabre how of Susan's investigations.' But *Coma* is not a classic detective story or 'whodunnit'. The film does not start with a criminal act, instead it begins by introducing us to its chief character, Susan Wheeler, first in her professional role, as a surgeon at work, and then in her personal relationship with Mark at his apartment; however, Susan leaves following an argument. This row is the first narrative event, so that the initial hermeneutic question posed in the film is whether the relation between Susan and Mark will succeed or not, suggesting a romantic comedy or melodrama film. The enigma heralded by the film's title – *Coma* – emerges only secondarily. The first victim is Nancy, Susan's best friend to whom she explains her problems with Mark while they share an exercise class. Nancy has an unwanted pregnancy and her gynaecologist has arranged for a therapeutic abortion, which Susan reassures her is a very safe procedure. Nancy, however, has a cardiac arrest during the operation and emerges from it in a coma. The enigma posed at this point is not one of murder and hence of who did it, but the problem of how a normal, healthy patient undergoing minor surgery becomes comatose following the operation. It is initially, therefore, a problem of medical knowledge and part of the project of the investigation will be the reconstitution of the problem as a criminal act. Susan has to show that the comas – for Nancy's is not an isolated case – *are* all unlawful deaths, since the film, despite the abundance of corpses, cadavers and moribund bodies, lacks evidence in terms of a body defined as murder victim. Of course the audience will presume that murder and sinister intent have been involved all along, reinforced by the prior publicity for the film which announced 'Someone's getting

away with murder.A suspense thriller. *Coma'*,[42] but the initial detection within the film is concerned with the *establishment* of this
possibility.

This has consequences for Susan's position in the narrative.
While it would be quite typical in a detective film for the protagonist to suspect sinister underpinnings where other characters deny it
– the suicide or accident which is really murder (though usually
they are fortunate enough to have a body) – in *Coma* Susan takes up
her investigation not because of suspicions, or in order to prove
murder, but in order to know. 'I just want to understand' she says,
which narratively is given as her response to grief over the condition of Nancy. As a result the narrative places Susan in a position
where, as it were, she doesn't know what she is doing – the knowledge she seeks is not the one she can or will obtain, since it is not a
medical knowledge. She is given a trait, the desire for knowledge,
which is conventionally coded as pre-eminently masculine, but she
is seeking a medical knowledge to understand a criminal act and
hence is doubly ignorant of what she seeks to understand though
her attempt to discover the truth of the first will bring about the exposure of the second. Susan's narrative position as detective is
qualified therefore by the narration which starts her off with the
wrong question. A similar process can be seen in Hitchcock's *North
by Northwest* (1959) where the hero, Roger Thornhill (Cary Grant), is
trying to find a man called Kaplan for whom he, Thornhill, has
been mistaken. Kaplan does not in fact exist but is a cover for a
female agent. Thornhill, like Susan, has the wrong question, or
quest, and he too takes on the role of a detective, seeking knowledge. His knowledge remains very partial until the facts are given
to him by the head of the government undercover agency. Once in
possession of full knowledge, however, Thornhill is able to act de-
cisively, and monumentally, when he rescues Eve and escapes
from the clutches of the villains on Mount Rushmore.[43]

In *Coma*, while Susan appears to be a place of knowledge, as the
agent of its discovery, she is consistently displaced from this position by a series of narrative situations which deny and dismiss the
knowledge she asserts or seeks, i.e. that the coma cases are at all
suspicious. For example, having obtained statistical evidence that
the frequency of coma cases is unusual, she observes a correlation
between random tissue-typing and medical procedures undertaken
in Operation Room 8, but when she checks the air lines and equipment in OR8 with Mark she is forced to admit that the diversity of

circumstances and variety of staff involved in the operations make it almost impossible that anyone could tamper with the supply of oxygen. Later, on discovering the conspiracy to sell organs orchestrated through the Jefferson Institute – the futuristic medical facility for 'caring' for coma cases – the head nurse's reference to 'Dr George' confirms Susan's suspicions of the Head of Anaesthesia. (The filmic narration has apparently supported Susan's inference by its inclusion of shots of Dr George watching Susan, and at the end he is shown beside her in the elevator as she goes up to see Dr Harris.) The moment that Susan has full knowledge, that Dr George Harris is the villain, she is returned to the role of woman as victim, and she spends the final minutes of the film prostrate, for, having been duped by Harris she is now doped by him to produce false symptoms of appendicitis, enabling him to arrange to murderously remove the supposedly malign organ in OR8. The ending where Mark replaces her as protagonist to bring about the final exposure of the villain – and rescue Susan – is therefore the culmination of this narrative strategy of displacement. At the same time this narrative strategy contradicts and conflicts with Susan's role as protagonist, contributing to that sense of an unsatisfying ending noted by reviewers and spectators.

THE CONSPIRACY OF *COMA*

If Susan is not a true detective in *Coma*, then what is the status of her investigation and of her as investigator? For it is as a detective that Susan Wheeler can have the role of dominant initiator and principal agent of the action and narrative – the active protagonist in fact – a role which has been viewed as progressive by feminists. There is no rival investigator. Mark is a poor stand-in at the end, his race to save Susan only embarked upon after her precipitating actions, and he only succeeds by following her account of finding the gas line – which Mark 'remembers' as we hear her voice-over – and which he follows. A mystery is posed and solved in the film by Susan, but *Coma*'s mode of narration moves between mystery and suspense so that the issue of knowledge in the film is not only the question 'what happened?' but also 'what will happen?'. In suspense the narrative concern ceases to be in the detection and solution, but lies instead in how the characters will act, and hence in the form of resolution. Suspense is the 'waiting to know'.

This shift is not, of course, motivated by the lack of a detective, since Susan is clearly offered as one. Rather, *Coma* seeks to operate through the conventions of both the detective and the suspense genre, the shift between them being effected through the narrative's construction of an enigma involving both a mystery – the coma cases – and a threat to Susan. This threat does not arise simply from the danger inherent in tackling the mystery and it changes her position from active protagonist within the detective narration to a passive position within the suspense narration. For the protagonist within suspense never has the 'upper hand' narratively, but is always a potential victim to the mystery under investigation.

As noted already, one of the problems within the film is that while the investigation is central its object has to be asserted and then justified in the process of the investigation. Susan's response to Nancy's coma following a straightforward operation is to try to understand why it happened. She establishes the issue of coma for herself and then asserts it as a general problem, since she cannot understand Nancy's condition within the (medical) knowledge she has. Checking all the cases of unexplained coma at the hospital over the past year, she discovers that the rate for these cases is far higher than could be statistically expected. The basis on which she is trying to make sense of Nancy's condition thus shifts from the purely individual to one of the enigma of unexplained coma cases in general. However, her investigation is never recognised within the film, in the sense of being either authorised or seen as reasonable by other characters. The hospital authorities reject the need for her investigation – claiming that all aspects of the coma cases have been explored already. As a result her continued investigation implies negligence on the part of the hospital and its staff, hence it is also viewed with hostility and is blocked by Dr George while by Dr Harris instructs her to cease her enquiries, and he also requires her to be seen by a psychiatrist.

Such an 'opposition of disbelief' is seen in many thriller-investigation films, where the hero must do battle against a bureaucracy as well as with the 'real' villain, for example in *Dirty Harry* (Siegel, 1971). However, these difficulties or 'trials' put before the protagonist may not only operate as simple forms of delay in the narrative, but, as in *Coma*, may be embedded to produce a significant complication within the narration. This arises because, first of all, Susan's investigation is not directed towards a suspected third party but at the hospital itself and, since she doesn't initially recognise the criminal nature of the cause behind the coma cases, it implies that hospital malpractice and a cover-up are involved, therefore the hospital management's response is logical and expected, in fact quite 'reasonable'. Secondly, not only her investigation but Susan herself is set up by the hospital as unreasonable – the opposition to her investigation becoming an opposition to her. At this point, because the justification for her investigation is not confirmed within the film, the film could simply be a psychological drama about the 'problems' of Susan Wheeler, about her personal difficulties as a woman doctor in an all-male world, and indeed the film offered this as its opening *fabula/syuzhet* structure with the row between Susan and Mark. The mystery of the coma cases comes to displace this, taking over as the focus of narrative action, thus it might be deemed a second story/plot structure. However I will try to show that this is not the case, and that instead the psychological drama is a plot device for the narration of the drama of the murders.

The status of Susan as protagonist is crucial here, for both she and the investigation must seem plausible, her suspicions well-founded and reasonable, and the investigation therefore necessary and justified, in order to sustain the story/plot structure. Two factors interrelate in confirming Susan's credibility as protagonist: first of all there is audience expectation – created through cinema advertising, prior publicity and reviews – that *Coma* is not a psychological drama, and that a conspiracy will soon be made apparent. The problem of the coma cases immediately fits as the 'sinister mystery', so that the audience will have accepted all along that the investigation is justified, and see its questioning in the film as a narrative twist. Secondly, this expectation will affirm Susan as the investigator in as much as she has already been offered within the film for identification as the protagonist. This can be seen in a number of ways: the film opens on Susan driving to the hospital, her place of work – which is a conventional way of introducing the chief character. The following scenes at the hospital, of Susan taking a conference on a patient, in the operating theatre etc., present her as a doctor, in charge, authoritative, in possession of knowledge. After her row with Mark at his flat, Susan leaves and the next scene shows her arriving home, the narrative thus following Susan rather than Mark, confirming the bias of the opening shots. In addition Susan is presented as having a number of positive traits which encourage identification with her as protagonist: she holds a position of moral rectitude in her rejection of the hospi-

tal politics and careerism expressed by Mark, or the political wheel-
ing and dealing of Dr Harris. Her care and concern for patients is
contrasted to the general theme in the film of the typical de-
personalised care given in hospitals, or doctors' insensitivity, for
while the surgeon operating on Nancy Greenly says 'I just want to
get this mother off the table', Susan is shown giving lollipops to a
small boy patient (he is waiting for a kidney transplant, a typical
example of narrative over-determination in *Coma*).

What then of the narrative twist, of the 'opposition of disbelief' to
her investigation within the hospital? I want to argue that this is
more than just a narrative twist, that it is a crucial narrative strategy
which in effect sets up a second, 'false' conspiracy within *Coma* on
to which the real conspiracy and threat are displaced for much of
the film. What makes this second conspiracy possible are the very
features which provided the basis for a feminist reading of the film,
that is, the construction of Susan as a strong independent woman
prepared to think and act on her own. As such she is shown continually as 'difficult' in relation to other characters in the film. Susan's
row with Mark at the beginning of the film both establishes her
strength and independence, securing the credibility of her investigation and of subsequent 'heroic' scenes, *and* sets her up as
difficult, as a problem as a woman. As she walks out of Mark's flat
she says 'I just want some respect' but he replies 'You don't want a
relationship, you run away from it. You don't want a lover, you
want a Goddam wife.' Against the reasonableness of her demands
for Mark to 'help out' is set his accusation that she can't handle her
femininity, can't cope with a relationship. Her independence is
identified with her problem with their relationship and thus also
portrayed as a weakness. This theme of her vulnerability as an independent woman recurs when she repeats Mark's accusation to
the psychiatrist. The question of acting in her own right and being a
woman is raised when, insisting on pursuing the investigation, she
says to Mark 'You think that just because I'm a woman I'm going to
be upset. I just want to understand. I wish you'd stop treating me
as if there was something wrong with me.' Dr Harris, too, says 'I
can protect you 'cos you're good. And a woman'; while Susan says
again, in reply, that people seem to think there's something wrong
with her, instead of seeing that the problem is the coma cases!

Susan is quite right. Her independence, as it is constructed in the
film, is played on in commonsense sexist terms: if she is so independent then there must be something wrong with her and this is

also a way in which her investigation is denied in the film by other characters. This collective male prejudice against the idea that a woman could be right, or that if a woman is saying something disagreeable she must be neurotic, appears as a kind of conspiracy. The 'opposition of disbelief' sets her up as overwrought and upset at her best friend's condition, as unreasonable and paranoid – shown by the way she does not react as a woman should, but yet over-reacting, as a woman would, while the psychiatrist's report is that she's 'rather paranoid and upset'. The sense of the independent woman as a problem to those around her, i.e. to men, is developed in the scene where Mark is exhorted by the Chief Resident (whose job he hopes, and is encouraged to believe, he will get) to 'Do something about her', though Mark can only repeat that 'she likes to do things her own way'. It is reinforced by Harris, after his second meeting with Susan, when he turns and comments: 'Women. Christ'. These scenes are unknown to Susan so that the audience is given a privileged position of knowledge in comparison to Susan, namely, of a sustained effort by the men in authority around her to control her and to stop her investigation. These scenes build up a sense of conspiracy around Susan.

The scene in which Susan is apparently followed by a suspicious-looking man culminates this narrative strategy. Following the frustrations of that day, and after her second meeting with Harris, she leaves to go home and finds that her car won't start. It's too much and she collapses in rage and frustration, uselessly beating the roof of the car with her fists. Her ineffectual violence emphasising her lack of control, her 'feminine' position as a victim. The camera stays with Susan's narrative perspective, presented by an 'omniscient' camera view cutting between medium-close shots in front of Susan or from to one side of her as she hits the car, and long shots from behind and to her left, until we see her turn around and notice something and now are we given a long reverse-shot from Susan's point-of-view (pov), which reveals a man standing in shadows opposite, watching her, and Susan leaves her car, exiting frame right. (See frame-stills from this scene : plate 2.) In the next shot the camera pans from a subway poster with a train entering obscuring the poster, to Susan waiting on a the platform. The camera pans back to follow as she enters the train and takes a seat opposite the door, then the camera cuts to show the platform through a train window and we can see the man arriving on the platform. There is a cut to Susan in medium-close shot, her face now registers a startled look, and the camera cuts to show the man reaching the train door, too late – it has closed again. The final shot shows Susan looking. These events lead Susan – and perhaps the spectator – to believe that this man tampered with her car and is following her, leading us to identify with her projection of threat from this man although such a reading is not yet narratively supported but could simply be further evidence of Susan's paranoid and hence unfounded fears. In fact the scene both introduces the first mark of the 'true' conspiracy – the man watching her later proves to be a hired killer – and completes the construction of Susan as paranoid: when she arrives at Mark's he reassures her saying her car is always breaking down, and then 'proves' the absurdity of her theories of carbon monoxide poisoning as the cause of the coma cases when they go and check the equipment in OR8.

After this Susan and Mark go away, so that Susan can 'recover', as Dr Harris proposed. Here, where the narrative requires it, Susan is weak and 'feminine', against character. The following montage of scenes suggests an idyllic weekend with its images connoting the classic romantic couple[44] while its portrayal of love and tenderness between the couple places Susan and Mark firmly within conventional male/active, female/passive roles. Susan has been put back in place so that the 'male conspiracy' view of her appears to be confirmed. This sequence is, though, a false resolution, a hiatus, which seems narratively unnecessary as well as unfortunate in terms of a progressive reading of the film, while an opposition is set up between this sequence where Susan is 'normal' – conventionally feminine – and the scenes where she is actively pursuing her investigation. This opposition is resolved at the end of the film with Susan's rescue by Mark and its closing images showing her prostrate on a stretcher, her hand held by Mark, ceasing to be 'independent' once the narrative ends.

Only at the end of this interlude does the trip away have a narrative function in advancing the investigation: happening to pass the Jefferson Institute, Susan makes Mark stop the car and she goes in to make enquiries while we are also shown through a series of shots the modernist – and connotatively ominous architecture – of the building, the camera returning to Susan via shots of the video security cameras, emphasising the role of surveillance. She is met by a woman who informs her that 'there is no staff' and that 'I am in charge', telling Susan that she must visit during official times. Here, where Susan will find the real conspiracy, she also finds a woman; this balances her as protagonist, setting the two up as adversaries. And it also avoids rupturing the 'male conspiracy' by not presenting at this point a man as bearer of the real conspiracy but a woman instead. It is as a structure of suspense that the 'false' conspiracy – the construction of Susan Wheeler as paranoid discussed earlier – is produced, but now understood not only in terms of an anxiety on the part of the spectator but more importantly as the production of a privileged knowledge for the viewer and different position of 'view', and hence of identification, than that within the detective strategy. From this point *Coma* becomes an action film, with Susan seizing the initiative to actively pursue her investigations. The next day, taking coffee with colleagues in a break between surgery, a maintenance man (seen earlier when she sought the files on the coma cases from Dr George) approaches Susan and arranges to meet her in the basement to show her how the comas are induced.

The 'detective' and the 'suspense' elements in *Coma* represent two different narrative strategies, two distinct codes operating in different sequences of the film, which employ differing systems of narration and importantly, as a result, producing differing placings of the spectator in relation to the actions and characters constructed. In the 'detective' narrative Susan knows more than the spectator, while in the suspense narrative the spectator knows more than Susan. Susan is most 'positively' represented in the moments of her role as detective, seen for example in her determined and effective action in investigating the coma cases, dispatching her attacker, and escaping from the Jefferson Institute. Narratively Susan is the source of action – when she finds the maintenance man dead she pursues the investigation, following the gas-lines he had mentioned and exploring the ventilation shaft. She initiates action, illegally entering Dr George's offices to check the records, while she takes effective counter-action when she is disturbed and then pursued by the hired killer. The narration is now characterised by camera positions which support our identification with Susan as active protagonist.[45] The camera consistently offers us Susan's optical point-of-view (pov) within the action, showing us Susan intercut with what she sees but without at this point introducing the alternative position of her attacker. Susan is presented as dominant, appearing in charge of the action because we only see it from her position, her viewpoint or in the place of her viewpoint. This filmic strategy (a combination of camera position, the placing of the characters in the mise en scène of actions, and editing in the alternation of these shots) pulls the spectator into identification with the place and source of action – Susan Wheeler. And through these devices her character is attributed a power to act, to take charge of the situation, within the scene. Our expectation is that she will deal with attacker and later that she will escape from the Jefferson Institute (she does), since no other possibility is created by any alternative position of view of the action.

When a shot which can be taken as the killer's pov is finally shown – as he follows her into the hospital lecture hall – we have always already seen her one step ahead or at any rate we never know more than Susan when we are given his point-of-view. 'Knowledge' is on the side of Susan, and when we return to Susan's point-of-view she is always already in charge of the events, taking action. She bursts out of the storeroom at the back of the lecture hall and attacks her pursuer with a fire extinguisher. Then, when the killer searches the cold-store room where Susan is hiding she is already in position to act – pulling the row of frozen cadavers down on top of him and making her escape. The next morning, visiting the Jefferson Institute for clues, Susan slips away after the tour to search the building and the audience again becomes at times less knowledgeable in relation to the action and events than Susan, that is we have the spectator-position typical of the classic detective narrative. When she is pursued into a room on the second floor of the Institute the camera shows her entering the room, then cuts to her pursuers, then in the next shot it returns to the room but Susan is not there; instead the camera reveals a broken window and we hear the guard's comments that she won't get far, so that we are not yet aware that she has ingeniously hidden herself above them in the ceiling cavity, and are *surprised* at her escape.

FROM IDENTIFICATION TO PARANOIA

The structures and positions of identification produced by the narrative strategy of suspense is quite different to that of the action/detective narrative. What is important is not the mere possession by the audience of more knowledge than the protagonist but its relationship to this knowledge and its unfolding. In his discussion of suspense Hitchcock emphasised that he wanted the audience to *care* about his characters, and referred to the importance of 'the intensity of the public identification with the person who is in danger'.[46] But this is achieved only by breaking up that identification, refusing any simple identity of character and specta- tor point-of-view within the action. The spectator is *engaged on behalf* of but not in the position of the character – a very dangerous place. Instead of viewing the action from the place of the protagon- ist with pov shots alternating with non-pov shots, in suspense the camera strategy will effect an undermining of the protagonists's pov and thus of her or his dominance over the action so that the scene will be equally or even predominantly viewed from *another* position.

The climax of the suspense strategy in *Coma* is the scene dis- cussed earlier in which Susan, upset and demoralised following a harrowing meeting with Harris, tries to start her car. Narratively Susan is not initiating or in charge of the action that follows and will eventually respond by trying to flee. The sequence contains 12 shots, and frame stills from shots 4, 7, 9, 10 and 12 appear in plate 2. Shot 1 shows Susan in her car, but it won't start and she finally gets out. The film cuts to a long-shot from behind and to the left of Susan (2), then it cuts to a medium shot along the same axis, and Susan begins to hit the car (3); the camera then cuts to a medium- close shot in front of her (shot 4, across the car and a reverse of the previous shot), alternating in shot 5 to a medium-close shot along the same axis as 3; shot 6 repeats shot 4, 7 returns to shot 2, a long shot, and 8 repeats 5. The camera initially functions as an objective, omniscient observer showing Susan's hysterical loss of control but the cut-in to medium-close shot pulls us into an identification with her response of frustration and helplessness, while since they are not narratively motivated as another character's viewpoint, the powerful mirror-identification arising with the close-up is made possible.[47] The long-shot/close-up alternation presents Susan's sub- jective responses and experience and while shots 1–8 do not show Susan's optical point of view, we are able to infer her psychological point of view through the close-ups of her.

We lack a look within the scene, therefore, of Susan's or another character's look. As a result an anticipation is set up – involving the question not only of what will happen next but of how, and from where and with whose look we will see it. The anticipation becomes anxious expectation when the question becomes: whose view is the camera's look? The narrative system of *Coma* has consistently worked through shot-reverse-shot combined with medium or long-shots and this has been the structure of the preceding sequence in Harris' office, where the camera alternated between Harris seen from or near to Susan's position, and the reverse, of Susan seen from or near Dr Harris's position, and medium-long shots from neither character's place, showing either both Susan and Harris – he gives her his handkerchief to wipe her eyes; or one character only, the latter giving the audience a 'privileged' or 'objective' view of the characters. Given this already-established system of editing the beginning of the scene with Susan's car is incomplete. The narrative expectation of 'what will happen next?' is exacerbated or doubled-over in the filmic narration. Anxiety in the anticipation arises from the lack of a signified, of meaning, to the narration at this point, which only the intervention of another look can break and resolve. At the same time such a 'view', or signified, is already implicit in its lack, we are aware of its absence, an absence which thus structures our viewing – held to the inescapable two-look structure of camera/our look and Susan's look seen by us but not seeing us. The 'sinister quality' or anxiety is an effect of this structure, for while the doubling structure of the two looks offers an imaginary relationship – Lacan's mirror identification which pulls us as spectators into an imaginary totality, an 'imaginary' fullness of view and knowledge – this apparent structure of full knowledge is incomplete. Narratively we don't yet know what the scene 'means' in terms of the overall narrative, nor is it clear what is going to happen or why this scene is happening.[48] Jacqueline Rose has shown that the apparent plenitude of the cinematic look is always already broken in so far as the look is reversible and it is this potential reversibility, of looking and being looked at, which Lacan defines as the paranoic alienation of the ego, leading Rose to argue that 'paranoia could be said to be latent to the structure of cinematic specularity in itself, in that it represents the radical alterity of signification (the subject spoken from elsewhere)'.[49]

The anxiety of suspense, its effectivity as an 'exacerbated form of delay' (Barthes) thus also lies in its drawing into play the paranoia of specularity latent in cinema through a narrational structure of camera views in which the third look is kept absent. Narratively, there clearly will be another look, and it is also one which will be discovered by Susan. At the end of shot 8 we see Susan look left and notice – glance at – something, and the next shot (9) from behind Susan is a reverse shot showing what she sees – a man standing in shadows across the road. This shot is also reverse field of shot 2 and shot 7 which had previously appeared to be an objective camera shot but are now revealed to be the place of a view, this mysterious man's look while at the same time it is Susan's point of view. Meaning now is in place: we infer that this man has been watching her for some time, perhaps has tampered with her car, and that maybe he is a potential threat. This meaning has been constructed through the form of representation – Susan is shown as a victim of circumstances which appear sinister rather than accidental once Susan's look draws the man into the narrative scene and we may infer, as Susan asserts later to Mark, that he could be the cause of the car's malfunction and a potential threat.

The sequence actualises the latent paranoia of the reverse-shot structure – Susan's look finds its answering return as a potential or imagined threat because the narration does not provide any further information to Susan, or the spectator, about the unknown man. The latent paranoia is here a device of the plot, of the narration, creating suspense and a sense of anxiety, while paranoia – Susan's unconfirmed suspicions – is also a narrative signified. At the same time the scene introduces a representative of the real conspiracy, the hired killer, but this will only be known later. On the one hand the scene completes the presentation of Susan as paranoid – as Mark tells her later, her car is always failing to start – and thus is the culmination of the 'false' conspiracy. This is possible because the position of Susan as place of narrative truth and knowledge has been undermined by earlier scenes emphasising her paranoia (the psychiatrist's report for example), that is, her 'false', unreasonable, interpretation of events and reality in the film, and because the spectator knows that she is upset. On the other hand the spectator has been given information not known to Susan which allows us to confirm that she should indeed be suspicious of the good intentions of those around her. Dr George Harris's remark 'Women, Christ' undermines him as the kindly avuncular or fatherly protector he purports to be, while Mark's discussion with the Chief of Staff casts suspicion on him too. Suspense – that is, anxiety about the fearful events which may befall Susan – arises then as a result both of our having the same suspicions as Susan, for we too may believe there is something suspicious in the coma cases and thus we identify with her view of events, and because we have even more reason than she to be suspicious and our knowledge makes us anxious for her, indeed paranoid since our worst fears are not yet narratively justified. The spectator's position of knowledge here is multiple and contradictory, for we know that Susan is a little paranoid, but all the same it's true, she is being persecuted, and moreover we may identify with her 'paranoic' response that people are out to get her – after all, tough and successful women are often the objects of male attack but while our knowledge in the film – the remarks by Harris, Mark and the Chief of Staff – justifies this judgement, this knowledge is unknown to Susan and hence the film at this point does not yet justify *her* fears.

The latent paranoia actualised in the reverse-shot structure as a plot or narrational device produces a further level (remembering here Barthes's 'storeys') for the enactment of paranoia is a game which is always twofold, of a projection of aggressivity onto the other, and the fear of that aggressivity returned upon oneself from the other. Within this Susan will be both the subject of her projected aggressivity – she places it outside herself in Harris and in the man watching her, and she will be the object of her projected aggressivity turned back on her – it is *she* who is being difficult and unreasonable, not all the men around her, so that it is in the place of these male figures that the projected aggressivity will find its point of enunciation. Paranoia is therefore constructed in the film at a series of levels, and in each case it involves both identification and a splitting of the subject's position.

CONCLUDING VIEWS

The narration in *Coma* is constructed through an oscillation between narrating through suspense, where Susan is victim to and passive within the 'false' conspiracy, and narrating through an active protagonist, with Susan as actively detecting and dispatching the villainy. We cannot, however, substitute the weighing up of images of women in *Coma* with a weighing up of the narrative construction, whereby one strategy is progressive for women and the other repressive, for these strategies are not discrete operations but interdependent, and, after all, there is considerable satisfaction in Susan being proved right, a satisfaction made possible and more poignant by the 'false' conspiracy and the narrative weight accorded to it (which is precisely the narrative purpose of this form of reversal). Nor can we assess Susan's character as if she were a real person, for her 'characteristics' are not independent of these constructions but a function of the plot and its requirements for the narration of the enigma of the coma cases. We might, however, speculate that it is only because the chief protagonist is a woman that the narration sets her up as a victim of suspense, but obviously suspense is not gender specific, and it is as protagonist that Susan is thus a 'victim', not as a woman.[50] And, despite the convincing verisimilitude of the motivation of Susan in the film as paranoid, drawing as it does on the reality of women's difficulties in their social and professional interaction with men, it functions in the film as a tactic of suspense, of delay, all the more transparent because it has no function within the real conspiracy plot.[51] It is only within the suspense strategy that Susan is 'out of place' as the difficult and independent woman, and by the end of the film this strategy has disappeared.

Suspense is created within *Coma* around a second, 'false' conspiracy, while the true one is elsewhere, the villain is Dr Harris, not Dr George, despite the clues foisted on us right up to the last minute when Susan meets Dr George in the elevator on her way to see Dr Harris! What are the consequences of this narrative manipulation? It produces a certain confusion in the ending since the 'false' conspiracy is not resolved but just disappears with the emergence and resolution of the 'real' conspiracy, located in the figure of Dr Harris who can now become the sole bearer of the 'false' conspiracy as well, and as a result the issue of Susan's 'independence' which the suspense narration drew upon is left hanging. While the film's closure places its characters back into conventional relations of sexual difference, as Mark embraces Susan and reassures her that Harris has been apprehended, the introduction of Mark as Susan's rescuer is an abrupt reversal of narrative expectations, not only because by this shift the film 'cheats' on its audience's identification with the active protagonist, but also because Mark has been presented repeatedly as an ambiguous and suspicious figure, so that he cannot readily appear as a convincing substitute protagonist. Something falls apart here, therefore. The plot fails to convince us of its manoeuvres, and the contrivance of its narrative devices becomes obvious. As a result, whether intended or not, the film's closure begins to appear parodic of the classical action film where the male hero rescues the threatened heroine. The reversal of Susan's earlier active role seems too pat, and the film's assumption that a woman protagonist cannot be allowed the final victory is made all too apparent so that the film's narrational strategy is laid bare. This arises not just because the film has set Susan up as a power-ful woman and then reverses this, but because it fails to resolve the narrative strategy it has set going around Susan as an active, independent but *difficult* woman.

Coma, as a commercial Hollywood product, tries to cover all the angles, to include as many elements as possible which will sell the film.[52] It has social relevance in its issue of spare-part surgery, and draws on genre elements of horror and suspense, it makes an appeal to feminists in its presentation of a woman investigator while playing to male perceptions of the 'difficulty' of independent women, and finally, it hedges its bets by reinstating a male as final protagonist (a disavowal of Susan's role which no doubt some spectators identify with).[53] But as a result the film, or rather the function of story-telling – of enunciation – takes up at this point the same position as both Mark and Dr Harris earlier, that is, it tries to put Susan back in her place, thus it occupies the same position in the narration as the 'false' conspiracy, and it will be subject to the same suspicions with which the audience may have viewed that 'conspiracy'. In other words the film narrates how sexist it is, just like the male-dominated hospital system! It is because the film fails to narratively recuperate Susan, that is, it fails to motivate her re-instatement back in her woman's place, subservient to the active male, while it asserts this subservience at the level of its visual dis-course, its narration – the image of Susan lying prone on the hospi-tal stretcher – that it thereby lays itself open to the very accusation of recuperation.

COMA'S IDENTIFICATIONS

The discussion of *Coma* has emphasised the position of the charac-ter as actant, a locus within the narrative and its set of actions, as both doing and being done to, which is presented as a position of view and hence knowledge in which we locate ourselves and *thus* identify with. Identification here is not as an appropriation by the spectator of an *identity*, but instead identification arises insofar as the narrative in its narratingness takes hold of us and puts us too, as spectators, in play in the story-world of the film. The organisa-tion of the filmic system, a vertical and horizontal organisation in time and space, finds us our place, or rather, is a process, a finding for us of places, which is neither arbitrary nor wholly given in advance. As a result we are involved with, care about (even if only for a moment) characters we may not like, nor necessarily wish to be like, but whose position and place within the narrative we adopt. And this against sexual difference as it were, for the gender of the character is not a necessary determinant of the identification thus produced; it doesn't matter here that it is a man or a woman.

In *Coma* this 'narratingness' involves both the suspense and the detective form of narrative, from which two forms of look and identification arise: on the one hand there is Susan's controlling look as the active protagonist pursuing detection, on the other hand the structure of suspense poses her as the object of looks – of other characters, and of the 'objective' camera's look. While this 'objective' view undermines the identity of character and spectator – for the spectator is in a place of view other than that of the character – it also constructs the basis for an identification by providing information about and, perhaps, understanding of the character – the close-up of a character's face for example which precedes the cut to that character's optical point-of-view look. The 'objective' camera look is therefore never properly objective, never simply a neutral observer upon the scene, for it takes its place within a system which is an interplay of objective and character-looks, this interplay coming to contaminate the camera's look, posing the spectator/camera no longer as an onlooker, evaluating the scene, but as an impassioned spectator – the spectator of Hitchcock's 'caring public' caught in the play of the narrating and the structure of identifications thereby produced. The privileged knowledge made available to the spectator through the 'objective' look intensifies the structure of identification established in as much as it is put in the service of that identification – our protagonist is being conspired against by her enemies – while placing the spectator out-of-place in relation to that character's position, an out-of-placeness which provokes an anxiety in that it poses a gap, precisely a space for the look which is returned. The cultivation of this anxiety, the paranoia of the look returned, characterises suspense as a narrative strategy. But this is only an exacerbation, an intensification of a tendency inherent in cinema, of the possibility of the omnipotence of the spectator/narrator's look being undermined by a look or view from elsewhere.

THE DESIRE FOR IDENTIFICATION

While sexual difference, and a certain sexism, are at issue in the narration of *Coma*, the film's structures of identification are not fixed according to gender. What has been emphasised in this analysis are positions of view and knowledge constructed by the narration for the characters within the film and for the spectator. We identify, I argue, in as much as we take up these positions of knowledge, of view, which are also positions in relation to another, a viewing other. Feminism, however, has more often focussed on identification as an issue of contents, and on identity as the effect of identification with a certain content of image or role. Positive images of women were demanded in order to enable a politically progressive identification by women with these images. But such a demand assumes an unproblematic assimilation of viewer to the film character and her image as sexed role in terms of a model for identity. The psychical mechanism involved in such an assimilation of, or modelling on, the personality of the character or film star on the part of the woman spectator – as a content which can be taken up or rejected – is not explained.

At the same time identification has been viewed as a central political issue insofar as it is taken to be the mechanism by which the viewer is assimilated to a film's particular system of meaning. 'Identification' here is held to be the means for forming or moulding opinion, reproducing existing sets of ideals, of ideologies, and this is taken to be the political stake in relation to film, by both the right and left as well as by feminists, with the question of control of films, television etc. thus becoming central. What is assumed is that the viewer 'loses' her or himself in the process of viewing – the 'ideology' working against the viewer's wishes or best interests in appropriating her or him to pleasure in 'being' the character whose perceived attributes are copied or in some way assimilated. Again the mechanism of such identification remains unclear.

In rejecting a view of ideology and identification as a simple content – sheer signified within the film – psychoanalysis has been looked to in order to describe the process by which the spectator is implicated within the film, that is, the way the viewer is constructed as a spectator-subject for film. But, following the work of Laura Mulvey in 'Visual Pleasure and Narrative Cinema', the question of sexual difference in the cinema was answered unilaterally, the gaze is masculine and our identification with it in the film places us in a masculine position.[54] This confuses the controlling camera's (objective) gaze and the active protagonist's look with a position of sexual difference and/or with gender, and a position of view within film has become endowed with a content – masculinity. The analysis of *Coma* shows, however, that this is not necessarily the case. There is, I argue, no single or dominant look in cinema with which we identify – neither the male look nor the identification with camera. Rather, there is a continual construction of looks, and hence a shifting production of spectator-position, so that it is the structure of the looks in a film which is determining of the spectator's place, not a content for that look. Identification in cinema is a continually shifting construction of subject-position across the determinants of the film system – the organisation of narrative and narration – producing a subject-in-process. Nevertheless the spectator-subject must be available to the constructions of cinema, to be able to come into its positions of identification, including positions of sexual difference. It is therefore necessary to look at the process of identification itself for the spectating subject – already pointed to in the notion of a mirror-identification referred to earlier – and the production of the identity of sexed difference. This is taken up in the following chapter, which examines the status of the viewing subject as a psychical subject – as someone who may be moved to tears or joy by a film.

3

Identifying in the Cinema

A path leads from identification by way of imitation to empathy, that is, to the comprehension of the mechanism by means of which we are enabled to take up any attitude at all towards another mental life. (Sigmund Freud)[1]

It is always through some transfer from Same to Other, in empathy and imagination, that the Other that is foreign to me is brought closer. (Paul Ricoeur)[2]

'You've always been like that, able to think with my thoughts and feel with my feelings' Thorley declares to her childhood sweetheart, Jeb Rand, in *Pursued* (Raoul Walsh, 1947).

In general speech, 'identification', as the noun of the verb 'to identify', refers to two processes which are apparently quite distinct. There is on the one hand the process of identifying things as objects, that is, as different or similar from each other in, for example, the categorising of species as mammals, insects etc. On the other hand the term refers to a process of making oneself the same as, to identify oneself with something else (the Latin root of the work means literally 'to make the same'). This can be summed up as the difference between saying 'I identify that man as my father' and 'I identify with my father'. These two processes in fact involve a common element, namely the statement 'I am not my father'. In order to identify, to make the same, an acknowledgement of difference is required implying a separation prior to any assimilation with the object of identification. As a result, and in this gap, a psychological process comes into play.

The following discussion will examine the ways in which identification is produced as a psychological process and its consequences for and on the subject who identifies. What will be emphasised is identification understood not primarily as an issue of identity, and a set of contents for that identity, but as the taking up of a position. The argument here draws upon psychoanalytic theory as offering the most complex account of identification; at the same time identification continues to be the subject of controversy and debate within psychoanalysis and for those drawing on psychoanalytic theory. In psychoanalysis identification is invoked as fundamental in relation to a number of psychical processes; however, several mechanisms of identification seem to emerge in the literature, alongside related concepts such as incorporation, internalisation and transference, and the relation and demarcation of these is not clear. The view of identification developed by Melanie Klein draws upon Freud's concept, but also posits distinct and different psychical processes, notably developing Sandor Ferenczi's terms of introjection and projection to describe modes of identification in relation to internal and external objects.[3] Klein's emphasis on the process of splitting arising in identification was clearly influenced by one of Freud's last, unfinished papers, 'The Splitting of the Ego in the Process of Defence'[4] and this, too, is central to Jacques Lacan's view of identification which my discussion here will draw upon.

The difficulty of identification as a concept in psychoanlaysis arises from its work as an explanatory factor in the formation of symptoms, such as hysteria, while at the same time (or rather, much later, as Freud develops the second topography) it is involved in the emergence of the subject as such in the formation of the ego/superego structure. As a result psychoanalysis does not offer a unified or singular account and indeed it cannot do so insofar as there is no unified subject to support identification as identity. At every point to speak of identification is to invoke a relation involving different psychical agencies as distinct participants and partisans *vis-à-vis* external objects. It is identification indeed by which the subject is constituted as a subject but this as a *split* subject, and as split not only between conscious and unconscious but also between different psychical agencies within each of these.

Identification for Freud is the starting point for the tracing out of a psychical process first begun in the analysis of hysteria. However, the concept undergoes a gradual transformation through the development of the ideas of oral incorporation and narcissism in relation to the theory of object-choices, and as a result a more complex notion of identification emerges whereby it begins to be seen as a founding mechanism for human subjectivity. Its importance is confirmed in the formulation of the second topography where the differentiation

of the agencies id, ego and super-ego occurs as a result of the transformation of object-choices into identifications. In particular Freud
describes the transformation which occurs in the Oedipus complex
as the result of the abandonment of the parents as love-objects and
the place of these cathexes being taken by identification.
Identification is both a constitutive mechanism *and* part of secondary
symptom-formation and it might appear therefore that several concepts of identification are necessary, corresponding to different
symptom-formations, and to the division between constitutive
identifications which bring about a fundamental change, and other
kinds of identifications which may be transitory.[5]

In *The Language of Psycho-analysis* Laplanche and Pontalis summarise identification as a 'Psychological process whereby the subject
assimilates an aspect, property or attribute of the other and is transformed, wholly or partially, after the model the other provides. It is
by means of a series of identifications that the personality is constituted and specified.'[6] Psychoanalysis has traditionally been concerned with the processes of identification as the production of
identity, suggested in the phrase 'I identify with my father' referred
to earlier, that is, with those mechanisms which involve the subject
making itself the same as another subject or an aspect of another
subject or object. As a result, the process of differentiation which is
also involved has not been addressed. It is Lacan's concept of
identification in the mirror-phase and his resulting theory of the
subject which brings into the centre-stage the issue of difference, in
what Lacan terms the alienation of the subject in the process of
identification. The reintroduction of differentiation as an element in
this process shows that what is central to and for indentification is
not in the first instance a set of contents, but a *position* in relation to
the other of identification – this even, or especially, in the case of
Oedipal identifications, for it is not simply a content – the father as
super-ego – which is involved, but rather the taking up of a position,
ultimately of the father in *his* acceptance of castration. As a result we
cannot distinguish between constitutive and transitory identifications
on the basis of supposed contents of identity arising thereby.

This distinction can, however, be seen in Freud's own discussions of identification. While his earliest discussion concerns what
he terms hysterical identification, with the development of the
theory of narcissistic identification and the splitting of the ego
which accompanies this giving rise to the ego-ideal, hysterical
identification ceases to be addressed. Narcissistic identification is

the basis of those processes which have a structuring function for the subject, whereas hysterical identifications would seem to correspond to transitory identifications and which, as transitory, are less important. This dualism has been translated into film theory in the work of Christian Metz in his investigation of cinema as the imaginary signifier, where the spectator's identifications with characters in a film are called secondary, while the cinema's primary identification is found by Metz in what he describes as the spectator's identification with the camera and which is at the same time an identification with the subject's own look (but as distinct and secondary to the mirror-phase identification with one's own image).[7] As a result, in Metz's framework, psychoanalysis does not offer a theory of identification in cinema, but a theory of the constitution of a subject for cinema.

The psychoanalytic subject is also always a subject of sexual difference and the constitutive identifications are central to the production of sexual difference in and for the subject. However, this arises not in relation to masculinity and femininity as such – as if these were simple contents available for identification – but in terms of the different positions and hence pathways through the Oedipus complex which the girl and boy may be subject to. What immediately arises here therefore is a dynamic structure of identification, rather than a system of identifications in place. It is the issue of sexual difference for the cinema spectator which Metz's account fails to address.

Moreover what remains to be accounted for here is the secondary or transitory identifications so summarily dismissed by Metz. Or, more precisely, what must be accounted for is the stake for the subject who identifies as well as the mechanism of the repetition, the 'replaying' of identification which film, and indeed all narrative, offers the spectator-subject. Freud addressed the question of these transitory identifications in 'Creative Writers and Daydreaming' and as a result – as the following chapter explores – the question of identification in cinema can be shifted from one of identity, of the constitution of the subject described by psychoanalysis, to an issue of fantasy and its multiple positions of identification. But the question of identification in fantasy itself remains. It is, no doubt, that form which Freud describes as hysterical identification but to view this as merely a transitory form, a self-contained and passing form, is to ignore the way in which it involves a re-making, a re-playing of identification. Further it becomes apparent, as the following discussion will seek to show, that what is central to identification is a position in relation to an other, and that this is equally the case in hysterial identification as in fantasy, and, therefore, in cinema. This is not to suggest that identification in fantasy is simply the same as the constitutive identifications but to point to the way in which the very structure of the constitutive identifications sets up the drive for their re-playing so that subsequent, apparently transitory identifications are the support for as well as the symptom of the difficulty of the constitutive identifications. They signify the incompleteness and insufficiency of the constitutive identifications in as much as these are not fixed places of identity but are themselves a scenario of positioning in relation to an other.

FREUD'S THEORY OF IDENTIFICATION

Freud's initial consideration of identification was in connection with hysterical symptoms: 'It enables patients to express in their symptoms not only their own experiences but those of a large number of other people.'[8] However Freud emphasises that the psychical process involved is not mere imitation, but a much more complicated '*assimilation* on the basis of a similar aetiological pretension; it expresses a resemblance and is derived from a common element which remains in the unconscious'.[9] As a result, similarity – the common element – is not the effect of identification but its basis. Laplanche and Pontalis suggest that 'This common element is a phantasy: the agoraphobic identifies unconciously with a "streetwalker", and her symptom is a defence against this identification and against the sexual wish that it presupposes.'[10] The agoraphobic's sexual wish leads her to put herself in, and hence identify with, the position of the prostitute as streetwalker, i.e. as a sexually available woman. Identification here is based on the common position arising from the wish to be sexually available or active, and not on the 'identity' of the streetwalker, for only one part of that 'identity' is involved and others, such as poverty or the acquisition of money via a sexual transaction, may not be.[11] The identification derives from a prior wish which finds support in the image or rather one aspect of the image of streetwalker, and this aspect is the position of the streetwalker in relation to others, i.e. a sexual relation to her potential clients.[12]

Freud suggests the hysteric unconsciously infers 'If a cause like this can produce an attack like this, I may have the same kind of attack since I have the same grounds for having it.'[13] That it is the *same* kind of attack is as a result of the process of communication set in play – hysteria is after all but a particular form of communication – whereby the particular symptom stands as trace of the cause, as its guarantor. For the 'imitator' it stands as a signifier, a material support for a signified which has an *arbitrary* relation to that signifier. The stake of identification for the hysteric is not the trait or symptom it utilises (the cough etc.) but the position – ultimately in relation to desire – which is involved. Identification is produced not through imitation but through fantasy. Lacan therefore echoes Freud when he writes 'Whenever we are dealing with imitation, we should be very careful not to think too quickly of the other who is being imitated. To imitate is no doubt to reproduce an image. But at bottom, it is, for the subject, to be inserted in a function whose exercise grasps it.'[14] To see identification as imitation would be to ignore the complex psychical processes which bring about identification and to privilege an apparent content – the other as imitated – rather than its function for the subject.

As a result of this approach to hysteria Freud was led to posit the unconscious as such, for the hysteric was clearly not faking his or her symptoms but nor did these have any discernible organic cause. The material of the unconscious is fantasy, the wishes and desires which have been subject to repression. Freud does not develop the concept of hysterical identification, but instead introduces a new theory of identification as a result of his work on the theory of narcissism.[15] The concept of narcissism is deceptively simple – the taking of the self as a love-object. The psychical processes summed up by the concept are however very complex. In his essay *On Narcissism: An Introduction*, Freud proposes two forms. One is a primary or constitutive narcissism involving an original libidinal cathexis of the ego, from which some is later given off to objects.[16] Two, a secondary narcissism arises as a result of the withdrawal of libido from objects back on to the ego. But how then is primary narcissism distinguished from infantile auto-eroticism which is defined as the obtaining of sexual satisfaction from the child's own body? Freud writes:

we are bound to suppose that a unity comparable to the ego cannot exist in the individual from the start; the ego has to be developed. The auto-erotic instincts, however, are there from the very first; so there must be something added to auto-eroticism – a new psychical action – in order to bring about narcissism.[17]

In infantile autoeroticism the satisfaction of a component (sexual) instinct (the sexual drive)[18] is obtained solely within the child's body, bound to the operation of an organ such as feeding or defaecation, or to the stimulation of an erotogenic zone such as the mouth, the genitals, or the skin; satisfaction is distinguished as an *aim* but the drives remain objectless. In narcissism, however, the sexual drives are organised in relation to an *object*: they are directed to an image of a unified body. Just like an external object, the ego is cathected, charged with libido. Freud is thus led to speak of primary or infantile narcissism as a stage in which the ego becomes cathected with energy, and can pass itself off as the source of libido.[19] But this is not simply a progression, of narcissism now supplying the object of the drive previously missing in autoeroticism. As noted above, Freud emphasises that 'a new psychical action' is involved, enabling the taking of the body-image as an object, and thus indicating a clear disjunction between the two mechanisms. For Freud, the ego, the human subject, is made and not born. The organising effects of this disjunction are given articulation in Lacan's concept of the mirror phase.

Primary narcissism is not discussed further by Freud. It is in a sense an enabling process, or moment, in which the ego is precipitated as a kind of resevoir of libido which 'lasts till the ego begins to cathect the ideas of objects with libido, to transform narcissistic libido into object-libido'.[20] More important for the discussion here is the concept of secondary narcissism which arises in three ways Freud says: as a response to organic disease in the withdrawal of cathexes onto the ego; or, in hypochondria, in which the same phenonema occurs but without any organic cause; and finally, in being in love. Freud distinguishes two forms of being in love, a distinction which, in its division between men and women has also become notorious; a person may love

    (1) According to the narcissistic type:
        (*a*) what he himself is (i.e. himself),
        (*b*) what he himself was,
        (*c*) what he himself would like to be,
        (*d*) someone who was once part of himself.

(2) According to the anaclitic (attachment) type:
    (*a*) the woman who feeds him,
    (*b*) the man who protects him,
and the succession of substitutes who take their place.[21]

The notoriety of Freud's theory here, for feminists at least, lies in
the way in which, while refusing any general sexual difference in
relation to narcissism – primary narcissism means that all humans
have originally two sexual objects, themselves and the person who
nurtures them – nevertheless Freud seeks to erect a sexual division.

Freud uses the concept of anaclisis to describe the way in which
the sexual instincts are propped upon the self-preservative instincts
and he argues as a result that 'the persons concerned with a child's
feeding, care and protection become his earliest sexual objects: that
is to say, in the first instance his mother or a substitute for her'.[22] He
now suggests that 'Complete object-love of the attachment type is,
properly speaking, characteristic of the male', while a different
course is followed by most women:

> With the onset of puberty the maturing of the female sexual
> organs, which up till then have been in a condition of latency,
> seems to bring about an intensification of the original narcissism,
> and this is unfavourable to the development of a true object-
> choice with its accompanying sexual overvaluation. Women, es-
> pecially if they grow up with good looks, develop a certain
> self-contentment which compensates them for the social restric-
> tions that are imposed upon them in their choice of object.[23]

Freud does, though, note 'quite a number' of exceptions where
women do love 'according to the masculine type'. His arguments
here seem, therefore, to appeal to commonsense knowledge about
women, that is, to his contemporary dominant ideological discourse about women, rather than being part of a theory of sexual
difference.[24] More accurately, Laplanche has argued, these two
forms of object-choice are open to both women and men, and will
moreover tend to appear in combination. This tendency is explained if we follow Laplanche's suggestion that the anaclitic
object-choice be viewed as metonymic and the narcissistic as
metaphoric. For the young child, the anaclitic object-choice de-
volves from a slippage, a progressive detachment along a chain of
objects – milk, breast, nurturer: the part for the whole, container for

the contained, a partial object. It thus has a contiguous relation to the original object. On the other hand the narcissistic object-choice is made on the basis of similarity, and the libidinal energy is 'veritably *transported* rather than imperceptibly *displaced*'.[25] The difference is between the love of the complementary as opposed to the love of the similar. These two forms of object choice come into play before sexual difference has yet emerged.

Laplanche points out, too, that the anaclitic object choice Freud sees as characteristic of the male is also posited by Freud as deriving from infantile narcissism for 'It displays the marked sexual overevaluation which is doubtless derived from the child's original narcissism and thus corresponds to a transference of that narcissism to the sexual object.'[26] In loving the woman he loves what he himself once was, Laplanche argues, for he is captivated by 'another "beautiful totality"': the self-sufficient woman, the beautiful and complete narcissistic animal loving only herself. Thus at the very moment in which man – and Freud – would yield to "objectality", he shifts dialectically into another form of narcissism.'[27]

Freud's central concern in this essay, however, is to use the notion of narcissistic love to develop the concept of the ego-ideal. This, he says, arises following the blows to the child's narcissism (such as the arrival of a sibling, or the Oedipal complex) as a result of which a repression occurs producing a dampening down of infantile narcissism. This repression is brought about by 'the self-respect of the ego',[28] that is, an idealised image of the ego is set up by which the actual ego is measured, and all the self-love, all the child's narcissism, is now given to this 'new form of an ego ideal'.[29] Freud uses the terms ideal ego and ego ideal interchangeably here but subsequently Freud uses the term ego ideal to refer both to the ideal which is set up for the ego by the censoring agency of repression and to that agency itself, and it is then used interchangeably with the term super-ego. (The ideal ego then referring to primary narcissism.)

It is in 'Mourning and Melancholia' that Freud brings together his theory of narcissism and the mechanism of identification. Freud describes mourning as a process involving the giving up of the lost, dead, love object – painfully and slowly – through the withdrawal of libido, of cathexes, from the object back on to the ego (just like the secondary narcissism arising with illness or hypochondria). He argues that the same process occurs with melancholia, or depression, which often accompanies the mourning of the death of a loved person but which may also arise without an actual death, or even of any apparent loss of a loved one, while it is also accompanied by an extraordinary self-deprecation. 'In mourning it is the world which has become poor and empty; in melancholia it is the ego itself.'[30] The depressive has turned one part of the ego – the repressive agency or conscience – against another part, which it takes as its object and judges critically.

This reproachful agency is clearly the ego-ideal, yet how has it been turned against part of the ego? The withdrawal of libido from the loved object into the ego has not thereby 'freed' energy but rather it has served to establish an *identification* of the ego with the abandoned or lost object which is incorporated and set up inside the ego.[31] It is henceforth judged by the ego-ideal as though it were the lost object, in all its vileness. The self-deprecation which arises is in fact an attack on the former love-object now set up internally.[32] Freud describes this as a narcissistic identification involving 'a *regression* from one type of object-choice to original narcissism'.[33] This does not simply involve a return to primary narcissism, for it follows after object-cathexes and the libido thus withdrawn returns not to the ego as such, as a unified entity, but to a part of the ego, namely, to that part set up through identification as the lost love object. Primary narcissism, however, now appears as a form of primary narcissistic identification, that is, to take oneself as one's own love object is to identify with oneself, to pose oneself as an object which is the same as oneself. This seems to be the basis of Freud's insistence that identification precedes object-choice and is distinct from it. He says that it is 'a preliminary stage of object-choice, that it is the first way… in which the ego picks out an object' and that this involves the ego incorporating the object into itself for, in accordance with the oral stage of development, 'it wishes to devour the object'.[34] Freud posits this form of identification on the model of oral incorporation – for example, the breast. It is not an object-choice in the way this term is used for subsequent object relations – the object is assimilated *to* the self rather than differentiated as an object *for* the self. But a process of separation is implicated, for in so far as 'the ego' identifies it is constituted as an ego – which Lacan describes in the 'mirror stage'. The ego arises from such identifications, but as a kind of precipitation rather than as the sum of such identifications, hence producing the id-ego structure.[35] True object-cathexes then arise as a result of the passing of libido from the ego to objects. Freud therefore asserts narcissistic identification as older than hysterical identification 'and it paves the way to an understanding' of the latter.[36]

In *Group Psychology and the Analysis of the Ego* Freud presents his most extended consideration of identification. It is a synthesis of his earlier discussions which he now sums up by outlining 'three sources' of identification.[37] First, Freud says, identification is the original or earliest form of emotional tie with an object. Freud had previously considered this in relation to the precipitation of the ego, but here Freud presents it as an identification with the father and says that the small boy 'would like to grow like him and be like him, and take his place everywhere',[38] and hence he also places it in relation to the early history of the boy's Oedipal complex. This is reiterated in *The Ego and the Id*, where Freud refers to 'an individual's first and most important identification, his identification with the father in his own personal prehistory', but he qualifies this in a footnote saying 'Perhaps it would be safer to say "with the parents"; for before a child has arrived at definite knowledge of the difference between the sexes, the lack of a penis, it does not distinguish in value between its father and its mother.' [39] This introduces a distinction between primary identification – with the parents – and Oedipal identifications. Freud also includes in this account of the 'earliest' form of identification the idea that the father is a model, of what the child would like to be, and this invokes the notion of the ego-ideal; however, the ego-ideal itself was placed in relation to narcissistic identification where object-choice has regressed to identification, and which Freud describes as the second source of identification.[40]

The second form of identification is the same as that which Freud outlined in 'Mourning and Melancholia', a regressive identification through the substitution of a libidinal object-tie by means of introjection of the object into the ego. But first Freud sets himself the task of disentangling 'identification as it occurs in the structure of a neurotic sympton from its rather complicated connections',[41] that is, distinguish it from hysterical identification.[42] To do this he takes the example of a girl's cough as a neurotic symptom. On the one hand he says this may indicate an identification with the mother whereby, as a response to Oedipal rivalry and the wish to take her mother's place with her father together with the guilt this gives rise to, the girl also takes upon herself her mother's sufferings, developing the same cough as her mother. This, Freud says, is the 'complete mechanism of the structure of a hysterical symptom' namely, the symptom of hysterical identification.[43] On the other hand the cough may be her father's, as in the case of Dora, that is, the symptom is the same as that of the person who is loved. Here Freud says *'that identification has appeared instead of object-choice, and that object-choice has regressed to identification'*.[44] It is important to note that the difference Freud is concerned with does not arise from the difference in gender of the person from whom the symptom is taken, but from the relation to the love-object.[45] Hysterical identification involves taking the same position as the model in relation to the love-object, whereas regressive identification incorporates the love-object.

Freud gives a second example of this form of identification, describing the case of male homosexuality where a young man, having remained fixed on his mother as a love-object as a child, at puberty renounces her only at the cost of identifying with her. In contrast to the earlier example, where Freud speaks of the identification as partial and extremely limited, borrowing only a single trait from the person who is its object, in this second case the identification is characterised 'by its ample scale; it remoulds the ego in one of its important features – in its sexual character'.[46] For the young man transforms himself into his mother so that he now looks for objects which can take the position of his ego, of himself, and on which he can bestow the love and care his mother gave him. However this 'content' of re-modelling is not the cause but the effect consequent upon identification; its aim is not to be the mother but to continue to have the mother as a love-object, and to be loved by her. In order to achieve this the young man takes up *her* position in relation to his new love-objects, who therefore occupy his former position. The identification is again a position taken up by the ego, but now it is an internalised position.

In each example it can be seen that identification does not promote a unified identity but a splitting, one part of the ego set against another as loving, or as self-deprecating. Freud now outlines a third form of identification 'in which the identification leaves entirely out of account any object-relation to the person who is being copied'.[47] In fact Freud has already outlined three forms of identification – as the original form of emotional tie with an object, as hysterical symptom (identification with the mother's cough), and as regressive identification (with the father's cough).[48] The middle form – hysterical identification – is not referred to as a form of identification in Freud's discussion; however, it is the basis, though unacknowledged, of the third form of identification which Freud describes as follows:

> one of the girls in a boarding school has had a letter from someone with whom she is secretly in love which arouses her jealousy, and ... she reacts to it with a fit of hysterics; then some of her friends who know about it will catch the fit, as we say, by mental infection. The mechanism is that of identification based upon the possibility or desire of *putting oneself in the same situation*. The other girls would like to have a secret love affair too.[49]

The symptom of the identification, the hysteria or mental infection (though it is not this that constitutes the identification as hysterical) is adopted because 'under the influence of a sense of guilt they also accept the suffering involved in it'.[50] But why should guilt arise? Is Freud assuming that the girls would feel guilty at wishing to transgress social and sexual norms by having a secret lover? Or is it that, following Freud's own argument, the pain of jealousy is not the 'price' of identification, but its signifier? The mark of the girl's secret love affair is precisely her susceptibility to jealousy, and thus the jealousy is the signifier of her position which is adopted by the other girls, i.e. to have been *replaced* in someone's affections is nevertheless to *have been* loved. At the same time, and in keeping with Freud's theory of bisexuality in hysterical symptoms and fantasy, we may understand the jealousy of the other girls as an identification not only with the girl of the secret love affair, but also with her lover, a wish therefore to take his position in the girl's affections, i.e. to love or be loved by her. However, Freud's reference to guilt suggests that a more archaic element is also involved, namely the Oedipal scenario and its attendant guilt (invoked in his earlier example of the cough as hysterical identification) arising from the wish to have the father.[51]

This third type of identification, Freud says, 'may arise with any new peception of a common quality shared with some other person who is not an object of the sexual instinct'.[52] It is this form of identification which Freud sees as central to group psychology where, in the absence of any sexual cathexis with the other persons, identification nevertheless arises and it does so on the basis of the (new) perception of a (repressed) common quality shared with the others.[53] This common quality, as far as group psychology is concerned, lies in the nature of the tie to the leader. Freud characterises the primary form of group as one where a number of individuals have put themselves in the same place as all the others in relation to the loved object – the leader – who, Freud argues, is introjected as an ego-ideal. The viability of a group founded in this way is based upon the condition that the leader loves *all* the members of the group equally.[54] Freud was drawing here upon his thesis in *Totem and Taboo* that human civilisation was founded on the murder of the primal father by the sons whom the father had excluded from access to the women, but with whom the sons also identified. Having killed the father whom they feared, their love for him becomes uppermost, and he becomes the absolute arbiter for the society then founded, as the totem which secures the rules by which they now live. The (dead) father is set up as the power and force over all the group, but the terms of his authority are inverted, and incest is now forbidden. It is this same relationship which Freud sees as in play between the small boy and its father, a fear of the father's power and an identification.[55] In *Civilization and its Discontents* Freud connects this explicitly with his concept of the super-ego:

> After their hatred had been satisfied by their act of aggression, their love came to the fore in their remorse for the deed. It set up the super-ego by identification with the father; it gave that agency the father's power, as though as a punishment for the deed of aggression they had carried out against him, and it created the restrictions which were intended to prevent a repetition of the deed.[56]

This process involves two moments of identification: firstly that between the brothers enabling them to come together as a band in relation to the father, and which subsequently enables them to act together to enforce the restrictions they submit to; secondly, that with the father himself. The first is clearly Freud's identification between people as a result of a common feature, and this common feature is not some generalised trait but their common relation of desire to a third figure, the leader or father. Thus what characterises this form of identification, as with the girls in the boarding school, is a desire in common, and it involves each member of the group taking up the same position as all the others in relation to the love object – it therefore has the form of 'hysterical' identification. The second moment of identification is the introjection of the love object as the ego-ideal. This ideal is not, however, the image of the father but his authority, so that what is internalised is not a model for behaviour, an ideal to live up to, but a voice of authority to which one must submit, for the father's incest is now forbidden the sons. A certain ambiguity arises, therefore, as to whether introjection here involves an ideal or a prohibition, and Freud is referring interchangeably to the process as the ego-ideal and the super-ego. Freud's subsequent discussion of identification is in relation to the second, narcissistic, identification through which he traces the emergence of the ego-ideal as a splitting of the ego, pointing to but not developing the role of the super-ego as a distinct element. It is Jacques Lacan who, in his 're-reading' of Freud, has clarified and developed Freud's concepts of ideal-ego, ego-ideal and super-ego, and it is these which will now be explored. In this, Freud's third form of identification, which I have identified as 'hysterical identification, will be important', for it this mode of identification by which the subject is able to take up a position in relation to the Other. Freud had pointed to this in *Group Psychology* when he suggests that in this third form of identification 'we are faced by the process which psychology calls "empathy" [*Einfühlung*] and which plays the largest part in our understanding of what is inherently foreign to our ego in other people'.[57] It is this 'empathy' – or 'hysterical' identification – upon which cinematic identification also depends as the final section of this chapter will seek to show.

THE IDEAL-EGO, EGO-IDEAL AND SUPER-EGO

Lacan places a new emphasis on the role and process of identification in his re-reading of Freud. He formalises the divisions ideal-ego, ego-ideal and super-ego, clarifying the way in which these are positions of identification for the subject, and as a result focusses on the process of splitting Freud pointed to as being the corollary of these identifications, and which Lacan terms the fundamental alienation of the subject in identification. He introduces a new topography in relation to these divisions, of the real, the imaginary, and the symbolic, which Metz has taken up in his discussion of the cinematic signifier as imaginary. Although the mapping of this topography and its relation to the psychical divisions arising in identification was continually under revision by Lacan, the central tripartite structure always remained. The subject's identifications, however, cease to be tied in any simple way to particular structures – the imaginary for example – and become a process across them, as a placing rather than a placement. Identification is less an arrival point after a journey, more or less fixed, than a positioning in relation to another, and the desire of an other, and hence the subject's identifications are a continual journeying. As a result it is impossible to simply map these identifications, or structures, on to the processes of cinematic identification, categorising some as imaginary, others symbolic. Instead a more dynamic concept of identification emerges, and it is through this that I shall try to show that cinema, as representation, is not a reproduction or re-presentation of identities and identifications, but a production and presentation. Cinema does not illustrates a process which has already occurred in the subject, but is itself that very process for the subject – this is also the scandal of cinema, that it moves us, just like real life or even more. Only in this way can the lure and desire involved in our relationship to representation be understood.

Lacan addresses more directly and systematically the emergence of the subject through identification. Freud had always insisted that the ego is made, not born, and that this must involve an identification which is both extremely early and also extremely sketchy, at first no more than a form conceived of as a limit, or a sack, 'a sack of skin'.[58] In *The Ego and the Id* Freud writes that 'The ego is first and foremost a bodily ego; it is not merely a surface entity, but is itself the projection of a surface.'[59] Lacan's account of the emergence of the ego as conditional upon an identification in his discussion of the mirror phase is thus prefigured in Freud. Lacan says 'We have only to understand the mirror stage as an *identification*, in the full sense that analysis gives to the term: namely, the transformation that takes place in the subject when he assumes an image',[60] and he comments that the human child of about six months, although with less instrumental intelligence than a chimpanzee, can nevertheless already recognise its own image in a mirror.

Laplanche points out however that 'The scenario of the child at the mirror is only the index of something that occurs, in any event, without that apparatus: the recognition of the form of another human and the concomitant precipitation within the individual of a first outline of that form.'[61] It is a moment in which the child recognises itself as constituted by a corporeal image, whether as in Lacan's example it is through the mirror-reflection of its own body, or through the agency of another's – its mother's or carer's look and address – who grants that image to the child. The moment of recognition is also one of identification: 'that's me, that's mine. I am that image' precipitating the I of the ego which emerges to claim the image as its own. Lacan therefore terms the child's recognition a misrecognition insofar as its narcissistic identification is with its mirror image, and this appears to present a unified, whole and coherent image. Lacan emphasises as key in this misrecognition the fact of the child's relative motor inco-ordination in comparison with the coherent, unified and whole image – an image which appears fixed and stable – presenting itself to itself in the mirror.[62] This constitutes for the child, Lacan suggests, an ideal-ego equivalent to Freud's position of primary narcissism. This ego is thus fictional, and alienated in that it comes to the child as *other*. It is also an other who sends back to the child the affirmation of its identity in its identifying with the mirror image, its ideal ego. This can be seen clearly in the case of the child who, when held up to the mirror, turns to the one who is holding it and appeals with its look for an affirmation of what it sees. It can also be seen in that form of address so dear to parents 'Who's my beautiful, clever, baby?' (or, perhaps, 'clever boy' and 'beautiful girl'). A rhetorical question finding its answer in the child's identification with the object of address. The other here is for Lacan the mother, but one may follow Freud and instead posit the parental couple in so far as sexual difference is not yet a stake for the child (although it is for the parents who will convey this to the child more or less directly). This other functions as the *Other* which is thus already present in the register of the imaginary.[63]

The child bases its desire in its alienating image as ideal ego, but that object is supported and guaranteed by (the desire of) the Other, and who is the addressee of the demand to be given its image as full, complete, as a plenitude. The Other is thus also itself taken as the site of a plenitude. What characterises the imaginary, then, is not a unity or plenitude as such but a demand addressed to an imagined plenitude which remains always unattained. The Other here is the condition of possibility for the demand for a full identity *and* its point of frustration.

However the mirror phase is not a stage of development but rather should be understood as a turning-point, for the precipitation of the ideal-ego is only fully apparent at the moment this phase comes to an end, through the extension of identification beyond merely the child's own image to the image of the counterpart. This arises because the child takes itself as an object – its mirror image – with which it identifies, and this process becomes the model of its relation to other objects, as can be seen for example in the phenom- enon of transitivism, where one child will cry when another has fallen down, or it finishes a gesture begun by a different child.[64]

What is precipitated in the subject is not only an ego/ideal-ego but also the ideal ego as an object of desire, and an already lost object, the demand for which, however, is addressed to the other through whom, after all, the object was constituted. Freud had commented that it is the loss of the object which characterises the infant's relation to the world, whereby the child's first utterance, its cry, is predicated on the missing object which it thereby represents.[65] Moreover he says 'the ego is formed to a great extent out of identifications which take the place of abandoned cathexes by the id'.[66] In Lacan's formulation it is the subject itself or rather a part of itself which is this lost object and which is also the infant's first love-object. In making itself the same as its image – by identify- ing – the subject posits this image as an object, and as other. Lacan's ideal ego corresponds to Freud's category of what the subject once was and its quality as ideal lies less in a notion of perfection (though it includes this), than of a lost unity and hence omnipo- tence, along with the presumption of an ideal which was simply loveable, and loved, before it was admonished. This is not, however, the regressive introjection of a lost love object, for here the lost object is only constituted as a result of the identification which precipitates the split ego/ego-ideal. Lacan thus posits a primary narcissism, and follows Freud in placing identification before object choice.

The first love-object is therefore the subject itself, as its ideal-ego which is instituted as separable – indeed lost – in the moment it emerges.

It is this erotic relation, in which the human individual fixes upon himself an image that alienates him from himself, that are to be found the energy and the form on which this organisation of the passions that he will call his ego is based.[67]

So that:

What we call libidinal investment is what makes an object become desirable, that is to say how it becomes confused with this more or less structured image [ideal ego] which, in diverse ways, we carry with us.[68]

We love, and desire, in so far as we place the object of our love in the same position as our ideal ego. Thus desire emerges in identification which figures it as fundamentally narcissistic.

The mirror phase and its corollary narcissism are therefore the scene for the emergence of three constitutive moments: the ego; of relations to objects on the model of the child's own image as its first object, which institutes the capacity to engender a potentially infinite number of objects in the world, that is, as libidinal object-choices; and the correlative function of aggressivity. In identifying itself with its image the subject emerges in a movement involving the recognition of itself as other, thus splitting its identity and its identifying in a process which alienates the subject from its image, and which can then potentially confront it, and confront it with all the aggressivity the child itself feels towards its objects. In his argument here Lacan refers to Melanie Klein's work for confirmation of the aggressive component of the original imaginary operation. Lacan grounds the boy's later Oedipal rivalry with his father in the prior alienating function of the constitution of the ego as other and thus itself as potentially rivalrous:

> the structural effect of identification with the rival [the father, in the Oedipal Complex] is not self-evident, except at the level of fable, and can only be conceived of if the way is prepared for it by a primary identification that structures the subject as rival with himself.[69]

The pleasurable narcissism of the ideal-ego identification must also include the terror of the rival – for it is as *other* that the subject recognises and identifies with its own image. This is undoubtedly a *mimetic* identification, and Lacan argues 'At first, before language, desire exists solely in the single place of the imaginary relation of the specular stage, projected, alienated in the other', but the only outcome possible from this 'absolute rivalry with the other' is the destruction of the other. 'And each time we get close, in a given subject, to this primitive alienation, the most radical aggression arises – the desire for the disappearance of the other in so far as he supports the subject's desire.'[70] Here arises what Lacan calls the see-saw of desire, in which the death drive is also situated. But, Lacan continues:

> thank God, the subject inhabits the world of the symbol, that is to say a world of others who speak. That is why his desire is susceptible to the mediation of recognition. Without which every human function would simply exhaust itself in the unspecified wish for the destruction of the other as such.[71]

Lacan shows how the subject's identifications are a series of moves by which the subject comes into existence as a result of the exigencies of lack and which correlate with his three registers of the real, the imaginary and the symbolic, giving rise to three forms of identification corresponding to those outlined by Freud. Privation, in the register of the real, is a demand which is directed to a lost object – the ideal self, and corresponds to Freud's primary object relation. It is here that a differentiation of the registers of the real and the imaginary also emerges. The ideal-ego as lost object belongs to the real. The real signifies not reality in general but the subject's cognisance of an outside which bears upon it but which is unrepresented and unrepresentable. It is nevertheless not originary but always constituted retrospectively, when the ideal-ego is formed in the emergence of the imaginary which thereby retrospectively constitutes the real.[72] Frustration, in the register of the imaginary, is a demand which cannot be given its object, a demand addressed to the Other from where it cannot be met, leading to Freud's regressive identification with a libidinal object and the development of the ego-ideal. Castration, in the register of the Symbolic, involves a demand for which there is no object and hence involves the acknowledgement, if not the acceptance, of lack. It corresponds to Freud's identification between egos – the possibility of putting oneself in the same position as all the other's in relation to a third term – and the consequent emergence of the super-ego. It is lack, the real, which sets in play the moves by which the subject attempts to deal with lack, yet it itself only comes into existence as a result of identification, which precipitates the splitting of the subject in its very constitution and sets the subject off on the path of desire as well as demand.

Each form of identification, however, would seem to be out of step with the register which gives rise to it, so that the ideal ego is placed in the imaginary, while both the ego-ideal and the super-ego are seen as symbolic formations.[73] It seems necessary therefore to consider these identifications not as characterising each register but as constituted on their very edges, on the cusp between. The ideal ego is the response to the demand directed to the lost object of the real but the identification thereby arising inaugurates the subject in the imaginary. Alienated from its ideal, the subject seeks to recover it by a demand directed to the Other, but from where it cannot be met.

The ego-ideal corresponds to Freud's category of what the subject would like to be *in order to retrieve what it once was*. It is formed in response to the inadequacy of the ideal ego perceived as a result of the onslaught of reality and the series of narcissistic wounds – not least amongst which must be counted the appearance of a sibling – arising therefrom. The subject identifies with, in the sense of adopting, an image arising from the demands of others, the Other, so that it will again be lovable by the Other, giving rise to secondary narcissism. The ideal ego is a projection, an image which the subject then identifies with, while the ego-ideal is a secondary introjection whereby the image returns to the subject invested with those new properties which, after 'the admonitions of others' and the 'wakening of his own critical judgement' are necessary so that the subject can recover the lost narcissism 'in the new form of an ego-ideal'.[74] It 'represents that by which the subject restores the lost narcissistic satisfaction, that is, it implies a fantasy of omnipotence'.[75] But this is undertaken as a response to the Other as a judgmental agency, it is what the child would like to be as understood through the desire and demands of the Other. As a result, Slavoj Žižek argues, 'imaginary identification is always identification *on behalf of a certain gaze in the Other*. So, apropos of every imitation of a model-image, apropos of every "playing a role", the question to ask is *for whom* is the subject enacting this role?'[76] Thus the image in which we appear likeable to ourselves, and which represents 'what we would like to be' – as an ideal – can only come into existence as a response to the demand of the Other and therefore the subject's relation to the image is already penetrated by the lack-in-being of the subject. The ego-ideal is the image of what the subject *should be*. The identifications involved here are complex.[77] The subject may identify with this image; however to do so would return it to the ideal ego as an achieved but then lost but now regained place of the ideal. Rather, or perhaps as well, the subject identifies in the sense of coming into the place from which it is loveable – in this case the features of the ego-ideal are the support and not the stake of the identification – for the stake is the desire of the Other, just as in the third or 'hysterical' mode of identification discussed earlier. At the same time there will be an identification as well with the place of the Other, the place from where we are being observed and from where we look at ourselves so that we appear to ourselves likeable, worthy of love. This arises because the demand to the Other – that is, the demand that the Other return to the subject an image of its completeness, its pleni-tude – is rejected. In its stead, and on the model of Freud's regres-sive identification, the subject identifies with the Other who had the power to respond to its demand, setting it up as an internal object. As a result there are as many identifications as there are rejected demands. We identify with the judging agency and therefore seek to become the image set before us in order to fulfill *its* demand. Identification here again has two modes – regressive identification with the judging agency which rejects our demand, and the adop-tion of the features of the ideal it requires us to be in order to be loveable – which is Freud's form of hysterical identification – that is, we identify with an image for the gaze of the Other, as the place from which we are desired by the Other.

The psychical import of the ego-ideal does not lie in the image as such but in its function as prescription of how to become *for* someone else. Žižek has referred to this as the adoption of a certain 'mandate', to do or to be this or that. Thus

> This interplay of imaginary and symbolic identification under the domination of symbolic identification constitutes the mechanism by means of which the subject is integrated into a given socio-symbolic field – the way he/she assumes certain 'mandates'.[78]

This 'integration' is seen by Žižek as equivalent to the interpellation of the subject into the social described by Althusser, but this now as a symbolic and not an imaginary relation.[79]

The imaginary cannot therefore be opposed to the symbolic as an order of plenitude to an order of lack, as has been assumed. What differentiates each register is the form of relation to lack. The sym-bolic, as the acceptance of castration and accession to the Law, re-solves the problem of lack by constituting it *as* an order, whereas the imaginary becomes the field of a struggle to deny and defy lack by posing the object as able to satisfy, but this satisfaction is never in fact achieved – which is confirmed by the continuing struggle and posing of the demand. Furthermore the imaginary is shown to already contain a look which returns to the subject, the look of the Other. Freud had already noted this when he commented of the ego-ideal, 'Recognition of this agency enables us to understand the so-called "delusions of being noticed" or more correctly, of being *watched*.'[80] Lacan emphasises that 'the point of the ego ideal is that from which the subject will see himself ... *as others see him*'.[81]

The distinction between the ego-ideal and super-ego is not fully present in Freud's writing; however the grounds for such a separation are clearly there. Freud notes that:

> The super-ego is, however, not simply a residue of the earliest object-choices of the id; it also represents an energetic reaction-formation against those choices. Its relation to the ego is not exhausted by the precept: 'You *ought to be* like this (like your father).' It also comprises the prohibition: 'You *may not be* like this (like your father) – that is, you may not do all that he does; some things are his prerogative.' This double aspect of the ego ideal derives from the fact that the ego ideal had the task of re-pressing the Oedipus complex; indeed, it is to that revolutionary event that it owes its existence.[82]

The ego-ideal commands the subject's narcissistic position and it is related to the specular register. In contrast the super-ego is related to the voice, not the look.

> the super-ego is essentially a demand presenting itself in the form of imperatives and prohibitions which are correlated with the model constituted by the ego-ideal.[83]

Both the ego-ideal and the super-ego are formations which belong to the symbolic, but in different ways.

> whereas the ego-ideal is sustained by a feature – *einziger Zug* – a feature that is of the order of the *insignum*, of the badge, that is, of something halfway between the sign and the signifier, on the contrary, the super-ego is more a matter of speech (*parole*).[84]

Both involve a relation to a demand, but this relation is different in each case. The ego-ideal consists in those identifications arising as a result of the rejected demands; it is fundamentally narcissistic and hence lies on the cusp of the imaginary and the symbolic. The super-ego, however, consists in the identification with the *demand*, and Catherine Millot has summed up the subject's relation to this demand from the Other as that 'to which the subject submits insofar as he thereby makes a compact with the paternal power. I can formulate this demand using Lacan's words: "Thou shalt not desire what was my desire".'[85]

The formation of the super-ego is a corollary of the decline of the Oedipus complex, Freud argues: the child stops trying to satisfy his Oedipal wishes, which have become prohibited, and he transforms his cathexes of his parents into an identification with them, or rather with the parental agency at the level of the prohibition which is thus internalised. It can now be said that it is not just the mother as love-object who is denied to the child, but the Other to whom the child directed its demand as a guarantor of its unity, its plenitude, that is, the phallic mother.[86] In this case the symbolic is the order of a castration which is not just loss or lack, but the impossibility of the demand addressed to the Other being fulfilled, and it is this which must be accepted and internalised, so that the demand is given up. This comes about through the intervention of the third term, the Name-of-the-Father. The imperative determining the accession to the Symbolic, the passage through castration, demands that the object as such be given up, rather than substituted. In a true dissolution of the Oedipus Complex the demand is renounced, but it may instead be repressed, in which case it will return as the basis of symptoms of neurosis and in this case the super-ego would, in Lacan's terms, be reduced to the identity of desire and law. Millot suggests that:

> This Freudian post-Oedipal super-ego is not the super-ego of transitivist retaliation, which is never anything but the turning on the subject of his own demand. It is the super-ego that, in the Lacanian perspective, hardly still deserves the name, since it results from the assimilation by the subject of the law in so far as that law frees him from demand and at the same time constitutes his desire.[87]

Freud remarked that 'Every such identification [of the super-ego] is in the nature of a de-sexualisation or even of a sublimation.'[88]

The castration complex demands not the acceptance of castration as such, as a literal fact for the subject, but the law of lack in the

Other. It is not lack as such, which the child has been trying to get around for a long time, but the law which inscribes, writes and names lack, that is identified with. Where the ego-ideal is formed on the model of love-objects, the super-ego is formed on the basis of dreaded figures, involving not the introjection of the love-object, but the internalisation of authority. 'Internalisation' here marks a differentiation in the process of identification, for the subject may be said to identify with objects, or part-objects – with things – whereas intersubjective relations are internalised, as in the internalisation of a prohibition or conflict, and hence involves more than one agency in the subject (primarily the ego and the super-ego). It is in this sense that the super-ego is described as the heir of the Oedipus complex, constituted through the internalisation of parental prohibitions and demands.

Internalisation is then that form of identification constituted in the register of the symbolic through the acceptance of castration and the submission to the Law through the Name-of-the-Father. It is identification insofar as the subject takes for itself, makes its own, not only the prohibition but, more importantly, the point of address, the subject of enunciation of the prohibition, in the Name-of-the-Father which is thus constituted internally as the super-ego. Yet it is not the addresser, the voice of authority which is identified with, but the position of addressee; it is a relation of prohibition which is internalised. To identify with that position is to give up the (secondary) narcissism still invested in the ego-ideal, for it is a position which is always also insufficient, in a word, castrated. This corresponds to Freud's third category of identification arising with a new perception of a common quality shared with someone who is not an object of sexual desire and which I earlier termed 'hysterical' identification. It is an identification with a *position*, of castration, lack, like all of the other subjects under the law, and specifically, like one's father. It is the point at which the subject recognises that the other, too, is castrated, and hence can never accede to it that which it desires. The paternal imago is introjected, then, not as (or not only as) a love-object but as someone with whom the subject perceives a common element – castration. And it is not the father as super-ego which is internalised, but the father's – or parent's – super-ego. It is as if the condition for accepting the Name-of-the-Father is that one's own father has accepted it. What will be determining here is not just a representation, or a recognition of lack, not just the loss of the object of love and object of the demand for love, but the acceptance that it can never be, has never been, obtained. The acceptance, therefore, not of a *frustrated* wish or demand whereby the object of desire is *withheld* – which would be imaginary – but the acceptance of castration, symbolically, as the impossiblility of the fulfilment of the demand, of the desire that is, for the mother or rather, for the *phallic* mother. It is therefore the experience that one's own lack is already the lack of the Other itself. The Other hasn't got it, either. Without this lack in the Other, the Other would be a closed structure and the subject forever caught in a demand which is frustrated. Such a total alienation is avoided not by filling out one's lack but by identifying oneself, one's own lack, with the lack in the Other. But more, the Other, who also doesn't have it, is itself blocked, desiring, and there is the question therefore of the desire of the Other who lacks. For if the Other is lacking, it must also desire and hence arises the question, what is the desire of the Other, which appears as the question: 'What do you want?' (*Che vuoi*?)[89]

The symbolic identification of the ego-ideal continues to guarantee the subject in its command 'Be this'. In contrast the super-ego identification is with the impossibility of the guarantee. It bears upon the subject as a requirement not because of the father's prohibition as such, but because as Žižek points out, 'the circular movement between symbolic [ego-ideal] and imaginary identification never comes out without a certain leftover'. The seamless movement of interpellation of the subject is challenged at the point when the subject asks of the Other, in order to situate itself, '*Che vuoi*? What do you want?' but which at the same time poses the Other as wanting, or, as Žižek puts it, 'You're telling me that, but what do you want with it, what are you aiming at?'[90] But this interrogation of the desire of the Other gains no answer and instead it opens up a gap for the subject which is only resolved – and this Žižek calls the final moment of the psychoanalytic process – when the subject 'gets rid of this question – that is, when he accepts his being as *non-justified by the big Other*'.[91] This is, too, the moment of identification with the super-ego which is therefore situated on the cusp of the symbolic and the real, for it is in the register of the real that the lack in the Other was first instituted.

The symbolic is posed in Lacan's work therefore in two apparently opposed ways. On the one hand, it designates the accession to the domain of the social, in terms of the rule of the Law, the Name-of-the-Father, of social relations and the rules governing them, most specifically, the incest taboo – that prohibition which in securing the circulation, the exchange, of women, thus establishes kinship relations and inaugurates culture. This implies a fixing of the subject. On the other hand, the introduction of the symbolic, and the intervention of the father as third term in the dyadic, imaginary relation of mother and child, is represented as a rupture and as a gap. This is not simply the rupture of the plenitude of the imaginary, for this has already been found wanting. Nor can the symbolic be equated simply with language or the social, rather it must refer to those relations, those structures which require the subject to submit his or her desire to a law, an order, which is constructed outside of them – the order of the Other. The Name-of-the-Father constitutes the figure of Law as a symbolic function and which is therefore never the real father as object of real familial relations or of narcissistic identification.

CINEMA'S IDENTIFICATIONS

Identification never involves unified or whole identities, as if it were the transportation of a self into the other or the other into the self, as an encounter between two fully present identities, two subjects. In cinema, too, therefore, identification cannot be taken to be the vehicle for a transportation of the spectator out of him or herself into another – temporary but nevertheless complete – dwelling. Identification institutes not identity as a unity but as alienated, partial, and multiple. However, while psychoanlytic theory accounts for the constitution of the subject through identification this does not offer in any straightforward way an account of the subject's identifications in the cinema. It is this which Christian Metz addresses in his essay 'The Imaginary Signifier', the title itself supplying his answer, that the subject takes up an imaginary identification in the cinema. Firstly Metz argues:

> More than the other arts, or in a more unique way, the cinema involves us in the imaginary: it drums up all perception, but to switch it immediately over into its own absence, which is nonetheless the only signifier present.[92]

For Metz it is not cinema's realistic illusions which qualify it as imaginary but the ontological nature of the cinematic signifier as a real perception (it is not an hallucination) but which signifies as present what is in fact absent. The images are real but they are not produced by light reflected from real objects; instead they are the effect of light projected through transparent celluloid which carries a thin film of chemicals containing a photographic record of the images. The cinematic image here, like the child's mirror image, is imaginary because the perceiver takes as really present what is absent. The imaginary, however, is not characterised simply by a making present what is absent, but rather the imaginary arises when the relation of desire set in play is the demand for presence, for plenitude, in the face of its absence – a desire, that is, to fill the gap.[93]

Secondly, and again drawing on the model of the mirror image, Metz says that the spectator identifies 'with himself as a pure act of perception'.[94] For Metz the cinema cannot reduplicate the mirror phase in the spectator since he or she has already passed through it, and the cinema screen does not offer the spectator its *own* body with which to identify with as an object. The ego, Metz says, is already formed: 'But since it exists, the question arises precisely of *where it is* during the projection of the film.'[95] Metz therefore asks '*with what*, then, does the spectator identify during the projection of the film? For he certainly has to identify.'[96] Metz rejects identification with characters in a film as merely secondary identification, for such identifications are intermittent in a film, or even absent. More importantly, Metz sees these as contingent upon a prior identification, one which enables the spectator to *be* a subject for cinema at all. This identification, Metz says, is an identification by the subject as all-perceiving, an identification 'with himself as a pure act of perception (as wakefulness, alertness): as the condition of possibility of the perceived and hence as a kind of transcendental subject, which comes before every *there is*'.[97]

This is not specific to the cinema. The identification of the mirror phase precipitates a place which speaks 'I' and nominates its image as 'me', and thus makes present to itself its image, implying its having-been absent. The subject comes into existence in its absence – over there, that's me (it is of course not yet a subject of the symbolic, but rather it is the ego of Freud, which is the point of imaginary projection and identification). This is also the structuring of language, which presents to us in its nominations what is thereby made absent. The moment of the subject's entry into the signifying chain as a subject also simultaneously fixes signification itself, for it is only a signifying chain at the point when it is signifying for someone, a subject. It is, therefore, the condition for any signifying system that the subject be the (imagined) site of unity of meaning for and of the message – the fiction of the unity of the subject is not abandoned with entry to the symbolic, but made relative in relation to lack. In so far as a film posits the spectator as a spectator and thus predicates its place as 'I' this is not a function of the cinematic signifier alone, but of human subjectivity as such. This function is already in place for the subject who takes her or his seat in the cinema, constituted in the mirror phase whereby the subject identifies with its own image *and* as one who looks.

What is specific to the cinema as visual performance is that all the spectators see from the same position – everyone sees Garbo's face as a profile – but this point-of-view will be continually changing: now close-up, now long-shot, now from this character's position now from another's. In other words, the spectator's look is aligned with and made identical to another look, the camera's, which has gone before it, and already 'organised' the scene. The spectator thus identifies with the look of the camera and becomes the punctual source of that look which brings into existence the film itself, as if it was by one's own look that the film unfolds before one in the cinema.

This process has been traced back to the very nature of the cinematic apparatus and the optics on which it is based, namely, the monocular perspective perfected in Renaissance painting. The *camera obscura* was developed as an aid to achieving 'correct' perspective and this, along with the 'vanishing point' used in such painting, inscribes, Metz says, 'an empty emplacement for the spectator-subject, an all-powerful position which is that of God himself, or more broadly of some ultimate signified'.[98] The spectator, it is said, identifies with the camera as an omniscient, omnipotent look. Metz then argues:

> And it is true that as he identifies with himself as look, the spectator can do no other than identify with the camera, too, which has looked before him at what he is now looking at and whose stationing (= framing) determines the vanishing point.[99]

In these few words Metz has locked the whole thing together. The misrecognition of the mirror phase is now allied directly to the cinematic signifier in the identification with the camera – hence the *same* illusion of control and mastery, which ensures for Metz that such cinema is indeed imaginary.

It is also, however, the mirror phase which inaugurates lack in the subject, its fundamental self-alienation, and to identify with one's image also always implies an identification with the place of looking – 'I am the image I am looking at' and which contains the supplementary position of 'I am looked at by an other'. The structure of specularity thus undermines the imaginary as the field of a unified subjectivity.[100] Voyeurism is not a relation of unmitigated mastery. In identifying with the other (the mirror image) we are also separated from it as other. It is this which allows us to both be and *not be* the camera. We take the camera's look as our own, yet we are not at all disturbed when it suddenly pans, although we have not turned our own heads. This does not require the transcendental identification with the camera which Metz claims. Rather, cinema depends on producing in the spectator an oscillation between two knowledges, between seeing events as if for the first time (identification with the camera) and knowing that the events which are being seen have already happened, in so far as the spectator is aware that the scene he or she is now seeing precedes scenes which are yet-to-be-seen *but which the spectator knows he or she will see*, implying a separation from the camera. What is involved here is a disavowal – 'I know these events have been rehearsed and recorded, but I will watch them as if they are happening here in front of me' which colludes with that other disavowal of the fictional narrative 'I know very well this is only a story, but all the same it is real.'

Classical Hollywood cinema, which has been characterised as seeking to efface in the spectator any sense of a camera which has looked before it, is also a master of the use of suspense, a form in which the spectator is only too aware of what he or she doesn't yet know or, worse, the spectator knows all too well what will happen, unlike the characters, but in relation to whom we are helpless and from whom the spectator is thus separated – as the discussion of *Coma* showed. The camera's look is not always or simply a look which is powerful, which knows and can thus control. It is sometimes a character's look, and it is this play of looks and the spectator's movement of identification between these looks which is one of the pleasures of cinema. Films which do not offer this are often felt to unsatisfactory by spectators, as suggested in the notorious failure of *The Lady in the Lake* (Robert Montgomery, 1947) which was filmed entirely in subjective camera from the investigator, Philip Marlowe's, point-of-view. A dissatisfaction is often also felt by audiences of films where the camera seems too independent of characters, such as in Jean Renoir's *La règle du jeu* (1939), which uses a moving camera but without point-of-view shots.

Metz's desire to theorise the metapsychology of cinema as a complement to his study of the semiology of cinema leads him to institute a fixed schema, and hierarchy, of identification. The spectator's identification with her or his own look is made analogous to his theory of semiotic codes in *Language and Cinema* by being erected as the general code of cinema, in which it is primary, all other identifications being secondary or sub-codes of cinema.[101] Metz places his 'primary cinematic identification' with what psychoanalysis terms secondary identification, for the cinematic subject is already a psychical subject, yet since in Metz's argument it is also imaginary, it must be derived from the primary identifications of the mirror phase. For psychoanalysis, moreover, the secondary identifications involve the ego-ideal and super-ego which stand in opposition to the ideal ego of the mirror phase. There is, therefore, an incommensurability between Metz's primary and secondary identifications and those of psychoanalysis.[102]

In contrast the following discussion assumes that identification in the cinema arises in relation to the different modes of identification which psychoanalysis describes. There can be no fixed hierarchy for these, although any particular film may privilege certain relations of identification. Indeed forms of representation are a field of engagement, of negotiation and even replaying for the subject of the difficulties and contradictions of its identifications. In what ways, then, are the identifications which psychoanalysis describes brought into play for the cinema spectator?

THE IDEAL OTHER OF CINEMA

The cinema does indeed offer visual representations of the other as an idealised image. Do we not identify with these ideal egos with all the narcissistic investment of the mirror stage? Are not film stars – those perfect and perfected images presented on the cinema screen – embodiments of our ideal egos? Yet this is not the process psychoanalysis describes, for in the mirror stage the child does not identify with a (or its own) ideal ego, rather it identifies with its image and thus produces that image as an ideal ego invested with all its narcissism. If film stars are identified with as a result of their idealisation then this will involve a judgement prior to identification on the part of the spectator, a recognition of the ideal-ism of the image and hence would suggest rather the function of ego-ideal, an identification with the image which appears to us as likeable from the place of the other.

In contrast the ideal ego is that image which restores to the subject its original narcissism, of being without flaw, omnipotent. It is not a set of ideal contents so much as a position, the place in which the subject is beyond reproach and, therefore, in a sense super-human. This image is the basis for subsequent identifications with heroic characters, and also with anti-heros, but only in as much as it is separated from ego-ideal demands. Identification here will be promoted not by the fine qualities of the character (though these may also be present) but by his or her position as hero, as the 'winner' within the narrative and as dominant in relation to the structure of looks within the film. In film examples are Sylvester Stallone as Rambo (*First Blood*, Ted Kotcheff, 1982) or Clint Eastwood in *High Plains Drifter* (Eastwood, 1973), but it is realised most purely when it is an identification with the all-powerful villain. Arnold Schwarzenegger in *The Terminator* (James Cameron, 1984) affords the basis for just such an identification, as the appar-ently invincible foe brutally but efficiently destroying anything in his way (except the heroine) and even arising unscathed although fleshless – as a mechanical skeleton – from the conflagration caused by the hero Kyle's explosive device.[103] This is heightened (and perhaps even enabled, in Freud's sense of the aesthetic bribe that draws the subject into the joke or fantasy, as explored in the next chapter) by the comedy of the ironic reversal of expectation early in the film when the Terminator confronts three punks whose clothes he takes, or when he 'pays' for the array of armaments he obtains by using one of the guns to shoot the salesman, or the indefa-tiguable disbelief of the police officers hopelessly combatting the Terminator.[104] Identification with the ideal ego, however, is also accompanied by the splitting of the subject and is the origin of aggressivity – as noted earlier – and in this aspect it affords an ambivalent and unstable basis for film identification.

The other mechanism of identification arising in the mirror stage, namely the phenomenon of transitivism, accords very closely with

what is expected of cinematic identification insofar as it is a trans-
posing of the self into the other's image, a conflation – 'You've
always been like that, able to think with my thoughts and feel with
my feelings' Thorley declares to her childhood sweetheart, Jeb
Rand, in Raoul Walsh's *Pursued* (1947). This is possible because, as
Jacqueline Rose argues, 'the subject never specularises its own body
as such, and the phenomenon of transitivism demonstrates that the
subject's mirror identification can be with another child'.[105] It is the
close-up, uniquely photographic, which would seem to be pre-
eminent in motivating transitive identification (the lens of the
human eye cannot focus or frame an object or person in close-up in
the way made possible by artificial optical lenses). But here also is
that side of the mirror stage which falls into the real, as Roland
Barthes describes:

> In the Photograph, the event is never transcended for the sake of
> something else: the Photograph always leads the corpus I need
> back to the body I see; it is the absolute Particular, the sovereign
> Contingency, matte and somehow stupid, the *This* (this photo-
> graph, and not Photography), in short, what Lacan calls the
> *Tuché*, the Occasion, the Encounter, the Real, in its indefatigable
> expression.[106]

To suggest that the image in the photographic close-up offers an
image of the other (small o), an interchangeable other, is not to
imply that the spectator is cast back to those early months of its life
and its primitive object-relations; the real, the imaginary and the
symbolic are not historical stages (although they may emerge as
such initially for the infant) but different registers of the subject's
relation to the other as lacking.

The cinematic close-up is however different from the photograph
in that it is part of a continuous moving chain of images. By close-
up here I mean a shot of the face or part of the face only; closer-in
shots came to be used to allow audiences to see better the actions
ar.d responses of characters, with the accompanying developing of
structures of cutting or editing between shots taken close-in on a
scene and others taken from further away. A further development
of key importance for narration in film was the device of motivating the cut from one shot to the next within a scene via a character's
look, a look established through a close-up. As a result films have
dominantly become not a series of views on to a scene, but a series

of views within the scene. Our reading of these views is motivated primarily not by what we are seeing but by what we have seen and the expectations of what we will be seeing that this has given rise to, so that if a character looks and the film cuts to another view we tend to assume it is a view of what the character was looking at. As the experiments of the Soviet film-maker Lev Kuleshov in the 1920s showed, the particular expression of the actor or actress can be a matter of indifference; the spectator's understanding or interpretation of the expression depends on reading the prior or subsequent shot, that is, of what we assume the character was looking at, and by implication, responding to.

Through editing the spectator may be given the visual viewpoint of a character (the point-of-view shot, considered earlier in the discussion of *Coma*), but to be given a character's pov look is not thereby to necessarily identify with the character. Identification, as distinct from narrative information, arises not with the visual view of a character but with a close-up shot of the character looking.[107] The use of a full-face close-up can invoke a transitivist identification not merely because we can then see the face clearly, but more importantly because in filling the screen it also obscures the space and time of the narrative. Perhaps this is also why they are comparatively infrequent in films. It is an identification of the order: I am what I see. In *The Termininator*, the scene when Schwarzenegger repairs his injuries, removing his eyeball to adjust its computer and stripping back the flesh on his arm to re-align its mechanical articulation, draws a gasp of horror from spectators. The audience's reaction suggests just such a transitivist identification, as if it were our own flesh being stripped, and despite the fact that we know it is only a machine. This therefore does not tally either with our idealised identification with the Terminator as *super*-human!

The transitivist identification with the image of the face is but a moment, and just like the mirror stage itself, it is no sooner constituted as identification than it is flipped over into identification in a chain of desire, and the figure of the Other intervenes. In the cinema it is the moment when movement, narrative, the shift to medium-shot from close-up, or to the object of the glance, breaks up the absorption in the image of the other and forces it to give way to the chain of signification, to the movement of desire which is figured. Even without movement – in the still photograph – the interruption of an action or gesture, or the glance alone will provoke the demand for a narrative, posing questions – who is this person, what is their story, what is the action interrupted?

THE FILMIC IMAGINARY AND THE EGO-IDEAL

The ego is precipitated through identification and remains the agent of identification, that is, the subject's ego-ideals do not identify with other ego-ideals; rather the ego will introject new, different and even contradictory ego-ideals in as much as each is forged in relation to the desire of the Other, which is the position from which the ego perceives itself. If the ego introjects a cinematic figure – a film star – as an ego-ideal it will become one of the 'standards' by which the subject seeks to live, and by which it maintains itself as lovable, for the ego-ideal(s) arise from the attempts by the ego to remain lovable – to repair the attacks on its narcissism – by being what it supposes (imagines) the Other wishes it to be, in order that it be loved by the Other. In this the subject wishes to be loved by the star, and not to be like him or her. Identification arises in response to the rejection of this demand so that the spectator's ego takes up the position of the loved object, and appearing like the film star will then be the support or trace of the identification but not its purpose. The stars and characters of cinema perhaps only rarely function as introjected lost love objects: instead identification arises as a result of existing ego-ideals with which the star or character accords, providing the basis for the multiple and myriad figures of identification the cinema trades in. It is an identification with the place in which we already believe we can be loved, lovable. It is thus also distinct from the ideal ego, the heroic or omnipotent figures, but it is an imaginary identification, for it is 'as this' that I am loveable.

Nevertheless this is brought into play not simply or primarily by a character who is already loveable but rather as the result of narrative vicissitudes which bring the character to this position at the film's conclusion. Thus many films – including and especially adventure films – involve protagonists for whom the narrative is a journey of self-exploration, in which they move from some position of indadequacy to a position of knowledge, and often marriage as well. It is an Oedipal journey, as Raymond Bellour describes in his analysis of *The Westerner* (William Wyler, 1940).[108] In this case the spectator does not start with an already achieved ego-ideal, and though this may be obtained at the end, nevertheless our relation to such a figure is an identification with the scenario presented, with the story of that Oedipal journey as if it were our own, it is an identification with the fantasy within the film.

In *Rio Bravo* Dean Martin plays a drunk, Dude, who is brought to resume his symbolic mandate as deputy to John Wayne's sherriff – John T. Chance – in the course of the conflict with the Burdetts, and a key moment in this is when Dude returns to the bar which was the scene of his humiliation earlier by Joe Burdett. Dude is seeking one of the Burdetts' hired killers whom he has winged, and this, after initial stonewalling, he achieves, reversing his previous shaming. Of course Chance/Wayne himself provides an ideal while he is also the voice of authority; however, early on in the film Hawks subverts Chance/Wayne's position as one of knowledge and power – and hence his position as omnipotent – in the scene where Feathers (Angie Dickinson) comes upon Chance holding up a pair of ladies' red bloomers, and later Chance wrongly accuses her of cheating at cards. Chance is a 'parental figure' both as carer for Dude (he kept his clothes cleaned, bought back his guns) and as enunciator of the symbolic demand. But, in the love-story between Chance and Feathers, he must also submit his desire to the Law.

THE SUPER-EGO OF THE CINEMA

We do not identify with the super-ego; it is not the basis for an internal remodelling; instead it is an internalised authority to which we submit; we identify with its demand, setting it up internally as an agency of judgement. It involves not an image but a voice. There can be no question of identifying with a figure who represents the position of the super-ego in a film, for this would immediately produce the figure as an ego-ideal, or even ideal ego. But the spectator can take up the position of that figure in relation to its enunciation (but not its desire), as the *voice* of authority, but not image of authority.[109] The correlative of this is that where any such figures are placed in the position of the super-ego, they appear castrated. This can be seen for example in the figure of Lincoln in John Ford's *Young Mr Lincoln* (1939),[110] and of Al (Frederick March), the former army sergeant returned home to resume his position as father and bank manager in *The Best Years of Our Lives* (William Wyler, 1946), as well as Wayne's John T. Chance in *Rio Bravo*, each of whom functions as the agent and voice of authority, yet, extraordinarily, each is also shown as a 'fool'. Al, during his key speech to fellow-bankers in which he argues for the rights of the returning service-men to a new start, a decent life, is also clearly drunk, but this, far from undermining his position in fact affirms it since it produces a separation between the statement and the character (as in the case too of the traditional 'fool').

The filmic enunciation itself may undertake the function of the super-ego, presenting to the spectator a demand that it submit its (narrative) desire to the Law, as emerges in Samuel Fuller's *Underworld USA* (1960). The film's hero, Tolly, seeks to avenge the gangland murder of his father, a minor crook. He rejects the law at the beginning of the film – he is a thief – and he refuses the help of the law in finding the men who killed his father – 'I'm no fink', he says. He comes to accept the law through his relation to Cuddles, a girl he rescues and whom he at first just uses to pursue his vengeance but later falls in love with, agreeing to marry her, to go straight and 'kick our way of doing things' – to become like other people – to submit to the Law, in fact. Tolly moves from acting in the present in his own interests alone, to seeking to ensure his future with Cuddles, and as a result he moves from invulnerability to vulnerability – he is killed. The film shows the legal system failing Tolly, without thereby negating the necessity of his choice. It is after all only from the point of view of the imaginary that the Law is omnipotent.

THE PLACES OF IDENTIFICATION IN FILM

> The subject painfully identifies himself with some person (or character) who occupies the same position as himself in the amorous structure...Identification is not a psychological process; it is a pure structural operation: I am the one who has the same place I have. (Roland Barthes)[111]

The structuring forms of identification that psychoanalysis de-scribes are not sufficient, either singly or together, to account for cinematic identification. What remains to put into place is the way in which we respond to the representations of cinema 'as if' they were our own. What is put in place, in fact – as Barthes emphasises – is the spectator itself. Identification for psychoanalysis arises as a positioning in relation to another producing a psychical transformation in the subject. In cinema this positioning also occurs, but without necessarily implying a psychical transformation.

Nevertheless it is through identification that film narratives are assumed to produce their emotional effects upon us. How does this square with the structural role of identification Barthes emphasises, and what role, if any, does the cognitive aspect of identification play? Hugo Münsterberg, one of the earliest writers to consider the psychology of the cinema, sees two modes of emotional response, one where we have the same feelings as the characters in the film, and the other where we have quite different and perhaps opposed feelings to the characters. In the first mode

Our imitation of the emotions which we see expressed brings vividness and affective tone into our grasping of the play's action. We sympathise with the sufferer and that means that the pain which he expresses becomes our own pain.[112]

Here imitation brings sympathy, but in neither case is the process of this explained. However, the experience by which the other's pain becomes our own has come to be more usually called empathy. Richard Wollheim also sees two different and distinct processes in play for the spectator. On the one hand the spectator may be moved to pity or to hope on behalf of a character – that is, seeing the character's terror or emotion moves the spectator to feel for the character, to feel pity, and this he calls sympathy. In contrast, empathy for Wollheim arises when the spectator imagines the feelings of the character, so that she or he feels *with*, that is, *as*, and not *for* the characters. Wollheim makes clear the role of the spectator, for it is her or his active imagining which must be involved. He says the spectator 'feels what he does not because of what he watches but because of what he imagines: but he imagines what he does because of what he watches'.[113] Something brings the spectator to feel as the character.

A scene from Fritz Lang's film *Fury* (1936)[114] provides an example of the distinction I think Wolheim is concerned with here. Joe (Spencer Tracy) and Katherine (Sylvia Sidney), unable to afford to marry, have been separated for a year, Katherine working as a teacher down South, while Joe establishes a business for himself and his two brothers. Now able to marry and bring Katherine back to Chicago, Joe sets off by car to meet her. Stopped at a roadblock set up to catch the kidnappers of a young girl, Joe becomes a suspect as a result of an array of circumstantial evidence. Arrested and taken to the nearby jail, the townsfolk become incensed by what they view as the sherriff's inaction, and are mobilised as a lynch-mob. They break into the jail but are unable to reach Joe in his locked cell, and instead set fire to the building. Meanwhile Katherine has been anxiously awaiting the long-overdue Joe at a diner up the road when chance information from a busdriver alerts her to the events in the neightbouring town and she hurries there by foot in time to see Joe amidst the flames at the window of his cell, jeered at by the jubilant crowd, before she faints. A sequence of shots establishes Katherine, not Joe, as the object of our 'empathy'. Joe is seen in his cell with his dog, Rainbow, crosscut with shots of Katherine running down the street. We see Katherine in medium shot (1), surrounded by the jeering crowd, looking slightly up and offscreen left. (Frame-stills of shots 1, 2, 3, 5, and 12 appear in plate 2.) The next shot (2) of Joe grasping wildly at the bars of his cell window in medium long shot is therefore motivated as Katherine's point-of-view so that in the close-up in shot 3 we assume we see her seeing him, but her look is now directly at the camera though perhaps focussed beyond it. Shots 4, 5, and 6 show members of the lynch-mob looking up out of frame – at Joe in the jail, we infer – in extreme close-up, with strong underlighting, appearing ghoulish and demonic in contrast to Katherine's look of horror in shots 7 and 12. Shot 8 shows Joe again, as shot 2 but now from a position closer in than before, but Katherine has not moved closer, so that this shot is not coded as her pov. Shot 9 shows an elderly woman in the crowd kneeling, praying, which contrasts with shots 10 and 11, of the laughing faces of a mother and baby with bystanders, and the medium shot of another spectator, open-mouthed as he is about to bite into a hotdog, all of whom are looking up and off frame left watching Joe. Shot 12 returns to Katherine in a similar framing to the previous shots but now in medium close-up, followed by shot 13, a repeat of shot 2 – her 'true' pov. In shot 14 the crowd begins to throw rocks at Joe at the cell window, and in shot 15 – a repeat of 2 and 12 – we see Joe now move back from the window. The next shot (16) of Katherine is from a new camera position, and she is now again clearly looking off left; she shakes her head slightly, and faints.

The sequence gives us views of Katherine and members of the crowd seeing Joe – their optical point of view – but we are not given

Joe's pov. Instead the film suggests the horror of his situation, of burning to death, *expressively*, his face barred at the jail window, the light of the fire playing on it, but this as sympathy, while it is with Katherine that we empathise. This is not because we are given her pov (we do not, after all, empathise with the bystander's delight), but because the film breaks the pov convention – Katherine is not looking up and off frame but directly at the camera. Her angelic, innocent beauty barely scarred by the merest shadow of a grimace of horror across her face, her very lack of expression, her immobility and the repetition of this image three times in the sequence of reverse shots, produces a transitivist identification. At the same time an identification with her psychological point of view arises, but this is not because we know or see what she feels but because we see *why* she feels, namely her horror at her lover burning to death. Yet it is not that Joe, the hero, is going to die that catches our emotions and provokes our empathy, but that he will be lost to Katherine and lost unjustifiably for his is innocent. The innocence of her look stands as signifier of Joe's innocence or rather for the tragedy that he is after all innocent, and it is this which moves us.

Can empathy and sympathy be used to distinguish between affective identification and a cognitive response which enables us to judge the worth of characters, to feel the justness, or not, of their condition? This is certainly a useful logical distinction, but it is much harder in practice to separate out affect and judgement, for in so far as sympathy *is* a feeling, and we *do feel*, if we are moved to support the justness of the character's cause or desire, we cannot assume this is based simply on cognitive information. To feel pity is to feel, and though we may wish to think that our feelings are 'justified', that our sympathy with the downtrodden and the good is because of an ethical judgement, it can never be definitively distinguished from our more messy feelings in relation to our ego-ideals, that is, how we can come into the position of what we should be to be loveable. Moreover it would not be surprising to find here a quite different feeling, namely the spectator's relief and pleasure in *not* being the wretched and oppressed figure depicted.

Münsterberg pointed to the complex role of cognitive information when he noted, of his second form of emotional response arising 'from the standpoint of [the spectator's] independent affective life', that the 'overbearing pompous person who is filled with the emotion of solemnity' in fact 'awakens in us the emotion of humor', and similarly, while 'We see the scoundrel who in the melodramatic photoplay is filled with fiendish malice, and yet we do not respond by imitating his emotion; we feel moral indignation toward his personality.'[115] Tomashevsky, too, referred to the plot's role in the production of affect in the tracing of characters as good or bad, and hence as drawing from us a response of support or hostility, so that the narration places us with characters – whether because they are the main actants, or they possess knowledge, or because we have their 'view' of the action.[116] Murray Smith has suggested that two processes are involved here. One is 'alignment', in which we are placed with a character by being given knowledge of and through a character – typically through a point-of-view structure. The second process, 'allegiance', arises from the spectator's moral evaluation of the information given through the narration about a character within the film, hence it does not depend on optical point-of-view.[117] That our sympathy is engaged can of course be ascribed to the film text which may give us a morally upright character who engages our allegiance as the 'good guy', that is our – or perhaps more correctly, society's – moral values are solicited by the film on behalf of this character. Or we may be drawn to characters we judge to be worthwhile as a result of narrative information, characters who deserve our interest and sympathy because of their struggles, hopes and desires – all of which are available to be judged as conventionally proper and socially approved.[118] However, morally good figures may also be so anodyne that perversely and by contrast we are more engaged by the bad characters. Moreover it is also these characters who can make the transformation from villain to hero, from lost soul to redeemed character, and around whom the narrative struggle and drive can be focussed, and therefore in relation to whom we have hopes and desires – that the hero come to realise his folly, to recognise the love of the heroine as his true path – desires not yet, if ever, enunciated by the character.[119] While our feelings for characters are certainly aroused by the narrative information we receive about them, our responses are not only judgements about that information; our emotions are not simply reasoned and reasonable reactions but involve our ego-ideals and our wish to come into the position from which we are loveable, are seen to be worthy, by ourselves and by others.

What then of those elements of ourselves we wish to have nothing to do with and instead push into and on to others? Projection is often cited as a form of identification. Certainly its correlative, introjection, is clearly involved in the ego-ideals we adopt. Projection is primarily considered as involving part-objects, bits of the self, implying a partial and particular role in identification. It is a structural relation with the other in whom the 'bad' bits are placed but who is thereby one's own other half – hence it is a 'projective identification', and it is a psychical relation authored by the subject herself or himself. If it occurs in films then we must consider whether the film is an unwitting vehicle for the subject's projections, or whether it constructs a scenario where typical and universal projections are played out to which we relate *as if* they were our own.[120] In the latter case it cannot be said that the spectator projects his or her fears, but, rather, enters into the scenario which involves finding one's fears realised in the figures who embody our most hated and – therefore – desired parts. What is involved here can perhaps be better termed as a relation of *transference*.

Transference is the 'as if' relation which Freud described as being fundamental to psychoanalytic practice as a 'talking cure' in which the patient identifies the analyst with a figure from her or his past, for example a parent, and relates to the analyst with all the hate and/or love felt for the father or mother, that is, transferring to the analyst the feelings felt for that past figure.[121] Considerable affect or emotion may thus be stimulated – whether it is a dreaded figure of fear or desire. At the same time the transferential relation may also involve identification in so far as the dreaded father is also what one wishes to be, his powers of mastery are what one wishes to have or take, and his retribution all the more likely as a result, so that there is a reciprocal relation between transference and identification.

Transference itself is not a structuring psychical process, but is something which is drawn into play within the analytic situation, that is, it draws on the forms of identification already in play for the subject. Moreover it always comes into play in conjuction with its answering response, the analyst's countertransference. Analysis is, after all, where we come into place in relation to the other and the desire of the other. Film, as a fictional narrative form, must however extend the 'as if' relation of the analytic transference so that the spectator can find not only figures who will play out the position of her or his dreaded and desired parental figures, for example, but also figures who can represent the spectator, that is, who 'stand-in' for the identifying spectator. It is because identification is a structural position that we can take the position of characters who have the same relation as ourselves to the figure/character in the fiction on to whom we have transferred our feelings – typically a filial relation. A film works as fantasy, just as in the dream, where feelings and desires are transferred and displaced on to other figures than those in relation to whom the desires have arisen.

It is transference which gets the anayltic process stuck, the analysand repeating and replaying his or her relation to figures of their past. But it is also, by the same token, the very means by which the analyst and analysand can work through the resistant and conflictual material, to approach the kernel of enjoyment, the fundamental fantasy through which the subject enjoys. In this the analyst comes to occupy the position of the one who is presumed to know the meaning of the symptoms, dreams and diverse signifieds of desire of the analysand. A similar position is given to the 'author' of a film, the supposed organising authority which or who has emplaced the meanings and images of the film, so that the film's unfolding narration is assumed to be the effect of authorial intention.[122] It is this position of knowledge which we expect to come to occupy at the close of the narrative. Yet, as Freud found, if analysis were only the transfer of knowledge between analysand and analyst nothing of the analysand's relation to her or his symptom would be changed. What is required is that the analysand comes into a new position in relation to her or his own and the other's desire. So too in film we may be affirmed in or displaced from our relation to the fiction's organising narration, that is, its fantasy.

The process whereby we take up a position as addressee of the enunciation,[123] of the film's unfolding narration – so that we are the place it comes to make sense – has been taken to be a process of identification in cinema and to involve a 'suturing' of the spectator. The term 'suture' was proposed by Jacques-Alain Miller to describe the psychical mechanism whereby the subject takes up a place, is stitched into, the signifying chain – just as a surgeon sews up a wound (which is the origin of Miller's metaphoric use of the term) and thereby constituting it as a subject. But, Miller argues, suture, is, like the role of the zero in Frege's theory of numbers, fundamentally a paradox, for it refers to the process of coming into being of the subject whereby the subject is the effect of the signifier and at the same the signifier is the representative of the subject.[124] The subject, as too the number zero, is non-identical to itself. The subject is present in the signifying chain not as something but as no thing until it has entered the signifying system – until it is sutured. The subject only exists in the chain of signification, yet the signification only exists for and in the subject: 'it is a circular, though non-reciprocal, relation'.[125] In precipitating an 'I' who recognises 'me', the mirror phase institutes a division in the subject in the moment it is forged, but that division and the lack in the subject it constitutes is resolved – sutured – in the voice of language which allows the 'I' to claim as itself its image – I am, after all, myself. This suturing of the division is, however, never over once and for all, but is a constant process and Miller refers to the 'flickering in eclipses' of the subject, an image now present now absent, just as the flicker in the cinema is the trace of the now present, now absent still image of the film as the projector's stop–go mechanism of intermittent motion passes it in front of the projection shutter.

The term suture found immediate favour amongst film theorists in order to describe the mechanism by which the spectator is positioned as a cinematic subject, as a process in which the viewer is stitched into, takes her or his place in the cinematic discourse, and as, therefore, a mechanism of ideology. But the term is more difficult to appropriate to film than has been acknowledged. The notion of 'stitching' implies that what was rent can now be made whole, the lacking subject can now be bound into a seamless unity, but the metaphor begins to break down here, for stitching produces the very seam itself, and so too the suture cannot be produced without the subject bearing its trace. Moreover suturing was identified as an imaginary process, and hence it was assumed there would be something beyond and outside the suture, and indeed Lacan's colleague, Serge Leclaire, proposed that the analyst be recognised as 'the person "*who does not suture*"', which introduces both the sense of *someone* who may or may not suture, and the sense that not-suturing – the therapeutic role of the analyst – is a good thing.[126]

In film theory the suturing of the subject also quickly became identified with the work of cinema as imaginary, producing in the spectator a misrecognition of itself as the centred subject of meaning for the film. Suture became the way in which the spectator was locked into, captured by the film for its set of meanings, in so far as suture was taken to be a tying down of signification. Unlike Metz's primary identification with the camera, however, the suture is taken to arise from the work of the filmic codes. Daniel Dayan, drawing upon an essay by Jean-Pierre Oudart, argued that suture was produced by the cinematic code of shot-reverse-shot and point-of-view, the reverse shot giving the spectator a view and a place in the scene, a place from which to understand. Suture for Dayan is the 'tutor-code of classical cinema'.[127] Suture therefore became an enactment upon the subject, and it became a 'bad' thing to do, or to suffer. Yet suture does not name only a closure in the signifying chain, but a process of closure and re-opening. Any closure must be provisional, more or less precarious, fissured by the trace of lack, and hence ultimately failing – from which the desire arises to start again, to watch another film.[128] Oudart, moreover, emphasised not the fictional unity afforded by suture but the trace of absence, of lack, which always remains and is remade, fissuring that unity.[129] As a result he imagines the emergence of a cinema of suture: 'The field of such a cinematic, not yet born, would be less the space of an event than the field of emergence of the symbolic.' This is not un-problematic, however, for it implies the symbolic as a field free or purged of 'subjective illusion', free of the imaginary and therefore – following Louis Althusser's view – of ideology. The subject sutured in the film text is then the deceived subject who 'misrecognises' himself or herself as a unified subject of knowledge, of the meaning of the film.

The problems with this view of ideology should not lead us to throw out the distinction between *énoncé* and *énonciation*, or the function of suture, for the process of communication, of signification must always propose an addresser and addressee. When someone says 'You know what', she or he is not only opening conversation and commencing communication with a question which seeks to confirm a channel of addresser and ad-dressee, but is also positing the addressee as not yet knowing and inviting them to come to know by listening. And in so far as we do come into position as addressee of the enunciation, we also come into a place of desire, constructed by the narration, the plotting. 'Every classical narrative inaugurates the captivation of its specta-tor by carving out an initial crevice between a desiring subject and his or her object of desire.'[130] The question arises of what is the desire set in play by the narrative. There is the desire for narrative itself as the wish to know, founded in the wish to know the desire of the other, for narratives provide a scenario of coming to know, exemplified in the detective story. Identification here is with the po-sition of coming to know. This does not depend on a particular content of the narrative or the subject's own identity, it is simply a placing, an identity as subject-position – a suturing no doubt, but as a process constantly remade. As a result the drive to mastery that is also involved in the desire to know in narrative becomes an oscillation between mastery and subjection.[131]

The desire for narrative has, however, more often been stressed as a desire for identity, as an identification *with* the narrative and its contents, and hence a desire for such an identification so that 'This capturing of the subject by a narrative, any narrative, reveals some primordial condition of identification by which every story told is, to some slight degree, our story.'[132] While Paul Ricoeur has argued that:

> Our own existence cannot be separated from the account we can give of ourselves. It is in telling our own stories that we give ourselves an identity. We recognise ourselves in the stories that we tell about ourselves. It makes very little difference whether these stories are true or false, fiction as well as verifiable history provides us with an identity.[133]

As a result there is also a desire for narrative. We wish to find ourselves in our stories. But identity is first an image, it becomes a story in the splitting of the subject – a story of refinding oneself as ideal or becoming an ideal for an other, so that I come into the position from which I am loveable, that is an ego-ideal. If narratives capture us, then no doubt it involves this capture to the story of how I will become loveable – with all the possible extensions of this, of how I will put the world to rights, how I will rescue X – whether X is a figure substituting for my father, my mother, or indeed myself. Telling a story, even one's own life story, is not to tell the tale of what one is, as a set of roles, or contents, but to narrate a scenario of relationships to others. Narratives set out stories not of how to *be* but of how to be *for* someone. Our social discourses provide a clothing for this, the roles of astronaut or doctor or whatever.

If stories did simply tell us our identities, or enabled us to become *something*, to take on or to find our identity, we would no longer go on wanting stories. But instead narrative sets out a becoming, it holds in play the desire to again come into place for someone, a playing which the *next* story will replay. Narrative is about positionings in relation to another, whether of mastery over the figure who stands in for the father, or submission to that figure; narrative does not produce *identities* of mastery or submission but a relation – hence the much-noted fluidity and indeed reversibility of narrative identification. Barthes, placing this relation to an other in an Oedipal frame, writes that:

> Death of the Father would deprive literature of many of its pleasures. If there is no longer a Father, why tell stories? Doesn't every narrative lead back to Oedipus? Isn't storytelling always a way of searching for one's origin, speaking one's conflicts with the Law, entering into the dialectic of tenderness and hatred? Today, we dismiss Oedipus and narrative at one and the same time: we no longer love, we no longer fear, we no longer narrate. As fiction, Oedipus was at least good for something: to make good novels, to tell good stories (this is written after having seen Murnau's *City Girl*).[134]

But 'Oedipus' here does not name just a masculine desire for the mother, hence referring to a role and a content for that role; rather it signifies a scenario, a series of relationships between Oedipus, the object of his desire – Jocasta, his mother – and the absent figure of his mother's husband and the missing knowledge of the relation of his object of desire, Jocasta, to the man he killed at a crossroads, as well as of his own origin as the fruit of their coupling. Oedipus, as an identity, is the effect of all that he does not know, to his cost. Oedipus, therefore, functions to name our relations of desire, and these are triangular as well as dyadic. (That they are masculine or feminine is a whole other story, itself never either complete nor over.)

This, of course, was Oedipus's story – so why does it move us, too? Why can it become our own? It is not that we can find ourselves in its particular set of events – which after all are not often met with – but its structure of relations of desire does offer us a place. That is, identification not because I am like Oedipus, but because I have the same structural relation of desire:

> The structure has nothing to do with persons: hence (like a bureaucracy) it is terrible. It cannot be implored – I cannot say to it: 'Look how much better I am than H.' Inexorable, the structure replies: 'You are in the same place; hence you are H'. No one can *plead* against the structure.[135]

But, as Barthes noted, this is not a singular place – a story of unrequited love moves us because we enter both the place of the other who loves without being loved, while also occupying the position – which is therefore both gratifying and uncomfortable – of the loved one who does not love in return. As a result the desire is not a singular desire.

It is in this scenarioisation of desire, with its stories of wish-fulfilment, of fantasies and dreams, that the hinging of identification as affect and as structure arises. Freud's account of the 'Smoked Salmon' dream of his 'clever woman patient' shows very well the process of this scenariorisation which is both structure and affect. Freud begins by showing that what was brought to him as an example of an *unfulfilled* wish – thus refuting Freud's own theories – was something more complex. Through the dream the woman not only fulfilled a wish to contradict Freud, but in addition Freud showed that what appeared to be unfulfilled – namely, her wish to give her friend dinner, which, although she was well-known for her good dinners, she was unable to do because all she had was a little smoked salmon – was in fact her wish. Her friend, who was admired by the patient's husband – although he like plump women while the friend was rather thin – had recently expressed a wish to grower fatter, and had enquired 'When are you going to ask us to another meal? You always feed one so well.' Freud writes 'It is just as though when she made this suggestion you said to yourself: "A likely thing! I'm to ask you to come and eat in my house so that you may get stout and attract my husband still more! I'd rather never give another supper-party".'[136] Thus she dreamt that she was unable to give a supper-party.

Behind this 'simple' wish Freud suggested there lay another, and one which was the result of an identification he characterises as 'hysterical'. For his woman patient did not simply wish for a negative occurrence – to not give a meal and so not help to make her friend plumper – rather it was also a wish to renounce a wish. For instead of wishing that the friend's wish was unfulfilled as the basis of her dream she had wished for one of her *own* wishes to be unfulfilled which, Freud suggests, shows that the dreamer had put herself in her friend's place and had identified herself with her friend.

The process might be expressed verbally thus: my patient put herself in her friend's place in the dream because her friend was taking my patient's place with her husband and because she (my patient) wanted to take her friend's place in her husband's high opinion.[137]

That the dream involves identification in this way is shown precisely by the role of the smoked salmon. Freud had asked his patient how it came to be in her dream, she replied that it was her friend's favourite dish, and Freud confirms from his personal knowledge that this lady 'grudges herself salmon no less than my patient grudges herself caviare'.[138] The wish for caviare at breakfast was the delicacy which Freud's patient was seeking to renounce or, rather, sought her husband to refuse her, for though he would gladly have granted it had she asked, she grudged the expense and thus asked him teasingly *not* to grant her wish. Freud noted that the patient was 'very much in love with her husband now and teased him a lot'.[139] The renunciation of caviare thus had an erotic colouring, precisely as the renunciation wished for in the dream. Caviare has been substituted by smoked salmon, and not to be given smoked salmon is to be in the same position as to not be given caviare, namely, lover to the patient's husband.

Freud comments that this is a 'subtler interpretation'[140] but one which is not necessarily contradictory with the first interpretation of the dream fulfilling a wish for the friend not to become plump. The patient's wish to have the position of her friend in relation to her husband disturbs her simpler wish for her friend not to have that position, so that, having wished her friend to renounce her wish to become plumper, that is, more attractive to her husband, she takes up the position of a wish to renounce a wish – hence the dream and the symptom in reality regarding caviare. Thus both the dream and the symptom secure the friend in her position in relation to the patient's husband, for it has become the stake of the patient's own wish, namely to take her friend's place in relation to her own husband, as the place from which she can be loved. But the dreamer of smoked salmon has also given her husband, too, an unsatisfiable wish, namely for the friend who is too thin to satisfy his wish for plump women, so that she has also identified with him.[141]

The 'hysteric' identifies with the figure whose place in relation to another, third person, he or she wishes to have. But this 'hysterical' identification is the very form of identification itself.[142] Where for the dreamer the fantasy presents a scenario of her or his structuring relations of identification, in cinema we take up a place in a ready-made scenario – a public and published form – as if it were our own. This arises through that process Freud described as being the basis of the group relation, namely 'the possibility or desire of putting oneself in the same situation' as another because we have some element in common.[143] This common element is not some trait or characteristic, it is a common wish.

For the members of a group, the common quality is their emotional tie to the leader, that is, the common wish to be 'loved' – appreciated, approved, recognised – by this figure, and it is a *social* relation. Identification arises because each member of the group takes up the same position as the others in relation to the object of desire. In Freud's example of the girls at boarding school, it is the wish for a love affair: however, the girls do not wish for the *same* lover but for the same form of relation, namely, they wish to be loved. Freud connects this form of identification with 'the process which psychology calls "empathy [*Einfühlung*]" and which plays the largest part in our understanding of what is inherently foreign to our ego in other people.'[144]

Identification is with the place occupied by the object of identification in relation to an other, a relation of desire, of a wishing, which is often most poignantly produced because the character has lost what they desired, as seen in *Fury*. The common element we may feel with another person, the sense of 'being like' them, or having had a similar experience, is not the basis for identification but its material support. For such a 'recognition' must ignore the many other elements or circumstances which are different in favour of the similarity, so that we can see here a *wish* to be like the other, to be the same as, and it is a wish not to *be* the other, but to be in his or her position in relation to another figure which is also a figure of desire. It is a wish to re-find or re-play our founding relation to subjectivity in our relations with others (a core fantasy through which we enjoy, Lacan says) and which is missing, deflected or turned around on the self in autism, in psychosis, and also in perversion. It is this which public forms of fantasy also satisfy. And, although the reader or viewer has willingly come to the film or play or novel, such ready-made scenarios must nevertheless ingratiate themselves by invoking a sense of recognition, of our being like the characters presented, or having been in the same situation. The sense of recognition – the 'common element' – which is produced is the support for identification, not its cause (here the importance of verisimilitude becomes apparent), it works as a 'forepleasure' to open the subject to identify, to bring him or her to say 'that could be me' and thereby to take up the position of the other and to enter the fantasy as if it were one's own. It is the role of fantasy, in public forms of imaginative writing as well as film, and as a political issue for feminism, to which I will now turn.

4

Fantasia

The notion of fantasy, when applied to film, has either designated a particular genre – the fantasy film – in which the term marks those films which figure the supernatural or an imaginary world unknown to us yet, as with the science fiction film. Or the term has been used pejoratively to dismiss cinema and especially Hollywood cinema as escapist and as unreal – notably in the words of Hortense Powdermaker – as the 'dream factory'.[1] Within feminism the discussion of fantasy emerged as a necessity in the context of the demand 'the personal is political'. The issue of fantasy, however, was never seen only in terms of male fantasy as a problem for women – whether in pornography, for example, or in the treatment of women by men as sex objects, or as an element in the sexism which divides women into virgins and whores, good girls and slags, wives (and mothers) and mistresses. Fantasy was also addressed from early in the modern women's movement as a problem in relation to our own, politically recalcitrant, fantasies – whether as secret pleasures in Mills & Boon-style romantic fiction, or as, before falling asleep, imagined scenes of romantic encounter or seduction, or the desire when making love for domination or submission. Such 'fantasy' was initially seen as the consequence of women's oppression in which we accepted and acted out the distorted fantasies and repressions of men. Once a woman was aware of this oppression, for example through consciousness-raising, such reactionary imaginings would be seen as simply as that – the trappings of male ideology which we hadn't been strong enough to throw off.

As a result what emerged in feminism were, broadly, two positions. The first is moralistic: it sees fantasy as simply a question of content which can be changed at will; as a result we are exhorted to have strength and to forsake fantasy, at least any sexual fantasy, altogether. Fantasy is condemned as invariably using another person as an object, and as fragmented and reductive in relation to the full identity of that person. A moral charge is made, that sexual fantasy dehumanises. The second position on the contrary accepts that fantasy is intrinsic to human nature and indeed is bound up with sexuality, although in a way which we do not yet wholly understand.

The first position appears most often represented as an aspiration in relation to which women (and men, for whom the aspiration allows a masochistic breastbeating, and which itself often seems part of a satisfying fantasy) bemoan their failure, or appeal for the discovery of a new feminist eroticism and fantasy, for which we are still waiting. And will continue to wait, in as much as such a position misunderstands the mechanisms of fantasy. The partialisation of objects in the external world, indeed the external world as a series of objects and parts of objects, is intrinsic to our relation with the external world. Yet it is clearly crucial that we also recognise the unity of objects in the external world, the mother as a whole object, as well as the part object, the (maternal) breast. But our relation to the whole is bound up in certain ways with our relation to the part, as in the example just given. We cannot remove that by fiat. But nor does this psychic structuring have simple or necessary consequences for social relations; and the intervention of moral norms, of social requirements through the agency of censorship by the super-ego will be involved in the organisation of such cathexes. It is the interplay of this organisation across public forms of fantasy such as films which I will be concerned to address later in this chapter in terms of the second position outlined above, of fantasy's intrinsic role in relation to sexuality.

The special issue of *Heresies* in 1981 on sexuality set a new agenda for debates about sexuality, femininity and feminism through its controversial reintroduction of the question of women's sexual pleasure.[2] Its writers challenged feminism's rejection of fantasy, instead seeking to affirm politically the important role it played in their sexual lives:

> But what is it that I really like? What is it that I really want, sexually? Why is it that I turn away from him even though I feel pleasure and rising lust? I do not know what I imagine when I masturbate. Yet my innermost sexual fantasies, with their emphasis on passivity and total male dominance are frightening, because they are so contradictory to what I, as a feminist, think.[3]

The fantasied scenarios suggested in this quote, with their implied sadism and masochism, are taken up explicitly by Pat Califia and defended as a valid form of feminist and lesbian sexual activity: 'The women's movement has become a moralistic force, and it can contribute to the self-loathing and misery experienced by sexual minorities... Like Victorian missionaries in Polynesia they [feminists] insist on interpreting the sexual behaviour of other people according to their own value systems.'[4] In no way do her criticisms imply a general disaffection with feminism, for she goes on to write 'I think it is imperative that feminists dismantle the institutions that foster the exploitation and abuse of women. The family, conventional sexuality, and gender are at the top of my hit list. These institutions control the emotional, intimate lives of every one of us, and they have done incalculable damage to women.' Yet while this argument might lead her to condemn sado-masochism as an oppressive structure, given the dominant patriarchal, capitalist society, she in fact argues that S/M relationships are egalitarian:

Some feminists object to the description of S/M as consensual. They believe that our society has conditioned all of us to accept inequities in power and hierarchical relationships. Therefore, S/M is simply a manifestation of the same system that dressed girls in pink and boys in blue, allows a surplus value to accumulate in the coffers of capitalists and gives workers a minimum wage, and sends cops out to keep the disfranchised down.

It is true as I stated before, that society shapes sexuality. We can make any decision about our sexual behavior we like, but our imagination and ability to carry out those decisions are limited by the surrounding culture. But I do not believe that sado-masochism is the result of institutionalised injustice to a greater extent than heterosexual marriage, lesbian bars, or gay male bath-houses. The system is unjust because it assigns privileges based on race, gender, and social class. During an S/M encounter the participants select a particular role because it best expresses their sexual needs... The most significant reward for being a top or a bottom is sexual pleasure. If you don't like being a top or a bottom you switch your keys. Try doing that with your biological sex or your socio-economic status.[5]

Califia's defence of S/M rests on the sexual pleasure obtained, the fact that it is always very clearly *play* ('Even a minor accident like a rope burn can upset the top enough to mar the scene'), and the interchangeability of the roles – 'You can always switch your keys...'

Choice, consent and free will to engage in S/M are all emphasised in the article, yet it opens with a powerful confession of the compulsive quality of her fantasies: 'Three years ago, I decided to stop ignoring my sexual fantasies. Since the age of two, I had been constructing a private world of dominance, submission, punishment and pain. Abstinence, consciousness-raising and therapy had not blighted the charm of these frightful reveries.'[6]

I will not centre my discussion of fantasy on sado-masochism as such, although certainly the opposition active/passive is central to fantasy. Rather, I am taking it as exemplary of the problem of fantasy for feminism, a problem brought out in Califia's article precisely because she wishes to argue for feminism *and* S/M practices. As a result, and because she is not prepared to make a simple defence of S/M, she is led to theorise the pleasure in S/M. She challenges the content of fantasy as a simple function of experience, for example in the idea that S/M fantasies are found in those who experienced corporal punishment as children. Califia writes:

> The key word to understand S/M is *fantasy*. The roles, dialogue, fetish costumes, and sexual activity are part of a drama or ritual. The participants are enhancing their sexual pleasure, not damaging or imprisoning one another. A sado-masochist is well aware that a role adopted during a scene is not appropriate during other interactions and that a fantasy role is not the sum total of her being. The S/M subculture is a theatre in which sexual dramas can be acted out.[7]

Califia comes close to psychoanalysis' view of fantasy not only in her suggestion of a splitting of the subject in S/M but also in her notion of fantasy as a scene, a theatre, involving role-playing and the interchangeability of roles, in her emphasis on the 'unreality' of fantasy as distinct from its 'seriousness', and in her assertion that fantasy involves not an object of desire as in 'I want X' but a scenario of activities which depend upon the partner's participation. All these are part of what is understood as fantasy in psychoanalysis.

Califia is clearly arguing for fantasy in terms of the second position outlined earlier, of fantasy as intrinsic to sexuality. But it is not a simple re-instatement of fantasy. Nor is it a declaration that fantasy is *unreal*, that the nature of our fantasies do not matter because they aren't real and we *know* it. But while Califia recognises this, her insistence on free will and on choice – with its consequent problems of knowledge and intention – prevent her from developing its full implication. Nonetheless she has opened up a space and debate which I want to explore more directly through the kind of understanding of fantasy suggested by psychoanalysis.[8]

FANTASY IN PSYCHOANALYSIS

(1) Fantasy[9] is the fundamental object of psychoanalysis, it is the central material for the 'talking cure' and for the unconscious: 'the psychoanalyst must endeavour in the course of the treatment to unearth the phantasies which lie behind such products of the unconscious as dreams, symptoms, acting out, repetitive behaviour etc.'[10] Fantasy is an imagined scene in which the subject is a protagonist, and which always represents the fulfilment of a wish albeit that its representation is distorted to a greater or lesser extent by defensive processes. Fantasy has a number of modes: conscious fantasies or day-dreams, unconscious fantasies such as those uncovered by analysis as the structures underlying a manifest content, and primal fantasies. These are not mutually exclusive modes; on the contrary, a day-dream will at the same time involve an unconscious wish underlying its manifest content and the structure of that unconscious wish will be related to the primal fantasies. This, Laplanche and Pontalis suggest in their essay 'Fantasy and the Origins of Sexuality', was the reason that Freud saw as the model of fantasy the day-dream, or reverie 'that form of novelette, both stereotyped and infinitely variable, which the subject composes and relates to himself in a walking state'.[11] The difference between these modes does not involve a difference in the objects of fantasy, nor primarily a distinction between conscious or unconscious, but a difference in their relation to repression, and the working of censorship.

(2) The word fantasy is usually understood as 'an imagined scene', with the associated meanings of: 'fabulous; fancy (now a separate meaning); imagination, mental image; love, whim; caprice; fantasia; preoccupation with thoughts associated with unattainable desires'.[12] The word derives through Latin from the Greek term meaning to 'make visible'. However, rather than a notion of revelation, making visible what we would not otherwise be able to see – as with a microscope allowing us to see bacteria etc. invisible to the

'naked' eye – fantasy has come to mean the making visible, the making present, of what isn't there, of what can never *directly* be seen.

In German *Phantasie* is the term used to denote the imagination, but not so much in the sense of the faculty of imaginings as in terms of the imaginary world and its contents, the imaginings into which the poet – or the neurotic – so willingly withdraws. As Laplanche and Pontalis note, it is difficult as a result to avoid defining the word in terms of what is not, namely, the world of reality. The opposition of fantasy and reality, however, cannot be reduced to the conventional opposition between the terms 'fiction' and 'real life'. Freud discovered the importance of fantasy, in particular its importance in the neuroses, when he abandoned his theory of sexual seduction by a parent or other adult as a real event which produces a trauma whose consequences can be found in adult life. Notorious as this has become for feminists, the importance of Freud's assertion is nevertheless extremely relevant for feminism. For what Freud came to understand in relation to the account of rape or seduction by the father so common amongst his women patients was not that the woman was making something up, was pretending or trying to dupe Freud, but that since the event had not happened – as he now believed – then sexuality in the woman could not be thought of as simply the 'effect' of outside events, of the seduction or rape, whether pleasurable or traumatic. Rather sexuality was already there, in play. Now viewed as fantasy, the account of seduction or rape and its attendant traumas were no longer the *result* of a seduction but of the *wish* for a seduction, implying sexuality already there motivating the wish. Freud is then concerned to elaborate on *how* it is already there. The consequences of this are important: for feminism, it shows that women's sexuality is not a simple consequence (again, whether traumatic or pleasurable) of male sexuality, of the seduction as a real event. Furthermore the wish is not simply passive – its object is the father and it also implies its inverse, the wish to seduce or rape the father. The father as sexual object is, of course, the consequence of the Oedipal scenario, and therefore of an earlier wish to seduce/be seduced by the mother. What Freud shows is that the issue is one of psychical reality, for which the reality or not of the event is not as such determining.[13] This psychical reality is not simply the internal world, a psychological domain of the mental, rather Laplanche and Pontalis argue that for Freud fantasy denotes 'a heterogenous nucleus within this field, a resistant element, alone truly real in contrast with the majority of psychical phenomena',[14] and they quote Freud, 'If we look at unconscious wishes reduced to their most fundamental and truest shape, we shall have to conclude no doubt that *psychic* reality is a particular form of existence not to be confused with *material* reality.'[15]

This psychical reality of which fantasy is the nucleus has an effect on and for the subject just as much as the material, physical world may have. In analysing fantasy, it is not a criterion that there be any factual basis for the fantasy 'in reality' or that there be a wish for it to 'really happen', but rather the criterion is the level of 'reality' the fantasy has for and in the psychical system of the subject. What is refused here, then, is any privileging of material reality as necessarily more important, more serious.

(3) Freud did not make a terminological distinction between conscious and unconscious fantasy, and Laplanche and Pontalis argue against such a division (but one which is made, for example, by Melanie Klein) emphasising instead the continuity between unconscious and conscious fantasy. Rather, they argue, following Freud, for a distinction between original fantasies and other, secondary fantasies, whether conscious or unconscious. These two modes are always found in combination in any fantasy, conscious or unconscious, hence Freud's emphasis on the day-dream as the model of fantasy. As a result what is brought into focus is fantasy as a scene. The importance of this idea cannot be overestimated, for it enables the consideration of film as fantasy in the most fundamental sense of this term in psychoanalysis. The same material, motivation and structure can be revealed in imaginary formations or day-dreams and in psychopathological structures as diverse as those described by Freud such as hysteria, delusional paranoia etc. as well as in public forms of fantasy such as film and the novel. And these forms are not just conscious re-workings, i.e. censored representations of unconscious, repressed fantasies, for Freud realised that it is conscious fantasy itself which may be repressed and thus become pathogenic. Laplanche and Pontalis argue that on the one hand fantasy 'is linked with the ultimate unconscious desire, the "capitalist" of the dream, and as such it is at the basis of that "zig-zag" path which is supposed to follow excitation through a succession of psychological systems', leading from the unconscious scenes of fantasies to the preconscious where it collects the day's residues. On the other hand, fantasy is also present at the other extreme, in the secondary

elaboration of the dream, the *a posteriori* re-working of the dream once we are awake, which seeks to place a minimum of order and coherence onto the raw material handed over by the unconscious mechanisms of displacement and condensation.[16] Imposing a scenario, a façade of coherence and continuity – in a word, a narrative – it will thus also draw on those ready-made scenarios, the subject's day-dreams. But this re-working is not simply a masking, a mistaken distorting and arbitrary revision, for it will draw on the same impetuses for fantasy as the dreams of sleep.

The distinction in fantasy is therefore not between conscious and unconscious or between censored and uncensored fantasy but between primal or originally unconscious fantasies and secondary fantasies which may be unconscious or conscious. The concept of 'primal fantasies' in Freud is controversial. Freud himself always saw these as human universals constituted through a phylogenetically transmitted inheritance, while later theorists such as Laplanche emphasise the role of 'originary' fantasies which organise subsequent fantasy. The primal fantasies are scenes of origins, and they 'theorise' or explain the problem of origins for the child. In the 'primal scene', it is the origin of the subject that is represented – in seduction fantasies, the origin of or emergence of sexuality, and in castration fantasies it is the origin of sexual difference or the distiction between the sexes. The concept of the 'primal scene' does not therefore imply a simple causality, nor a primacy of origin or original content. Rather it is to be understood as originary in the instituting of a structure of fantasy, a scene of fantasied origins: of the origin of the child in its parents' love-making; it is the scene of the wish to take the father's place and have the mother, or to usurp the mother's place and have the father. The primal fantasies are not so much an inherited pre-history, as a pre-structure, which is actualised and transmitted by the parents' fantasies.

In their content, in their theme (primal scene, castration, seduction…) the original fantasies also indicate this postulate of retroactivity: they relate to the origins. Like myths, they claim to provide a representation of, and a solution to, the major enigmas which confront the child. Whatever appears to the subject as something needing an explanation or theory, is dramatised as a moment of emergence, the beginning of a history… There is a convergence of theme, of structure, and no doubt also of function: through the indications furnished by the perceptual field, through the scenarios constructed, the varied quest for origins, we are offered in the field of fantasy, the origin of the subject himself.[17]

The original fantasy explains the beginnings of the child but thus always pre-exists the child, for to pose a beginning is also to pose a *before* the beginning; and there is always an already-there for every child – its parents, grandparents, a history. The original fantasy then as structuring rather than a structure, for it is activated by contingent elements. Laplanche and Pontalis make this clear in their discussion of Freud's first reference to primal fantasies in 'A Case of Paranoia Running Counter to the Psychoanalytic Theory of the Disease'. Here Freud describes the case of a woman patient who declared that she had been watched and photographed while lying with her lover. She claimed to have heard a noise, the click of a camera. 'Behind this delirium Freud saw the primal scene: the sound is the noise of the parents making love, thus awakening the child: it is also the sound the child is afraid of making lest it betray her listening.' The role of this noise in the fantasy is difficult to assess, they suggest, for in one sense Freud says that it is only a provocation, an accidental cause, whose role is solely to activate the 'typical phantasy of overhearing' which is a component of the parental complex, but he immediately corrects himself by saying 'It is doubtful whether we can rightly call the noise "accidental".. .. such noises are on the contrary an indispensable part of the phantasy of listening and they reproduce either the sounds which betray parental intercourse or those by which the listening child fears to betray itself.'[18] In fact the sound alleged by the patient was, according to Freud, a projection, the projection of a beat in her clitoris, in the form of a noise which, Laplanche and Pontalis suggest 'reproduces in actuality the indication of the primal scene, the element which is the starting point for all ulterior elaboration of the fantasy. In other words, *the origin of the fantasy is integrated in the very structure of the original fantasy.*'[19] The primal fantasy then as the instituting of this structuring, as a scene in which the child is also present interchangeably with the other participants as onlooker, as one or other parent, or even as the person who will discover the child looking-on. Moreover Laplanche and Pontalis argue that the primal scene, 'this "foreign" body which is to be internally excluded, is usually brought to the subject, not by the perception of a scene, but by parental desire and its supporting fantasy'.[20]

(4) What is shown here is the originary structuring of fantasy, but it presupposes a structuring of *wishing* already present in the subject, raising the question of the origin of fantasising as such. This, Laplanche and Pontalis argue, cannot be isolated from the origin of the drive itself. Reinterpreting Freud's concept of *the experience of satisfaction*, they locate this origin in auto-eroticism, which they define not as a stage of evolution but as the moment of a repeated disjunction of sexual desire and non-sexual functions. That is, 'the experience of satisfaction' is separated from the object which satisfies, and the latter is represented as a sign. For the baby, the 'breast' becomes the object of desire – as giving the experience of satisfaction – but it is so not as itself but as a signifier of the *lost* object which is the *satisfaction* derived from suckling the breast, but which comes to be desired in *its absence*. This is the emergence of auto-eroticism, for the sexual drive is separated from the non-sexual functions, such as feeding, which are its support and which indicate its aim and object. The feeding still nourishes the child, but the experience of satisfaction in feeding has been split off through the function of representation and moves into the field of fantasy and by this very fact starts existing as sexuality. It is auto-erotic because the external object has been abandoned, the drive is 'objectless' and satisfaction is derived from 'organ-pleasure' – the motions of sucking, rather than the instinctual act of sucking and obtaining nourishment.[21]

The importance of relating fantasy to auto-eroticism is to show that desire is not purely an upsurging of the drives but comes to exist as sexual through its articulation in fantasy.

(5) As noted earlier, fantasies are wishful; however they are not about a wish to have some determinate object, making it present for the subject. Lacan writes that

> The phantasy is the support of desire, it is not the object that is the support of desire. The subject sustains himself as desiring in relation to an ever more complex signifying ensemble. This is apparent enough in the form of the scenario it assumes, in which the subject, more or less recognisable, is somewhere, split, divided, generally double, in his relation to the object, which usually does not show its true face either.[22]

Similarly, Mustapha Safouan notes 'instead of being co-opted to an object, desire is first co-opted to phantasy'.[23]

Fantasy involves, is characterised by, not the achievement of desired objects, but the arranging of, a setting out of, desire; a veritable mise en scène of desire. For, of course, Lacan says, desire is unsatisfiable, much as Freud commented that there is something in the nature of sexuality which is resistant to satisfaction. The fantasy depends not on particular objects, but on their setting out; and the pleasure of fantasy lies in the setting out, not in the having of the objects. Within the day-dream and more especially in fictional stories, the demands of narrative may obscure this, for the typical ending will be a resolution of the problems, the wars, feuds, and so on, bringing about the union in marriage of the hero and heroine. Yet inevitably the story will fall prey to diverse diversions, delays, obstacles and other means to postponing the ending. For though we all want the couple to be united, and the obstacles heroically overcome, we don't want the story to end. And marriage is one of the most definitive endings. The pleasure is in how to *bring about* the consummation, is in the happening and continuing to happen; is how it will come about, and not in the moment of *having happened*, when it will fall back into loss, the past. This can extend into producing endings which remain murky, ill-defined, uncertain even. It is thus not modesty which veils the endings of romantic fiction by wise caution. Sternberg's film *Morocco* is perhaps an extreme example in cinema of the refusal to narrate an ending, to consummate the narrative, for it concludes with another repetition of the setting out of a lack to be fulfilled, which has already been played twice over and more, namely, of Dietrich leaving an anguished Adolphe Menjou for an unknowing Gary Cooper.[24] Fantasy as a mise en scène of desire is more a setting out of lack, of what is absent, than a presentation of a having, a being present. Desire itself coming into existence in the representation of lack, in the production of a fantasy of its becoming present. It can be seen, then, that fantasy is not the object of desire, but its setting. As a result:

> In fantasy the subject does not pursue the object or its sign: he appears caught up himself in the sequence of images. He forms no representation of the desired object, but is himself represented as participating in the scene although, in the earliest forms of fantasy, he cannot be assigned any fixed place in it... As a result, the subject, although always present in the fantasy, may be so in a de-subjectivised form, that is to say, in the very syntax of the sequence in question.[25]

The subject is present or presented through the very form of organisation, composition, of the scene. It is perhaps only the most re-worked, conscious, day-dream which is able to impose the stabilisation of the ego, so that the subject's position is clear and invariable as the 'I' of the story, which the subject, as it were, 'lives out'. Nevertheless it is not only in the 'original' fantasies that this de-subjectivisation takes place. Both the day-dream 'thoughtlessly' composed, and the more complex fictional narrative join with the 'original' fantasies in visualising the subject in the scene, and in presenting a varying of subject position so that the subject takes up more than one position and thus is not fixed.

This is made clear in Freud's analysis of fantasy in '"A Child is Beaten": A Contribution to the Study of the Origin of Sexual Perversions'. This fantasy was produced by both male and female patients of Freud and he shows that in each case there is an earlier stage or stages, with corresponding subject-positions. It is the version found in women that Freud most fully describes, however, and this is the version which my account here is based upon. Freud shows that three phases lie behind this fantasy for the woman, each involving a different subject-position. In the first phase the fantasy is: 'my father is beating the child, *whom I hate*', thus 'He (my father) loves only me, and not the other child, for he is beating it'. But the child is also fantasising that it is making its father beat the other child to show that the father loves only itself, and thus the subject erases the other, rival child, from the father's affections. It is thus egoistic, identifying both father/self-love and father/self as beater of the other child. For this to become transposed into 'A child is being beaten' with its third-person syntax, Freud proposed a second phase 'I am being beaten by my father'; while the first phase may be remembered through analysis, this second phase is wholly unconscious and can only be inferred from analysis. However it produces the move from sadism to masochism. (Though the first phase is not yet properly sadistic, or erotic, inasmuch as it is pre-genital.) The implicit incestuous desire of the first phase is subject to repression in the second phase to produce a reversal: No my father does not love me (you), for he is beating me (you). The beating is not only the punishment for the incestuous wish but is also the 'regressive substitute for that relation, and from this latter source it derives the libidinal excitation which is from this time forward attached to it'.[26] Guiltiness and punishment are thus attached to the sexual desire; to be punished is to have had the forbidden sexual relation, for why else would you be punished? In the third phase, the consciously remembered fantasy 'A child is being beaten', once more appears sadistic:

> But only the *form* of this phantasy is sadistic; the satisfaction which is derived from it is masochistic. Its significance lies in the fact that it has taken over the libidinal cathexis of the repressed portion and at the same time the sense of guilt which is attached to the content of that portion. All the many unspecified children who are being beaten by the teacher are, after all, nothing more than substitutes for the child itself.[27]

The fantasy escapes repression by a further distortion, the disguise of the third-person syntax. Out there, there are children being beaten (like I should be, for my forbidden wishes). Apparently sadistic, in as much as it represses the parenthesis. The stake, the effectiveness, of this third phase of the fantasy is the interchangeability of the subject and the other children being beaten. Laplanche and Pontalis cite the seduction fantasy as a similar example, which they summarise as 'A father seduces a daughter', emphasising the 'peculiar character of the structure, in that it is a scenario with multiple entries, in which nothing shows whether the subject will be immediately located as *daughter*; it can as well be fixed as *father*, or even in the term *seduces*'.[28] The fantasy scenario always involves multiple points of entry which are also mutually exclusive positions, but these are taken up not sequentially – as in a narrative – but simultaneously or rather, since the unconscious does not know time in this way, to take up any one position is also always to be implicated in the position of the other(s).[29]

(6) It is to the extent that desire is articulated in fantasy that the latter is also thereby the locus of defensive operations – it facilitates and can become the site of the most primitive defensive processes, such as turning round upon the subject's own self, reversal into its opposite, projection and negation. As a result, where a wish has undergone repression a fantasy may provide a satisfaction not by presenting a scenario for the achievement of the wish but, on the contrary, by enacting the failure and frustration of that wish or even its reversal into its opposite. This has been seen in the example of 'A child is being beaten'. Defences are inseparably bound up with the work of fantasy, namely, the mise en scène of desire, a mise en scène in which what is prohibited is always present in the

actual formation of the wish.[30] Freud's most famous example of a wish for an unfulfilled wish is the smoked-salmon dream, discussed earlier in the chapter on identification. However an example he gives in his essay on hysterical fantasies is also, I suggest, an instance of a wish which is unfulfilled, or more accurately, one which is initially fulfilled, then appears to be reversed, turning out badly. Freud described the day-dream, which had been produced by one of the women patients, as a case of an involuntary irruption of fantasy. The patient recounted that on one occasion she had suddenly found herself in tears in the street and that, rapidly considering what it was she was actually crying about, she had got hold of a fantasy to the following effect: in her imagination she had formed a tender attachment to a pianist who was well known in the town (though she was not personally acquainted with him); she had had a child by him (she was in fact childless); and he had then deserted her and her child and left them in poverty. It was at this point in her 'romance', Freud says, that she burst into tears.[31]

Freud does not give any analysis of the fantasy himself, but I would like to suggest that it is an example of the fantasy subject to defensive processes. Consider the moment of the tears, narratively appropriate, tears of self-pity at her imagined loss. But why has she produced a story to make herself cry, and may the tears be a response not to the pathos of the story but to its satisfactions? The crying thus acting as a defence, bringing her fantasy to an end in the same way Freud speaks of waking oneself up from a dream. This becomes even more plausible if the possibility of multiple subject positions in the story is considered. It commenced with a pleasant and typical erotic wish in relation to the pianist, together with its happy consummation. But the fruit of the affair, a child, places the fantasy into an Oedipal context, for the child is the one wished for with the father. A forbidden desire has found expression in the fantasy, that it is forbidden is marked by the punishment immediately meted out – the man deserts her and the child and in addition they are left in poverty. This doubling marks that it was not enough punishment for the man to desert her; another hardship must be given to her. But even this is not enough, for tears intervene to halt the fantasy. This might suggest that the man's desertion is *not* the punishment, but part of the wish, i.e. for the eviction of the father, so that the child has the mother to herself, and it is *this* wish which provokes the final censorship of tears. (The day-dream bears an astonishing resemblence to Max Ophuls's 1948 film

Letter From An Unknown Woman, although in the short story by Stefan Zweig on which it was based the lover was a writer.)

Summarising his conclusions on the nature of hysterical symptoms in 'Hysterical Phantasies and Their Relation to Bisexuality', Freud suggests not only that 'Hysterical symptoms are the realisation of an unconscious phantasy which serves the fulfilment of a wish', but also that 'Hysterical symptoms are the expression on the one hand of a masculine unconscious sexual phantasy, and on the other hand of a feminine one.' Freud draws here on his view of the innate bisexual disposition of the human and he says, 'In one case which I observed, for instance, the patient pressed her dress up against her body with one hand (as the woman), while she tried to tear it off with the other (as the man).'[32] But what is shown here, I would suggest, is not a mixing of the masculine and feminine but the juxtaposition, side by side, of both the feminine and masculine as distinct sexual positions of desire.

FANTASY IN THE REALM OF THE PUBLIC

Fantasy has, of course, never been simply a private affair. The public circulation of fantasies has many forms, from the publishing of psychoanalytic case studies, to feminist articles such as those in the issue of *Heresies*, or speaking-out in consciousness-raising groups. There are also those anthologies such as *My Secret Garden*[33] which, besides their pseudo-scientific claims of extending human knowledge, are also offering forms of circulation of fantasy just as much as do the letters in *Forum*, *Men Only*, *Penthouse*, etc. But by far the most common form of public circulation of fantasy is what Freud described as 'creative writing', which I take to also include film. Unlike confessional forms, such as letters, diaries etc., in the novel or the film the subject of the fantasy and the 'author' are differentiated. Fantasy, as a mise en scène of desire, will nevertheless be at work in film, but how, and with what implications? Laplanche and Pontalis have shown how all fantasy involves original fantasies which are limited in thematic, endlessly re-worked through the material of the everyday, that-day, experiences:

> The day-dream is a shadow play, utilising its kaleidoscopic material drawn from all quarters of human experience, but also involving the original fantasy, whose *dramatis personae*, the court

cards, receive their notation from a family legend which is mutilated, disordered and misunderstood.[34]

And Barthes writes:

> If there is no longer a Father, why tell stories? Doesn't every nar-
> rative lead back to Oedipus? Isn't storytelling always a way of
> searching for one's origins, speaking one's conflicts with the Law,
> entering into a dialectic of tenderness and hatred?[35]

This appears reductive, for there cannot now be anything more to
say of fantasy in general, whether in film or the novel, which is not
merely banal. And this is supported by the realisation of the enormous repetition of cinema: the stories replayed before the cameras,
always the same but differently, which has been the key to cinema's
success as a mass form of entertainment. On the other hand there is
the rich diversity of cinema, presenting the world on the screen
through a range of genres, narrative devices, and cinematographic
techniques.

Between the 'limited thematics' of original fantasy and the
diverse, often complex webs of modern forms of representation,
how should we pose the question of fantasy in film and the role of
narrative for and in fantasy? My starting point here, before considering in detail particular films, is Freud's essay 'Creative Writers
and Day-dreaming'.

Freud asks what the role of conscious fantasies, of day-dreams
is, and argues that they function for adults as play had done in
childhood, with all the same seriousness:

> In spite of all the emotion with which he cathects his world of
> play, the child distinguishes it quite well from reality; and he
> likes to link his imagined objects and situations to the tangible
> and visible things of the real world. This linking is all that differ-
> entiates the child's 'play' from 'phantasying'.
>   The creative writer does the same as the child at play. He
> creates a world of phantasy which he takes very seriously – that
> is, which he invests with large amounts of emotion–while sep-
> arating it sharply from reality.[36]

And behind the play, behind fantasy, is a wish: for the child, to be
grown-up, which is acted out in its scenarios; for the adult,

ambitious and erotic wishes are fantasied (in scenarios). These can be infinitely various and varied, shifting with the new impressions received every day, changing to fit the new situations and contexts of the subject – the kaleidoscopic material to which Laplanche and Pontalis refer. The day-dream/fantasy, Freud suggests, moves between three time periods: the present which provides the occasion and hence the material elements of the fantasy as well as the provocation which arouses the wish, which is not new but an existing wish that relates back to a past time in which the wish was fulfilled, whether in reality or in fantasy; the fulfilment of the wish is imagined in a new situation, in the future. Freud's example is of a poor orphan boy going for a job interview imagining not only obtaining the job but being so successful that he is taken into the employer's family, marries his daughter and succeeds him in running the business. This time structure implies a sequencing of events, but the logical and causal relationships of narrative may not be present; instead, events appear motivated by coincidence, that is, appear uncaused. As noted earlier, it is secondary revision which imposes a logic and order on the fantasy scenario, whereas in the unconscious the fantasy scenario has no time periods, or rather, its time is simultaneity. And, while ambitious and erotic wishes are both fulfilled, whether in dreams of sleep or consciousness, censorship and secondary revision will intervene; in various ways, more or less, the fantasies are tailored to and address 'reality' – in the sense of Lacan's symbolic, a domain of prohibition, and in the sense of 'reality-testing' and actualised social relations. Fantasy is therefore a privileged terrain on which social reality and the unconscious are engaged in a figuring which intertwines them both.

Our day-dreams and fantasies are normally very private affairs (which is why their rare forms of public circulation are so fascinating) and a certain amount of 'shame' and embarrassment is involved whenever our fantasies are found out, or when we fear being found out in them. A shame not only for being childish (and hence for a denial of reality) as Freud suggests, but also surely because of the cathexis deriving from the archaic, original wishes involved. Despite censoring, the very existence of the fantasy bears witness to the pressure of a desire itself absent (or rather, which is not represented as such). Yet, as Freud suggests, a publicly sanctioned form of fantasy does exist – creative writing – in which all this is in play. In his discussion Freud addresses initially the most despised form of creative writing, popular fiction, where he notes the recurrent feature of an invincible hero 'for whom the writer tries by every means to win our sympathies', and that 'through the revealing characteristic of invulnerability we can immediately recognise His Majesty the Ego, the hero alike of every day-dream and of every story'.[37] This remains true even for 'serious' literature, where the hero may die nobly on the scaffold, or indeed be no hero at all. The anti-hero, too, is a centred ego, the privileged character and the site of a celebration, however negative. Freud similarly suggests that the psychological novel, where there is no centred hero, 'owes its special nature to the inclination of the modern writer to split up his ego, by self-observation, into many part-egos, and, in consequence, to personify the conflicting currents of his own mental life in several heros'.[38] Creative writing is thus seen to be the presenting in a public form of the author's own fantasies – and the same time structure as that of the day-dream can be seen to operate.

Freud's theses, while opening up the study of fantasy in public forms of representation, seem, however, to lead back to the author as origin of the fantasy in the text. If fantasies *are* 'personal' in this way, how can they work for a general public, for a mass audience? For Freud is very clear that what is at stake is not that the reader can see and be entertained by the author's fantasies, but that the reader *enters* into those fantasies. He or she can do so not only because fantasy-scenarios involve original wishes which are universal but also – and more importantly – because a fantasy-scenario is a structure of positions, of loving and/or being loved, of being the father and/or mother, child and/or onlooker. Any one position implies another – as father for a child, as a son or daughter to a parent. It is because these are not reciprocal relations but are marked by lack that desire arises. We enter the fantasy-structure and identify *as if* it were our own. This is not a cognitive mistake, we are not deluded or deceived by the fiction, we have not misrecognised or disavowed the otherness of the film's fiction. Films and stories offer us a contingent world for their events and outcomes, and, just as we draw on the events of the day to produce our own fantasies, so too we can adopt and adapt the ready-made scenarios of fiction, as if their contingent material had been our own. We do not take the character's desire as our own, but identify with the character's position of desire in relation to other characters (just like Freud's case of the boarding-school girls' identification with their jealous friend). If we adopt the same objects of desire, or the character traits of the figures of the fiction, this is as support for our identification, as its symptom and not its cause.

Another question arises here, of how the reader or spectator can overcome the internal censorship which fantasy in the adult – and especially material related to primal fantasies – is subject to. This is made possible in two related ways, Freud suggests. First of all the fantasy origin of the material is disguised. The author – whether the single author of the literary text, or the collective 'authors' of a film – reworks his or her fantasies, drawing upon literary and filmic conventions of the novelistic to produce a figuring of those fantasies which will lead us to accept what would otherwise appear as rampant egoism by altering, softening and disguising the characters of the fiction. The far-fetched, unrealistic aspect of fantasy is replaced by conventions of narrative realism, of 'properly' motivated cause and effect within the plot, and by verisimilitudinous, 'believable' characters. Paradoxically, therefore, a film will seek to reassure the spectator that it isn't fantasy or mere wishfulness but is properly subject to the reality principle, while the spectator similarly disavows the possibility of fantasy of the film – 'I know this isn't real, is only an illusion, but all the same I want to treat it as real...', with an attendant demand for and pleasure in the *realism* of the illusionism, to the extent that it is the most typical aesthetic criteria for good film. Notwithstanding the fact that realism, the realistic, are the effects of, are produced by, filmic and literary conventions,[39] it is still held to be axiomatic by critics and audiences alike that some films are realistic – and good – while others are mere fantasy. The vehement demand – itself a wish – that we should be able to tell the difference between reality and fantasy even in fiction bears witness perhaps to the fear involved in apprehending the reality of fantasy. But in as much as this wish is located in relation to representation it is condemned to a hopeless circularity: reality is realistic in representation in so far as it conforms to the accepted conventions of representing reality.

Secondly, our access to fantasy in the work of representation is brought about through what Freud describes as the way in which a writer

> bribes us by the purely formal – that is, aesthetic – yield of pleasure which he offers us in the presentation of his phantasies. We

give the name of an incentive bonus, or a fore-pleasure, to a yield of pleasure such as this, which is offered to us so as to make possible the release of still greater pleasure arising from deeper psychical sources.[40]

The notion of fore-pleasure here derives from Freud's account of two forms of pleasure arising in the sexual act:

This distinction between one kind of pleasure due to the excitation of erotogenic zones and the other kind due to the discharge of the sexual substances deserves, I think, to be made more concrete by a different nomenclature. The former may be suitably described as 'fore-pleasure' in contrast to the 'end-pleasure' or pleasure of satisfaction derived from the sexual act.[41]

Freud draws on this distinction between two types of pleasure to explain the kinds of pleasure which arise from jokes. The simple joke, a pun for example, gives pleasure by the shift of meaning, the substitution implied, which produces a comic effect by juxtaposing an appropriate and inappropriate meaning (just as cinema audiences unused to subtitles may laugh and titter at any misspellings). In the tendentious joke, that is those jokes which have an object or butt of the humour, there are additional sources of pleasure through the satisfaction of erotic and/or aggressive feelings, but the means to this additional pleasure is via the simple joke which opens the way to the substitution of meaning in relation to the object. Freud gives a number of examples among which are the following:

Serrenissimus [the name conventionally given to Royalty under the German Empire] was making a tour through his provinces and noticed a man in the crowd who bore a striking resemblance to his own exalted person. He beckoned him and asked 'Was your mother at one time in the service of the Palace?' – 'No, Your Highness', was the reply, 'but my father was.'[42]

The question formally admits the reply, the man naming the correct relative instead of the one wrongly suggested by Serrenissimus, but the substitution of father for mother turns the implicit insult back upon his exalted person, making both a joke against authority and a sexual joke (it also contains some of the elements of the 'Family Romance' scenario in the mutual imputation of bastardy[43]). Another example Freud gives is the quip spoken by Herr N of a public personage, 'he has has a great future behind him', whereby the substitution of one word, behind, for before, presents an amusing 'mistake' since futures cannot lie behind us, while also succinctly summing up the man's career, for he once had a great future in store, but no longer has.[44] Another Herr N joke is a simile, making a – slightly inaccurate – appeal to (Roman) history with reference to a man who had been Minister of Agriculture with the sole qualification of having been a farmer and who proved to be the least gifted minister there had ever been. On resigning and returning to farming, Herr N remarked that it was said that: 'Like Cincinnatus, he has gone back to his place before the plough.'[45] (In this case *before* substitutes for behind, and thus likens the former minister to an ox!)

Fore-pleasure, then, is that small pleasure of word-play, substitution or whatever in the joke, which enables another, greater pleasure. It lifts inhibitions – aggressive or erotic – which are on the one hand social and on the other hand unconscious. In a film the audience is opened to the 'greater pleasure' of the fantasy by a fore-pleasure produced through the aesthetic or formal presentation rather than by an *a priori* identification with the fantasy as such. The 'realism' in representation can now be seen both as a *defence* against fantasy and also as a 'hook', involving the spectator in the fantasy structure 'unawares', and thus functioning as fore-pleasure. The aesthetic is then another level on which conventions of representation are brought to bear, but in this case it does not function in the service of censorship, through disguising fantasy, but enables censorship to be *undermined*.

Conventions are thus a means by which the structuring of desire is represented in public forms, in as much as, following the arguments of Laplanche and Pontalis earlier, fantasy is the mise en scène of desire. What is necessary in public forms of fantasy for their successful collective consumption is not universal objects of desire, but a setting of desiring in which we can find our place(s). And these places will devolve, as in the original fantasies, on positions of desire: active or passive, feminine or masculine, mother or son, father or daughter. Two films will be considered in some detail in order to explore the spectator's relationship to the scenarios of desire presented.

NOW, VOYAGER

The production of films centering on romantic stories or addressing family relations and their problems – the 'woman's film'[46] – was a staple element in studios' year plans in Hollywood in the 1930s and 40s and *Now, Voyager* is an exemplary 'quality' production within that genre and even those reviewers who dismissed the film nevertheless admired the acting of Bette Davis, Paul Henreid and Gladys Cooper.[47] These films were characterised not only in the way they centred on women but also by the foregrounding of the wishfulfilment scenarios thereby presented, the 'worst' examples being described by Molly Haskell as filling 'a masturbatory need, it is soft-core emotional porn for the frustrated housewife'.[48] The following discussion, however, will be concerned to explore precisely the working of such fantasy in *Now, Voyager* and *The Reckless Moment*.

In *Now, Voyager* the traveller of the title is Charlotte Vale (Bette Davis), the not-so-young spinster daughter of a wealthy Boston family. A 'late' child whose justification for being born, so her domineering widowed mother (Gladys Cooper) says, was to be a comfort in her old age. Charlotte's sister-in-law Lisa, worried about her mental health, brings an eminent psychiatrist and therapist, Dr Jacquith (Claude Rains), to persuade her to have treatment at his sanatorium and, despite her mother's condemnation ('No Vale ever had a nervous breakdown before'), Charlotte agrees. Two lines of poetry from Walt Whitman are later used by Dr Jacquith to herald her 'cure', 'Untold want by life and land near granted/ Now, voyager sail thou forth to seek and find'. Charlotte's recovery is rewarded by an ocean cruise arranged by Lisa, including a new wardrobe (she has lost weight), lent by the glamorous Renée Beauchamp. The cruise presents definitively the ugly duckling-become-beautiful-princess, the caterpillar-turned-butterfly. Turning the tables on her mother, Charlotte transgresses every prohibition Mrs Vale had imposed during their previous cruise together, from acting like a common tourist, to consummating a love affair with fellow-passenger Jerry Durrance (Paul Henreid). A new impediment now separates Charlotte and Jerry, for he is married. They part in Rio de Janiero after three days together, she to rejoin the cruise, he to begin his architectural commission.

On her return she is met by Lisa and niece June, both of whom can barely conceal their amazement at her transformation.

Charlotte is surrounded by male admirers and greeted by friends who compliment her as the most popular passenger on the cruise. Her niece, having cruelly taunted her old-maid aunt before, now gets her come-uppance when she asks Charlotte who her boyfriend is and receives the reply 'Which one?' Arriving back home, Charlotte confronts her mother with her transformation. Meeting disapproval, she is about to submit despite Dr Jacquith's advice, until she receives a present of a single camelia – a gift from Jerry whose special name for her was Camile. This determines her to remain 'true to herself' and she gives away the old drab dress her mother has had altered for her and instead puts on a newly-purchased stylish, gown for the family dinner. Mrs Vale, rebuffed again after demanding that Charlotte return to her role as dutiful daughter, falls on the stairs, twisting her ankle. Her mother now confined to her bed, Charlotte takes charge at dinner with huge success, symbolically marking the change in the household by lighting the drawingroom fire, until now left unlit on her mother's instructions because of the smoke. Her transformation is admired not only her by her relatives but also by another guest, Elliot Livingstone – recently widowed – and who asks why they had never met before. (At a later meeting Charlotte reveals to him they had – they were partners at dancing classes and later he stood her up on her graduation!) Charlotte's 'rise' is matched by her mother's 'decline' into physical illness and invalidism. Then Elliot proposes marriage to Charlotte, delighting her mother at the prospect of thus joining two of Boston's oldest families, but after accidentally meeting Jerry again she realises that Elliot and she could not be happy together. Ending the engagement provokes a row with her mother which brings on a fatal heart attack. Feeling responsible, Charlotte relapses and goes back to the sanatorium, only to find there Jerry's daughter, Tina, also the victim of an uncaring mother. Taking up the goal of curing Tina, Charlotte confesses to Dr Jacquith the reason for her interest. He agrees to her idea of taking Tina home with her only on condition that she forswears any relationship with the father, Jerry. The film's closing scenes are of the Vale house transformed by the happy laughter at a party for Tina who has blossomed into a delightful and pretty young girl under the care of the lovely and kindly Charlotte. Jerry, visiting for the first time, refuses to let her sacrifice her life, saying that he's ashamed at taking so much from her, but she stops him and says that he will be giving her everything in giving her Tina, that they can be together in the child, and therefore: 'Don't let's ask for the moon when we can have the stars', she says.

Even from this summary it is clear that a series of wishes, both erotic and ambitious, are presented in the film. First, that of being recognised – as somebody, as worthwhile. This role is initially fulfilled by Dr Jacquith; he is a fellow transgressor of Vale prohibitions on smoking, and he takes Charlotte's part against her mother both in recognising her illness and and rescuing her from the house. Then there is the triumph of the cruise, with Charlotte's social and erotic successes, and the subsequent achievement of independence from her mother, aided not only by Dr Jacquith's words (Charlotte's voice-over repeats them) but more importantly through the love of a man, Jerry, signified by the flower he sends. Elliot Livingstone, however, represents a different fantasy, of achieving the love of a man who had previously rejected her, only to be then able to refuse him in turn. Within this there is also the fantasy of remaining true to the 'absolute' love, the grand passion which, in being unattainable, is also unsullied by the banality of marriage, housekeeping, and so on. The film ends with an apparently unfulfilled wish, however, for Jerry and Charlotte cannot marry, and their love must remain unacknowledged in the world. The fantasy scenario is thus the desire for a secret love, passionate and fulfilling as 'reality' can never be, and this mise en scène is not closed off at the film's end, but remains in place. In contrast marriage with Elliot had been impossible because it could not be passionate (shown by Elliot's discomfiture when Charlotte displays her disorderly desire in wishing to go to a 'bohemian' restaurant).

Under the guise of these banal wishes, however, a far more 'serious', seemingly perverse fantasy arises as the film progresses.[49] Charlotte not only frees herself from her mother; she also displaces her mother, becoming as powerful but charming and kindly where her own mother had been cruel and domineering. Charlotte becomes the pretty, loving mother her own and Tina's had never been, while the wish to have a child (to be a mother) is fulfilled. On the one hand the film must displace Jerry in order to bring together mother and child; on the other hand this is narratively motivated by Charlotte's claim that through his daughter, cared for by herself, she and Jerry can be together, for in Tina she will have a part of him! The perversity of this claim is barely concealed. Sexuality is renounced, and Charlotte has

Jerry's child without having sex with him. At the same time motherhood is sexualised by this association, the child standing in for Charlotte and Jerry's passionate love as both a sign and a replacement. This follows the narrative's eviction of Mrs Vale – it kills her off – so that the film presents a clear Oedipal trajectory for Charlotte, but with a further twist. For instead of transferring her desire from her mother – the child's first love object – on to her father, and hence on to his substitutes by whom she can have a baby/phallus, Charlotte obtains the child but evicts the father (she promised Dr Jacquith to give up Jerry) and sets herself up as the 'good' mother against Mrs Vale's 'bad' mother. Here, no man is the agent of the Father, no man successfully intervenes into the trajectory of Charlotte's desire; on the contrary, the narration marshalls Dr Jacquith, as well as Jerry, *for* it.

Charlotte does not, however, tell her own story of desire: rather, as Lea Jacobs has shown, it is constructed through an 'objective', descriptive camera view and 'spoken' by men.[50] Her wish to defy her mother is first realised through Leslie, Charlotte's first shipboard romance, who, she recounts to Dr Jacquith, defied her mother and declared his love for her so that he had, she says, 'placed me on a throne. And before a witness.'[51] Dr Jacquith then succeeds – where Leslie failed – in rescuing Charlotte from her mother, and Jacquith's words continue to echo in her mind as guidance and support for her later. And, when Jerry writes to his daughter Tina about his 'new friend Charlotte' after their first meeting, he says that he has learned from her that 'Even after a person grows up she can be alone.' Here, as Lea Jacobs notes, 'Her narrative, as well as her desire, is claimed *for* Charlotte through this man's eyes.'[52] But at the same time Jerry's discourse here – as that of the other men – is articulated by the narration for Charlotte's fantasy. For example the aligning, indeed *identifying of* Charlotte and Tina as mirror images by Jerry is repeated near the end of the film – but no longer spoken by Jerry – in the scene where Tina, pretty as a picture in her first party-dress, is seen at the top of the staircase beside Charlotte before running down to be greeted by her father at the foot of the stairs (a mise en scène which echoes the earlier staircase shots of Charlotte); as Jerry hugs Tina he looks up towards Charlotte and we see him say 'I love you'. What is enunciated here is not part of Jerry's story – for example Jerry is not shown loving Charlotte as his daughter; the stake of this identification of Tina and Charlotte is in relation to Charlotte and the spectator who is positioned in relation to the fantasy structure enunciated for Charlotte/Tina.

The male discourses within the film are produced for this fantasy structure but these men are ultimately displaced or rather superseded by Charlotte.[53] In a sense Dr Jacquith and Jerry are both substitutes for the phallic mother, the mother of unconditional love, and they are finally unnecessary once the conditions are set for Charlotte herself to be the phallic mother. (Charlotte is 'phallic' for the narrative in being bound to and signified within pre-Oedipal relations, rather than because of any male, 'phallic' imaging of her.) The topsy-turvy way in which the film's apparent discursive construction is subverted or reversed is exemplified in Charlotte's appeal to Jerry that they forgo the moon for the stars, implying that they should accept the lesser or more reachable goal of the stars than reach for the moon, yet of course the stars appear lesser than the moon only because they are further away. When Charlotte forgoes the moon for the star, however, she fulfils every child's wish for its mother to forgo the father.

There is of course another reason for this outcome in *Now, Voyager*. Hollywood censorship will not allow Jerry to divorce his wife and marry Charlotte, nor may he and Charlotte continue an adulterous affair, but this could easily be resolved by the ailing wife conveniently dying (a narrative motivation already made possible in the characterising of Jerry's wife as an invalid, while the narrative has already similarly evicted Charlotte's mother). That this device is not adopted turns the narrative back on to the excluding of the father in favour of the mother/child relationship now represented as admirable and all-fulfilling. As a result, while the film refuses to allow its couple the future together we all wish for them, rather than leaving us empty-handed this 'lack' is repaired by a replacement: instead of the couple Charlotte/Jerry, we have Charlotte/Tina, in a beautiful narrative move which replays the fetishistic structure of disavowal and substitution. No, indeed, why ask for the moon when you want the stars! Here, in a gesture of narrative economy, the film affirms a romance of true love, unfulfilled but undying, and an image of feminine sacrifice of this love for a greater good, the child. Lea Jacobs says of this:

> In a gloriously perverse gesture the narrative does not bring Charlotte's desire to fruition and an even more perverse sub-text would lead one to suspect that she likes it that way.[54]

The narrative economy operates between the overt level of story – a kind of conscious level – and the level of narration whereby the constraint of censorship – the Hays Office in Hollywood, well-known to audiences – enables a different structure of wish to arise in the eviction of the paternal from the game, leaving the dyadic couple of mother and child. The convention of social morality, of censorship, thus operates as a kind of fore-pleasure device, for it motivates the setting up of a structure of substitution – not the heterosexual couple, but instead this *other* couple which is the inverse of the first and thus opens us to this perverse wish.

Such a reading implies a desire played across the film to have and to be the powerful and good mother, and if this is the case (and my reading is not too far-fetched), it can be seen that this desire has pleasures for the masculine as well as feminine spectator, at least in the position of the child who has the mother, since the film figures the eviction of the father and the reinstatement of the now 'good' phallic mother. Of course if this is the woman's desire, it is not conventionally 'feminine' insofar as it is a desire for the mother.[55] By suggesting this I am also assuming that the place of the spectator is not one of simple identification with Charlotte Vale. Nor is my suggested reading an attempt to psychoanalyse her character. Rather it is an attempt to grasp how the film makes a series of narrative moves between its fantasy scenarios (which themselves are not only successive, but also imbricated). Apparently fulfilling banal wishes, the fantasy of *Now, Voyager* thereby sets the terms for another ('unconscious') scenario of desire, clearly Oedipal, but where the subject positions are not fixed or completed. Charlotte is both mother and daughter, Mrs Vale and Tina. This is not Charlotte's fantasy, but the film-text's fantasy. It is an effect its narration (of its *énonciation*). If we identify simply with Charlotte's desires, namely the series of social and erotic successes, then the final object, the child Tina, will be unsatisfactory. But if our identification is with the playing out of desiring in relation to the opposition (phallic)mother/child, the ending is very much more satisfying. A series of 'day-dream' fantasises unfold an Oedipal, original fantasy. The subject of this fantasy is then the spectator; in as much as we have been captured by the film's narration, its *énonciation*, we are the only place in which all the terms of the fantasy come to rest.

The scenario, the mise en scène of desire, thus emerges for us not just in the story, but rather in its narrating: that series of images bound into the narrative structures, the devices, delays, co-incidences etc. that make up the narration of the story. The plea-sure then not in *what* wishes Charlotte obtains but *how* – a how which refers to the positioning, ultimately of the spectator – rather than Charlotte – in relation to a desire which is an oscillation between mother and child. The conscious fantasies are these 'banal' wishes through which much more archaic unconscious wishes are realised, that is, are *figured*. However, in order to bring about such a position the narration must 'bribe' us, as Freud puts it, to admit the *repressed* wish. The series of banal fantasies embed another scenario: the eviction of the father and the usurpation of the mother, a scenario which forepleasure opens us to. This is partly achieved through the preliminary of the more 'normal' erotic and ambitious wishes, but whose banality often provokes re-jection by 'sophisticated' audiences (as shown in some of the con-temporary reviews). But the film also produces a fore-pleasure through its aesthetic devices which open us to, hooks us into, the play of desire. Freud pointed to the role of puns and word substi-tutions in the joke in producing fore-pleasure, and *Now, Voyager* presents similar devices – the parallelism, for example, produced by the shots of Charlotte's shoes, first seen as she descends to join her mother and Dr Jacquith at the beginning of the film: the close-up of her feet operates metonymically as a synecdoche for Charlotte and connotes her as an 'old maid' – the shoes are sturdy brogues, her legs fat, her stockings are thick lisle. The same order of image is presented later, at Charlotte's first appearance on the cruise: other passengers are awaiting her (so that they can all go ashore), speculating about the mysterious Renée Beauchamp (for the ticket was booked in that name), and the cinema audience waits too, for we last saw Charlotte in her usual unflattering clothes, when Dr Jacquith removed her ugly spectacles and spoke about 'signposts'. This second shot reiterates, puns, the first but with a difference: Charlotte's ankles and feet are again the object of view but now slender, clad in sheer stockings and smart high-heeled shoes. The camera quickly pans up to her face (quickly, so that a salacious connotation is not produced), and a *beautiful* Charlotte is revealed. The same metonym, but different connota-tions. The shot ends with another 'bribe', for Charlotte's face is de-lightfully now hidden, now revealed by her huge-brimmed hat, evoking our wish to *see*. The hat continues to offer a hide-and-seek effect when she first meets Jerry and later as they lunch.

The device of a surrogate audience within the film is also used for the repeated signifying of Charlotte's social success on the cruise when Lisa and June meet her at the dockside. There is a further bonus of fore-pleasure here in its *excess*: not one but several fellow-passengers come up to say goodbye, and not one boyfriend but several. There is also the humour of the come-uppance delivered to June and the pleasure of the reversal in Charlotte's gentle teasing when she comments that June is becoming a 'roly-poly'.

The trite staging of Jerry and Charlotte's enforced night together 'bundling' as a result of the car accident during a shore trip in Rio de Janeiro is presented as a comic incident in the device of the incompetent and incomprehending Brazilian driver who misunderstands their instructions and eventually crashes the taxi. Coincidence and chance are central elements of cinematic forepleasure in melodrama. In this example, the accident results in Charlotte missing the ship, and hence remaining with Jerry for three days before flying on to rejoin the cruise. Later, on the train to the sanatorium, Charlotte wishes she could hear Jerry's voice just once more. Chance fortuitously intervenes for when she arrives she finds Tina and, taking her to town for an ice-cream, she obtains her own wish when, helping Tina telephone her father, she dials his number and hears him answer.

Finally, there is the example of cigarettes, which works through a series of transformations. First of all smoking links Dr Jacquith and Charlotte as something they have in common, and as a common transgression in the Vale house (when he first entered he had knocked his pipe against a vase, the ash spilling on to the floor). Later, when Charlotte is showing Dr Jacquith her room he finds the cigarette ash in her wastepaper bin which she had earlier covered over, and this discovery leads to Charlotte's angry confession of another secret when she shows him her diary record of the cruise she and her mother had taken and the sexual repression imposed on her by her mother. Connected to transgression and then to sexuality by its metonymic association with the confession, cigarettes come to signify Charlotte's and Jerry's sexual desire: on the balcony of their hotel in Rio de Janiero, late at night, Jerry lights two cigarettes and Charlotte, taking one, affirms her love for him and, we may infer, spends the night with him – the sharing of cigarettes veiling and substituting for what Hollywood cannot show directly, leaving it open to audiences to understand as much or as little as they wish. This gesture is reiterated at their leave taking in Rio the

next day, and again at their meeting in Boston, and then in the final
sequence of the film; but this time when Jerry lights up the two cigarettes it now signifies his agreement to forswear his sexual desire
in order to enable their union through Tina. The gesture of smoking
thus accumulates a meaning of transgression and sexuality across
the film, which is reorganised at the end to claim an asexual commitment which can therefore be nothing of the kind.

Now, Voyager however keeps in play both meanings, both the
desire for Tina instead of Jerry, and the desire for Jerry. It is in
order that Charlotte may keep Jerry's daughter Tina that Charlotte
and Jerry agree to abide by Dr Jacquith's prohibition and to give up
their love in its carnal realisation. As a result at one and the same
time they affirm the love they deny in forswearing it. In addition
Jerry and Tina (rather than Charlotte and Tina) have been made
equivalent through this exchange, for while Charlotte will
have/love Tina instead of Jerry this very act will also symbolise the
love between Charlotte and Jerry. The film restates two meanings
which it presents as mutually exclusive – Charlotte really wants
Tina, not Jerry, or Charlotte only wants Tina because she is Jerry's.
The film forces the spectator to oscillate between these two possibilities – or to disavow one of them, for after all Jerry's wife is
ailing, so might not she soon die and enable Charlotte and Jerry to
truly realise their love?

THE RECKLESS MOMENT

This film presents some further aspects of the workings of fantasy
in film and illustrates most clearly Laplanche and Pontalis's thesis
that 'Fantasy is not the object of desire but its setting. In fantasy the
subject does not pursue the object or its sign: he appears caught up
himself in the sequence of images. He forms no representation of
the desired object but is himself represented as participating in the
scene.'[56] The subject of *The Reckless Moment* as fantasy is at one and
the same time Lucia, Donnelly (the film's principal characters) and
the spectator.

The Reckless Moment[57] is centred on an American family, white,
middle-class, and living in a seaside suburb of Los Angeles. It opens
with a man's voice-over (which does not recur in the film) describing the town and its inhabitants and speculating on how little it
might take to shatter the peace of a family. The scene cuts from

shots of boats to a boy fishing, he looks up and calls 'Mother, Mother, where are you going?' The mother is Lucia Harper and she is driving to Los Angeles to see Ted Darby, a man of dubious character, to persuade him to stop seeing her daughter Bea. She is unsuccessful. On returning home she is greeted in turn by her son David, the grandfather, and Sybil the maid, each of whom ask her where she has been, and we now learn that her husband Tom is away working in Europe. She goes upstairs to tell Bea of her meeting with Darby and to forbid her to see him again, saying that he had asked for money as payment for not seeing her anymore. Bea disbelieves her mother, and has indeed already arranged to meet with Darby that night in the adjacent boathouse. But Darby shows himself to be the no-good sponger that Lucia portrayed him as and Bea, horrified, rejects him. He struggles with her but she hits him with her torch and runs out. He stumbles after her, stunned by the blow, and clutching at the rail of the stairway which we see is broken, he falls to the beach below.

The hysterical Bea is met by Lucia who goes out to check if Darby is still in the boathouse. Finding no one, she returns to put Bea to bed. Very early next morning Lucia goes for a walk and discovers Darby's body speared by their boat anchor. She drags the body into their boat and ferries it to marshes some way away. Having covered up the killing, she is visited later that day by Donnelly who blackmails her over love-letters Bea had sent Darby and which came into his hands as collateral on a loan to Darby. Lucia tries to raise the $5,000 demanded by Donnelly but she cannot draw on her back account without her husband's signature and she adamantly refuses to contact him. Instead she raises some but not all of the money by pawning her jewellery. Meanwhile Donnelly has fallen in love with Lucia but he cannot withdraw the blackmail demand because of his partner Nagle. When she meets Donnelly again he tells her that her problems are over since Darby's killer has been arrested. Conscience-striken, Lucia tells Donnelly that the man couldn't have done it, and, taking the blame herself, confesses that she killed Darby. Donnelly, disbelieving, tells her that it doesn't matter and that she should let the man take the rap since he might have done it anyway. Later Donnelly finds out that the man had an alibi after all, and that Nagle has gone to see Lucia himself. Donnelly goes after Nagle, finds him in the boathouse with Lucia and after an argument strangles him in a struggle. Lucia finally believes in the now-wounded Donnelly and wants to clear him by going to the police and taking the blame. Donnelly, out of love for her, refuses to let her do so and drives off with Nagle's body, but crashes his car. Lucia has followed him but he demands she take the letters he has retrieved from Nagle and leave him to await the police alone or else his sacrifice will have been for nothing. She returns home. Crying on her bed, she is called down by the family to receive a phone call from her husband Tom while Bea tells her that Donnelly was found by the police and died after confessing to killing Darby and Nagle (see stills 8–10, plate 3).

A synopsis such as this, of the main elements of the action – the *fabula* we construct in retrospect – elides the narrative drive of the film which spurs it on and ensnares us as spectators, and which I will summarise as: extraordinary events intervene into an ordinary family's life as the result of transgressive sexuality on the part of the women of the family. Bea's transgression, her liaison with the no-good Ted Darby, puts Lucia 'out-of-place' – as marked by her son David's anxious calling as she drives off to Los Angeles at the beginning of the film. Lucia seeks to confront Darby and takes on the role of the absent father in seeking to be the keeper of her daughter's sexuality. But Darby flirts with her, commenting on how like Bea she is, how young she is to be Bea's mother and Lucia's endeavours to warn Darby off appear impotent.

Later, arguing with Bea, Lucia shifts between acting the stern father who nevertheless wants to talk things over reasonably, and playing the irrational mother who hysterically demands that Bea obey her without question in one breath as she instructs her to tidy her room in the next. And in addition mother and daughter are identified as she laments that 'I've been stupid and indulgent, your father wanted you to go to college and I took your side and persuaded him to let you go to art school... (shot changes from Lucia to Bea)... he was right, and I was wrong. You'd never have met Darby if we'd have listened to him.' And later she says '...I probably would have felt the same way at your age.' The moment of identification is interrupted by Tom's phone call giving her the news that he will be in Germany for Christmas – building bridges for the Marshall Plan – and he is not told of Bea's misdemeanours (see stills 1 and 2, plate 3).

That evening Lucia sits down to write to Tom but is interrupted by her son David. She hides his Christmas presents, then asks him why he isn't wearing slippers (this reference to his clothing is an invariable element in each encounter of mother and son until the end of the film when Lucia is most out of control, and David proudly informs her as he is about to go to a movie that he is properly dressed; it is an example of the economic way in which the film narrates Lucia as mother and housekeeper). Lucia begins to write that she wishes David were older, or Tom's father younger, or that Tom were there to deal with Darby himself. The signifying of the lack of the father here is intercut with shots of Bea leaving the house to meet Darby – the cause of Lucia's 'need' for the father. Lucia tears up her letter and writes another, anodyne, one; thus the father's absence is underscored at the same time as he is *excluded* by Lucia's keeping him in ignorance.

Lucia takes charge of Bea, hysterical after her meeting with Darby, and firmly reassuring her, she takes another torch to go out to check the boathouse in an action which precisely mimes that of Bea minutes earlier. Lucia is authoritative after her investigation – 'He's gone' (but which she will later find is not the case) – and motherly in putting Bea to bed (she makes Bea hot milk) and also identified with Bea through the repetition of their actions. The next day, by concealing Darby's body, Lucia assumes the responsibility for his death. This is her reckless moment. And the import of sexual transgression which originated with Bea is transferred to Lucia. Bea now ceases to be central to the narrative, which has always in any case been focussed on Lucia. Meeting Bea on the stairs, Lucia orders her to forget about Darby after first ascertaining that Bea had not told anyone of the relationship. Bea, unaware of his death, is mortified at the thought of him, but Lucia tells her 'Stop it Bea, I know how you feel but you musn't talk against him or about him to anyone. You musn't even mention his name. Do you understand?' Lucia asks if there was anything else. Bea after a pause replies 'No', and Lucia continues on upstairs as Bea goes to her breakfast. For Bea, but not for Lucia, it is over.

Later that day, at the post office mailing her letter to Tom, Lucia hears that Darby's body has been found. The scene economically narrates both events of the thriller narrative and the melodrama-detail of Lucia's role as 'Mrs Harper' (distractedly, she buys the family's Christmas tree). Arriving home, a man – Donnelly – has been waiting for her. Donnelly is initially presented as a threat, with a deep-focus shot of him in the darkened, shadow-filled room. Lucia at first attempts to deny the significance of the letters but, after her talk with Bea in the kitchen which confirms the damaging nature of the letters, she accepts the blackmail in order to protect

Bea from the possible sexual scandal and – we may infer – to avoid an investigation which might reveal Darby's visit to their house. But, given the identification I have suggested above, Lucia is equally guilty and thus she is also protecting herself, and this is the motivation for her adamant refusals to contact Tom.

At the same time the filmic narration figures the family and the home as a mise en scène of containment in the interconnecting tracking shots and framings which always place Lucia within her family, a visualisation of the narrative information that she is prevented by her family's demands from taking decisive and independent action against the external threat. Donnelly, however, is visually drawn into the family by the same means that Lucia is shown as entrapped: Lucia leaves Donnelly (introduced as a friend of Tom's) talking to the grandfather, framed together, and goes to talk to Bea; when she returns the camera follows her, revealing Donnelly in big close-up next to the grandfather as she joins them (see stills 2 and 3, plate 3). By this camera-movement Donnelly has been included in the family, a portent of later events. As he leaves, Donnelly also gives the grandfather a racing tip and the latter subsequently repeats his request for Lucia to 'invite that nice man' to dinner.

Seeing Donnelly off outside the house, Lucia tries to stall for time (a sign of her weak position), but refuses to contact Tom, and says that she cannot act precipitously for fear of worrying the family. These elements are replayed in their meeting the next day, adding the further element of Lucia as the site of morality when she berates Donnelly for his way of earning a living, comparing it to David's honest work (for a pittance) during his vacation. 'You'd never know about that' she says. He replies 'Do you never get away from your family?' 'No.' The external threat represented by Donnelly and Nagle's blackmail is split into good and bad as Donnelly falls in love with Lucia, but it will ultimately be shown that he does so precisely in terms of her role in the family, as mother and wife. The scene at the drug-store, for example, shows Donnelly in the part of the husband as Lucia rushes up to him for change for the telephone (she's arranging a visit for Bea). The camera remains with a pensive Donnelly as he turns to buy a cigarette filter for Lucia, whose heavy smoking he has already disapprovingly remarked upon (see stills 5 and 6, plate 33). Driving back, she again refuses to contact Tom and the theme of Lucia's entrapment by her family is repeated, while the *new* position of

Donnelly is represented when he tries to assure her that but for his partner he'd not pursue the blackmail, but he has his Nagle just as she has her family. Lucia angrily denies the comparison, and refuses to believe he has a partner. Donnelly comments that Bea is lucky to have a mother like Lucia, but she retorts 'Everyone has a mother like me. You probably had one.'

In this abbreviated gloss of the film I am forced to emphasis dialogue over the staging of the scenes. But staging, camera movement, the image track as a whole, etc. are crucial to the film's narration and to producing fore-pleasure. For example Donnelly, having promised her more time, phones Lucia later that day to tell her Nagle won't agree. We see Lucia take the phone from the grandfather who has answered the call, and then the film cuts to Donnelly in a phone booth saying he understands that she can't talk because her family are there. There is no cut back to Lucia, so that we hear only Donnelly's words to her, repeating his wish to her earlier that she believe him, *in* him: 'I wish things could have been different in many ways. Only one good thing came of it. I met you' – as the camera cuts in to a close-up of Donnelly's face. Donnelly leaves to joins Nagle at a bar, thus Donnelly's good faith is proven to the spectator before it is to Lucia. (Here, as in suspense, the audience is given greater knowledge than a character; however, this knowledge is not of a potential threat, but of a desire; nevertheless it equally implicates the spectator.)

Lucia's meeting with Donnelly at the bus station to give him the little money she has raised presents her repositioning in relation to Donnelly, as he tells her that Darby's killer has been arrested. The scene is orchestrated by alternating tracking shots and reverse-field close-ups as they go to get a coffee, then sit down as Lucia 'confesses', and finally when Lucia leaves to catch her bus. The scene implicitly narrates Lucia's acceptance of Donnelly in the role of 'protector', of surrogate father, as Lucia had been to Bea. He takes charge morally and practically, telling Lucia in words which echo her own to Bea earlier 'Forget about him [the arrested man]. What's the use of sacrificing your family for a man that's no good, that deserves what's coming to him?... It's the right thing to do Lucy. The right thing. Just you forget this.... I'll have it out with Nagle. I'll have the letters back and bring them to the house.' Lucia accepts his help but denies him as part of her world when she replies 'No, please. No please mail them. I'm sorry but...' Donnelly has filled the place of the absent father but the place of the absent husband remains empty. Her denial is a delay, and sets up the audience to expect its retraction, desiring Lucia to recognise Donnelly as worthwhile, as we have done!

This is brought about in the scene following the killing of Nagle (the boathouse is the repeated site of death). To Donnelly's implicit declaration of love 'I never did a decent thing in my life, never wanted to until you came along', Lucia responds with a corresponding offer of sacrifice 'I can't let you take this on yourself and be hounded for murder the rest of your life. I got you into this. It was my way of doing something that made everything wrong.' Lucia is positioned as lover and mother to Donnelly after the car crash (see stills 7 and 8, plate 3) when, cradling his head and speaking through her tears, she tries to tend his wound (she makes no verbal declaration, however). Donnelly, after earlier speaking of his mother's unconditional love for him – 'she would never learn that I was the bad one' – has finally done something she could be proud of. In dying, he has the mother.

SUBSTITUTION, EXCHANGE AND EQUIVALENCE IN FANTASY

A number of fantasy themes are present here, including the fantasy of nullifying an external threat by sexual seduction, along with the fantasy of an illicit love affair, as well as the wish to finally be or to do what one's mother had desired, and with this, the corollary of the wish for one's child to finally act as one wishes! Embedded in this wish – the term is appropriate – is also the desire for the mother as lover. But more importantly for the discussion here is the way in which *The Reckless Moment* clearly presents a series of positions which are presented through pairings and equivalences the terms of which are successively taken up by Lucia and Donnelly, the two main protagonists. This is not as a manifest narrative content, but signified through the narrating. Thus

 – Bea is to Darby as Lucia comes to be to Donnelly (lovers)
 – Lucia is to Bea as Donnelly comes to be to Lucia (father).

Donnelly is the helpful father to David, showing him how to fix the car horn, and he is the helpful son to the grandfather with his racing tips. But Donnelly is not shown with Bea, this exception tending to confirm the system insofar as Bea and Lucia are identified as interchangeable. Thus

- Donnelly is to the family as Tom is to the family (father)
- Donnelly is to Lucia as Tom is to Lucia (husband/lover)
- Lucia is mother to Bea (and her family) as she comes to be to Donnelly.

The work of the film is to transform Donnelly from being 'bad' insofar as he substitutes for the no-good Darby in the first set of equivalences, into being 'good' as the father and husband/lover.[58] But the sliding of positions is unstoppable, and Donnelly's gestures of 'caring' for Lucia, his concern over her smoking, as well as the formal motivation of inverted parallelism, bring him too into the position of the mother.

A further structure of equivalences arises in the film in the paralleling of the opposition and pairing of Donnelly and Nagle with that of Lucia and her family, a parallel made explicit in Donnelly's comment 'We all have our Nagles' in which he compares his own relation to Nagle with Lucia's to her family, and he does so in terms of constraint, of something 'owed'. For some writers this appears to present a critique of the family and its constraints,[59] though of course it is this very element that Donnelly seeks to affirm in his final sacrifice whereby he secures for Lucia her family intact, unblemished. One term of the equivalence, Nagle, is evicted in order to ensure the other, Lucia and her family, thereby affirming the structure of equivalence and undoing any possibility of critique. But this is not the whole story.

We have seen that in *The Reckless Moment* the hermeneutic, the problem of Bea's letters to Darby and the resulting blackmail, is displaced by the other hermeneutic, of the story of Donnelly and Lucia. At the end, Lucia has the letters back, on behalf of her daughter, but is crying over a new lack – Donnelly, we may assume. Here are the 'storeys' of narrative Barthes has referred to, the vertical structuring which arises from the film's linear narration. The staging of desire emerges through the series of figures, the exchanges and equivalences set up, produced, by the narrative. Donnelly's death has only halted this exchange, it does not resolve it. The film concludes conventionally enough, for Lucia at the end is returned to the feminine position as wife and mother. The original lack which 'causes' the narrative, the absence of the father, appears to be made good, filled by the final phone call from Tom Harper. The 'rightful' father makes himself heard as the third term, putting an end to the imaginary play of dyadic relations, the pairings. But the mise en scène narrates something more, for the final shot of the film shows Lucia on the phone at the bottom of the stairs beyond the bannisters so that their wooden supports appear like prison bars. Moreover Tom is only heard by Lucia; the cinematic audience receive no direct aural or visual sign of the father. We simply hear Lucia's declaration to him of how much she loves him! The symbolic law is not asserted by the filmic narration; instead it is again present only through Lucia. The possibility of the imaginary play continuing thus remains.

What is restated here is the fantasy structure with which the film began – the wish for the eviction of the father. This of course has two sides, at least. One place for this wish, and the place from which Lucia's position as wife and mother is questioned, is that of the other man, of the son, of Donnelly. If there is a critique of the Lucia's entrapment by her family, it arises from this position and therefore cannot be easily hijacked by feminism. The other place of the wish for the father's eviction is that of Lucia/Bea, each of whom wishes to replace the father, Bea with Darby; while Lucia first of all seeks herself to replace the father, later Donnelly comes into position as the protective father and hence by association and extension (visually anticipated in the scene of taking change from Donnelly in the drugstore), as husband/lover. Lucia's predicament – her daughter's transgressive sexuality and its consequences in Darby's accidental death – constructs the wish for something outside the family, elsewhere – precisely realised by Donnelly as lover – while her very role as mother is affirmed, for it is also Lucia's role in the family and her attempts to protect her family which is the basis for Donnelly's love and sacrifice for Lucia. Thus the fantasy of seducing the mother away from the father/being seduced is achieved and preserved, while the reality principle is also satisfied, for Donnelly dies – that is, nothing *really* happens, and there are no messy further consequences – at the same time constituting the fantasy of self-sacrifice for the loved other.

All this seems quite conventional, if tragic, for the male hero, Donnelly. On the woman's side, however, on the side of femininity, things are different. For Ophuls suggests for the woman here – as in many of his films – a desire which is split, which has two objects, the one supplying what is perceived as missing in the other.

Donnelly replaces Lucia's husband as father and lover. It is a split-ting of feminine desire as profound as that ascribed to men by Lacan:

> If it is the case that the man manages to satisfy his demand for love in his relationship to the woman to the extent that the signifier of the phallus constitutes her precisely as giving in love what she does not have – conversely, his own desire for the phallus will throw up its signifier in the form of a persistent di-vergence towards 'another woman' who can signify this phallus under various guises, whether as a virgin or a prostitute.[60]

Lacan derives this point from Freud who, in an essay baldly titled 'On the Universal Tendency to Debasement in the Sphere of Love', also discerns a splitting of the love-object in men. This arises where the man, unable to resolve his Oedipal attachment to the mother, fails to be able to transfer both loving and sexual feelings to substi-tute figures and instead splits the two sets of feelings so that love is divided 'in the two directions personified in art as sacred and profane (or animal) love. Where they love they do not desire and where they desire they cannot love.'[61] And again the split is between a virgin, Madonna/mother and a prostitute. A split in the woman's attitude to love and sexuality is also noted by Freud in 'The Taboo of Virginity',[62] and again an Oedipal element is sug-gested, but for Freud the woman's hostile response to the man who first substitutes for her father – her husband who deflowers her – is the result of her infantile penis-envy, not the ambivalence of her re-pressed loving feelings. In which case we can see the same wish as the man's, now on the woman's behalf, namely to have as well as to be the phallus, and indeed Lacan confirms this 'For if one looks more closely, the same redoubling is to be found in the woman.'[63]

What this implies, for both the man and the woman, is a contin-ual circulation of exchange and substitution (the subject of Ophuls' *La Ronde*, 1950). In this way *The Reckless Moment* sustains the logic of its fantasy structure, which is a logic of paradox. Lucia has loved, loves, Donnelly *and* she willingly embraces her role in her family again, her place as her husband's wife. She eats her cake and has it, too. While for the man, Lucia both represents the mother he wishes to seduce away from the father, and she re-enacts the mother's be-trayal – suggesting here Freud's account in 'A Special Type of Choice of Object Made by Men' which describes a repeated pattern

in certain men who fall in love with a married or otherwise attached woman but who is unfaithful yet must also be rescued.[64]

The exchanges and re-positionings in *The Reckless Moment* are
not, however, simply the substitution of Tom by Donnelly, but
involve the diverse positions – father, mother, child, lover, wife,
husband – each of which are never finally contained by any one
character. And each position only has meaning by its relation to the
others, which is seen most clearly in the sliding of 'meaning' of the
role of 'mother'. Thus while there are multiple positions of
identification, these are not alternative choices. For each will imply
the other and their interrelationship is changing through the film as
new meanings are constructed. Father, mother, phallic mother, are
not roles but positions of desire defined as positions insofar as they
are related to other, different and opposing positions: the other to
whom I address my demand, the other by whom I am addressed,
the other who is my rival, the other whose judgement I submit to.
To take up any one position is to be also implicated, to identify
with the other places within the structure, for the multiple positions
of a fantasy scenario are an organised structure of places, each determined by and determining of the other in an array of binary or
triangular oppositions.

The plural positions of fantasy do not produce a pluralism;
whether the fantasy is our own or ready-made we are not able to
pick and choose at will. For the subject who fantasises, the scenario's positions are necessarily fixed by her or his own psychical
history. In the ready-made fantasy the positions are orchestrated
not by the spectating-subject's psyche, but by the narration. Firstly,
narration in the film, just like secondary elaboration of the dream,
organises the material, restoring a minimum of order and coherence to the raw material and imposing on this heterogeneous as-
sortment a façade, a scenario, which gives it relative coherence and
continuity. A holding down, a fixing, is performed in this production of coherence and continuity; the narrative seeks to *find* (that is,
produce) a proper place for the subject. Of course at the same time
the narration presents a fantasy-scenario whose very logic of existence as representation, as fantasy, is the overturning of fixity in a
play of subject-positions, multiple and mobile, but, and hence secondly, this is also an orchestration, a playing which is organised by
the narration. The pleasures of the fantasy arise in its particular
game-positions which are structural relations, of being for an other
and the other being for me. We may play beyond those centred by

the narration, but we will do so because of our own psychical investments, whether through transference or projection.[65]

THE SEXUAL DIFFERENCE OF FANTASY

Film has long been considered a domain of wishfulfilment and fantasy; what has been argued here, however, is that this is not a retreat to unreality, an avoidance of life's harsh truths, or an unfortunate hangover of childhood and typical of the foolish, the weak, and of women. Fantasy is as necessary an aspect of adulthood as of childhood. It not only involves the satisfaction of wishes that are unrealisable in reality, but also and perhaps more importantly, public forms of fantasy involve the representation of the impossibility of the wish but which, of course, also makes possible the very scene of the wish. Fantasy is first and foremost not a wish for X, but a scenario, a structure of positions and relationships for the subject, and the 'apparent' wishes may tell us little or nothing about this scenario and its relationships. But nor can we assume that the 'deeper' wishes covered over by the overt fantasy-structure are the 'truer' wishes, or are more important than the 'surface' wishes, for the stake of the fantasy-scenario is that all are possible and all are desired. Thus it is not that Charlotte really wants a child instead of Jerry, rather the wish is for the mother to choose the child over the father *and* to have the father *and* to be the now-loved, adorable good mother *and* to be the now-loved, adorable child. There is a core element, however, which drives the fantasy, for in order to have or to be the mother, Charlotte and Tina must disavow the role of the father in relation to the mother's desire.

While, as Barthes claimed, every story leads us back to Oedipus, the fantasies of *Now, Voyager* and *The Reckless Moment* do not provide the Oedipal resolutions which Freud wished upon us. But nor can we call these desires pre-Oedipal, for there is not simply another, full and complete scenario or story competing with the Oedipal. There is the wish – on all sides – in these two films to both have and to be the father, and to both have and to be the mother. And a certain phallicness is also involved in each. Addressing film as a fantasy structure has therefore introduced the issue of feminine as well as masculine fantasy and desire into discussions of representation in film, but the placings produced by the narration may not reproduce the fixed positions of gender or, to put it another way, of the man as masculine – the father – and of the woman as feminine – the mother. Fantasy fails therefore to produce the fixed and polarised positions – and identities – of men and women required for a feminist politics basing itself on a theory of patriarchy. Indeed, while the issue of feminine desire is introduced – in the films as well as the theoretical consideration here – the question now arises as to the nature of this 'femininity' and in what sense it is an attribute of women, and if it is, how far it is always and only an attribute of women.

The concept of fantasy also allows us to understand cinema as an institution of desire and as a scenario for identification which avoids the models of the cinematic apparatus arising in the work of Christian Metz or Jean-Louis Baudry so aptly dubbed 'the bachelor machines' by Constance Penley, insofar as they posit a centred and unitary subject of desire, a masculine subject.[66] The linear progression of narrative is disturbed and re-ordered by the drive of fantasy, disrupting the possibility of a coherent or unified enunciating position. A fantasy-scenario itself is not a simple progression to satisfaction, but a composite of positions of desire, so that we can no longer speak of *a* position of fantasy, and certainly not a *masculine* fantasy as simply dominant, as the 'organising' fantasy. Thus, to take Raymond Bellour's example, while in Hitchcock's *Marnie* (1964) we are indeed brought to occupy the position of Mark Rutland/Hitchcock as the 'enunciator' of the desire for Marnie, it is a desire for a 'perverse' woman who cannot desire him/Hitchcock. As Marnie acidly comments – focalising the spectator through her viewpoint – Mark's (Hitchcock's) obsession with her, a liar and a thief, itself needs psychoanalysis.[67] That Mark 'brings' Marnie to desire him is only possible if he also 'loses' his object of desire – Marnie-as-thief. And Hitchcock reorganises the enunciative structure which has privileged Mark in the scene where Marnie is raped when he shows Mark 'bearing down' on Marnie through a shot which is not her optical point-of-view, for it is the camera which is moving in on Mark. The film then cuts to a shot of the ship's porthole – a richly suggestive but also finally enigmatic image, not locatable as the view of either Marnie or Mark, and hence marked as 'Hitchcock's look'. It is excessive, hence disturbing further the 'logic' of male desire signified in the rape.[68] As a result it can be seen that there also arises a fourth look in fantasy, for while we are interchangeable with the figures in the scene, and with the onlooker to whom the scene is presented or who 'sees' it, so too our view upon the fantasy-scene also implies a place from which we are seen seeing, that discovers us in our desiring and thus poses it as forbidden, and shaming.

The concept of fantasy does not of itself provide the means to an alternative meta-psychology of cinema, it does not secure a plural and mobile subject for film in opposition to the fixed – and masculine – spectator-subject of Metz and Baudry. Fantasy, insofar as it is also the field of play of the death drive, defines the limits of the subject, not its infinite dispersal, and it is therefore as well a repetitive play of a certain fixing/unfixing. Fantasy is a form of representation, of thinking, which can be read as a symptom. It emerges at the same time as the drive, as desire, and it is this which forms and structures fantasy and hence the drive and its vicissitudes must be examined to open out further the questions of fantasy and sexual difference which this chapter has begun to raise. Within film theory, however, the drive has primarily been considered in terms of scopophilia and the gaze, and in relation to castration and the emergence of fetishism as a disavowal of castration by the man. It is therefore these debates which will be the concern of the following chapter.

5

The Partiality of the Drives and the Pleasures of the Look in Cinema's Voyeurism

INTRODUCTION

Far from showing how the spectator is in place for the cinema, psychoanalysis forces us to consider cinema, representation, as a *placing* of the spectator, implying both a fixing and an unfixing – in the present tense. The imaginary, with which cinema has so often been identified by film theorists, is not a full, fixed subjectivity; it comes into existence in the loss of any such full subjectivity, the regaining of which is in fact the central fantasied scenario of the imaginary. Within this process, the gaze is critical, for it is the gaze, the structure of specularity as such, which undermines the imaginary. The gaze for Lacan is a paradox: both instituting and undermining the unity and hence the possibility of subjectivity. It has a structural function for identification within the mirror phase but it is also, as in scopophilia, one of the component drives of sexuality and thereby part of the instition of desire in the subject.

It is this duality which has made the concept of scopophilia and the function of the look of such interest to film theorists, for where more than in cinema is the pleasure in looking provoked and played to? As a result these have been seen as crucial concepts to the understanding of the pleasure of cinema for the spectator. Two problems have thereby arisen, however. The first concerns exactly this 'obviousness' of cinema as visual pleasure. The second concerns the way in which a theoretical orthodoxy has arisen which declares that the cinematic look, at least in the classical film, is partriarchal and works only to satisfy the fetishistic and voyeuristic pleasure of the *masculine look*. Mary Ann Doane writes that:

166

In the structures of seeing which the cinema develops in order to position its spectator, to ensure its own readability, an image of woman is fixed and held – held for the pleasure and re-assurance of the male spectator.[1]

It was Laura Mulvey who first formulated this thesis on the cinematic look in relation to psychoanalytic theory in her highly influential article 'Visual Pleasure and Narrative Cinema'.[2] Of course, feminists had many times in the past taken issue with the way woman's image has been constructed, manipulated and packaged 'for men', especially in relation to pornography. Laura Mulvey's essay, however, was not simply a humanist critique of the objectification of women in images for men, for it brought together new work on ideology in the cinema and the theories of Freud and Lacan on the institution of sexed subjectivity in the human infant.

> Going far beyond highlighting a woman's to-be-looked-at-ness, cinema builds the way she is looked at into the spectacle itself. Playing on the tension between film as controlling the dimension of time (editing, narrative) and film as controlling the dimension of space (changes in distance, editing), cinematic codes create a gaze, a world and an object, thereby producing an illusion cut to the measure of desire.[3]

This desire is masculine, insofar as cinema is held to be voyeuristic or fetishistic, two alternative poles producing a continual play between affirming and disavowing the fact of castration, a fact which is 'found' on the body of the woman, and endlessly displayed to and investigated by the camera's gaze and, by extension, by the (masculine) spectator.

Psychoanalytic concepts and theories are used in order to describe the mechanism of the patriarchal organisation of visual pleasure in cinema and to show the dynamics of this pleasure: 'Psychoanalytic theory is thus appropriated here as a political weapon, demonstrating the way the unconscious of patriarchal society has structured film form.' This gives Mulvey her founding premiss in the article, the role of castration in human societies:

> the function of the woman in forming the patriarchal unconscious is two-fold, she first symbolises the castration threat by

her real absence of a penis and secondly thereby raises her child into the symbolic. Once this has been achieved, her meaning in the process is at an end. It does not last into the world of law and language except as a memory, which oscillates between memory of maternal plenitude and memory of lack ... Woman's desire is subjugated to her image as bearer of the bleeding wound; she can exist only in relation to castration and cannot transcend it.[4]

This premiss is aligned with the sociological observation that woman's image has been used by men for male pleasure, and that the dominant representations in our culture serve this purpose: 'In a world ordered by sexual imbalance, pleasure in looking has been split between active/male and passive/female.'[5] The ways in which social and political structures of sexual inequality have given rise to a psychical split of visual pleasure between men and women is not explored further, leaving open the question of the relation of the social to the psychical structures psychoanalysis describes. Mulvey's argument centres instead on understanding visual pleasure in cinema through Freud's concept of scopophilia, or the pleasure in looking, which he defined as one of the component drives, that is, one of the elements of the sexual drive or instinct, which is experienced as a wish to *see*. Mulvey argues that cinema exploits and engages this pleasure in looking. Further she outlines the way in which this pleasure is important for a quite separate psychical development, namely the emergence of the ego in the process of identification inaugurated in what Lacan has called the mirror phase. In this moment the subject emerges *as* a human subject, but also as split between the subject who identifies and the image identified with, giving rise to the ego and the idealised ego, the latter having two elements – the ideal ego narcissistically invested as without flaw, as, in a sense, before sin, as what the subject once was; and the ego-ideal, an image of what the subject would like to be like. As a result the spectator identifies with the image seen as an ideal ego or ego-ideal.

In these two ways Mulvey outlines the lure and pleasure of cinema; however, neither scopophilia nor identification are specifically or only masculine, though the relation of both of these to femininity remain the subject of theoretical debate. Dominant ideology, however, Mulvey argues, requires that it is the male hero of the film who is the active controller of the film's fantasy, and who has the look. Active scopophilia and its investigative, sadistic, enquiring look, are aligned with the male hero of the film as the active protagonist and the spectator projects his look on to this screen surrogate and identifies with the power of this figure as he controls events. As a result:

> The determining male gaze projects its phantasy onto the female figure which is styled accordingly. In their traditional exhibitionist role women are simultaneously looked at and displayed, with their appearance coded for strong visual and erotic impact so that they can be said to connote *to-be-looked-at-ness*.[6]

In the cinema the drive to mastery underlying the scopophilic drive, and which always implies a distancing of subject and object in which the object is controlled by a look, becomes a male drive, involving male control of the woman's image for and as a function of male desire – 'styled accordingly': Woman displayed as sexual object is the *leitmotif* of erotic spectacle: from pin-ups to strip-tease, from Ziegfeld to Busby Berkeley, she holds the look, plays to and signifies male desire.[7]

What is introduced here is the issue of a content – woman as erotic object – and an exploitation: 'Woman, whose image has continually been stolen and used for this end.'[8] Mulvey argues that this woman-as-spectacle is inadequate and insufficient to real women and our representation, but that this distorted and partial representation is taken to be the true one. While the rhetoric of images as possessed and stolen is powerful it is also misleading, for it implies that our images are things, fixed and stealable. Both the complex structures of identification for the woman through which she encounters and acquires her images, and the nature of representation itself, suggest a different story however. There is no image which can be adequate to 'real' women for there is no simple and singular subject-position for women, and any image must institute, and be part of, a discursive construction of woman. Moreover the lure of images is that they both are and are not the original, and a gap is always introduced between the representation and the represented, a gap in which desire arises. As a result the pleasure of the look in cinema is not only the desire for erotic spectacle, though no doubt it will include the erotic, and it also requires something of the woman (as Raymond Bellour has argued[9]).

Scopophilia should not be so quickly hijacked to a politics of representation. Visual pleasure is not a straightforward affair. It always implies specularising the object, whether another human being, an inanimate object, or a part of another human being, or even part of oneself. And this is as true of women as of men. As a result it does imply an active mastery involving a distancing of subject and object in which the object is controlled by a look, but only so far, for the subject is also always looked at and as a result the 'omnipotent gaze' is unstable, difficult to sustain. Nor can visual pleasure in the woman or her image as the gaze's object be taken for granted, for such a presumption of a simple stimulus-response blinds us to the complex signifying process set in play by what is termed 'sexual imagery' as well as the fantasy-scenario involved. Sexual arousal is not merely a bodily affair but first and foremost a psychical relation so that it is not a matter of nature but of signification. What arouses is already a highly coded entity. However, this signifying process is not a set of contents – of socially learned conventions of sexuality – rather it is what psychoanalysis has termed fantasy. The assumption of the image which arouses, as if a simple content of anatomy stimulates desire, effaces the complex system of signification involved, and the complex fantasy implied.[10]

The woman and her image, lacking a penis, is also the term of sexual difference which secures the male identity as possessing the penis, but she is at the same time a sign of castration, so that her image may also be a threat. Visual pleasure is thus subject to the vicissitudes of constructing sexual difference, and this is equally at stake in narrative representation. Mulvey addressed this in the second half of her essay, arguing that the problem of castration constituted by the woman's penis-less body requires a modification in male visual pleasure, giving rise to either fetishism or voyeurism, either a disavowal of castration, or a re-enactment and investigation of the woman's 'castration': on the one hand the fetishistic display of Dietrich in Sternberg's *Morocco* and on the other hand the hero's sadistic investigation of the woman in Hitchcock's *Vertigo* (1958). The woman is passive victim to all this, for once she has functioned as the representation of castration for the male child, her meaning is 'at an end'. Fetishism and voyeurism appear here as alternative and incompatible strategies, since the voyeur is seeking to see again the woman's castration, while the fetishist is piling up an elaborate display which disavows that very knowledge. The look is male now not because it is active but rather and much more because it is implicated in the subject's relation to castration. But for the woman – psychoanalysis told us – that relation is very simple and unproblematic – since she lacks a penis, she is already castrated, and there can be no loss to fear, nor can it be disavowed without falling into psychosis. Thus her relation to castration is established and completed very early on and indeed this inaugurates her entry into the Oedipal complex, and the only consequence or symptom which arises is her relation to her child as the penis she never had or was given, and which is usually taken, or mistaken, for natural mother-love. In contrast, for the man castration is a continuing anxiety never fully accepted and resolved in the Oedipus complex, and it is this which gives rise to fetishism and voyeurism.

Mulvey's article was an important intervention into debates in 1975, and, bringing together as it does film theory, psychoanalysis and ideas from feminist debates, it was a vigorous theoretical challenge to the dominant forms of thinking about cinema which continued to ignore the imbalance in the representation of men and women in film. It achieved enormous political success because it offered at once a conceptual understanding of male exploitation of woman's image and a theoretical account of sexual division in cinematic representation. However, while stimulating a new body of work on film, by men as well as, crucially, by women, it also produced something of an impasse since no alternative route of visual pleasure seemed available to men, and no route at all to women (a route was proposed, however, in Mulvey's later discussion of *Duel in the Sun*[11]), while the essay itself argues against visual pleasure as such for the spectator. The essay is, as Mulvey herself has made clear, very much a polemic of its time, as, too, its dualistic or binary structure, but its legacy has been to circumscribe the terms in which subsequent work has been undertaken.[12]

The following discussion re-examines the imbrication of the look and masculinity in a reconsideration of the 'obviousness' of visual pleasure. Firstly, and putting aside the issue of the visual and cinema for the moment, the place of scopophilia as one of the partial or component drives or instincts is re-examined, while at the same time the notion of the drive itself is addressed in Freud's writings and, using the view of the drive presented in Jean Laplanche's study *Life and Death in Psychoanalysis*, a different account of passivity and activity is suggested. The consequences of this for the career of the drive in the woman are explored together with the concept of bisexuality, and women's scopophilia is reintroduced into the scene through Freud's own examples. The place of scopophilia in relation to castration is then examined and with this the emergence of voyeurism as perverse scopophilia and its relation to fetishism and to the mechanism of disavowal. Disavowal is shown to not only be a solution to the anxiety of castration, but to also institute the theory, or fantasy, of castration itself, and hence it appears to be determining of both voyeurism and fetishism. These are not, then, opposed solutions to a singular problem, and indeed, as has been widely noted, many films involve both in a way which cannot be explained through Mulvey's account. In emphasising disavowal, rather than simply fetishism, both fantasy and Lacan's concept of the *objet petit a* come into view as central elements in the play of the drives, including scopophilia. From this revised perspective the theories of masculinity and femininity which psychoanalysis gives us will be questioned, although in a way which is nevertheless from within psychoanalytic theory.

THE DRIVES

Scopophilia, the term Freud used to designate pleasure in looking, seems an obvious, commonsense concept, guaranteed as it is by the eye as physical organ and erotogenic zone.[13] It is described by Freud as one of the component drives or instincts of sexuality, together with the pleasure of touching, and epistemophilia or the pleasure in knowing. Epistemophilia, however, in contrast to scopophilia, though a pleasure also given its own term unlike the pleasure of touching, cannot be said to have a clear-cut physical organ constituting an erotogenic zone as source of pleasure. But scopophilia too is not characterised primarily by its erotogenic zone, rather it is a pleasure in looking at *something*. Freud writes that from the first, despite the dominance of erotogenic zones, infantile sexuality 'exhibits components which from the very first involve other people *as sexual objects*. Such are the instincts of scopophilia, exhibitionism and cruelty, which appear in a sense independently of erotogenic zones.'[14] Scopophilia is also involved with epistemophilia, being a means to satisfy curiosity through looking and hence produce mastery by 'seeing how things work'. These contrast with the other component drives, the oral, anal and genital, which are attached to erotogenic zones and which Freud relates to stages of development in the infant. The component drives are not, therefore, simply different manifestations of the drive, different but comparable parts of a single structure. Each has its own specificity, while nevertheless remaining an instance of the drive.

In order to consider the relation of scopophilia and voyeurism in cinema, and the way in which the latter term evicts the former in discussions of the look in film, the following discussion re-examines what, quite, Freud meant by the drives or instincts. This will introduce as well the issue of the division of: active/looking at, versus passive/being looked at, and its relation to sexual difference.

Freud's theory of the drives remains one of the most controversial aspects of psychoanalysis in as much as it theorises the relation of bodily phenomena and mental experiences which have never been and may never be, verifiable.[15] The theory of the drives in Freud is formed at the conjunction of two of his most fundamental premises, first, that mental functioning is not a biological imprint but emerges as a construct. Freud, however, also consistently strove to delineate the probable biological origin and nature of the affect which played a part in that construction, and he also always retained phylogenetic theories such as the notion of inherited primal fantasies. Second, at the same time and from the very beginning of his work, Freud assumed a binary structure and a conflictual model for the drives, initially as the sexual drives in opposition to the drive for self-preservation, later as the life versus death drive – Eros versus Thanatos.

It is in 'Instincts and Their Vicissitudes' that Freud presents the outline of his theory. His discussion there commences with an a priori assumption in his thesis of the principle of constancy:

> the nervous system is an apparatus which has the function of getting rid of the stimuli that reach it, or of reducing them to the lowest possible level; or which, if it were feasible, would maintain itself in an altogether unstimulated condition.[16]

External stimuli can be dealt with by the organism through a purely physical response, such as by fleeing, but this is ineffective for internal stimuli and as a result, Freud argues, the organism must find other ways to allay the stimulation in order to re-establish a state of constancy. Moreover, these internal stimuli 'maintain an incessant and unavoidable afflux of stimulation' which forces the nervous system to abandon its attempts to keep off all stimulation, and leads to the development of a drive to accommodate it by actions through which 'the external world is changed so as to afford satisfaction to the internal source of stimulation',[17] and this leads Freud to write of the organism 'mastering stimuli'. (Mastery had already been cited by Freud in *Three Essays on the Theory of Sexuality* as a drive.) What arises is a complex structure which is able to eliminate stimulation only indirectly. The drives are a result of this structure and are, therefore, constructed rather than biologically imprinted. As a result Freud conceives of the drives as a pressure to action, and hence in opposition to the general principle of the drive to constancy within the organism. From this arises Freud's second structuring principle, a polarisation which is conflictual.

The source of the drive is the somatic process which occurs in an organ or part of the body while the drive itself is the psychical representative of the stimuli originating in the organism; it is a pressure for activity and the aim of the drive is constant, namely a satisfaction which can only be obtained by removing the source of stimulation. The object of the drive is the thing in regard to which or through which the drive is able to achieve its aim but neither this nor the pathway of the drive are given in advance by its source. The object is not originally connected with the drive but becomes assigned to it only because it is peculiarly suited to enabling satisfaction. As a result the object is highly variable, it may be extraneous but it can also be part of the subject's own body, and it can be *changed* any number of times in the course of the vicissitudes which the drive undergoes. In other words we know nothing necessarily of the drive by knowing, or supposing we know, its object.

Further, Freud makes a sharp distinction between the drive and its psychical representative or delegate when he states that

> An instinct can never become an object of consciousness – only the idea [*Vorstellung*] that represents the instinct can. Even in the unconscious, moreover, an instinct cannot be represented otherwise than by an idea.[18]

Freud posits two distinct orders of the drive: 'the *ego*, or *self-preservative*, instincts and the *sexual* instincts'[19] and the component drives are seen as part of the sexual drive. However, this polarity is reorganised in *Beyond the Pleasure Principle*, where the concept of the death drive emerges from Freud's thesis of the principle of a return to constancy inherent in all organisms, and which itself was part of Freud's concern to see mental functioning as ultimately part of a biological, or even *mechanical* system. The concept is part of a recognition of the destructive tendency – for example in sado-masochism – as an irreducible datum. It is now placed as the fundamental principle of psychical functioning and as a result the tendency to destructiveness is seen as a normal and unavoidable reality of the human psyche rather than as an aberration. This binary structure of antagonism is not superimposed on the topography of id, ego, and super-ego in any simple way, although there is a tendency for Freud to posit the id as the agency of all demands of the drive, in opposition to the ego, but this will be the demands of both the life and death drives. However, the death drive does not have its own energy: its energy is libido, or sexual energy, which Freud now places with the life drive, and this implies that the death drive is a subsequent development, in contrast to Freud's assertion of the primacy of the death drive. It is the failure or impossibility of the drive to constancy which leads, Freud says, to the emergence of the drive as such. In this sense *both* the life and the death drive emerge at the same time, but whereas the aim of the life drive is 'to establish even greater unities and to preserve them thus – in short to bind together; the aim of the [death drive] is, on the contrary, to undo connections and so to destroy things'.[20]

These ambiguities and even contradictions in Freud's account of the death drive, despite the centrality he gave it, have led to it being widely ignored by psychoanalysts. Lacan reinstates this centrality but displaces the biologism of Freud's dualism, referring to it as 'a stumbling block for so many of us'.[21] Lacan uses the concept to emphasise the destructive or negative movement inaugurated at the same time as subjectivity. He describes this in two related ways. As discussed earlier in relation to identification, Lacan defines aggressivity as emerging in the same moment as subjectivity in the mirror stage, in the rivalry inaugurated by the splitting in which the subject comes into existence as such. Secondly, he takes up Freud's account of his grandson's game of *'fort-da'* and its structure of repetition, which was central to Freud's view of the death drive,[22] and shows how the subject, in coming into being for itself as a desiring subject, does so only in terms of the desire of an other, 'of an *alter ego* who dominates him and whose object of desire is henceforth his own affliction'.[23] This *'alter ego'* arises insofar as the game of *fort-*

da creates for the child the relations of subject and object, which are interchangeable and interdependent. The child comes to know its desire for its mother's presence *as* desire in the moment not of her absence, but in the making of her absence, symbolised in the reel being made to go, *fort* (gone) and return, *da* (there), and in so doing makes other to itself its desire in the very moment that it 'makes' its desire (which Lacan describes as also the moment of entry into language). Insofar as the subject thus experiences itself as a slave to its desire, its recourse can only be to withdraw from desire, and while this will ultimately involve biological death, it is a gesture whose aim is on the contrary an affirmation of life or 'being-ness' on the part of the subject. For it is in refusing the desire of the other that I most concretely experience myself as a self. Thus in death the slave defeats its master since by this death the master is unmade precisely as master of the slave. Aggressivity is not the result of the death drive, here, but part of the same structure. A human experiences a sense of existence only in the moment he or she can imagine, can 'realise' his or her own non-existence, so that in the assumption by the subject of its original splitting 'it might be said that at every moment he constitutes his world by his suicide' and which is 'the psychological experience of which Freud had the audacity to formulate, however paradoxical its expression in biological terms, as the "death instinct"'.[24]

Freud in his own writings on the drive does not offer a fully realised theory of the sexual drive, its essential nature or of its genesis in the infant. Moreover Freud's view of the relation of the sexual drive to other psychical structures underwent substantial transformations. Initially it was seen as a disruptive force which produced an unbinding in contrast to the self-preservative instincts or ego-instincts which defended the ego against sexuality. With the development of the theory of the death drive, sexuality was identified with Eros and seen as a principle of cohesion in opposition to the death drive. It is the riddle in Freud's writings concerning the emergence of the sexual drive and its relation to self-preservation which Jean Laplanche addressed in his book *Life and Death in Psychoanalysis*. Central to his project in that book, which also involves a reconsideration of the emergence of the ego and narcissism, is his recovery of the concept of *anaclisis*, or 'leaning on' (Freud's *Anlehnung*, previously translated as propping).

Freud had introduced this concept, though not the term, in his earliest discussion of the sexual drive in *Three Essays on the Theory of*

Sexuality in order to describe the way in which 'The satisfaction of the erotogenic zone is associated, in the first instance, with the satisfaction of the need for nourishment. To begin with, sexual activity attaches itself to functions serving the purpose of self-preservation and does not become independent of them until later.'[25] As noted in the discussion of identification, Freud used the term anaclitic to describe and distinguish a type of object choice (*Anlehnungstypus*), that is, an object which satisfies the function of self-preservation and which is based on the model of the mother, in contrast to the narcissistic form of object choice.[26] The use of the term disappears with the later topography of id, ego, and super-ego introduced in 1923 – although the concept of an anaclitic object choice is retained – and Freud assigns self-preservation to the agency of the ego, although this is clearly a later structure for the subject.[27] Laplanche argues that in fact two forms of self-preservation are in play here: a 'primary' self-preservation prior to the emergence of any psychical agency; a 'secondary' self-preservation, emerging with the ego, as 'self-love' (narcissism). This 'primary' – in the sense of being first, and not in the sense of being determining – self-preservation, namely the functioning of the 'vital order', is nonsexual but nevertheless involves *activities*, feeding, digestion, defaecation etc. It is from these excitations or functional pleasures that *organ* pleasure arises.[28]

Freud does not develop the concept of anaclisis in relation to the emergence of the drive, but it is this concept of 'leaning on' which Laplanche takes up precisely for its explanatory value in relation to the emergence of sexuality. The drive, he says, is always a sexual drive: 'it is sexuality which represents the model of every drive and probably constitutes the only drive in the strict sense of the term'.[29] This sexual drive leans on the 'vital order', the functions of the body in its sustaining of the living being's existence, as opposed to the sexual register, and Laplanche reserves Freud's term *Instinkt* for this function of the vital order. This does not, however, involve the body as such, that is, as a body-image, since the bodily functions are not yet organised into a body-image, nor can they be until the emergence of the ego in the mirror stage. Biological function *is* involved, but not as a topography, not as an organised space or image.[30]

The primacy of the self-preservative instinct as defined by Laplanche is not thereby determining. There is no linear progression from an originary point which remains both intact in its original mode, and implicit in every subsequent stage which it has given rise to. Thus 'Whilst self-preservation does have a role to play, it must be quite categorically stated that it is not a protagonist in psychical conflict.'[31] Once the sexual drive emerges, self-preservation as an instinct will be wholly displaced, and its role played instead by the sexual drive as represented in the narcissism or self-love of the ego.

This move and the emergence of the sexual drive as such derive from the moment when the self-preservative instinct *loses* its object and a *representation* arises in its place – the breast replaces milk in a metonymic displacement which is also at the same time a metaphoric condensation, for when the baby cries out of hunger it anticipates milk which will satiate its need, milk which is identified with the breast which thereby becomes the signifier of its desire to be satisfied. As soon as need becomes desire it is adrift from mere function, of feeding in order to live. The experience of satisfaction in feeding has been split off through the function of representation, and moves into the field of fantasy, of a wish not for the life-sustaining milk which the breast provides, but for the experience of satisfaction obtained, instituting at the same time a *drive* for satisfaction, which is thus sexuality.

The source of the drive is not the body as such except insofar as it is the 'source of a process which mimics, displaces, and denatures it'.[32] The somatic zones become erotogenic with the emergence of the drive as a satisfaction split off from simple self-preservation, and Laplanche emphasises here Freud's notion of sexual excitation as a concomitant effect, marginal or by the way, so that 'any function, any vital process, can "secrete" sexuality; any agitation may participate in it'.[33] He affirms here not only the polymorphous character of sexuality but also that the drive, sexuality, is not determined by its source in the body. Moreover Laplanche suggests, in an anticipation of his later development of a theory of seduction, that these erotogenic zones 'focalise parental fantasies and above all maternal fantasies' and that through these is 'introduced into the child that alien internal entity which is, properly speaking, the sexual excitation'.[34] Seduction produces a split in self-preservation; it 'peels away' a layer and this then constitutes the sexual drive. Once instituted in the subject, the source of this drive is no longer the vital order as such, but a psychical representative, a residue of primal repression, but this is 'anchored in the erotogenic zones as a result of the phenomenon of seduction'.[35] This does not, Laplanche emphasises, make the sexual drive originally biological, and it is only later – if at all – that it is joined to the biological function of reproduction.[36] For Laplanche, then, the internal excitations which Freud referred to are the primal and traumatic 'enigmatic' signifiers inserted into the child by its adult carers.[37]

Lacan distinguishes three modes of the drive corresponding to the three orders of the subject's relation to the other which he proposes – the real, the imaginary, and the symbolic. Need arises as a biological imperative in the real, signalled as a cry of hunger which once made and responded to becomes a call to the carer, a sign for and between the child and its carer, and thus it moves out of mere need into a demand put to the other, that is, a wish or want which we imagine can be satisfied, hence it is the mode of the drive in the imaginary. Finally there is desire, which emerges as a result of repression and in particular the repressions of the Oedipal complex and the internalisation of prohibition. It is a 'wish' which cannot be satisfied, and it correlates therefore with the symbolic, and it is unconscious.

The drives are not fixed or determined in any originary way. Once in play they are extremely vulnerable to being transformed. The concept of the drive, however, is a composite; it involves not only the force which is exerted on the mind, and perhaps body, in relation to a 'demand for work', but also an aim and an object for that 'pressure'. The aim of the drive 'is in every instance satisfaction'[38] but, as Lacan says, 'When you entrust someone with a mission, the *aim* is not what he brings back, but the itinerary he must take.' The aim is the trajectory or path of the drive. The object is not the goal of this trajectory, it is simply the thing through which the drive can reach its goal. It is the most variable element and, Freud says, it is not originally connected with the drive but arises as an object for the drive insofar as it appears 'peculiarly fitted to make satisfaction possible'. The object is, then, not fixed but may change in the course of the career of the drive, and the same object may 'serve the satisfaction of several instincts simultaneously'.[39] Lacan emphasises that the object is not the end point of the drive, for the drive's aim is a circuit, going out from the subject towards its object and it is only in returning to the subject that the drive reaches or achieves its 'goal', that is, its objective.

A number of points can now be established. First, the drive is always the sexual drive. A corollary of this is that the two forms of the drive which Freud subsequently posited, namely the life and death drives, both *'exist within the field of the sexual drive'*.[40] Second, it is not characterised by and in any one organ or several particular organs or even by the erotogenic zones as such – the oral, anal and genital drives are not determining of sexuality as a result of their bodily origin but as a result of the specific organisation of sexuality. While the drive can only be known or analysed through its emergence as a *partial drive*, these do not thereby together produce a unity or unification of the sexual drive; the partial drives simply name particular pathways for the organisation of the sexual drive and not a 'content' of the drive, or its objects. Moreover the oral, anal and genital drives are not simply stages of maturity but transformations in the subject's relations to its objects and its others. Third, scopophilia is no more guaranteed as a drive because it is posited in relation to a physical organ than any other drive.

The central concern of Freud's discussion in 'Instincts and Their Vicissitudes' is not with the drives as such but with the forms and consequences of the vicissitudes encountered by the drives, most obviously repression, which bear primarily upon the aim and the object of the drive. The vicissitudes to which the drive is liable are not simply external constraints or imposed limitations from a coercive society. On the contrary, the most important vicissitude for the drive is the external world itself and the very fact of its externality.

Freud argues that the transformations to which the drive is liable are not arbitrary but involve four distinct processes: 'Reversal [of the drive] into its opposite. Turning around upon the subject's own self. Repression. Sublimation.'[41] Freud does not discuss sublimation here, and in fact he does not consider it again, although it may have been the subject of one of the lost metapsychological papers. Repression is the central vicissitude of the drive and Freud devoted a paper to this topic alone. It is of course through repression that the unconscious is constituted, so that the pressure of the drive following repression will nevertheless continue in relation to unconscious representatives. Repression occurs when satisfaction of the drive, though likely to be pleasurable in itself, would incur the risk of provoking unpleasure because of other requirements. Freud says that 'the essence of repression lies simply in turning something away, and keeping it at a distance, from the conscious'.[42] What is repressed is a wish, and the Oedipal and castration complexes constitute universally a core of repressed material. Repression may be extensive, so that the drive is severely inhibited: for example, in a case of repressed scopophilia cited by Otto Fenichel, contact with

GERTRUDE

FORT APACHE

1.

3.

5.

COMA

FURY

Shot 4.

Shot 1.

Shot 7.

Shot 2.

Shot 9.

Shot 3.

Shot 10.

Shot 8.

Shot 11.

Shot 12.

THE RECKLESS MOMENT

2.

4.

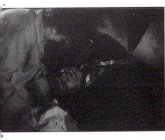

6.

8.

10.

MOROCCO

Shot 8.

Shot 9.

Shot 13.

Shot 14.

Shot 49.

Shot 50.

Shot 51.

Shot 52.

Shot 62.

Shot 90.

MOROCCO

ot 83.

Shot 86.

ot 87a.

Shot 87b.

ot 101.

Shot 118.

ot 119.

Shot 121.

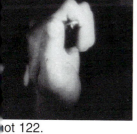

ot 122.

Shot 123.

BLUE STEEL

1.

2.

5.

6.

9.

10.

13.

14.

BLUE STEEL

4.

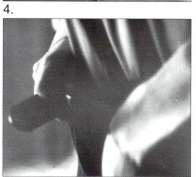

8.

12.

16.

SMOOTH TALK

1.

2.

3.

4.

5.

6.

7.

8.

9.

10.

the world through looking was replaced by other senses, and by concepts and words.[43] Or repression may produce a displacement and substitution, as in the following account of voyeurism. As a child the patient had in the winter months shared his sister's room (she was one year younger) – a measure by his parents to economise on fuel costs – but despite the opportunity thereby offered

> he avoided watching her undress and was disturbed by the least sexual sensation or thought, but he often watched a girl in a distant house undress, and wondered why this had been so important to him since he could see practically nothing.[44]

The wish to see his sister undressed, to see her genitals, is repressed but nevertheless finds a new object in the distant neighbour, yet what characterises the pleasure is that the patient *cannot* see anything (she is too far away). The wish has turned into its opposite, the wish *not* to see. Freud had noted this type of outcome in 'The Psycho-analytic View of Psychogenic Disturbance of Vision' where he comments that it is 'as though a punishing voice was speaking from within the subject and saying "Because you sought to misuse your organ of sight for evil sensual pleasure, it is fitting that you should not see anything at all".'[45]

Freud's concern in the remainder of 'Instincts and Their Vicissitudes' is with the two processes he described as 'reversal into its opposite' and 'turning around upon the subject's own self'. And it is these which will be the main focus of this discussion, for it is here that Freud presents the mechanism for the emergence of the drives as either active or passive on which he then bases his theory of sadism and masochism. It is this account which Laplanche re-reads in order to resolve the ambiguities surrounding the emergence of aggressivity and its role in the death drive. At the same time this offers, I think, a new perspective on the issue of feminine passivity.

In both these two vicissitudes, Freud says, the drive is manifested but subject to a structural change in regard to its object or aim or both. The reversal into the opposite is the change of the drive from active to passive, a change in the aim from a wish to do something to a wish to have something done to one. Freud's example is the drive to mastery which thus appears as a pair of opposites – sadism/masochism: 'The reversal affects only the *aims* of the instincts. The active aim (to torture, to look at) is replaced by the passive aim (to be tortured, to be looked at).'[46] The choice of example is important, for in fact Freud is primarily concerned to understand the move from active to passive, and the correlative sadistic or masochistic positions produced. It is this which is also of central interest here, in relation to the subsequent twinning of passivity/masochism with femininity. The turning around of the drive, however, involves a change in the *object* of the drive, and can be a change from an external to an internal object: the ego itself. But for both the examples he considers here – sadism and scopophilia – Freud notes that the 'turning round upon the subject's self and the transformation of activity and passivity converge or coincide'.[47] This appears to produce a simple binary opposition and, as Laplanche points out, it suggests a complementarity between the two positions and a reversibility comparable to the grammatical move from an active to a passive proposition,[48] so that sadism /masochism and voyeurism/exhibitionism are seen as pairs of opposites. In his discussion of scopophilia, however, Freud proposes a preliminary stage:

(a) Oneself looking at a　＝　A sexual organ being looked
　　 sexual organ　　　　　　　at by oneself

(b) Oneself looking at an　　(g) An object which is oneself
　　 extraneous object　　　　 or part of oneself being
　　 (active scopophilia)　　　 looked at by an extraneous
　　　　　　　　　　　　　　　 person (exhibitionism)

This preliminary stage, represented in the schema as (a), Freud defines as autoerotic. This stage, he argues, is 'the source of *both* the situations represented in the resulting pair of opposites, the one or the other according to which element in the original situation is changed'.[49] This preliminary stage has two possible modes in Freud's schema, oneself looking at a sexual organ, and a sexual organ being looked at by oneself, but in each case the sexual organ is part of the subject's own body, so that in this stage the two modes are equivalent, and Laplanche proposes that it should be described as 'reflexive'.

Freud initially doubted that such a preliminary stage existed in sadism but he later revised this view, arguing that sadism too followed from an earlier moment, an 'original, erotogenic masochism', a primary masochism.[50] Drawing on this revised view, and using the notion of a preliminary 'reflexive' stage Laplanche reformulates Freud's schema for scopophilia and shows how its two stages lead to the emergence of both sadism and masochism. The first stage involves a turning around of the initial drive for mastery. Laplanche sees this initial drive as simply a hetero-aggression leaning on the vital order and with no necessary sadism, that is, it is not linked to sexuality. Freud implies this when he states that:

> Psycho-analysis would appear to show that the infliction of pain plays no part among the original purposive actions of the instinct. A sadistic child takes no account of whether or not he inflicts pains, nor does he intend to do so.[51]

This hetero-agression is turned around to produce self-aggression or a primary masochism and only now does it emerge as sexual in as much as pain, a perturbation like any other, can 'produce a pleasurable condition'.[52] This stage for Laplanche is the primary form of the sexual drive and he designates it as reflexive masochism: 'sexuality emerges only with the turning round upon the self, thus with masochism, so that, within *the field of sexuality*, masochism is already considered as primary'.[53]

This primary masochism or self-aggression is not yet passive, however, since no reversal of aim has occurred. It is, Laplanche argues, an intermediate stage in which, as Freud says, 'The active voice is changed, not into a passive, but into the reflexive, middle voice.'[54] It is in this reflexive, auto-erotic phase that sexuality emerges, leaning on the vital functions but in which there is no object as such. This primary masochism is the basis for the second stage, so that it is only with a second turning around that the active drive, and sadism proper arises. In this second turning-around an external object is again the object of the drive. Sadism is then the active position producing a search in the external world for an object capable of being substituted for the original object while the passive position of masochism requires that another subject be substituted for the subject's own self.

The passive drive and masochism as such only arises with the reversal of the drive, when the active *aim* is replaced by a passive aim, which implies the search for another person as 'object', that is, object of the drive but who will be the subject of the action.[55] It is through the object of the drive that the aim, satisfaction, can be achieved. Where this primary or reflexive masochism is reversed in its aim, from active to passive, the subject itself is now the 'object' of the action giving rise to a satisfaction occurring on the subject's own body – an action by an external object which is thus also the aim of the drive. There are therefore not one but two aims of the drive here and, one must suppose, two forms of satisfaction, the first in relation to having the other do something to oneself – the pleasure, one might say, of bringing the other to undertake the action in relation to oneself. The second is the sensation the action as such brings about on the body of the subject itself – which may or may not be pleasurable in itself. In the passive position, then, the object of the drive is also the subject itself, but acted upon from the place of another. Here, unlike the position of reflexive masochism, in which there is no object as such differentiated, the subject is its own object.[56] This 'self-as-object' is constituted through the action of the other upon the subject, whereby the agent of the action stands in for the subject itself, so that this is thus also an identification. Identification is also involved in that particular turning around of the active drive which Freud describes as regressive identification – the drive turns away from the external object, but now the internal object to which it is directed is not simply the subject's ego, but the external object introduced as an internal object.[57]

Sadism and masochism, voyeurism and exhibitionism, are not, therefore, simple opposites, and the complement of the masochist is not a sadist but a person who can be brought to or put in the position of the subject itself.[58] Similarly the exhibitionist is not the complement of the voyeur.[59] Moreover Freud himself commented that the transformation of the drive is never exhaustive and that the different stages, the auto-erotic as well as passive and active forms, co-exist alongside one another.[60] Laplanche's re-reading of Freud not only resolves many of the ambiguities in Freud's theory of the drive. It also implies a radically new view of the relation of active and passive in the emergence of the drive, namely that the drive is first constituted in relation to passive aims. Laplanche then maps this reading onto Freud's analysis in 'A Child is Being Beaten' of the genesis of a sado-masochistic fantasy. He argues in conclusion, and this is a fundamental tenet of his work as an analyst and a theorist, that fantasy in the position of reflexive masochism involves taking in, internalising and making the fantasy enter oneself. 'To fantasise aggression is to turn it round upon oneself, to aggress oneself: such is the moment of autoeroticism, in which the indissoluble bond between fantasy as such, sexuality, and the unconscious is confirmed', and as a result 'the passive position of the child in relation to the adult is not simply a passivity in relation to adult activity, but passivity in relation to the adult fantasy intruding within him.'[61] This new understanding is closely allied to Laplanche's development of a theory of primal seduction. This both draws upon Freud's rejected supposition of infantile seduction and transforms it by relating it to the emergence of the drive and the unconscious. Primal seduction, for Laplanche, describes 'a fundamental situation in which an adult proffers to a child verbal, non-verbal and even behavioural signifiers which are pregnant with unconscious sexual significations'.[62] These signifiers are, however, enigmatic for the child, and hence are not fully symbolisable; instead Laplanche argues, there is a residue of signification which is yet 'to be translated' and as a result is repressed by the infant and this forms the core of the unconscious. The intrusion of these enigmatic signifiers upon the child – and this has no necessary relation to the adult's conscious intentions, but may figure unconscious desires – is experienced both as an excitation and as a pressure, a demand upon the child which produces a concomitant drive for meaning in the child. As a result the very origin of the drive lies in this coming into the child of these signifiers which are experienced as irresolvably enigmatic. The corollary is that this origin is constituted as passivity.

FREUDIAN FEMININITY AND THE CAREER OF THE DRIVE IN THE WOMAN

> The mechanism of the turn from the active to the passive, moreover, pervades woman's entire instinctual life. (Helene Deutsch[63])

The drive and its energy, libido, is always active, it is not divided as such into active/masculine, passive/feminine. What then is the role of this equation which is at one and the same time one of the most disputed but also most resilient premises within psychoanalytic theory? If it is simply true, then as feminist theorists we will have to pack up our books and go home, for how can psychoanalytic theory be used to argue against the equation passivity=femininity which it has instituted for itself?

Laplanche's revised theory of the drive has important implications for our understanding of *feminine* passivity, for it suggests a
new approach to the stumbling block in Freud's theory of femininity, namely, that it requires the little girl to replace her original
active aims with passive aims in order to become properly a
woman. Freud's views on femininity and the 'fact' of feminine passivity contain a series of discontinuities, and even downright contradictions, so that he appears to give with the right hand what he
takes away with the left. In 'Femininity' Freud rejects the equation
active/masculine and feminine/passive saying 'I advise you
against it. It seems to me to serve no useful purpose and adds
nothing to our knowledge.'[64] Instead, and although he acknowledges that 'we must beware in this of underestimating the influence
of social customs, which similarly force women into passive situations', Freud says that femininity may be characterised psychologically as giving preference to passive *aims*.

> This is not, of course, the same thing as passivity; to achieve a
> passive aim may call for a large amount of activity. It is perhaps
> the case that in a woman, on the basis of her share in the sexual
> function, a preference for passive behaviour and passive aims is
> carried over into her life to a greater or lesser extent, in propor-
> tion to the limits, restricted or far-reaching, within which her
> sexual life thus serves as a model.[65]

He continues:

> All this is still far from being cleared up. There is one particu-
> larly constant relation between femininity and instinctual life
> which we do not want to overlook. The suppression of women's
> aggressiveness which is prescribed for them constitutionally and
> imposed on them socially favours the development of powerfully
> masochistic impulses, which succeed, as we know, in binding
> erotically the destructive trends which have been diverted
> inwards. Thus masochism, as people say, is truly feminine. But if,
> as happens so often, you meet with masochism in men, what is
> left to you but to say that these men exhibit very plain feminine
> traits.[66]

While affirming that passivity is always a question of the aim of the
drive, Freud has introduced a constitutional element in relation to

the passivity of femininity, and allied this with social convention, producing 'masochistic impulses'. Masochism is then identified with femininity, for the display of masochism in men is described as a 'feminine trait', although the argument here is quite distinct from any thesis of bisexuality.[67] However, this constitutional pre-scription arises not at birth for the little girl, but in consequence of 'castration', which is not the case – or not in the same way – for the male masochist. For Freud, femininity is not a biological inscription but a psychical construction arising as a result of the little girl's per-ception of her lack of a penis as 'castration'. Freud's thesis is that up to a certain point the girl has 'lived in a masculine way', with active wishes towards the mother and genital pleasure through clitoral masturbation. But as a result of her sense of lack in the face of 'the boy's far superior equipment' she loses her enjoyment in her phallic sexuality, and thus 'renounces her masturbatory satisfaction from her clitoris, repudiates her love for her mother and at the same time not infrequently represses a good part of her sexual trends in general'.[68]

The little girl's original active aims must be replaced by passive aims, then, in order for her to achieve femininity. This, Freud says, is brought about by her penis-envy which causes the girl to give up her active aims, and thus leads to a 'wave of passivity'. Freud's ar-gument here slides together repression with the reversal and turning around of the drive, in order to produce a 'wave of devel-opment' whereby 'passivity now has the upper hand', which will 'smooth the ground' for femininity. Freud, however, discusses the reversal and turning around of the drive only in relation to scopophilia and sadism/masochism, so that it is difficult to under-stand their role for femininity in producing the 'wave ' of passivity. Moreover Freud's reference to the role of repression seems to assume the existence of an original reservoir of instinctual drives in the little girl which have both an active *and* a passive aim with only the active aims being repressed.[69]

By contrast, Laplanche's account of the drives has shown that the active and passive are not inversely related in this way, but rather are two *distinct* forms of the drive. Both forms emerge from a primary masochism, involving auto-eroticism, which is structurally prior to the emergence of the active and the passive aim. As a result there can be no 'pool' of active and passive drives or aims. In addition, in Laplanche's account the passive aim emerges not through the turning around of the active, but of the auto-erotic or primary masochism – the subject moves from being its own object to being an object for someone else. Masochism, as self-aggression, is primary for the subject, and represents the tendency towards zero or the death drive. If there is a feminine passivity, it is a complex affair and not simply from a move from the active to passive.

The role of repression in producing passivity as femininity is also problematic in Freud's account.[70] Freud says that the repression of the active in the little girl arises because of the abandonment of a satisfaction as a result of penis-envy, but why is envy able to transform a pleasure into an unpleasure? If it is on the basis of the analogy that bigger is best, as Freud suggests, this can only be as a result of a sense of lack in being in the child which exists prior to castration. In this case the little girl's pursuit of sexual pleasure in her clitoral masturbation brings her up against the knowledge of her lack and hence produces unpleasure (the body is not a sufficient condition for desire), so that the repression of the wish for genital satisfaction removes the risk of that unpleasure. However, this will apply to both the active and the passive aim, to the wish to take pleasure in her genitals and to be pleasured in her genitals. Of course the boy, too, experiences an inadequacy in relation to the much larger penis of his father, and gives up masturbation as a result of the castration complex, but this is not described by Freud as a renunciation of activity.

Repression, moreover, acts not on the drive as such or in general, but on an idea, a wish, whose satisfaction would be pleasurable in itself but at the same time would risk incurring unpleasure as a result of other requirements.[71] Repression itself does not produce a passive aim, but an inhibition of the drive, whether active or passive. More likely for women in the sexual domain, repression will produce frigidity, which of course has so often been confused with passive sexuality. Indeed Freud seems to acknowledge this for while he asserts that where activity remains, femininity is not fully achieved, at the same time he notes that not too much must be lost through repression for a normal pathway to femininity to be achieved.[72]

In fact the girl's passivity is posited by Freud not in relation to the repression of masturbation, but in relation to a new wish, and one which is not repressed, namely the wish for a penis (this is also a form of turning around of the drive, from an object on the subject's own body, the clitoris, to an external object, the penis).

The aim of this wish may be active, the wish to take the penis from the mother or the father. Freud, however, sees the aim of the wish for a penis as passive in so far as it is a demand to – in the first instance – the mother, the phallic mother – from whom the little girl expects to receive a penis. It is only with the mother's refusal of the demand, or as Freud puts it 'the discovery that her mother is castrated'[73] that she turns to her father. The final transformation, Freud says, will then be the substitution of a wish for a penis by a wish for a baby.[74] In order to distinguish this as a passive aim – whether for a penis or a baby – Freud very clearly rejects confusing the little girl's post-castration wish for a baby with her earlier games with her dolls, for these, just as they do for the boy, 'served as an identification with her mother with the intention of substituting activity for passivity. *She* was playing the part of her mother and the doll was herself: now she could do with the baby everything that her mother used to do with her.'[75] Instead, in Freud's account this is a new wish and it must involve a passive aim, since the girl has repressed her active aims and thus has given up her phallic activity. If this has not occurred – as with the masculinity complex – it is because of 'a constitutional factor, a greater amount of activity, such as is ordinarily characteristic of the male'.[76] But there is no pool of active or passive drives; if there does arise on the part of the girl a wish for a penis, it must be shown why and whether the aim is passive rather than active. No doubt this may arise as a defensive reversal of the drive so that the little girl will be *given* the penis/baby, and hence avoid the feared retribution of her father, or mother, for her wish to take the penis. The reversal of the drive therefore enables the wish to escape repression. But this does not account for the *general* turn to passivity Freud claims for the girl. For what must be repressed by the little girl, just as much as by the little boy, is the active wish for the phallic mother; the role of castration is first of all in the realisation of the *mother's* lack and hence her loss to the child as phallic. As a result what must still be explained is the specific relation to active and passive aims – if any – which is brought about by the instituting of sexual difference in the child, whether boy or girl.

The inadequacy of Freud's description of female sexuality has long been acknowledged, but, as Juliet Mitchell has pointed out in her introduction to *Feminine Sexuality: Jacques Lacan and the École Freudienne*, many of the attempts to resolve it by offering alternative accounts are hardly more palatable. Alternatively, the account is accepted as fact, while it is also observed that many women do not fit the description and hence are not fully feminine – a strategy outlined by Freud himself in two different ways. On the one hand Freud draws upon the concept of the masculinity complex, arguing that the 'wave of passivity' which 'opens the way to the turn toward femininity' is avoided where

> the girl refuses, as it were, to recognise the unwelcome fact [of castration] and, defiantly rebellious, even exaggerates her previous masculinity, clings to her clitoridal activity and takes refuge in an identification with her phallic mother or her father.[77]

And the reason for this, he suggests, 'is a constitutional factor, a greater amount of activity, such as is ordinarily characteristic of the male'. This proposes a quantitative factor – repression fails because the active aim is too strong – which not only introduces the problems noted earlier of a notion of a 'reservoir' of active and passive aims but is not justified by Freud's arguments elsewhere on repression. On the other hand Freud invokes bisexuality:

> For the ladies, whenever some comparison seemed to turn out unfavourably to their sex, were able to utter a suspicion that we, the male analysts, had been unable to overcome certain deeply-rooted prejudices against what was feminine, and this was being paid for in the partiality of our researches. We, on the other hand, standing on the ground of bisexuality, had no difficulty in avoiding impoliteness. We had only to say: 'This doesn't apply to *you*. You're the exception; on this point you're more masculine than feminine.'[78]

It is precisely Freud's emphasis on and commitment to a notion of bisexuality which has always made Freudian psychoanalysis so interesting for feminists. Freud's theory of bisexuality, which he adopted from Wilhelm Fliess, is, however, determinedly biologistic for, drawing on the model of an original hermaphroditism, it asserts that there are two determinate sexualities, masculinity and femininity, *both* of which are constitutionally present in men and women. Nevertheless Freud, while always averring the psychological importance of the notion of bisexuality, also recognised difficulties in the concept because it presupposes a clear distinction between male and female, a distinction which Freud admitted did not clearly exist in relation to the psychological meaning for 'masculine' and 'feminine'. Instead he suggests that 'the contrast between the sexes fades away into one between activity and passivity'[79] but, although he affirms the importance of this view in a note to *Three Essays on the Theory of Sexuality*,[80] he later questions it as being 'by no means universally confirmed in the animal kingdom' and comments:

> The theory of bisexuality is still surrounded by many obscurities and we cannot but feel it is a serious impediment in psychoanalysis that it has not yet found any link with the theory of the instincts.[81]

In fact, though Freud's references to the notion of bisexuality tend to be essentialist, his theory of the sexual drive in the human subject as constructed, as propped on the vital order, contradicts this and in contrast to the biological notion of bisexuality two different ideas of – if not bisexuality – an intermixing between the sexes can be distinguished in his work. Firstly, there is Freud's view of the sexual drive as originally undifferentiated and hence as neither masculine nor feminine, but characterised as active (though its aim may be passive). Second, a bisexuality arises with the emergence of sexual difference in the subject insofar as this is defined as split between active/masculine, passive/feminine but where this never maps on to individual men and women in a unilateral manner. Laplanche's re-reading of Freud's theory of the drive has emphasised the constitutive role of passivity for the subject, whether male or female, and this has important implications for understanding the construction of sexual difference. For the complex identifications arising for the subject as a result of the castration complex in the context of Oedipal relations are not already determined by passive or active aims. It is the encounter of passive and active aims with the transformations demanded by the Oedipus complex which, regardless of whether it is resolved or not, can be said to produce a post-Oedipal sexuality and which is therefore always in some sense a bisexuality. Post-Oedipal sexuality can now be understood as arising from the encounter of passive and active aims – in which passive aims are primary – with the transformations demanded by the Oedipus complex.

It is this sense of bisexuality which seems to me to be of value to feminist theory, rather than an appeal to an originary state, which would return us to all the problems of an essentialism, even if a dualist essentialism.[82] Freud's appeal to bisexuality in his discussion in 'Femininity', however, simply opens up a Pandora's box, for how can it be determined whether and to what extent one is masculine or feminine, or is this simply defined by the extent of active or passive aims? In addition, however many instances Freud cites in which active wishes survive in women, however many exceptions he can claim, these remain *deviant* in respect to the normal path of femininity which he outlines. A 'progressive' reading of Freud, drawing upon such examples, can therefore be no more acceptable, since feminism can hardly find salvation for psychoanalysis in the fact that the 'normal' course of masculinity and femininity it describes is rarely achieved by men or women (or rather is *only* ever achieved by some women, and never at all by men). An emphasis on the *precariousness* of the psychological institution of sexual difference in men and women in no way dislodges the fixity of the fixing which is made only more stronger by its very difficulty; every failure of the fixing only proving the very fact and necessity of its existence.

Lacan affirms the importance of the equation activity/passivity with masculinity/femininity – 'it is only with activity/passivity that the sexual relation really comes into play' – but he suggests that for Freud 'the polar reference activity/passivity is there in order to name, to cover, to metaphorise that which remains unfathomable in sexual difference. Nowhere does he [Freud] ever say that, psychologically, the masculine/feminine relation is apprehensible otherwise than by the representative of the activity/passivity opposition.' But, Lacan adds, 'As such, the masculine/feminine opposition is never attained.'[83] As a result the precariousness of sexual difference now appears to be an aspect of sexual difference, rather than its failure, and Lacan writes elsewhere of the impossibility of the sexual relation.[84] Two distinct processes (at least) are involved: the emergence of passivity as an aspect of the drive, and the emergence of femininity as a subject position involving, and defined by, a passive aim which appeals to and is in turn appealed to by the active masculine aim but which is nevertheless never complementary. Lacan does not, however, propose simply lining up men and women under these same polar opposites, for activity/passivity is drive, a pushing and not a position, which is 'poured, moulded, injected', hence he says 'It is an arteriography, and even the masculine/feminine relations do not exhaust it.' As a result 'what we are dealing with here is precisely this injection, one might say, of sado-masochism, which is not at all to be understood, as far as its properly sexual realisation is concerned, as ready money'.[85]

But given current investment structures, ready money is exactly what feminists have demanded, and what psychoanalysis has seemed to fail to hand over. Nevertheless, the famous passivity of women which Freud's description seems to so neatly confirm has been shown to be a much more complex affair. It involves, as Juliet Mitchell puts it, the girl most actively devoting herself to this passive aim of being loved.[86] Lacan, too, emphasises that 'In fact, it is obvious that, even in their supposedly passive phase, the exercise of a drive, a masochistic drive, for example, requires that the masochist give himself, if I may be permitted to put it in this way, a devil of a job.'[87]

Two confusions have nevertheless dominated the debate. One is that, by having a passive aim, the woman (or man) is 'being' passive in the sense in which a dictionary might define it, of inert, bearing no interest, acted upon. This sense brings with it the assumption that what is acting upon her (or him) is not wished for, is imposed, thus reviving the obsolete meaning of passive, that is, 'suffering', but now in its modern sense of receiving some harm. In other words passivity is identified with being a victim to another's actions. The second confusion is, more properly, a conflation in which the fact of woman's biological receptivity – her vagina – is transformed into a metaphor of the woman as passive, awaiting penetration and subject to the man's active entry, with all its implicit possibilities of *forced* entry. Thus, men do it and women have it done to them. The truism, that there are always two sides to a question, is particularly apt here. To say that one agent is active is to say nothing about the position of any other agent involved in the action. In any case for psychoanalysis the division active/passive refers to the *aim* of the drive, of the sexual wishes, and not to a specific male/female interaction. And a passive aim – a man's perhaps – to be enclosed, surrounded, taken in, may require considerable activity to bring about, activity which would conventionally be identified as masculine.

Furthermore, heterosexuality does not seem to be secured by the extent to which the woman's or man's drive is dominantly passive or active (Freud's analysis of the Wolf Man illustrates this[88]) but rather seems to be significantly independent of such a factor. This is clearly possible in as much as sexual difference is constituted in and by castration, which is not equivalent to the activity/passivity opposition, the latter, Lacan noted, simply being the metaphor constructed to handle the relation to castration instituted as sexual difference. The precariousness of sexual difference lies in the difficulty which arises in the taking up of a position as a sexed subject, as masculine *or* feminine.

WOMAN'S SCOPOPHILIA

Whatever the career of passivity for the woman in the sexual relation this can no longer be understood as constituting the woman, or femininity, as having only passive aims. Active scopophilia remains a powerful drive for women, as it does for men, nor can this be seen as a failure to be feminine. Freud confirmed the continuing role of scopophilia for the woman in his account of a dream by one of his women patients of visiting the theatre with her husband.[89] Freud suggests that in the dream 'Going to the play appeared as a substitute for getting married' and the wish fulfilled by the dream was the wish to *see* what is to be known in marriage, for he notes that on marriage young girls are then able to go to the theatre, to all the plays which had been hitherto prohibited, and will be allowed to see everything, and he comments:

> The pleasure in looking, or curiosity, which is revealed in this was no doubt originally a sexual desire to look [scopophilia], directed towards sexual happenings and especially on to the girls' parents, and hence it became a powerful motive for urging them to an early marriage.[90]

Nevertheless Freud's later theory of femininity as passivity, as well as the views of psychoanalysts such as Deutsch, has meant that women's scopophilia has subsequently not only rarely been addressed, but it has often not been perceived as such.[91] As a corollary Mulvey's early polemical essays confirmed the woman's exclusion from the pleasures of the look in cinema, or found her pleasures in the remnants of her pre-Oedipal masculinity. Woman's relation to her pleasure in looking is now being re-viewed and re-imaged by women in the visual arts.[92] At the same time we are beginning to see how the cinema in Hollywood and elsewhere has represented and played to women's pleasure in looking, including their gaze at men. John Ford's classic Western, *Fort Apache* (1948), for example, makes this clear: a close-up shows the obvious visual pleasure of Philadelphia Thursday (the teenage Shirley Temple) when she accidentally happens upon the half-naked young Lieutenant Michael O'Rourke (John Agar) at a staging post on the way to Fort Apache. He is re-joining his non-commissioned father at the fort after his West Point training. She is travelling with her father Colonel Thursday (Henry Fonda), the new commander of the fort. Later, seated beside her father on the stagecoach while the young Lieutenant and other troops follow on horseback (plate 1), Philadelphia wants to satisfy her wish to see him but when she turns to look back at him (frame-still 2) her desire is censored by a glance of reproof from her father (frame-still 3), so instead she resorts to subterfuge and, opening her vanity box whose lid encloses a mirror (already shown to us in an earlier scene), her gaze finds its target in the young man's reflection imaged there (frame-still 4), to her clear satisfaction (frame-still 5). Of course, as a fantasy scenario what is presented here is also the wish to be seen, with the satisfaction – for the man – of finding himself seen by the woman, a satisfaction only available, at this point in the film, to the spectator, for the young man does not see Philadelphia seeing him.

In challenging Freud's account of the career of the drive in the woman as a simple move from activity to passivity, I have sought at the level of theory to open up new ways to understanding active scopophilia, and the active drive as such, in the woman. The issue of her femininity is returned to in Chapter 6. It is to the question of scopophilia itself that I now turn, together with its attendant term, voyeurism, and its companion-in-arms, fetishism.

SCOPOPHILIA, VOYEURISM AND FETISHISM

Freud's description of the splitting of scopophilia into active voyeurism and passive exhibitionism as a result of the reversal of the drive and turning around on the self, as with the pairing sadism/masochism, introduces an unresolved ambiguity around the relation of these to perversion. Woman's passivity becomes woman's masochism without this being related to Freud's later work on perversion, namely its relation to castration whereby perversion is a disavowal of castration. Voyeurism together with fetishism have been central to much recent film theory as two modes of visual pleasure and which, because of their relation to castration, are taken to be male pleasures. The role of perversion here, too, remains ambiguous. Moreover the two terms are treated as a couple yet this relation, if there is one, is not explained; voyeurism arises in relation to a specific component drive, so that the couple voyeurism/exhibitionism arise initially as active/passive aims of the drive, and Lacan emphasises that the scopic drive – active or passive – is not perversion.[93] In contrast fetishism is not a component drive, it is not divided into active and passive forms, and it is always taken to be a perversion. The following re-examination of these terms seeks to place them in relation to psychoanalytic theories of perversion and as a result proposes a rather different understanding of their role in visual pleasure. The problem of castration is affirmed through the role of disavowal, but it is now shown to be a much more complex affair for the man and for the woman, and as something which, for both, is never a real fact. It is disavowal which gives rise to the theory of castration, and it is equally central to both femininity and masculinity.

For Freud, in *Three Essays on the Theory of Sexuality*, both fetishism and voyeurism seem to be conceived as merely versions of normal behaviour which are more extreme because of some event – usually a childhood trauma – which has either fixed the adult at an earlier, regressive, sexual phase, or as a result of a prohibition has inhibited the drive, as with fetishism. This implies a 'continuum' theory. Freud reiterates this view of perversion as a more extreme form of normal behaviour in his paper 'On Narcissism'. Writing of the narcissist who takes his or her own body as source of satisfaction he says, 'Developed to this degree, narcissism has the significance of a perversion that has absorbed the whole of the subject's sexual life.'[94] Perversion at this point is also seen by Freud as distinct from and opposed to neurosis and its repressions. Perverse scopophilia or voyeurism appears to be different from the notion of scopophilia in 'Instincts and Their Vicissitudes' where Freud described the turning around of the drive to give an active (voyeur) and passive (exhibitionist) form, but where, in neither case, was this described as perverse. Something more is required for the drive to become perverse. A theory of the perversions must also address the fact claimed by psychiatrists and psychoanalysts as exemplified in their case studies, namely that women are very rarely, if ever, either fetishists or voyeurs (or exhibitionists) although we are told that women do exhibit one perversion, homosexuality and perhaps another – sado-masochism.[95]

In *Three Essays on the Theory of Sexuality* Freud saw voyeurism as a specific perversion of the scopophilic drive which arises when it is restricted exclusively to the genitals, or is connected with the overriding of disgust (looking on at excretory functions), or if instead of being preparatory it supplants the normal sexual aim. Exhibitionists, Freud says, exhibit their own genitals in order to obtain a reciprocal view of the other person's.[96] Not until 1920, in a footnote added to the *Essays*, does Freud refer to castration anxiety as a cause, though only one among 'a surprising variety of motives', and only in relation to exhibitionism, though it would presumably apply to voyeurism as well.[97]

Fetishism is described by Freud as arising when 'the normal sexual object is replaced by another which bears some relation to it, but is entirely unsuited to serve the normal sexual aim'.[98] The substitution may be some part of the body, such as the foot, or the hair, or an object related to the person, usually to their sexuality, such as a piece of clothing or underwear. Where such substitution occurs the sexual aim, whether normal or perverse, may be entirely abandoned.[99] Alongside this Freud distinguishes other transitional cases in which the sexual object is required to fulfil a fetishistic condition 'such as the possession of some particular hair-colouring or clothing, or even some bodily defect – if the sexual aim is to be attained'.[100] Indeed he concludes that 'A certain degree of fetishism is thus habitually present in normal love.'[101] Fetishim develops from the normal overestimation of the sexual object and everything that is associated with it. It becomes pathological when the fetish object replaces the normal aim, and when the fetish is detached from the person and becomes the *sole* sexual object.

Freud does not attach fetishism to a particular drive; rather, any of the drives may be diverted from their normal aim to become attached to a substitute object. Freud cites smell as one component drive typically involved in foot and hair fetishism. In a footnote to *Three Essays* added in 1910 Freud mentions scopophilia, again in relation to foot fetishism, which

> seeking to reach its object (originally the genitals) from underneath, was brought to a halt in its pathway by prohibition and repression. For that reason it became attached to a fetish in the

form of a foot or shoe, the female genitals (in accordance with the expectations of childhood) being imagined as male ones.[102]

Freud does not suggest the cause of fetishism here, though he mentions a 'constitutional factor', as well as the function of repression and prohibition, and he also cites the sexual theories of children 'the foot represents a woman's penis, the absence of which is deeply felt'. However all these refer to the particular fetish choice rather than to the phenomenon as a whole.

It is not until his paper 'Fetishism' in 1927 that Freud made specific the connection that the fetish is a metaphorical (and not only metonymical) substitute that stands in for the *mother's* missing penis. In that paper Freud gives castration anxiety as the sole cause of the construction of the fetish(es), arguing that 'the fetish is a substitute for the woman's (the mother's) penis'.[103] The notion of a continuum, of a normal to perverse 'overvaluation of the sexual object' is discarded here and instead Freud introduces a specific mechanism. Castration anxiety may, however, be more or less severe Freud says, leading to degrees of fetishism in which the sexual aim may not be supplanted and instead the fetish 'saves the fetishist from becoming homosexual, by endowing women with the characteristic which makes them tolerable as sexual objects'.[104] As a result a new form of continuum is introduced in relation to castration anxiety itself, and this will apply to both fetishism and voyeurism, for it is castration anxiety, too, which gives rise to voyeurism. But, in contrast to fetishism, the voyeur needs to see the fact of female castration in order to defend himself against the anxiety of his own possible castration by the obsessive looking and looking again at the woman's genitals for what is *not* there, a penis.[105] And, because a continuum argument has been introduced, it has been argued that the look of the man at a woman (at her body) will *always* include a reassurance against castration; voyeurism is now equivalent to the pleasure in looking – for the man. Similarly, fetishism is seen as a general and typical feature of male sexuality. However these two pathways out of castration anxiety, voyeurism and fetishism, appear to be mutually exclusive: a man cannot be both a voyeur and a fetishist, as the one would give what the other seeks to deny, one desires to know the woman's castration, the other to not know. Such a voyeurism must, as well, exclude women; for what feminine pleasure can there be in the reassurance of one's own castration – and indeed why go to the cinema to find it out?

Freud defined the scopic drive as looking at one's sex or rather, as having one's sex looked at – by oneself or, later, by another. Lacan sums this up: 'what is involved in the drive is *making oneself seen (se faire voir)'*.[106] All this is lost to the girl with the narcissistic blow of castration – she has nothing (to show).

This picture is not at all clarified, on the contrary it is shown to be much more complex, in the light of the concept of disavowal which Freud introduced in his paper on 'Fetishism'. Moreover the concept of disavowal as it subsequently develops in Freud's later writings fundamentally disrupts any possibility of a 'continuum' of normal to perverse.

Disavowal arises, Freud says, when the boy refuses to take cognizance of the fact of his having perceived that a woman does not have a penis: 'No, that could not be true: for if a woman had been castrated, then his own possession of a penis was in danger',[107] and the boy's narcissistic attachment to that part of his body gives rise to a rebellion against this knowledge. The knowledge is not destroyed, however, but rather a compromise is reached between the unwelcome knowledge and the force of the boy's counter-wish.

> Yes, in his mind the woman *has* got a penis, in spite of everything; but this penis is no longer the same as it was before. Something else has taken its place, has been appointed its substitute, as it were, and now inherits the interest which was formerly directed to its predecessor. But this interest suffers an extraordinary increase as well, because the horror of castration has set up a memorial to itself in the creation of this substitute.[108]

The boy disavows the perception in the erection of the fetish substitute which is thus a monument to the woman's castration, and thereby represents an acknowledgement of the perception it disavows. This is in contrast to a *denial* (or foreclosure, in Lacan's terms) which would be supported by an *hallucination* of the mother's penis. The fetish now exists as the *representative* of the mother's absent penis. Freud affirms that it is the *mother's* penis which is 'found' in the fetish, and not just any old penis, and that this substitution wards off castration anxiety. However, Freud's account seems to imply a simple relation between the perception of the woman's lack of a penis, and the resulting identification of the woman as castrated, and the fear (another, though different, identification) that he, too, might be so castrated. But the idea that the woman has been castrated must surely already be part of a process of disavowal, for the boy is assuming she did once have one, but 'lost' it.

> We know how children react to their first impressions of the absence of a penis. They disavow the fact [this is Freud's first use of the term] and believe that they *do* see a penis, all the same. They gloss over the contradiction between observation and preconception by telling themselves that the penis is still small and will grow bigger presently; and they then slowly come to the emotionally significant conclusion that after all the penis had at least been there before and been taken away afterwards. The lack of a penis is regarded as a result of castration, and so now the child is faced with the task of coming to terms with castration in relation to himself.[109]

Freud's reference here is to the case of Little Hans. The fear of castration for himself arises for the small boy as a result of his desire for the mother which he perceives as forbidden – ultimately, forbidden by the father. As sexual pleasure becomes organised in the genital stage, it is the boy's penis which he wants to use as the instrument of desire in relation to his mother and thus the boy becomes vulnerable to the fear that if he misuses it he will lose it – a castration threat constructed not so much out of any literal threat which there may have been, but rather out of the general form of prohibition and punishment he has already met with, that is, if a child keeps banging its toy drum, even after being told to stop, its carer is likely to remove the drum. (Little Hans's mother had threatened to send him to 'Dr A to cut off your widler' in order to stop him masturbating.)[110]

Castration is the representation in fantasy of the consequences of continuing with a forbidden desire. It is, Laplanche and Pontalis suggest, a theory constructed by the child, and they take issue with Freud's claim that the mother's castration is 'a piece of reality':[111]

> If the disavowal of castration is the prototype – and perhaps even the origin – of other kinds of disavowal of reality, we are forced to ask what Freud understands by the 'reality' of castration or by the perception of this reality. If it is the woman's 'lack of a penis' that is disavowed, then it becomes difficult to talk in

terms of perception or of reality, for an absence is not perceived as such, and it only becomes real in so far as it is related to a conceivable presence. If, on the other hand, it is castration itself which is repudiated, then the object of disavowal would not be a perception – castration never being perceived as such–but rather a theory designed to account for the facts – a 'sexual theory of children'.[112]

The Oedipus complex is the context or network of relations in which this fantasy is produced – that is, the wish to have the mother; the child must confront and accept the rejection of this demand. What will make him accept this? A young child is rarely sympathetic to the sort of logical arguments for the emergence and maintenance of human culture by which Lévi-Strauss explains the universality of the incest taboo. Rather the wish is given up – as all such wishes are – in so far as the child perceives a danger to itself as a result of the wish, i.e. the consequences outweigh the advantages. The fantasy of castration is the way in which the child gives itself a reason to give up its wish, and this also – for the boy at least – affords it a certain satisfaction. It is a fantasy not primarily because it is unreal, but because it organises reality to fit subjective desires. The fantasy is arrived at as a result of the experience of rivalry with the parent of the same sex – for the boy, its father – and desire for the parent of the opposite sex – his mother (the positive form of the Oedipal complex), but the Oedipal complex includes as well the boy's desire for its father and hence its rivalry with its mother (the negative or inverse form); thus it involves hostile and loving responses to both parents, and Freud emphasises the bisexuality of the relation here. Freud says that the boy's acceptance of the possibility of castration, his recognition that women were castrated, makes an end of the possibility of obtaining satisfaction within the Oedipus complex, for love for either the father or the mother will entail the loss of his penis – the masculine attachment to the mother will bring down on him the punishment of his father, while he may suppose that in order to have his father's love in the way his mother does, he too must be castrated (Freud describes this as the feminine attachment). Freud assumes in this last point that the boy will now expect that his father only desires the other as castrated but this may be a further and separate step which may or may not be included within the castration fantasy. At any rate, Freud concludes:

If the satisfaction of love in the field of the Oedipus complex is to cost the child his penis, a conflict is bound to arise between his narcissistic interest in that part of his body and the libidinal cathexis of the parental objects. In the conflict the first of these forces normally triumphs: the child's ego turns away from the Oedipus complex.[113]

For Freud the very sight of the woman or girl's genitals provides the confirmation for the boy of the possibility of castration – as he says, such an observation lends truth to the threat he had earlier laughed at and he is now forced to believe in the reality of the threat.

Freud in his writings on this subject always sees this conclusion as logical and natural. But this is only a further step into unreality. For nothing is missing in the little girl, or in the mother; rather what is confirmed for the boy is the reality that his mother's desire lies *elsewhere* than in him, and which he may surmise lies in the supplement represented by his new-born sibling, or ultimately and more importantly, in his father's penis. The fear of castration is not motivated by reality, rather it is a fantasy arising as a result of the child's desire for its mother and which it is beginning to realise is impossible; the child attributes this frustration to an external power which will punish it for its forbidden desires, a punishment of castration. Within this scenario, the mother's absence of a penis confirms for the child *not* the reality of the possibility of castration, but the reality of the impossibility of its obtaining its desire, the mother. For what is presented to the child is the reality that the mother's desire lies elsewhere. But no, this can't be true – 'they must have taken it away' the boy says to himself. It seems that the boy – and perhaps the girl – prefers to believe in the mother's mutilation, her castration, the taking away of her penis, rather than accept that she has never had a penis. The logic, perhaps, is something like this: because she has lost her penis, she has turned to my father; he has the penis she wants (because it is bigger than mine...). However at the same time the fantasy also figures the child's aggression, his rivalrous hostility in relation to his father, as well as anger at his mother for having 'submitted' to this castration, and thereby exposing him to the same danger. For, as suggested earlier, there is a satisfaction as well and it has a sadistic form, since the fantasy is also a *punishment* of the mother for her betrayal of the son; in becoming castrated in her son's eyes she is denigrated and made worthless. It is this aspect of the belief in the mother's mutilation which later gives rise, in certain men, to the 'horror of the mutilated creature or triumphant contempt for her'.[114]

The acceptance of 'castration', however, which is demanded of the child is not simply the 'castration' of the mother, or of women, but of humankind. It is an acceptance of a limitation on one's desire. The entry into the symbolic in Lacan's terms involves an acceptance of the lack in being of the self, and not just a lack in the woman. Thus castration is not the mutilation of women which I too, as a man, might succumb to, but the radical insufficiency in being of every subject, and it is the signifier of a radical prohibition on my desire. Moreover if castration is a fantasy in this way, and a disavowal, it is also a disavowal for the little girl, too, if as Freud argues, she takes the absence of a penis in her mother as castration.[115]

The belief in the mother's castration is therefore a constructed fantasy which disavows the reality of the mother's absence of a penis insofar as this has come to represent her desire as lying elsewhere than in the child. But such a move on the child's part has horrendous penalties, for it raises the possibility of the same thing happening to itself, or having happened. The solution to the Oedipus complex, of the relinquishing of the wish for the mother by the child, is of only limited relief in this, for it removes only this one reason for receiving the same punishment as the mother and does not do away with the threat as such. Simply giving up the parents as libidinal objects through a repression will thus keep intact the castration anxiety. Fetishism can become the solution to this anxiety: at its simplest, for the boy, a substitution for the missing penis is found and the mother's castration is disavowed. As a result castration as such is also disavowed. But this is a second and subsequent disavowal, for the thesis of castration of the mother arrived at by the child already disavowed the knowledge of anatomical difference between men and women, and substituted a penis which has been 'lost' by the mother for the knowledge that she has never had one.

Fetishism has come to be seen by psychoanalysis as 'paradigmatic of all perverse formations, i.e. it demonstrates in exemplary fashion the way in which the gap left by the disavowal or destruction of sexual truth is subsequently compensated'.[116] If this is the case, then voyeurism too must be founded on disavowal in so far as it is a perversion.

Voyeurism is a perversion for Freud when it supplants any aim of sexual intercourse, and this definition is broadly used by other writers. The concept is a standard entry in books on psychopathology and the following account is a useful summary of the classical view:

> The true voyeur is almost always a male whose behavior goes far beyond ordinary visual stimulation; his urge to look is stronger than his urge for sexual intercourse. He obtains a maximum of sexual excitement from clandestine observation of a female in a state of undress or in a sexual or excretory act.[117]

The voyeur may not necessarily experience orgasm; if he does this may be a spontaneous response or it may be the result of masturbation. Perverse voyeurism is clearly complex:

> Not only do voyeurs fear heterosexuality – contrary to popular superstition, they rarely attack women – but they seem to need constant reassurance that they are able to respond sexually. The excitement they experience in observing women convinces them that they are not asexual. In addition, many seem to identify with the women on whom they spy, so that a homosexual component is present. There is also an aggressive element in voyeurism which stems from its forbidden and stealthy character and from direct hostility toward the sexual object. Thus, a voyeur may get a special thrill out of social interaction with a woman whom he has previously spied on: he 'knows a secret' about her and therefore feels a hostile type of superiority.[118]

Voyeurism here may be operating to reassure the man of his own possession of a penis through the seeing again of the woman's lack,[119] but it also includes regressive sexuality in the concern with excretion (involving an overriding of disgust, which Freud also emphasised), and it involves fantasies of the primal scene, perhaps with anal intercourse as the model, as in childish theories of sexual relations. It also includes sadism (as well as masochism); sadism not only if at all as an action by the voyeur against the woman but rather the watching of sadistic acts undertaken by others. This suggests the scenario described by Freud in the 'A Child is Being Beaten' fantasy, but it also suggests a scenario of the mother's punishment imagined by the son, of her castration by the father which is both her punishment for turning to the father and also the cause for her turning to the father and thus, in each case, she is lost to the son's own desire.

That the scene may have a different function for the perverse voyeur is suggested by the account given by Joyce McDougall of a patient's fantasy of twenty years which she describes as 'a classical fetishist script', in which an older woman publicly whips her daughter. The patient enacted this scenario with his wife whom he asked to dress in ritualised clothing which hid her genitals but revealed her buttocks; he would then whip her on the buttocks and the sight of the marks would bring him to a sexual climax. He would also replay this scene on his own, donning the clothing and whipping himself, then watch anxiously for the whip marks. The patient claimed to be merely a spectator but McDougall argues that in fact he took the role of alternatively mother or daughter.[120] McDougall suggests that the whip represents the fictitious penis, the mother's penis, and the buttocks replace the female genitals. The whip marks are looked-for as the – further – proof of the reality of the penis.[121] McDougall sees the fantasy as involving fetishistic disavowal, but her case is very similar to an example, cited as voyeuristic sadism, of a city banker in London in 1792 who was said to have paid the headmistresses at two girls' schools to allow him to peep in from another room while the children received their accumulated punishments, as 'one after another each girl was brought in, bared behind and chastised with the rod'.[122]

But what is the disavowal of the voyeur? For surely the voyeur keeps wanting to know it all, the mother's castration that is, over and over again.[123] If, however, the castration of the mother is understood as a constructed fantasy it is also thereby already a disavowal. The mother *did have* a penis, but no longer has one. A displacement and substitution has occurred, thus Lacan says of the voyeur, 'What he is trying to see, make no mistake, is the object as absence.'[124] The disavowal of the voyeur is the same as that of the fetishist, namely the disavowal of the difference of sex, the voyeur reaffirming that she *is* castrated and not simply *different*.[125] 'What he is looking for', Lacan reiterates, 'is not, as one says, the phallus – but precisely its absence.'[126]

The disavowal is motivated by a wish, the wish for the mother. The reality involved is the anatomical distinction between men and women which signifies at the same time the structure of desire which is also that of the parents' desire. The recognition of the anatomical distinction is also then the recognition of the parental sexual relation and which precedes the child's desire, indeed which has engendered the child itself, much to its chagrin. As a result the child's desire for its mother (and equally for its father) is effectively disqualified, it is shown to be outlandish, and ultimately outlawed. A threat of castration by the father as such is not required then, but arises insofar as the theory of castration is constructed by the child, this functioning as a disavowal of anatomical difference. The fantasy of the mother's castration then punishes her for her desire for the father, while it recognises the complementarity of the father's penis and the mother's lack of a penis and her possession of a vagina but disavows this by seeing the latter as the effect of castration. And of course, as will be considered further in the following chapter, the little girl, too, may disavow the mother's castration and for the same reasons as outlined for the boy.

My argument here has put disavowal at the heart of the construction of sexual difference for the subject, and not as a marginal possibility depending on the severity of the boy's castration anxiety. This seems to me to be justified, moreover, by the importance Freud himself came to give the process of disavowal, namely as a process which produces a split in the subject's ego, for what Freud emphasises in his discussion in 'Fetishism' is that disavowal involves not a denial or negation but a process of knowing and not knowing at the same time. By tracing the development of Freud's thinking in relation to the concept of disavowal I hope to show the relation of disavowal to fantasy as another and related form of handling of disagreeable reality. As a result I will argue that it is necessary to distinguish – following Joyce McDougall's arguments – between the processes of disavowal which are fixed and routinised and those which involve a continuous and energetic remaking of disavowal, of fetishising, in new ways and forms. The process of equivalence and substitution of one knowledge for another, and one object for another, is also central to representation. It is in this way that the fetishism of representation will be reconsidered in the penultimate chapter in this book, but first I will try to place this process of substitution within fetishism, and the concept of disavowal which Freud develops in his last writings, in relation to Lacan's notion of the *objet petit a*.

DISAVOWAL, FANTASY AND THE *OBJET PETIT A*

In 'Fetishism' Freud says that the boy does not simply disavow the reality of the mother's lack of a penis, for in addition 'a very energetic action has been undertaken to maintain the disavowal'.[127] This is the fetish substitute, and it not only secures the disavowal by its 'alteration' of reality, but is also a memorial to the disavowed knowledge. The fetishist should now be secure from the unwelcome piece of reality – the fantasied castration of the mother, and behind this the knowledge of the mother's desire for the father. However, Freud points to a more complex outcome whereby the disavowal and fetish substitute are accompanied by an avowal of castration and the two knowledges are held side by side but without the one displacing the other:

> This was so in the case of a man whose fetish was an athletic support-belt which could also be worn as bathing drawers. This piece of clothing covered up the genitals entirely and concealed the distinction between them.[128]

Analysis had shown that the fetish signified that women were castrated and that they were not castrated, and also allowed the idea that men were castrated, too, since all these possibilities could equally well be concealed under the belt.

Freud also suggests that this mechanism of avowal/disavowal is found outside fetishism, and refers to two young male patients, each of whom had failed to take cognisance of his father's death, and had erased it, though neither became psychotic.[129] But, Freud notes, just as with the fetishist, neither of his two patients had simply erased this knowledge wholly, but only in relation to certain areas of thinking and activity, while in other areas it was clearly acknowledged – one patient for example complained that his father was still alive and hindering his activities, while he also acted as entitled to regard himself as his father's successor.

As a result Freud sees disavowal not as a simple refusal of reality but rather as involving two different mental attitudes, one which takes account of reality and another which does not, and he says that what is involved here is a splitting of the ego. There then arises the construction of a substitute for reality, without displacing the knowledge of the reality. This is a splitting within the ego and hence subsequent to but nor unrelated – in Lacan's view – to the form of splitting which arises with the emergence of the agencies of id, ego and superego as a result of identification.[130] It is also distinct from the other major form of defence, namely repression, where the unacceptable idea is rejected from consciousness and becomes the material of the unconscious but which also remains capable of returning in some displaced and re-cathected form. This new conceptualisation is developed in two later papers, 'Splitting of the Ego in the Process of Defence' and *An Outline of Psycho-Analysis,* in which Freud is seeking to distinguish and understand the processes of psychosis and neurosis. Fetishism is again the example, but Freud now argues that the splitting in the ego arises not with the creation of the fetish substitute, which Freud describes as 'a compromise formed with the help of displacement, such as we have been familiar with in dreams',[131] but rather it arises in certain special cases of fetishism – which may also be the most common – in which psychoanalysis has 'come across fetishists who have developed the same fear of castration as non-fetishists and react in the same way to it. Their behaviour is therefore simultaneously expressing two contrary premisses.'[132] Freud argues that the fetish-substitute signifies the belief in the female penis, while fear of castration is an acknowledgment that women have no penis. In another example in 'The Splitting of the Ego in Defence', Freud describes how, simultaneous with the creation of his fetish, the child no longer showed any anxiety in relation to his masturbation, but instead 'he developed an intense fear of his father punishing him'[133] which took the form of a fear of being eaten by him, an oral regression, which replaced the fear of castration. Thus 'The two contrary reactions to the conflict persist as the centre-point of a splitting of the ego.'[134]

It is this structure which Freud now says may be properly seen as involving the splitting of the ego, and from this he argues it is possible

to understand how it is that fetishism is so often only partially developed. It does not govern the choice of object exclusively but leaves room for a greater or lesser amount of normal sexual behaviour; sometimes, indeed, it retires into playing a modest part or is limited to a mere hint. In fetishists, therefore, the detachment of the ego from the reality of the external world has never succeeded completely.[135]

Freud goes on to point out that this splitting of the ego through disavowal occurs as well outside of fetishism as such:

Disavowals of this kind [of the perceptions which bring to knowledge an unpleasant or unacceptable demand from reality] occur very often and not only with fetishists; and whenever we are in a position to study them they turn out to be half-measures, incomplete attempts at detachment from reality. The disavowal is always supplemented by an acknowledgement...[136]

This is the structure which Octave Mannoni has described in his formulation 'I know very well but all the same'.[137]

The relation to reality and the mechanism of splitting in the ego are also at issue in Freud's discussion of fantasy, as well as in his distinction between psychosis and neurosis. Freud had described the relation of fantasying to reality as a process of splitting in 'Formulations on the Two Principles of Mental Functioning':

> With the introduction of the reality principle one species of thought-activity was split off; it was kept free from reality-testing and remained subordinated to the pleasure principle alone. This activity is *phantasying*, which begins already in children's play, and later, continued as day-dreaming, abandons dependence on real objects.[138]

In 'The Loss of Reality in Neurosis and Psychosis' Freud is also concerned with a division between an external world and its demands and an internal world constructed by the subject but here he draws upon the concept of disavowal to distinguish psychosis from neurosis. Freud argues that both neurosis and psychosis are a rebellion on the part of the id against the external world and are the result of its unwillingness or perhaps incapacity to adapt itself to the exigencies of reality. However, in psychosis, the reality is re-modelled, whereas in neurosis there is an avoidance or flight from the reality. As a result of such flight the neurotic's relation to reality, or a specific portion of it, may be severely damaged, however the structure of this deformed relation to reality is nevertheless different from that found in psychosis. Freud sees disavowal as the process which distinguishes psychosis from neurosis, for he says,

> neurosis does not disavow the reality, it only ignores it; psychosis disavows it and tries to replace it. We call behaviour 'normal' or 'healthy', if it combines certain features of both reactions – if it disavows the reality as little as does a neurosis, but if it then exerts itself as does a psychosis, to effect an alteration of

that reality. Of course, this expedient, normal, behaviour leads to work being carried out on the external world; it does not stop, as in psychosis, at effecting internal changes. It is no longer *autoplastic* but *alloplastic*.[139]

Freud modifies this view in his discussion in 'Fetishism', however, for he now sees disavowal as involving both a repudiation and an acknowledgement of the refused reality, so that, as noted earlier, two knowledges are held side by side. Disavowal in this sense now characterises neurosis (one of the young men who had disavowed his father's death developed 'a moderately severe obsessional neurosis'),[140] while in psychosis only the knowledge which suited the internal reality would be present, while the knowledge which fitted in with external reality would be absent. Bearing this is mind, Freud's brief discussion in 'The Loss of Reality in Neurosis and Psychosis' nevertheless suggests an important interrelation between fantasy and disavowal. The example Freud gives there, however, relates not to a piece of reality in the first instance, but to a wish. The case is of a young woman patient:

> Standing beside her sister's death-bed, she was horrified at having the thought: 'Now he [her sister's husband] is free and can marry me.' This scene was instantly forgotten, and thus the process of regression, which led to her hysterical pains, was set in motion.[141]

Freud argues that whereas the neurotic patient represses the desire and its wish, so that in this example the implications of her sister's death, that her brother-in-law is free to marry her, are not allowed into consciousness, in contrast the 'psychotic reaction would have been a disavowal of the fact of her sister's death'.[142] The disagreeable reality in both cases, however, is not the sister's death; rather it is this reality penetrated and formed by the patient's wishes in relation to her sister's husband, the reality of a forbidden or transgressive wish.[143] Because the fulfilment of the wish is predicated on another event – the sister's death, and which is not itself desired – the neurotic, Freud says, represses the wish, and instead acquires a hysterical symptom, while the psychotic, rather than giving up the wish, would deny the reality of the sister's death, i.e. deny the event which is what would enable the fulfilment of the wish. Freud's example here is therefore extremely complex.

Moreover the neurotic, too, will attempt to replace a disagreeable reality with one which is more in keeping with his or her wishes, and this Freud argues is made possible by the existence of the world of fantasy, that domain which became separated from the real external world at the time of the introduction of the reality principle. Freud now describes it as a kind of reservation, accessible to the ego but only loosely attached to it:

> It is from this world of phantasy that the neurosis draws the material for its new wishful constructions, and it usually finds that material along the path of regression to a more satisfying real past.[144]

Fantasy appears here as a process quite distinct from the repudiation arising in psychosis. However, the demands for rigour and logical consistency in Freud's work are implacable; thus he goes on to say:

> It can hardly be doubted that the world of phantasy plays the same part in psychosis and that there, too, it is the store-house from which the materials or the pattern for building the new reality are derived. But whereas the new, imaginary external world of a psychosis attempts to put itself in the place of external reality, that of a neurosis, on the contrary, is apt, like the play of children, to attach itself to a piece of reality – a different piece from the one against which it has to defend itself – and to lend that piece a special importance and a secret meaning which we (not always quite appropriately) call a *symbolic* one. Thus we see that both in neurosis and psychosis there comes into consideration the question not only of a *loss of reality* but also of a *substitute for reality*.[145]

This is also the process involved in disavowal, for it is this construction of a 'substitute for reality' in the fetishist's disavowal which produces elsewhere – as the shine on a nose – the missing mother's penis, and which is central to the splitting of the ego. Fantasy thus involves a similar relation to reality as disavowal, for it involves two knowledges – one of reality and one fantasy – and the production of a re-making of reality, as well as a process of substitution. In this case forms of representation, as forms of fantasy, are also clearly forms of disavowal, and we may expect to find their attendant fetish substitutions. Nevertheless disavowal cannot be subsumed to what we know of fantasy; rather it designates a particular process within fantasy, a way of acting with fantasy.

Disavowal, however, is clearly now no longer a singular form. Freud's discussion of fetishism in *An Outline of Psycho-Analysis* poses *two* forms of fetishism, one in which castration anxiety persists and another in which it does not. The former is characteristic of neurosis – for Freud has abandoned his assumption that where perversion has appeared, neurosis is avoided, while the latter is perverse fetishism. As a result Joyce McDougall suggests that perversion can be seen as a third form lying between neurosis and psychosis but without this implying that it is a bit of both, or that it may fall one side or the other. It is a distinct structure in so far as it is precisely neither neurosis or psychosis. It lies between on the one hand a magic denial 'I saw a penis there', which can only be dealt with by the creation of a new reality to fill the gap followed by some manipulation of the outer world, and on the other hand an acknowledgement with a corresponding refuge in fantasy ' there is no penis but...' in which reality is taken account of but the subject 'autoplastically creates imaginative, internal fantasy ways of dealing with the painful knowledge'.[146] In this 'third way' the subject not only disavows but must also obliterate the knowledge causing the disavowal, bringing about a quite different kind of mental activity in order to sustain the fiction of the mother's penis, and hence exclude the father from a position in relation to the mother's desire.

> In his attempt to know nothing of the relation between the parents, in his attempt, that is, to maintain a fictional introjected primal scene, the pervert is facing a losing battle with reality. Like trying to repair a crumbling wall with scotch tape – it has to be done every day. In this perspective his sexual act is a form of continuous acting out of a compulsive kind. For the pervert has created a sexual mythology whose true meaning he no longer recognises, like a text from which important pieces have been removed. (As we shall see these missing pieces are not repressed for this would have given rise to neurotic symptoms; instead they are destroyed, rather in the style of someone cutting the telephone wires when the news is bad.) Thus many perverse patients complain of not understanding human sexuality.[147]

McDougall argues that this does not imply psychosis, for what has been denied or disavowed has not been recovered in the form of delusions, but is retrieved through a form of illusion contained within an act. The endless repetition of the fiction in an acting out helps to avoid the danger of a slide into delusion, but it also indicates an inability to 'create an inner fantasy world to deal with intolerable reality'.[148] Laplanche, too, has distinguished between 'being able to enter the fantasy from the many entrances that are possible, which is after all the flexibility of fantasy, and the disavowal of splitting where maybe two entrances are privileged but are completely distinct from each other'.[149] What characterises perversion then is that not all the entrances of the mise en scène of fantasy are available to the subject.[150]

In this case, the perverse structure does not derive simply from 'deviant' sexual behaviour, it is a distinct psychical organisation of desire marked by the rigidity and limited scope of its scenarios. Sexual relations may be imagined only from one limited perspective which the individual feels immediately impelled to act out in reality; he or she has little erotic freedom, whether in act or in fantasy.[151] By contrast, so-called deviant sexuality, which is usually defined by the nature of the act alone, may be found as easily in neurotics and psychotics, while the same act may have different meaning in different contexts for different people. (In this sense homosexuality and lesbianism are not necessarily perversions; rather one might need to speak of the pervert who may be heterosexual, lesbian or homosexual.)

McDougall's notion of perversion as a third way clearly distinguishes it from perverse fantasy which, as she observes, might be considered to be the prerogative of the neurotic.[152] In this case there is no simple continuum of fetishism and voyeurism as defences against castration anxiety for two forms of fetishism have now been recognised, one where anxiety remains and the other where it is replaced by a compulsive sexuality, but in each disavowal rather than foreclosure is involved.[153] The problem of sexual difference and the mother's desire is present as much for the girl as for the boy, and she too may take the path of perversion. As perversions, therefore, voyeurism and fetishism are not paradigms of male sexuality.

In representations, in cinema, it is primarily as fantasy that we encounter the perversions. The cinema presents scenarios of desire, narrative structures of delay and fulfilment both repetitive and endlessly varied. But more, what is central to cinema is the

multiplicity of views set up within a film, and the multiple positions of identification – camera, character, different characters, authorial enunciation. The masochist or sadist, too, may reverse roles,
but will never pluralise them; there is no room, for example, for the
place of the father, for any third term which would disturb the
closed structure of the dyadic exchange. The disavowal, 'I know
but...', functions in cinema not merely in the spectator's disavowal
that the film is only an illusion, but which all the same he or she
will take as reality, but also and more importantly disavowal functions within the representation as part of the fantasy structure, acknowledging and disavowing its very status as fantasy; for
example a certain knowledge of the rules of real life may be disavowed and a more acceptable reality substituted by a fantasy
structure. Nevertheless the fantasy will retain the trace of its disavowal and hence will include the alternative and opposed knowledge, with all its attendant anxiety.

Hitchcock's *Vertigo*, a film frequently described as perverse in its
central theme of the hero, Scottie, re-making the image of his lost
love 'Madeleine' in Judy, and which Hitchcock himself called
necrophiliac in its sexual obsession with a dead woman,[154] nevertheless presents multiple positions of view, and hence of knowledge and of identification. Scottie's subjective look at 'Madeleine' is
itself figured for the spectator as we watch him watching her, and
even subverted as when, in the scene of his first glimpse of
Madeleine in a restaurant, the camera cuts from a shot of
Madeleine to what we expect will be a reverse angle of Scottie
looking but which proves to be a mirror image showing both
Scottie looking and also Madeleine being looked at by Scottie. Later
when Hitchcock reveals the plot to the audience – in the scene
where Judy, struggling between her love for Scottie and her conscience, writes a letter revealing her impersonation of Madeleine in
order to portray as suicide the murder of the real Madeleine by her
husband, only to tear up the letter – we are suddenly brought to a
new point-of-view in the film. This device wholly transforms the
narrative drive, first, as Hitchcock describes:

> Though Stewart isn't aware of it yet, the viewers already know
> that Judy isn't just a girl who looks like Madeleine, but that she *is*
> Madeleine! Everyone around me was against this change; they
> all felt that the revelation should be saved for the end of the
> picture. I put myself in the place of a child whose mother is

telling him a story. When there's a pause in her narration, the child always says, 'What comes next, Mommy?' Well, I felt that the second part of the novel was written as if nothing came next, whereas in my formula, the little boy, *knowing* that Madeleine and Judy are the same person, would then ask, 'And Stewart doesn't know it, does he? What will he do when he finds out about it?[155]

Second, it introduces the wish – through Judy's words – that Scottie might achieve his desire, might find his lost love Madeleine, whom – as Judy – we know truly loves him, and thus also introduces Judy's desire. The sadism apparent in Scottie's efforts to make over Judy into Madeleine is sharpened by Judy's anguished plea that he love her for what she is and not for what he wishes her to be. But this wish is impossible because Judy *is* Madeleine, a Madeleine who only existed as a deception upon Scottie. Scottie has lost Madeleine now more surely than at her death, for she is here revealed as an illusion. His subsequent discovery of Judy's duplicity imposes on Scottie the acceptance of the loss of his idealised love, Madeleine, and in the same moment returns to him his potency, his masculinity, whose loss was represented in his vertigo and which enabled the murderous deception to be successful – for the conspirators knew that Scottie could not climb the stairs of the tower from which 'Madeleine' – the murdered wife's body – would fall. He now drags Judy back up the stairs of that same tower and from which she too falls. Scottie's cure, his resumption of a whole identity, thus brings about another woman's death. The cost of Scottie's recovery is Judy's life; within the film's diegetic structure this knowledge is disavowed – Judy's death was only an accident poignantly depriving Scottie of his love just when he had finally recognised it – but it is avowed by the narrative structure which has required the woman's death, for the film's logic narrates that the object of desire remain an impossible object.

Freud's text *An Outline of Psycho-Analysis* is one of his last works, and, while complete in the arguments it presents, it is unfinished – not merely in the sense that Freud was interrupted in his work on this paper and was never able to return to it, but more, in the sense that it suggests developments in Freud's thinking in relation to certain concepts and mechanisms which open onto new directions, and it is these new directions which seem central for Lacan's re-reading of Freud, in particular for his concept of the ego and the role of splitting in his theory of the fundamental alienation of the subject. The following discussion will consider the relationship of Lacan's concept of the *objet petit a* to the psychical mechanisms arising in disavowal and exemplified in fetishism.

The *objet petit a* is Freud's object of the drive, but its additional designation 'little other' marks its function for the subject as representing the 'otherness' of the object, and thus causing desire. It is therefore distinct from the many object-choices the subject will subsequently have, the many objects of desire. This object was in the first instance the subject's own body, or a part of its body but which was split off from the subject as a result of the emergence of the drive as a demand for satisfaction, and which thus opens the subject to the field of fantasy, that is to the anticipation or imagining of a satisfaction which removes unpleasure. From this initial separation desire arises and returns to the subject as other, for the constitutive splitting of the subject also engenders a part which is lost and the drive emerges as the setting off on the long journey for the other. For Lacan this is the movement from need to demand from which desire emerges, as well as *jouissance*, that enjoyment or satisfaction – carnal and abstract – of the child *before* it is sundered by knowledge and introduced to lack in the field of the other. The enjoyment of *jouissance* exists – if such it does – outside of the symbolic, the order of law, and it remains unrepresentable, an element of the real. Lacan places it, therefore, on the side of repetition, of the death drive. In the same moment as the emergence of desire, the insufficiency, the lack, which engenders unpleasure is also inscribed for the subject, and the *objet petit a* is its monument.[156]

The *objet petit a* signifies the alterity of the other, its very otherness, but as a result at the same time it is the embodiment of the other. As the breast in the first instance, it is that which is separated from the subject but which can be imagined as returning to it; however, the 'returned-breast', which would make the subject whole again, completed, is the object of fantasy, the object of desire. The *objet petit a* is not this 'returned-breast' but the 'lost-breast'; it is not the object of desire, the breast itself and which has been lost, it is the object lost, that is, it is the breast insofar as it is missing, and hence it also represents the subject to itself in as much as the subject experiences itself as lacking. The *objet petit a* functions as cause of desire, not as an origin but as the supplement, as the figuring of a relation to the missing, and this is the primordial relation to subject and object. The *objet petit a*, however, does not form a dyadic relation with the subject, it does not complete the subject but always remains in the field of the other. Taking Freud's example of the game played by his small grandson (and through which Freud posited the role of repetition in the death drive) Lacan argues that the reel which the child throws away and pulls back is a 'small part of the subject that detaches itself from him while still remaining his, still retained'.[157] The reel is not the mother who comes and goes – now at the will of the child – but the child, or a part of it, which is here *and* over there as other, subject *and* object. This object is the *petit a*. The mastery of the mother's absence by making himself the agent of it, which Freud argued was the function of the game, is, Lacan says, of secondary importance, for what the child enacts is an internalisation of the mother's absence, an identification with her as absent. Hence the reel-game is not about making present, then absent, but about a making absent-to-be-present, or present-to-be-absent. When the reel is here it is only in order for it to be over there again. The reel is therefore an *objet petit a*, that is,

> something from which the subject, in order to constitute itself, has separated itself off as organ. This serves as a symbol of the lack, that is to say, of the phallus, not as such, but in so far as it is lacking. It must, therefore, be an object that is, firstly, separable and, secondly, that has some relation to the lack.[158]

The *objet petit a*, whether it is the breast, or the penis, or one in the long line of subsequent objects – the lock of hair, the glance, the mole just there above her shoulder blade – causes desire by signifying the object as separated, as now-absent, but able to be made present again. It is therefore a monument to that process of separation through which the lost object is constituted as missing. Desire is the organisation of the drive in relation to the object the lack of which is represented for the subject in the *objet petit a*, hence it is lack which causes desire, not the object as such. Desire emerges in relation to symbolisation in contrast to *jouissance* which consists in an unsymbolisable or unsymbolised enjoyment.

Freud's concept of the fetish does not at first sight seem to correlate with Lacan's account of the *objet petit a*, for the fetish stands in for the object lacking in the mother – it represents what has fallen away from the mother, her penis – while the *objet petit a* represents the lackingness of the object to the subject, and represents something fallen away from the subject itself.[159] But each is an attempt to deal with a piece of knowledge in which the other is shown as lacking in relation to the subject who is thereby also confronted as lacking, and this relationship to lack is invested in something outside the subject. Moreover both are most typically invested in the detritus of the body, the inconsequential and the discarded of the body. The *objet petit a* is a necessary condition for desire; it represents the relation to the missing object and thus sets off the desire for what will replace that object. It seems to function like a fetish, therefore, since it is the supplementary and separable but nevertheless necessary element for desire, and indeed Catherine Clément indicates as much when she writes of the *objet petit a*:

> Growing in the Hommelette desire takes root in a specific place: preferably in some minute detail, such as a slight infirmity, a winking eye, an out-of-place curl, a minor defect, a tiny feature, a leather whip, or an artificial penis – a fetish in short.[160]

Yet there is also a difference – Lacan continues to refer to fetishism as a specific and distinct psychical mechanism, and as a perversion involving a reversal of the drive and a splitting of the subject: 'It is the subject who determines himself as object, in his encounter with the division of subjectivity.'[161]

What we have here is then perhaps the same situation Freud referred to when he observed that there are in effect two forms of fetishism – where it appears together with castration anxiety, and where it has successfully displaced castration anxiety. The *objet petit a* is comparable to the fetish in the first form, insofar as it figures as a separable object, one of a series of substitutable elements which secure the loved object as loveable, which enable desire, but not because it adds in what is missing, the penis, but because in signifying absence it also signifies a possible making-present. It represents an avowal, a recognition of the knowledge of separation, but it does so in a movement which opens the subject to fantasy, to the imagining of the object which will disavow separation. The *objet petit a*, moreover, arises as a signifier of difference prior to sexual difference, although it is as its mother's *objet petit a* that the child first encounters itself as being for an other.[162]

It might seem as if the *objet petit a* is a first order of object, originally part of but then separated from the body, while the fetish is another object standing in for the one missing (on the mother's body), so that a substitution has occurred. This can only be the case, though, if there were a first order object, i.e. if there already was a unified entity from which the *objet petit a* became separated, or, with fetishism, if there really was a maternal penis. But in each case there isn't an object, except as already 'missing' or lacking. The first order object is an imagined object and the *objet petit a* is its stand-in by which in its role as substitute it affirms that the original object, the subject or the maternal penis, was really there. The *objet petit a* is two-faced: it signifies lacking but in doing so it makes something present, that is, the lost object in its absence – the *objet petit a* is a *monument* to lackingness, to a non-existence of the subject. Fetishism arises when the *objet petit a* is invested as signifier of presence-ness, of the continuing reality of the mother's penis, rather than its lostness.[163] In perversion the *objet petit a* is played as disavowal, the absent object is taken as condition of truth of its presence, and its lack is thereby disavowed. The fetish (and the symptom, which is what Lacan finally says A Woman is[164]) is addressed to an Other who can reply, a non-barred, consistent big Other. As a result, in perversion the circuit of the drive is closed; insofar as castration anxiety remains, however, what arises is a fetishising, a making-over of the *objet petit a* as fetish but which is sustained only for a moment. Such fetishising is characterised by a lack of fixity, a mobility and playfulness, in contrast to perverse fetishism.[165]

Desire, including sexual desire, is a process of avowal and disavowal involving the production of substitutions by which a part of reality is denied and re-modelled through that substitution as a normal process of dealing with reality. Fantasy, as the scenarioisation of desire, is the structure in which this process is played out; as a result it constitutes the frame through which we experience the world as consistent and meaningful. For Lacan, once the subject enters the realm of the signifier 'From then on, everything is played out for him on the level of fantasy', but it is also a fantasy 'which can perfectly well be taken apart so as to allow for the fact that he knows a great deal more than he thinks when he acts'.[166] As a result, fantasy always includes the Other as lacking, as a crossed-out, blocked and barred, non-whole element. Within the fantasy scenario, the *objet petit a* appears as a magical element which 'makes it so', and fixes it as 'true'. Here the *objet petit a* begins to appear like a fetish, playing out only one side of its structural role for the subject, in its making something present. This fetish-in-fantasy then sustains a fantasy as 'the fantasy' so that it become the subject's 'lived reality'. But not quite, something is left out, and this bears on the subject as the 'real'; unsymbolisable, the real is experienced as an internal limit on or interruption of enjoyment, it is the internal excitation Freud posited, but from which the subject cannot flee and the drive emerges as the movement to attain satisfaction in relation to this excitation, but which always fails. It is the *objet petit a* which constitutes this point of the real intruding in the subject, for it signifies lack in the subject – and in the signifier. At one and the same time it is the bridge or access to reality, the element which breaks open the subject to social reality, while it also carries a little bit of the real into symbolisation, so that it too is unrepresentable, a remainder – and reminder – which bears upon the subject as a left-over of every signifying operation.

Though fetish-like, the *objet petit a* is not a fetish. While objects and people (including women) can be *objets petit a*, they are so only in as much as they come to figure the object as lacking. The fetish is supplementary, not a residue; it supplants representation by over-turning the play of absence/presence in favour of one only of those terms, presence. Through the fetish the subject disavows lacking-ness; thus while both the fetish and the *objet petit a* stand in for another object, the fetish does so in order to disavow the lack, whereas the *objet petit a* signifies lackingness. The *objet petit a*, then, is not a replacement based on analogy or a displacement for some-thing which never was (or is), but is the figuring of a relation to the missing, and this as the primordial relation of subject and object.

Fetishism must now be understood in rather different ways according to whether it is part of a 'middle way' between psychosis or neurosis (the route now termed 'perverse') and hence radically refuses lack while signifying it in the fetish object which is identified with, or as *objet petit a*, as the magical 'thing' which causes desire but also signifies the subject as lacking. In a rather back-to-front form of argument, therefore, women can return to the scene as subjects, and not only objects, of disavowal, for certainly we women too, have our *objets petit a*, though they may not be the same as men's.[167] As a result, something of disavowal is involved in general in representation – including the cinema – and it operates for both women and men. But this is not quite or rather not only fetishism. And while men and women may equally fetishise, this is not the only point, for a difference and asymmetry in relation to the fear of castration remains. However the argument presented in this chapter suggests that this asymmetry is not quite as we have always assumed. For, if castration is not a fact but a theory constructed to discount a sexual difference which gives privilege to the parental sexual relation, it is the latter which is central for the child psychically – girl and boy – and in relation to which having or not having a penis must be accepted. That this is no easy matter has nothing to do with the value of penises, and everything to do with rebelling against what is also involved in accepting anatomical sexual difference, one's exclusion from the mother, or the Other, and the limiting of one's desire. Castration is thus a theory constructed as well by the little girl as the little boy, and for the same reason although with quite different consequences. These issues are the concern of the following chapter.

6

Female Sexuality, Feminine Identification and the Masquerade

THE FREUDIAN ACCOUNT

What, then, is the girl's relation to castration and the Oedipus complex and how far does this make of her a woman, that is, feminine? For Freud it is castration which impels the girl into the Oedipal complex, whereas for the boy it is what impels him, more or less, out of the Oedipal complex. In each case what is involved is not a real event – though Freud often writes as if it were – but a perception which is both an acknowledgement and an interpretation of the anatomical distinction between the sexes. For the girl, unlike the boy, it involves a simple cognition; she 'makes her judgement and her decision in a flash. She has seen it [the boy's penis] and knows that she is without it and wants to have it.'[1] Freud says that the girl will initially see her deficiency or castration as only applying to herself. Later she will understand that it applies to all girls and women and as a result 'it follows that femaleness – and with it, of course, her mother – suffers a great depreciation in her eyes'.[2] Freud does not enquire into what impels the girl to interpret or accept this cognitive event as castration, but does suggest that she may disavow it, that 'a girl may refuse to accept the fact of being castrated, may harden herself in the conviction that she *does* possess a penis', although he sees this as a disavowal of her own 'castration', not, as the boy may do, of the mother's castration.[3] It is this failure to account for the movement of desire in the girl, as he does for the boy, which seems to me to be at the centre of the problem of Freud's account of female sexuality. Freud's later acknowledgement of the importance of the girl's pre-Oedipal attachment to her mother only exacerbates this problem of what brings the girl, at the level of the drive, to give up her mother.[4]

222

Freud argues that there is no originary biological femininity and it is this which has been a central focus of interest to feminists. He insisted that the infantile sexuality of the boy and girl is the same; his problem was then to show how the paths of the boy and girl diverge, how asymmetry arises from an initially symmetrical position. Both boy and girl are attached to the mother, both suffer the slights and disappointments in love, the jealousy of a sibling, the seduction followed by prohibition of the mother. What is required, Freud says, is 'something that is specific for girls and is not present or not in the same way present in boys'.[5] Of course, there is something specific, but on the body of the boy, and Freud justifies this by arguing, 'After all, the anatomical distinction [between the sexes] must express itself in psychical consequences.'[6] Freud assumes that the little girl makes what amounts to an intellectual decision – she makes her observation, evaluates her data, its import and significance, and comes to her conclusion:

> Her self-love is mortified by the comparison with the boy's far superior equipment and in consequence she renounces her masturbatory satisfaction from her clitoris, repudiates her love for her mother and at the same time not infrequently represses a good part of her sexual trends in general.[7]

Thus the girl feels inadequate for lack of a penis and blames her mother. There is a certain convenience in this argument for Freud, since it neatly motivates as well the girl's turning to her father and hence the emergence of heterosexuality, which Freud always assumed to be the normal goal of the human organism. But this is a bodged account. Freud does not explain why the penis is seen as superior except through social value, a socially perceived greater power of the penis, and its superior facilities as a 'widdler' – in fact invoking our little girl as a scientist, indeed a social scientist. Nor does he indicate why the girl should understand her inferior powers of micturation as a lack and as a castration.[8] And the child's similar envy and distress at the arrival of a sibling, another 'disappointment' in the mother, is located quite differently by Freud, as an anger with the mother in relation to the specific loss of the mother's love, for this envy is also experienced by the boy.[9]

The problem of castration for the little girl, however, just as much as for the boy, is not her own lack but her mother's. The mother too is the girl's first love-object, and the girl enters castration, like the boy, through the realisation that the cause of her mother's desire is elsewhere – in the phallus which her father has. The castration complex is entered by both boy and girl not when the anatomical distinction is recognised, but when this lack in women is connected to the mother's desire, and as a result, to a lack in being in the child who now knows – boy or girl – that it can never be its mother's desire.[10] What is involved is not a simple knowledge of the body, or even of the mother's body, but a knowledge of her desire. The narcissistic wounding to the girl is not the effect of the knowledge of anatomical difference but of the meaning of that difference, that the girl – just as much as the boy – is forever excluded as being sufficient to the mother's desire.

A corollary of this may be that we can hardly call the phallic mother a woman, and if this is the case the problem of the girl's change of object from her mother to her father, i.e. from someone of the same sex to someone of the opposite sex, can be resolved. For it is only now that the mother is a woman, only now that sexual difference is properly in place for the child insofar as he or she is fully inaugurated into the human structure of desire. Moreover the boy, too, changes his love-object – with equally great difficulty – from his (phallic) mother to a woman. Anatomy as such is not a sufficient condition for desire.

As a result the castration complex for both the girl and the boy involves a reorganisation of their relation to the mother. At the same time psychoanalysis suggests two other developments are occurring. Firstly, there is the organisation of desire in relation to the genitals as the place where the child seeks to be pleasured. But the child meets a prohibition: its parents refuse to pleasure it in this way – masturbation by the child in modern families may be tolerated but the wish to be masturbated by a parent is not – and refuse to allow the child to demand it.[11] Second, there is the attempt by the child to separate itself from its parents, from its mother's control, with the child trying to control the mother instead; each child seeks to *have* what the mother wants, and no longer 'be' it – to have the phallus. From this he or she is impelled into castration.[12]

At first the girl experiences this as a frustration which she can resolve by turning to her father to acquire the penis, and thereby have what the mother wants, that is, *to have it for her mother*. The turning to the father by the little girl is therefore motivated by the girl's desire in relation to her mother, who continues to be an object of desire. For, as Freud argued, the earliest wishes are never given up; however this is exactly what he seems to assume to be the case for the girl, when he says that she abandons the mother as a result of her disappointment at discovering castration.[13] In contrast, I am suggesting that the girl continues to seek the imaginary plenitude of sufficiency for the mother, just as the boy disavows his mother's lack of a penis so that he remains sufficient to the mother's desire. But to acquire her father's penis will involve the girl in a mutilation of her father – she castrates him. The idea of the body in parts, of incorporation and fantasies of devouring, are widely documented in analytic case studies, and Freud's own metaphor of faeces–penis–baby implies such transformations and equivalences at the level of fantasy in relation to the penis.[14] This wish, and solution, is also pointed to in the version of the primal scene fantasy which figures the mother's incorporation of the father's penis. Two stages are involved here for the girl: firstly a wish for a penis in relation to the phallic mother, thus denying the role of the father's penis; secondly, a wish for a penis in relation to the 'castrated' mother in order to repair the mother, or to replace the father. However, turning to her father to have from him what will repair the mother will make the girl a rival with her mother for the father. The mother therefore stands in her way in relation to this wish for the father's penis, just as the father does for the boy, so that the girl must defer this wish into the future, as well as substituting other men for her father. She also puts herself at risk of retribution from both parents in retaliation for her aggression.

The acceptance of the phallic mother's lack and with this acceptance of the loss of the mother as a love-object to whom she can put her demand for exclusive love, is not easily achieved and can lead to several different outcomes for the little girl, all of which must therefore be understood as 'femininity'. For Freud the consequence of the little girl discovering the reality of her mother's, and her own, 'castration' may lead her along one of three pathways. The first will lead her to abandon sexuality altogether, in the flood of repression to which she is now subjected as a result of her recognition of her inferiority. But, as shown in the chapter on the drive, Freud posits repression here not as the repression of a wish but as arising as the result of a wish, the wish for a penis like the boy's. If sexuality is abandoned it would seem to be as a result of this wish itself, and thus related to the second pathway. This second pathway corresponds to the masculinity complex or penis envy which Catherine Millot says 'consists in her non-renunciation of the possession of the phallic organ, either in the form of a persistent expectation of it or in the form of a disavowal of her deprivation of it'.[15] The third pathway is the one that, for Freud, leads to proper femininity in 'orienting the girl toward the man from whom she will receive, in the form of a child, the symbolic substitute for the penis she lacks'.[16] These three pathways are not such straightforward alternatives as Millot suggests. The third pathway is in fact simply a variation of the second as well, but in which the wish for a penis has undergone a process of substitution from a wish for a penis from the father to a wish for a baby from the father, to finally, a wish for a baby from another man, although how this process of symbolic substitution is set in play for the girl is not explained in relation to any psychical mechanism, but rather the prior pre-Oedipal equivalence 'faeces/penis/baby' made by both boys and girls seems to be the model for this. As Rachel Bowlby has put it, 'If it seemed at first that there were three roads, of which only one led to the "final" destination of femininity, it now seems that all roads lead to the same destination, or rather the same non-destination, the same repudiation.'[17] The 'masculine' path, the repudiation of femininity – which ought to be the furthest from normal femininity – has come to characterise all three, including that of femininity itself.

Freud refers to the wish for a penis as being 'entirely unfeminine' but which, when transformed into a wish for a baby, becomes true femininity. Freud saw the implications of this view and, contradicting to some extent his earlier claim, he later stated that 'perhaps we ought rather to recognise this wish for a penis as being *par excellence* a feminine one'.[18] Femininity is now defined not by castration as such but by the wish to undo castration in the wish for a penis. Freud, as noted earlier, describes as 'disavowal' that process, following on from penis-envy, in which 'a girl may refuse to accept the fact of being castrated, may harden herself in the conviction that she *does* possess a penis, and may subsequently be compelled to behave as though she were a man'.[19] The woman's disavowal here is not correlated with fetishism, however, but with a remodelling of reality, thus the woman must 'be' a man.

For the woman, however, having a penis may have nothing to do with being a man; rather she is a woman with a penis. The wish for a penis is not simply a wish to be a boy. The wide variety of fantasies of possession of a penis, which often take the form of a fantasy of incorporation of the penis inside the girl, show this clearly. Otto Fenichel cites a patient of his who fantasised that she was 'wholly transformed into her father's penis and shared in his masculinity', and another who experienced her lover's penis as part of her own body (when her lover was unfaithful her thought was 'How could he. He cannot possibly do it without me').[20] In fact, just like Freud's neurotic fetishist, a woman may both avow and disavow, and will produce her own fetishes, her own monuments to that disavowal.[21] Nor does the basis of this fetishism lie in her bisexuality – for this would imply that it is in her masculinity that the woman fetishises.[22] Instead a certain fetishism and disavowal are characteristic of positions of sexual difference.

For Freud, what he terms penis-envy and the masculinity complex in the girl parallel the castration complex for the boy, yet it is not – as Freud suggests – an attempt by the girl to hang on to her masculinity, or to adopt a masculinity, but rather it is an attempt to evade the meaning of lack in the mother and, finally, in the father too. To evade the terms of a sexual difference is to appear within only one term – masculine. The term 'penis-envy' no doubt gets to the heart of the matter but for all that it also misses the point. What is at stake is a wish – to have what makes one sufficient for the other. The penis comes to be the signifier of that 'sufficiency', as that which the mother desires in the other, the father. 'Envy' then arises for both boy and girl because their desire arises in a triangular relation, and the penis is always playing a *figural* role. Penis-envy at its mundanest is probably more apparent in men, in the anxiety which continues as to whether theirs is good enough, big enough. Or, like the blonde curls of a sister, the penis is envied as a *cultural* marker of something in the other which makes them sufficient to the mother, or father. But if for women there is disavowal, then envy will not arise. What is involved for the girl in the castration complex, just as for the boy, is the lack in the other.

The positions of desire of the parents may present additional vicissitudes for the child here, and therefore penis-envy, like the castration complex for the boy, is the bedrock of neurosis in women. The masculinity complex, as the non-renunciation of possession of the phallic organ, is a *disavowal of castration* and, just as for the boy, it takes a double form.[23] The mother's lack is disavowed and instead she is perceived as 'castrated', as having lost the phallus, in the fantasy that the penis was once there but has been taken away.[24] And, as for the boy, the stake of the disavowal is not the lack in the mother but the lack in the subject this engenders in the child as a result of the realisation that the mother's desire lies elsewhere and forever excludes the child, girl or boy. The second disavowal arises in the girl's continuing expectation that she will acquire a penis, or that she indeed has one, for if the mother can 'lose' hers, the daughter may acquire one – that is, the disavowal or fantasy assumes a 'penis' which is separable and mobile, perhaps the mother's 'lost' phallus.[25] This may become the 'perverse fetishism' already seen in the boy, a radical refusal of knowledge in reality, leading to a revulsion and denial of the role of the vagina, much like the male perverse fetishist's horror, and a refusal of the role of the father's penis.[26] But the 'penis-envy' of the perverse woman, Joyce McDougall argues, does not involve the father's penis, which she argues has been divested of phallic significance, but rather is addressed to certain women who are magically endowed, namely with the maternal phallus.[27] The fetish is addressed, therefore, to an Other who can reply, a non-barred, consistent big Other. Alternatively, and more prosaically, the girl, like the boy, continues to be subject to castration anxiety, to avow as well as disavow, giving rise to a certain fetishism when the *objet petit a* is invested as signifier of presenceness – of the continuing reality of the mother's penis, rather than its lost-ness – but which is then invaded and displaced by the avowal of lack. There is a *fetishising*.

Turning to the father is not, then, the first step on the road to femininity for the girl – in the sense of accepting her lack – but another means to disavowing the mother's and therefore her own lack by getting a penis from the father, and hence also displacing the father since he will no longer have what the mother wants. But, meeting with the father's refusal, or for fear of his retribution for her castration threat, Millot says that the girl renounces her demand 'and thereby identifies with that Other that has refused her satisfaction, and especially with the insignia of his power, thereby constituting a paternal, masculine, ego ideal'.[28] This, she says – citing Lacan – presents a completed Oedipus complex, but with a resolution that is atypical and neuroticising.[29] However the identification Millot refers to is not so simple. For Millot it is based on the introjection of the lost love-object, but if it arises as a result of the girl's rejection by the father and if she acquires the attributes of her father – his penis – it is on the basis Freud described in a case of homosexuality in a young man, that is, as support for the identification and not the cause. Nor can this endow the girl with the phallus – any more than it does the boy, who similarly identifies with his father (following the outcome of the so-called 'negative' Oedipus complex). Identification with the father, or seeing oneself as a man, is not a simple corollary of the wish for a penis (it is also distinct from the originary masculinity Freud assigns the girl and which is in fact simply the active drive). Is it in fact an identification with the father or only with his penis, the 'insignia of his power'? For after all, the girl turns to the father here not as an object of love, but in order to obtain the penis from him.

Freud saw two processes in penis-envy – firstly the girl refuses 'to accept the fact of being castrated, may harden herself in the conviction that she *does* possess a penis', and secondly she 'may subsequently be compelled to behave as though she were a man'.[30] Freud associates having a penis with behaving like a man. This does not, however, require a regressive identification with the father as lost love-object (although this may nevertheless also be present). Rather it may be an 'hysterical' identification on the basis of an element in common – here, the common wish to be the desire of the mother or, even more rivalrously, identification may be based on having the penis for the mother, just as the father does. The nature of the identification in the 'masculinity complex' is made more complicated when Millot points out that 'writers such as Ophuijsen and Müller-Braunschweig noted that these women do not necessarily demonstrate masculine behaviour',[31] while Freud suggested that identification could also be with the phallic, non-castrated, mother.[32]

For Freud the Oedipal triangle and the castration complex are central elements in the emergence of the boy's identifications, but while he acknowledges the possibility of the boy identifying with his mother as lost love object he simply sees this as a less normal outcome.[33] There are, however, two losses – the phallic mother and the 'castrated' or lacking mother – and, as well, there are two fathers – the phallic, castrating father, and the 'castrated' father who desires, and who is subject to the law. Moreover two psychical processes are involved – the object may be identified with and therefore sustained as an object, even if now set up internally – the ego-ideal. Or the object may be renounced, so that its 'lostness' is internalised – the super-ego. The loss of the phallic mother as love-object will have similar consequences for the structure of identifications emerging for the girl and this is also related to what will be termed her femininity.

It is often assumed that the little girl wishes to be or recognises that she is like her mother and thus identifies. Eugénie Lemoine-Luccioni has emphasised the position of the daughter as the double of her mother, and she sees this as characterising femininity.[34] Similarly another analyst, Raquel Zak de Z. Goldstein, suggests 'The boy is very early separated by his mother from closeness with her body and desire. The girl instead is held in that closeness, this making her consequently run the risks of dual identity with the mother.'[35] What is involved here, however, is not identification, but a problem of separation and one which may give rise to psychosis, not the neurosis of the so-called masculinity complex. Nor can we assume that the girl identifies with her mother because she is the same, has the same body, as her mother, for of course she doesn't – yet. In any case the mother's body is not a single image and it is subject to a radical shift for both the girl and the boy between an image of the phallic mother, and the 'castrated' mother without a penis. No doubt the little girl may identify with either or both, but it will hardly be on the basis of a simple 'similarity'.

In 'Femininity' Freud distinguishes two strata in a woman's identification with her mother. The first is the pre-Oedipal affectionate attattchment whereby the girl takes her mother as her model – this is therefore the form of primary identification Freud outlined in *Group Psychology*, for he emphasises that from this she will acquire the characteristics 'with which she will later fulfill her role in the sexual function and perform her invaluable social tasks'.[36] (That the pre-Oedipal mother is also a phallic figure is not considered by Freud here.) The second 'strata' is the girl's wish to replace her mother and take her position in relation to the father, that is, a 'hysterical' identification with the position of desire of the other. Here the common element between mother and daughter is not the lack of a penis as an object, it is a *wish*, to be the phallus for the father, or to have the phallus from the father (for the mother). Traits of the mother will then be adopted – which may or may not be recognised as culturally defined traits of femininity – as the support or signifier of this identification but whose aim is not to be the mother, but to be in the place of the mother's desire (in relation to the father). This 'identification' easily sits with the feature of the daughter's denigration of her mother which Freud and other analysts have observed, for it is not an identification with the mother, who is now viewed as worthless, but with the mother's *position* in relation to the father. Freud also pointed to another, and more psychically structuring identification. The loss of the mother as a love-object may bring about an identification with the mother on the model outlined by Freud as a result of an introjection of the lost love-object which is now set up internally, 'This mechanism now comes to the little girl's help. Identification with her mother can take the place of attachment to her mother.'[37] But it may also give rise to a corresponding denigration of the love-object and anger as a result of the abandonment by the love-object (as outlined in Freud's discussion of melancholia). As seen in Millot's discussion of the masculinity complex, this form of identification in women has more commonly been recognised in relation to the father, as a masculine identification, but one which Millot described – following Lacan – as neuroticising, because, she says, 'Identification with the father has as a corollary the fact that the paternal Other is reduced, precisely by that identification, to the status of the little other, while the mother is restored to the place of the big Other.' It is this form of identification that is involved in the acquisition of ego-ideals and the super-ego, but which Freud had excluded as a feature of femininity in his earlier discussions. Thus Millot too shows that where the woman has ego-ideals she has no femininity. This, however, as suggested earlier, runs together two processes as one: regressive identification with a lost love-object – the father – and 'hysterical' identification – the wish to take the father's position in relation to the mother by having what the father has.

A FEMININE RESOLUTION

For Freud there was no structural reason why the girl should give up her father as love-object since she has already been castrated and, lacking the motive 'which leads boys to surmount the Oedipus complex', she 'enters the Oedipus situation as though into a haven of refuge'.[38] There is for the girl no apparent resolution equivalent to the boy's. Instead there is only a gradual acceptance of reality through the passage of time, although this can be put in jeopardy as a result of the upheavals of puberty and adolescence. As a result Freud also assumes that the woman never gives up her wish for her father, and hence also her wish not for a baby but for a penis from her father. Therefore, as noted earlier, the foundation of 'proper' femininity is the wish for a penis.

Yet a resolution of the Oedipus complex is both necessary and available to the woman. And it requires of her the same as of the boy, namely the symbolisation of castration. In his discussion of feminine sexuality Moustafa Safouan poses a series of questions: of how it is that the girl experiences the same phallicism as the boy and, following this, what it can mean for the child to call itself a girl or boy, or rather, since children do not call themselves a boy or girl so much as repeat it, what it means for us to call them different? Further, he displaces the question of how it is that the little girl transfers her genital satisfaction from her clitoris to her vagina (which she may not), to the question of how she transfers her desire or preference to an object of another sex to that of her mother (which she often does).[39] Safouan argues that it is the function of castration which is central and universal, whereas the Oedipus complex is culturally specific. The girl, too, is subject to the phallic function and

> this fact [of the function of the phallus] stands less in the way of our understanding as soon as it is related, not to the sex of the girl but to her status or condition as speaking subject. The problem then is that the same function has to be explained similarly or along the same lines for the boy: since he too shares that condition.[40]

Safouan says that the castration complex involves not one but two states. The first is the creation of an ideal or model with which the subject identifies – to the satisfaction of his or her narcissism – but with respect to which he or she feels castrated.[41] This ideal is a phallicism, which at first relates to the phallic mother and then later to the father as the phallic function is taken over by the father alone on 'discovery' of the mother's 'castration'. The experience of castration arises in comparison, but Safouan emphasises it does not arise from that comparison, for if it did,

> the feeling would have to be resolved eventually for the boy and never resolved for the girl. Even less can this comparison give rise to the origin of the ideal as such. In fact, the function of the ideal, insofar as it penetrates the whole economy of desire, is rooted in the promotion of the phallus, that is, precisely, of that whose insufficiency is discovered for the boy and its non-existence for the girl, at an early age, in an attribute of the father.[42]

However there is something more; the second state is 'a break in this capture by the ideal', for without such a break,

> the feeling of castration would become everlasting in the subject, motivating his revulsions and discouraging in him any erection of his desire.[43]

The third term intervenes for both the boy and girl as that break in the capture by the ideal on the part of he who has what it takes to possess the mother. Safouan thus emphasises the role of the father and not simply the mother in the Oedipus complex. For both the boy and the girl there must be enough of the paternal function, but not too much:

> let me say that it is incumbent on whoever carries out the function of the third party to spare the child, as far as can be, the effects of the strange prestige that designates him, the third party, as having what is necessary to possess the mother, and hence the woman (every woman or any woman); in other words, as having the phallus, on the one hand insofar as it is signified in the metaphors of absolute weapon and card that never loses, and also in that of colour and brilliance, and on the other insofar as it stamps desire with its metonymic structure.[44]

This will not be simply a matter of good parenting or generosity on the part of the father or whomever: something more is needed of this figure, or else

> The failure of this second moment sometimes goes so far that a belief in a mythical figure who alternately exalts and mortifies the subject becomes for him the very condition of his existence, or of his assent to existence.[45]

What is required is that the position of the third party must be realised as symbolic, and not just – or at all – as an actual relation. In other words what is necessary is for the father, or whoever comes to occupy the place of the third term, to accept his own castration.

As Lacan confirms, 'The woman has to undergo no more or less castration than the man.'[46] The consequences of the castration complex for the girl and boy are nevertheless different. The problem of how asymmetry emerges from symmetry, which Freud resolved through the reintroduction of biological difference, can be seen to arise instead as a result of the sexual difference already in play for the parents. As a result the boy experiences himself as 'insufficient' (his penis is too small) and the girl is 'without' it. This arises either because the father, in having the phallus, is a prior and privileged object of desire, or because the father intervenes in the dyadic relation to claim the mother for himself against and in opposition both to the child and to the mother who has privileged the child. Both boy and girl must give up their first love-object, the phallic mother, and transfer their desire to an object of 'another' sex. The resolution of the castration complex is the acceptance of castration; for the boy, this is his own 'castration' not his mother's, since what is involved is the symbolisation of castration and, as I argued earlier, the belief in the mother's 'castration' is a form of disavowal. (Thus the expectation of a bigger, sufficient penis in the future is no resolution.) Similarly, the girl must accept castration symbolically, not just her own or her mother's with its corollary of the turning to the father in order to obtain a phallus, but her father's as well. This hinges on the Oedipal scenario, with its presumption that the father has what the mother wants, the phallus. Nevertheless, as Safouan emphasises, the father does not 'have' the phallus but by 'bestowing' it – by having what the mother desires – he gives proof of it. At the same time the father's very desire for the mother marks him as 'castrated', as Granoff and Perrier note:

> If there is no desire that does not suggest the significance of a mark, the trace of a cut, then it is clearly the father, in his desire for the mother, who is marked by that castration.[47]

It is thus by accepting the father's desire for its mother, and hence as 'castrated', that the child can resolve the Oedipal complex. And for the girl, just as for the boy, the considerable vicissitudes of the Oedipal scenario involve the mother–father relation as well as father–daughter relation and the way in which the father accepts, if at all, both his desire and the Oedipal prohibition in relation to his daughter. The problem of the 'inferiority' of the son's penis will appear overwhelming where the father refuses to accept his castration, for he thus appears monstrous to the son and all-powerful; similarly for the girl, if the father refuses to accept his castration she, too, will be locked into her Oedipal relation to him, and as a result into a rivalry with the mother, whether directly or through an hysterical identification as double with the mother. The father may in fact be a cock-teaser, in a sense which is the inverse of the conventional meaning of this in English. That is, the father may present himself to the daughter as able to give her the phallus, but nevertheless always withholds it (as he must) and he thus plays out being phallic, whereas with his wife, in his desire for her he reveals himself as castrated. It is for this reason perhaps that many fathers denigrate their wives insofar as they are also objects of desire. The father truly castrates his daughter in this way, but also opens the possibility for the daughter to castrate him, since he affirms his possession of the phallus which she seeks. If the father reveals his desire for the mother, his castration, she could also then take her mother's place, but it is now a different place. Not of plenitude and completion simply, but of being what the father wants, i.e. the phallus, and hence the relation is figured through castration. Of course, insofar as the father desires the mother the daughter cannot take her mother's place, a solution similarly prohibited by the mother herself, and a limited rivalry arises. Thus, like the boy, the girl is promised in the future the relation reserved between her parents in the present. If the father suggests otherwise then difficulties ensue for the girl, just as much as have been shown in relation to the mother's desire for her son.

The acceptance of castration is not, however, simply a requirement for self-abnegation of the type 'I know I am nothing, I am castrated', though it may be so for many of us, insofar as we are not enabled at the same time to embark on a career of 'substitution' in relation to this lack. What is required is that the parents – both father and mother – let go of the child in relation to their own desire, so that he or she may substitute other objects as both equivalent and as in some sense attainable (and not forbidden) objects of desire. Castration must therefore be resolved in terms of Safouan's 'second state', for otherwise the child will be subject to the castrating super-ego of its parents.

The girl will therefore achieve symbolisation in the same way as the boy, through the realisation of the father's castration, of his desire for the mother, and will identify with the father as lost love object. Her super-ego, just as the boy's, is formed as the result of identifications with both parents, and it is an identification with the function of prohibition.[48] It is now that another form of 'penis-envy' arises. This is also a wish for the penis, but no longer as the magical object which will repair the lack in the other, the mother; if castration in the father as well as the mother is accepted, the woman may resolve her wish for the penis into a wish for the phallus, and thus enter the dialectic of desire of being or having the phallus. The woman will be the phallus in order to have it from the man, and the man wants the phallus in order to have it for the woman. By having the woman who is the phallus, he has the phallus. The man does not 'have' the phallus except in this dialectic, this sexual duet which, Lacan emphasises, is no relation. (Freud too commented on the lack of complementarity in the sexual relation, saying that a woman's and a man's love are a phase apart – the woman loving her son as her son will seek to be loved by another woman but who in turn will give that love to her son.[49]) That is, the man does not 'have the phallus' in general, but only as a function of a structure of signification, and thus femininity and masculinity are not strictly complementary. And being or having the phallus are positions of desire, and not identities; they are interchangeable and hence in some sense also 'roles', a play or masquerade.[50] Lacan comments that 'It is no doubt through the mediation of masks that the masculine and the feminine meet in the most acute, most intense way.'[51]

Sexual intercourse resolves the lack – for the moment – insofar as the man has the penis/phallus for the woman who in thus receiving it therefore 'has' it. Lacan says that as a result 'the organ actually invested with this signifying function [the signifier of her desire] takes on the value of a fetish'. It represents a disavowal and a substitution; this penis 'stands in' for another one which remains absent, and the woman identifies as the phallus in coitus, but, just as for the man, once achieved it is also undone. ('Perverse' fetishism is not, or not necessarily, entailed.) Lack in being thus comes to be related to a difference which becomes sexual difference since through this difference is symbolised a relation to lack which engenders desire. Having or being does not, either, imply an active versus passive relation; rather each are both active and passive, as the way in which men and women put themselves forward to be loved, to be or to have the desire of the other, and as the way the other of the demand for love is constituted as having or being the object of desire. For Lacan desire is always the desire of the other, the desire for the other – to have the other or what is in the other – and the desire to be the other's desire. Desire is therefore the desire for the other as cause of desire – the other who causes me to desire to be or have its desire. The demand for love is the address to the other to be given what one lacks and this is met by the lover not by giving anything but by giving love, which Lacan defines as giving what one does not have. There is then what Lacan describes as a dialectic of demand for love and desire in both the man and the woman, but there is a further dialectic involved, that of sexual difference in being or having, so that I would add that what is given in love is one's lackingness addressed to the other as having or being what one lacks. What is returned in love is the other's desire, for the other's demand poses the lover as having or being that desire. The dialectic of demand and desire exists for both the man and the woman but Lacan argues that for the woman there is a 'convergence onto the same object of an experience of love which as such ideally deprives her of that which it gives, and a desire which finds in that same experience its signifier'.[52] In contrast for the man there is a divergence, in as much as the woman cannot be both an object of desire, as being the phallus, and object of the demand for love, as having the phallus. It is a splitting of desire in relation to the object giving rise to the deprecation of women Freud had also observed, producing a persistent divergence towards 'another woman' who can signify this phallus under various guises, whether as a virgin or a prostitute. But the woman, too, may experience a divergence between the demand for love and desire such as Lacan describes for the man, and he notes 'We should not, however, think that the type of infidelity which then appears to be constitutive of the masculine function is exclusive to the man. For if one looks more closely, the same redoubling is to be found in the woman.'[53]

THE FANTASY OF THE SEXUAL RELATION AND ITS GUISES

That the sexual relation is not a complementary affair is apparent nowhere more clearly than in the sexual act, for each, in being or having what the other desires, also lacks it. The spectre of the lack of the Other reappears at the very moment each had thought it annihilated, irrevocably alienated and alienating. But it does so for both the woman and the man and, in a way, each fails the other as a result – as the man falls asleep or turns away to light a cigarette and the woman feels abandoned, while the woman's re-posed demand for love re-places her as other which their very love-making had annihilated, presenting to the man the issue of castration. This is only resolved through fantasy, that re-modelling of reality which Freud saw as central to human-kind, whereby an unacceptable element in the external world is re-worked to become acceptable. 'This fantasy, in which the subject is caught, is the support as such of what Freudian theory explicitly calls the reality principle', Lacan observes.[54]

Lacan makes all this very clear, from the side of the man, when he argues that what he relates to is the *objet petit a*, 'and that the whole of his realisation in the sexual relation comes down to fantasy'.[55] And as a result, 'A Woman is a symptom', that is, something of the unconscious but which serves to ward off the unconscious, and it is something which requires to be deciphered, thereby presupposing a meaning which might be read, symptomatically giving rise to the question, indeed demand, that the woman tell us what she wants.[56] This symptom wards off the way in which the other of the sexual relation is thereby radically other – 'By her being in the sexual relation radically Other, in relation to what can be said of the unconscious, the woman is that which relates to this Other.'[57] As a result the question is never answered – that is, whatever the woman might say will make no sense to the man for he requires the non-sense of her desire, since to make sense of it reveals his own absence in relation to her desire. This is equally the case – though differently – for a woman, and this is testified to not only in case studies but in works of fiction, both in literature and films. It is because desire arises in relation to the *objet a*, and not in relation to woman or man that, seeing desire in the other, any particular woman or man feels or fears that it arises despite, not because of them.[58] Lacan's account of the *objet a* in the analytic context describes this process of love and desire as a deformation (or objectivisation) of the other of love:

> This paradoxical, unique, specified object we call the *objet a*. I have no wish to rehash the whole thing again, but I will present it for you in a more syncopated way, stressing that the analysand says to his partner, to the analyst, what amounts to this – *I love you, but, because inexplicably I love in you something more than you – the* objet a *I mutilate you.*[59]

Thus too, the *jouissance* of the other remains ineffable. However, Lacan now introduces a radical difference, for he says that insofar as *jouissance* is defined as phallic the woman has nothing of this but rather has her own, supplementary, *jouissance*, 'a *jouissance* beyond the phallus....'[60] For Lacan *the jouissance* of the woman exists insofar as it is 'something more', a 'more' which, Jacqueline Rose argues, 'Lacan locates in the Freudian concept of repetition – what escapes or is left over from the phallic function, and exceeds it.'[61] But it is not clear that this *jouissance* which goes beyond, and which a man may also know of (since 'when you are male' you don't have to put yourself on the side of the phallus, of the all, 'You can also put yourself on the side of not-all'[62]), is the one which, in the course of what passes for love, women experience. Indeed we may wonder here to what extent this is another aspect of the *fantasy* of ~~The~~ Woman (which does not exist) – 'What was seen, but only from the side of the man, was that what he relates to is the *objet a*, and that the whole of his realisation in the sexual relation comes down to fantasy.'[63] Rather, this *jouissance* of ~~The~~ Woman appears to be the *jouissance* of the Other, but is it the *jouissance* of the lacking Other or of the woman as not-all who, because not-all, does not lack, either? For lack can only arise, logically, where there was an all from which a part is taken. Nevertheless the woman as a speaking subject is also subject to the division of language, to the splitting of subjectivity and its lacks. If there is no answer here to the nature of women's *jouissance* it is perhaps because 'it is elsewhere that she upholds the question of her own *jouissance*'.[64]

The Woman does not exist, Lacan says, because in the phallic function the woman is not-all and therefore he says, punningly, there can be no general category of The Woman designating all women. Instead ~~The~~ Woman, for both women and men, is barred, crossed through in the same way that The Other is barred, crossed out; it is radically inaccessible. Little girls do, however, grow up to be women, and Lacan does say that A Woman exists, though it is a symptom of the man, and therefore it is one which women may or may not identify with. Lacan refuses here the feminist demand that he tell us what the woman is because the demand assumes that women are *something*, and a universal identity. Lacan does not consider here women's relation, if any, to The Man, the category of 'the all' in which – through the phallic function – a man can find himself inscribed. Nevertheless if A Woman is a symptom for the man is it not also the case that, correlatively but not equivalently, A Man is a symptom for women in the sexual relation, that in fact 'Woman' and 'Man' are something only in the game, the masquerade, of sexuality? Lacan says:

This representation of the Other is lacking, specifically, between the two opposed worlds that sexuality designates for us in the masculine and the feminine. Carrying things as far as they will go, one might even say that the masculine ideal and the feminine ideal are represented in the psyche by something other than this activity/passivity opposition of which I spoke earlier. Strictly speaking, they spring from a term that I have not introduced, but of which one female psycho-analyst has pin-pointed the feminine sexual attitude – the term *masquerade*.

Masquerade is not that which comes into play in the display necessary, at the level of the animals, to coupling, and in any case display is usually to be seen on the side of the male. Masquerade has another meaning in the human domain, and that is precisely to play not at the imaginary, but at the symbolic level.[65]

Lacan's use of the term masquerade is drawn from Joan Riviere in her article 'Womanliness as Masquerade' which was published in 1929.[66] Riviere concluded that there is no difference 'between genuine womanliness and the "masquerade"….whether radical or superficial, they are the same thing'.[67] It is this idea of femininity as an adopted guise that Lacan took up:

Paradoxical as this formulation may seem, I would say that it is in order to be the phallus, that is to say, the signifier of the desire of the Other, that the woman will reject an essential part of her femininity, notably all its attributes through masquerade. It is for what she is not that she expects to be desired as well as loved.[68]

Moustafa Safouan summarises this as

she [the woman] invests the man as having the phallus. But she cannot thus invest him without the wish to be, herself, for him, the phallus…in the end she finds her being not as woman but as phallus (this is the sense of the fundamental alienation of her being).[69]

In being the phallus for the man the woman affirms, signifies, that she does not have it – she is castrated. Lacan says in relation to the woman concealed behind her veil:

it is the absence of the penis that turns her into the phallus, the object of desire. Draw attention to this absence in a more precise way by getting her to wear a pretty wig and fancy dress, and you, or rather she, will have plenty to tell us about: the effect is guaranteed 100 percent, for men who go straight to the point.[70]

And, as Stephen Heath argues, it implies that 'she becomes the woman men want, the term of phallic identity, phallic exchange', so that 'Disguising herself as a castrated woman, the woman represents man's desire and finds her identity as, precisely, a woman – genuine womanliness and the masquerade are the same thing, as Riviere insists.'[71] This appears to subordinate the woman's desire to the man's, to pose femininity as a fundamental subjection to the masculine. Lacan's adoption of Riviere's intuition, however, involves a displacement of her use of the term. Following Freud, Riviere argues that femininity is defined by a penis-envy which is never fully resolved.[72] This is not, therefore, the same as the desire to *be* the phallus attributed to the woman in the masquerade by Lacan.[73] For the masquerading woman of Riviere's account masquerades because she believes she has a penis, not because she wishes to display that she doesn't. She writes 'women who wish for masculinity may put on a mask of womanliness to avert anxiety and the retribution feared from from'.[74] Joan Riviere described her patient in the following way:

> her excellent relations with her husband included a very intimate affectionate attachment between them and full and frequent sexual enjoyment; she prided herself on her proficiency as a housewife. she had followed her profession with marked success all her life. She had a high degree of adaptation to reality, and managed to sustain good and appropriate relations with almost everyone with whom she came in contact.[75]

Nevertheless, she suffered from one symptom, from acute anxiety after every performance of public speaking, but which she was required to undertake as part of her work. (She had in fact taken up the same work as her father.) She was assailed by self-doubt, excited and apprehensive, and obsessed with the need for reassurance. This led her to seek approval and compliments from any important man at the occasion of her public speaking. These figures, Riviere says, were clearly father-substitutes. In fact two forms of reassurance were sought, one being directly about the nature of her performance in the speech, the other more indirectly in the nature of sexual attentions from these men. She would attempt to obtain these sexual attentions from the man through flirting and coquetry 'in a more or less veiled manner'.[76] The incongruity of this behaviour had become a problem leading her to seek analysis. Riviere analyses her patient's behaviour in the following way:

> The exhibition in public of her intellectual proficiency, which was in itself carried through successfully, signified an exhibition of herself in possession of the father's penis, having castrated him. The display once over, she was seized by horrible dread of the retribution the father would then exact. Obviously it was a step towards propitiating the avenger to endeavour to offer herself to him sexually.[77]

But note that the woman's response was both anxiety *and* excitement, the latter pointing to the woman's satisfaction at her successful display of her possession of the penis, immediately bringing in train her fear of retribution. And, by offering herself sexually she not only might placate the father but she also proclaimed herself castrated. As Catherine Millot puts it, 'By disguising herself as a castrated woman she assumed the mask of innocence and guaranteed her impunity. Her behaviour with men after lectures thus constituted the obsessional cancellation of her intellectual performance.'[78] As a result, she observes:

> Thus we have a three-fold construction: a woman regards herself as a man who passes for a woman, a construction which cannot fail to evoke the Jewish joke reported by Freud: 'If you say you're going to Cracow, you want me to believe you're going to Lemberg. but I know that in fact you're going to Cracow. So why are you lying to me?'[79]

But does the woman go to Lemberg or Cracow? If femininity is, as Heath summarises it, the woman disguising herself as castrated as a result of which, in representing man's desire, she finds her identity as a woman, it begs the question of what the woman is *before* she dons this disguise. In Riviere's account, she is phallic, in Freud's sense, of having the penis. As a result two categories of 'woman' are involved here, the woman who regards herself as having a penis (but without necessarily regarding herself as a man), and the 'woman' she passes herself off as. The first is not 'castrated', the second is 'castrated'. The masquerade is a disguise of appearing castrated, and this can be understood as meaning one of two things: either, as is the case with Riviere's patient, that the woman is not 'castrated' insofar as she believes she has a penis; or, that the disguise is necessary because the woman is not 'castrated' insofar as she has never had a penis which she might lose. The disguise veils this knowledge which thus becomes constituted as the real. (Castration of the mother is the fetishistic disavowal which both the boy and the girl construct to negotiate the problem of the gap opened up in the structure of desire by the knowledge of insufficiency.) These two positions of the masquerade may be summed up as: the woman will be the phallus in order to disguise the fact that she already has it; the woman will be the phallus in order that she may receive it, from the man. Moustafa Safouan similarly distinguishes the masquerade which is based on rivalry for the penis from what he calls the 'game' of sexuality: 'when Joan Riviere's patient falls into the masquerade, it is out of rivalry. What I call playing the game, is abandoning the masquerade in as much as it covers over such a rivalry.'[80]

Riviere's account is very much of the first form of the masquerade, and it cannot be subsumed to the second. By this masquerade the woman seeks to ward off the dangers of her unresolved rivalry with her parents. She is caught in the vicissitudes of castration within her Oedipus complex: 'Both parents are rivals in this stage, both possess desired objects; the sadism is directed against both and the revenge of both is feared.'[81] Riviere, following Klein, suggests another path, arguing that the girl fears, and hates, the mother most of all as the agent of castration, and hence 'she must retire from rivalry with the mother, and if she can, endeavour to restore to her what she has stolen'. As a result, she goes on to say:

As we know, she identifies herself with the father; and then she uses the masculinity she thus obtains by *putting it at the service of the mother*. She becomes the father, and takes his place; so she can 'restore' him to the mother.[82]

And this could be seen in the lavish self-sacrifices undertaken by her patient, but, as Riviere observes:

The recognition desired was supposed by her to be owing for her self-sacrifices; more unconsciously what she claimed was recognition of her *supremacy* in *having* the penis to give back.[83]

Riviere here confirms the structure of having the penis – or phallus – *for* an other, while she introduces a new perspective on the meaning of woman's self-sacrifice. Giving up something 'proves' that you have it, for only then can you give it up.

Riviere introduces another point which is also in contrast to the second form of the masquerade, for she says that while 'this woman's mask' is transparent to other women it was very successful with the men to whom she addressed herself for attention. But, Riviere goes on to say,

> Closer examination showed that these men were of the type who themselves fear the ultra-womanly woman. They prefer a woman who herself has male attributes, for to them her claims on them are less.[84]

In other words, these men are not duped by the masquerade but, on the contrary, take it for what it is, namely a disguising of the fact that the woman does have the penis. And thus, that she was never castrated, and, thus too, she does not seek to take mine.

In contrast, the second form of the masquerade involves the guise, the apparel, by which the woman can show what she does not have, a penis, and thus will be the phallus for the man. Here she is not covering up the truth of what she *does* have, but, if anything, covering up the truth that she has never had what she presents herself as having lost, the penis, and which is the meaning of castration. She takes on the apparel of a castration which is the fiction by which the impossibility of desire is negotiated by both the man and the woman.[85] This will, presumably, also be distinct from that appearance of the woman that proclaims her castration as a reality which she believes in, unlike Riviere's patient.[86]

There is also a corollary of the masquerade in the representation of the man's relation to having the phallus, and it too is not a singular form. Heath notes that 'To the woman's masquerade there thus corresponds male display (parade is Lacan's term).' It is a display in which 'All the trappings of authority, hierarchy, order, position make the man, his phallic identity.' He goes on to quote Lemoine-Luccioni who says 'if the penis was the phallus, men would have no need of feathers, or ties or medals ... Display [parade], just like the masquerade, thus betrays a flaw: no one has the phallus.'[87] As a result, and ironically, the representation of the insignia of the phallus has the contradictory consequence of the figuring the man *as* the phallus, rather than having it. Now this, as argued above, is not necessarily to a man's displeasure. He too wishes to be loved as the phallus, and not only as having it but, as Lacan observed, 'in the human being, virile display itself appears as feminine'.[88] This is not, as he suggests, a 'strange' consquence of 'The fact that femininity takes refuge' in the mask, as if display itself by its association with femininity might thus metaphorically transform male display, too, into the feminine. Rather, just like the masquerade, what is signified in a making present of something is in fact a statement of what is absent. Thus if the woman's masquerade displays her castration and therefore, in one form, that the woman *does* have the penis, then equally the parade that displays the man's phallicism will display that the man *does not* have the phallus, but is it. But there will also be the parade which the man dons in order to play the game of sexuality, corresponding to the second form of the masquerade in women. However, and as a further irony, it also seems to be the case that the man cannot be represented as having the phallus as such – this always in fact leads him into being the phallus – rather, his possession can only be figured through the desire of the other: he has the phallus insofar as the other, the woman, or man, desires it.

Representation is thus central to the sexual relation, but as a result it is, as Lacan emphasises, not a relation, for it is conducted through masks – a masquerade in which each constructs a fantasy of the other and herself or himself for the other. It is indeed, therefore, a signifying system, but one in which the metaphor is still assumed to relate to a real content of sexuality. For, insofar as the metaphor is discerned, it is assumed that there is something which exists as the likeness of the metaphor, whereas, on the contrary, the metaphor exists to produce a content which it thus guarantees. Though as the saying goes, after all, there's no smoke without a fire, this is however the fallacy.

A CONCLUSION

It begins to be apparent that the phallus as privileged signifier in Freudian and Lacanian psychoanalysis is not the upholder of patriarchy that feminism has supposed. It is not the cause of the conspiracy by men to subordinate women, nor its support; rather the subordination of women, with all its many forms, is also the attempt by men, as perhaps by women as well, to evade the phallic signifier. What is constructed in its stead is a phallic signified. Jacqueline Rose points out that:

> The subject has to recognise that there is desire, or lack in the place of the Other, that there is no ultimate certainty or truth, and that the status of the phallus is a fraud (this is, for Lacan, the meaning of castration).[89]

The power of the phallic fraud lies in the extent to which it supports an Other who holds the truth of the subject and has the ability to make good its loss. The failure of the phallic fraud (but not its exposure, for we still believe in it) gives rise to the most extreme denigration of the Other. In this women are not only victims but – we must acknowledge – may also themselves be perpetrators and hence perpetuators of such denigration. This fraudulent phallus institutes a disavowal of lack, but a disavowal which never wholly succeeds, and whose failure then leads to a production of woman no longer as a symptom (itself a fantasy but one we can live with), but as The Woman, as myth. Its correlative is the mythologised phallus, the phallus as symbol of life, as divine, as symbol of the unity and cohesion of the body etc. But this mythic phallus is not the phallus of psychoanalytic theory. On the contrary psychoanalysis reveals it to be a joke. Safouan writes 'To be more rigorous, what is the phallus if not that which renders vain and derisory the regressive positions of the ego ideal…. In other words, the phallus is the very point where the Other of Truth (capital T) is seen to be without truth (small t).'[90] The mythic phallus of phallocentrism is an *objet petit a*, a kind of stamp taken from the body which 'authenticates' the subject and becomes the lauded guarantee of identity.[91] In contrast, Lacan states that the objective of his teaching 'in as much as it aims at that part of analytic discourse which can be formulated, or put down, is to dissociate the *a* and the O, by reducing the former to what belongs to the imaginary and the latter to what belongs to the symbolic'. And, because the *a* has become confused with the signifier of the Other 'It is here that a rupture or severance is still needed. And it is in this precisely that psychoanalysis is something other than a psychology.'[92] Yet, given the arguments presented in the discussion of fetishism and representation, it would be another fantasy to imagine the abolition of the imaginary in the symbolic.

The account of femininity in both Freud and Lacan is of a construction, not an essence or biological origin. This also means that for Lacan there is no feminine outside language because, as Jacqueline Rose notes, first 'the unconscious severs the subject from any unmediated relation to the body as such... and secondly because the "feminine" is constituted as a division in language'.[93] But if the feminine is other, this does not mean it has another essence. Thus for Lacan men and women are only ever in language, and all speaking beings must line up on one side or the other of the division that is sexual difference although, because this is no longer anatomical difference but a difference in language, subjects may line up on the opposite side from that to which they are anatomically destined – this would not however be to take up the position conventionally designated as that of the 'homosexual', but the position of the transsexual. If sexual identity is the position taken up and identified with in the opposition having/being the phallus, where having is 'masculine' and being is 'feminine', we must also enquire for whom the subject seeks to be or to have the phallus? For, Lacan affirmed, desire is the desire of the other. And is the other of this address a subject who is or who has the phallus? Of course since, as noted earlier, both the man and the woman wish to be as well as have the phallus and since none of us wholly give up or transform our earliest attachments, this wish will also be in relation to the figure for whom the lover is a stand in (the metaphorical substitute). This figure may be either or both the mother or the father, however the mother and father are only sexually different psychically for the child as a result of the Oedipus complex and thus are likely to bear pre-Oedipal meanings as well, namely as phallic mother and phallic father, in relation to whom the child/adult may experience itself as castrated, or also phallic, hence having or being the phallus. Thus it seems necessary to enlarge upon Freud's comment in a letter to Fliess in 1889 that 'I am accustoming myself to regarding every sexual act as an event between four individuals'.

The subject can seek to be and/or to have the phallus for the phallic mother and/or for the 'castrated' mother, or she or he can seek to have and/or to be the phallus for the phallic father and/or for the father who is also subject to castration. The subject may seek to play out the oscillation between having or being in relation to the same love object, or it may be divided between two objects of the same or opposite biological sex in that splitting noted by Lacan and Freud between love and sexual desire.[94] Moreover that a sexual act ensues does not allow us to assume that the other has been 'interpellated', that she or he has taken up the position of the addressee as a place of her own or his own desire, although the enactment may provide support for the fantasy of such a fulfillment.

In each case, however, the subject must take up a position as either a man or a woman since she or he is a post-Oedipal subject, yet this cannot be taken as determining of the subject as homosexual or heterosexual. Lining up on one side or the other of sexual difference in language is the result not of subjective choice, but is the outcome of the subject's psychical history, of the career of his or her lost love objects in the unconscious, and the vicissitudes of Oedipal identifications. Neither the terms bisexuality nor homosexuality, in their specifying of a binary division between sameness and otherness in object-choice, can capture the complexity of this. Anatomical sexual difference can be no more determining for the homosexual than for the heterosexual.[95] Heterosexuality as well as bisexuality and homosexuality must be understood as the position of a subject in whom pre-Oedipal wishes and positions continue together with post-castration identifications.[96] What is involved is not a set of choices between which a subject may alternate but rather the subject's sexuality is a concatenation, a palimpsest, realised in the context of the contingency of the other who responds to our demand for love. There is therefore no simple mobility between such positions for the desiring subject. One enacts the emplacements of one's psychical history. The apparent mobility of sexual fantasy, whether enacted or imagined, can only arise with a – relative – fixing of the subject's position of sexual difference and its identifications, whereas the noted seeming fixity of sexual activity and fantasy of the so-called pervert marks the threatened and fragile position of that subject's sexuality and its identifications.[97]

THE SEXUAL DIFFERENCE OF CINEMATIC IDENTIFICATION IN *GERTRUD*

It is the positionings of men and women within cinema's scenarios and our identification with all or some of these as positions of desire that this book has been concerned to address, and to which I will now return. The masquerade, fetishism and the disavowal of sexual difference are explored in the analysis of Joseph von Sternberg's film *Morocco* in the following chapter. Here, the interrelation of positions of desire, of identification and of sexual difference in Carl Theodor Dreyer's *Gertrud*[98] are investigated.

Dreyer's film is based on a play by the Swedish writer, Hjalmar Söderberg (which is itself based on his own unhappy affair with Maria von Platen), and deals with the story of a former singer now married to an ambitious politician, but whose marriage has become (or always was) empty and meaningless, though not without sexual passion. She seeks love with a young composer who is shown to be unworthy of her by Lidman, her former lover and a celebrated poet returned home to receive the honours of his country and, perhaps, to persuade Gertrud to return to him. However, Gertrud had left Lidman when she discovered that he saw her love for him as a distraction from his work and hence as secondary to his more serious project as a poet. At the end of the play she leaves all three men, none of whom can meet her demand for absolute love. Dreyer follows the play closely, retaining its original dialogue although not using it all, but he adds an entirely new section in the epilogue in which we see Gertrud, now very elderly, meet for a last time with her old friend Axel Nygren. Dreyer commented:

> The epilogue was not in the play. But there is not a word in the dialogue which Söderberg has not said before in other connections. You see, I was a little in doubt with the end. In the play it was alright, excellent to end with Gertrud running away, but for the film it would have been impossible. The public would not have been in the clear what had happened. I was sure the public would have sympathy for Gertrud, and because of this sympathy they certainly would like to know what happened to her. And therefore I made the epilogue and the public had the satisfaction to see this woman didn't break down and she didn't regret. She had chosen solitude and she accepted it.[99]

Dreyer refers here to the sympathy for Gertrud which he was trying to evoke in his audiences, and indeed the central concern of many of his films is with their women protagonists: 'I'm interested in generally a single person in the film – *Joan of Arc*, *Gertrud*, and generally women.'[100] By 'sympathy' here I take Dreyer to mean identification in the sense I have discussed earlier in this book:

> In all art, human beings are the decisive thing. In the artistic film, it is the people that we want to see and it is their adventures of the spirit that we want to experience. We want to enter upon and into the lives we see on the screen. We hope that the film will set ajar for us a door into these other worlds. We want to be placed in a suspense that originates less from outside action than from the unfolding of inner conflicts.[101]

In *Gertrud*, identification is important both in relation to its female protagonist and to its several male characters. However, Dreyer does not draw upon the conventions of classical narrative film and its continuity style of editing to produce identification; instead *Gertrud* avoids the point-of-view shot and its system of looks exchanged or relayed, so that it refuses the spectator this form of access to knowledge about and identification with characters. This is part of the larger formal system of the film through which the issue of knowledge and sight, of the look and the relation it posits with its object, are presented. The rigour of Dreyer's style, pared down and simple but at the same time foregrounded, produced a hostile response on the part of even art cinema critics who, after its première in Paris following a retrospective of Dreyer's films, dismissed *Gertrud* as just 'photographed sofa conversations'. Others have seen *Gertrud*'s eschewing of conventional forms not as an affront to the spectator but rather as an attack on the illusionism of those forms. Noël Burch and George Dana have suggested that the film's form succeeds in putting in conflict its ideological content ('the petty-bourgeois ideology of Absolute Love, Transcendental Poetry, and Disinterested Science'), bringing out its contradictions so that the film on the one hand presents a correct analysis of the place of women in society while on the other hand it shows the dilemma in which that ideology places the heroine. They conclude that 'It is not too far-fetched to speak of Dreyer's adoption of a Brechtian attitude [in] this extreme alienation which one cannot help but feel relative to a dialogue which in turn tends in every way to be produced as surface.'[102]

David Bordwell has addressed the role of form in his book-length study of Dreyer's films. He argues that *Gertrud* is the culmination of a stylistic approach by which the structuring of space and time creates an *excess* in the way that the narrative is subjected to the work of cinematic representation:

> We know that Dreyer's films open up a gap between causal logic and spatio-temporal structures. What happens in *Gertrud* is that the 'very slow continuity' initiated in *Day of Wrath* and continued in *Ordet* now becomes more than the narrative can bear. Narrative events – dialogue, gesture, character confrontations – become swallowed up in cinematic structures, like pennies tossed in a canyon.[103]

For Bordwell, *Gertrud* anthologises and thus estranges, in Shklovsky's sense, the classical narrative cinema. This radical eschewing of classical conventions while laying them out in the film, he says, *empties* it of meaning because of the excess of signifiers without signifieds.

The look, so central to the organising of space in classical cinema, is transformed as a device in *Gertrud*. The opening of the film immediately sets this up: at the end of the first shot Kanning and Gertrud are seated together behind his desk, there is a cut to a medium-close shot of Kanning looking left; the camera pans left to show Gertrud, but she is *not* the object of his gaze, which is directed slightly further centre-frame, while Gertrud is looking off left, as well. The camera pans back to Kanning, then to Gertrud again, and then as Kanning speaks off-screen the camera pulls back to a medium shot of both characters, who are still not looking at each other and it is only as Gertrud goes to get up that an inter-character look is shown, Kanning to Gertrud.

There are only four points in the film at which Dreyer draws upon the familiar shot/reverse/shot and eyeline-match structure (there is also one point-of-view insert, a close-up of a newspaper photograph of Lidman), but it is only the fourth and last of these that is a true pov shot when, at the very end of the film, as Gertrud bids farewell to her old friend Axel, shots of her looking at him are alternated with shots of him seen from her vantage point.

The filmic strategies in *Gertrud* continually distance the spectator to produce a sense of separation: the very long takes result in a sense of elongation or extension to scenes unrelieved by shot changes or point-of view 'insights', while the similarity of scenes organised around dialogue exchanges – with characters moving between chairs, sofas, chair arms, benches, etc. as they talk to each other but rarely gazing at one another or shown exchanging glances – produces an awareness of repetition. Dreyer constructs an extremely theatrical effect as a result of the relentlessly frontal camera he uses, yet within the film space is never given once and for all, as it is on a stage, but opened up – often very confusingly – through camera movement after a scene has begun, using pans with medium-close shots, or using a travelling camera across rooms to follow a character. Camera movement often substitutes for cuts, suddenly swinging away from the character to find another space, as when, after Gertrud has spoken to Kanning in the ante-room at the banquet, he leaves right while the camera moves left to end on a door, but not the one Kanning is leaving by, rather it opens to reveal Lidman entering.

The effect of this may be to bring the film close to Brechtian strategies of alienation, as Burch and Dana suggest. But it is also rather different, and the thesis of alienation seems hardly sufficient to an understanding of the film's textual system. Dreyer's own views on the relation of form and content in his films is complex. Taking the stance of a modernist he says 'I am glad for every deviation from the standard form. The standard form I hate. We cannot go forward if there are no deviations, no new forms, even if they are not perfect.'[104] Dreyer does not see this as a simple emptying of meaning, however, as if form alone were sufficient, but rather it seems to be for him a way of stripping bare meaning from the detritus of everyday perceptions – to bare the soul, 'I must at once define abstraction as something that demands of the artist to abstract himself from reality in order to strengthen the spiritual content of his work.' And 'the artist must describe inner, not outer life. The capacity to abstract is esssential to all artistic creation. Abstraction allows the director to get outside the fence with which naturalism has surround his medium. It allows his films to be not merely visual, but spiritual.'[105] The emptying of meaning which Bordwell sees in *Gertrud* is the marking by Dreyer of a space of the spiritual, a space but not a content.[106]

At the same time cinema is, for Dreyer, a narrative form and at the centre of the film stands the actor. But space is used to emphasise and focus the character psychologically, rather than in terms of narrative action, and hence mere continuity of spatial relations may be ignored. Dreyer sought to emphasise human expressivity, and saw cinema as a special means to uncovering its essence; for him this was as a psychological truth, not as 'realism'. But while cinematic style is put in the service of the characters this is not to promote a simple naturalism, for the acting of the characters is highly controlled and stylised – Dreyer instructed the actors' every gesture, their style of delivery and of intonation of speech and of look. Given such an aesthetic, form in Dreyer's films is not used symbolically or expressively, as a metaphorical substitute for the actor's expression etc., but becomes the rhythm and texture of the representation. In *Gertrud*, this is dominantly one of separation, space opened, filled, then emptied; characters coming together only to separate across the space again. Dreyer, while anti-illusionist, seeks the reality of essence and pursues an abstraction of reality in which representation signifies only significance. As a result the characters appear hypostasised, separated out from the continuum of space and time, from reality. And thus, at one and the same time, the image is made full of meaningful gestures but without any fixed meaning.

The placing of a tapestry-like picture of a naked woman being chased by hounds behind Gertrud as she talks to Axel in an ante-room at the banquet, which I discussed in the Introduction, is an example of this excessive significance. The picture condenses visually a series of references in the film. It reiterates the scenario of Gertrud's dream recounted to Erland the day before, while dreams are also the subject of Axel's current studies in Paris, which Gertrud will later join him in. Its thematic reference of a wilful woman who rejects the love of her suitor is also Gertrude's own situation in the film, but the punishment it thereby implies for Gertrud is not forthcoming in the film. Finally, the picture's fateful and coincidental presence punningly counterpoints their discussion of the issue of free will, which itself is also the theme of Axel's new book. Thus excessively doubled-up, the picture has no singular meaning.

Two questions arise therefore. First, what is the relation of the film's form to its 'story' (*fabula*)? and second, how is the spectator placed for and by the film if the classical system is discarded? On the one hand the film's form does not work to simply 'express' the narrative, complementing or supplementing characterisation and dialogue etc.; rather it tends to be read as 'distancing', as pulling the spectator away from identification with characters and emphasises relations between characters as spatial rather than psychological relations. Objects and gestures become even more marked because no simply metaphorical meaning is produced. A kind of poetic skewing is effected which unravels the threads of the story, displacing the drive, the thrust of the narrative. Of course, this very 'distance' itself could be seen as the theme of the film. The abstraction of the mise en scène, the acting, the use of camera etc. continually isolate individuals from one another, as if posing an unbridgeable gap between characters, however close. Yet the film's narrative, insofar as it is centred on Gertrud, is not about loneliness as such (unlike Lidman's story and his loneliness of the soul), but about an ideal of love – for which Gertrud would rather accept loneliness than compromise her demand. The function of form in the film seems almost to be a realisation of an observation made by a character in another work by Söderberg, his novel *Dr Glas*, which Dreyer had also considered making into a film. Glas, his friend Markel and others are talking together at a restaurant when Markel comments 'that doesn't mean it's true that everyone seeks happiness. There are people who haven't any gift for it at all and are painfully and ruthlessly aware of the fact. Such people don't seek happiness, only to get a little form and style into their unhappiness... Glas in one of them.'[107]

Form and style in effect re-mark the fact of unhappiness but in so doing they introduce a figuring, a representing which is also thus a displacement. What is emphasised is the 'unhappiness' and thereby what is lost is the 'lacking' which caused the unhappiness and a kind of disavowal is instituted, form and style becoming its fetishistic monument, since they come to offer a presence, a sufficiency, in the face of lack.

On the other hand reviewers of the film tended to dismiss the 'story' or 'argument' of *Gertrud*. Kirk Bond writes of it as a soap opera in which 'the woman cannot or will not understand the man has interests of his own that are necessary in the scheme of things. She must have the man's total devotion...Here is the suffering, the rather gratuitous suffering of a "woman's story".'[108] Yet he is also brought to conclude that each of the three men must 'give way to the basic demand of life for love...Dreyer is saying...that man must once more know really what love is'.[109] (It is clear that he means men rather than people.) Similarly Tom Milne says 'the film is about a rather tiresome woman mid-way between an Ibsen bluestocking and a Strindberg shrew whose behaviour seems almost like an advertisement for women's rights'.[110] Rejecting the story and what he calls its 'almost dogged literalness' of treatment he sees beneath 'its naturalistic surface, its near-Ibsen conflicts, that it is Dreyer's most mysterious and personal, most supernatural film, glowing with a more secret magic than any previous work' and 'the whole film echoes like counterpoint for two voices – "I love you" and "Come with me" which never quite coincide'.[111] Something trivial, soap opera-ish, is set aside while an essence is valorised. Gertrud's ideal of love absolutely is seen as foolish, her girlish sixteen-year-old's poem is plain embarrassing, but rejecting literal meaning, another meaning is obtained, and thus Milne comes to find a position, a place of address or *énonciation*, of the impossiblity of the two discourses, which are one might say, the masculine and the feminine (though not always spoken only by men or by women).

This ascribing of a meaning to the film which transcends its surface signified implies and invokes an origin for that meaning elsewhere than the spectator, namely in the director-author. And by this kind of reading the spectator can thus find a position, a place of address which is also at the same time an identification with the director who, as the authorial source of the organisation of images and sounds in the film, is thus also the place from which the film can be understood. That is, in receiving (de-coding even) the authorial message we come to take up the position of the author in relation to the film-text – we too come to 'write' it. Dreyer, however, makes very little room for such 'writerliness' (which in Barthes's terms is on the side of the 'readerly'[112]). In *Gertrud*, even less than earlier films such as *Vampyr (1932)* or *Joan of Arc (La Passion de Jeanne d'Arc,* 1927), the authorial organisation through the camera as its delegate does not address us by giving the spectator privileged views or knowledge in relation to the film's events (unlike the ironic Fordian discourse in *Stagecoach,* 1939). Even where such views are given there is always a level of hesitation about how to see, to understand, and even to believe – for example, the miracle in *Ordet* (1954). While the very style of *Gertrud* signifies 'authoredness', disrupting any simple 'realism', it does not provide a separate unified and coherent statement – of irony or whatever.[113]

It is, however, Gertrud herself who emerges as the dominant means by which the spectator can 'follow' the film, can find his or her place *as* a spectator, for, while the film's form separates us from her it also insistently centres Gertrud. The story is about her search for an ideal love. Her speech is allowed to be the dominant discourse of 'truth' within the film; her view of her husband and of Lidman is not challenged in the film, and hence can be read as supported by the film, while no other character's actions or statements are given more weight. Nor is an alternative ironic interpretation given by the image track itself; the film does not ironise or otherwise comment on Gertrud's assertions. We are asked to follow, to understand the film's events primarily from *her* narrative and psychological point of view, and in one sense, certainly in Dreyer's sense, the success of the film depends on this, on the audience coming to sympathise with her and her desire.

In *Gertrud*, as in many of Dreyer's films, the female character stands opposed (even at the cost of her life, as in *Day of Wrath* (1944) and *Joan of Arc*) to masculine hypocrisy, to the oppressive structures of church, state, and patriarchal family. Such characters are therefore to some extent delegates of the authorial voice, through whom Dreyer appears to urge us to be open to the woman's desire, rather than seeking to possess it or recoiling from it when it is shown to exist independently of the man's desire. These are the noted feminist aspects of Dreyer's work and they raise the question of what it means for this male film director, almost invariably adapting male authors, to give voice to the woman in this way. That is, what is the implication for the position of the spectator of the sympathy for Gertrud which Dreyer is concerned to evoke in the spectator and in what way does this become an identification, if at all? Identification, it has been argued, is with a position, it is a relation to a scenario and thus not in the first instance, if ever, an appropriation of an identity as a content (or gender). And our relation to the scenario is predicated on desire – identification, in fact, with a wish.

What is Gertrud's desire, then? Her desire is active – she propositions Erland and initiates the relation; and it is strongly sensual – she says to Erland after their love-making that she is alive, has lived again, in their love. Gertrud remains faithful to Lidman's ideology of love, which he has long-since abandoned. At the banquet in his honour the student's speech praises Lidman for bringing new freedom and understanding with his idea of love: 'We discover infinity and eternity in sexual ecstasy. This is the greatness of your concept of eroticism. This love without boundaries. For this love man was created and called upon.' Lidman, however, responds in a quite different manner, citing truth and philosophy as man's true goals. An irony, then, in this man's ideal being realised by a woman. The object of Gertrud's desire in the film is Erland Jansson, but what we see of him hardly supports her choice. Even at their first meeting, Erland seems to be insincere, too eager to go to bed with her and too slow with his protestations of love, and here the film provides a rare moment when a different reading of the scene is possible for the audience compared with Gertrud's. Two other men, Lidman and Kanning, have been previous objects of Gertrud's desire, but the film narrates how all three men come to fail her demand for absolute love. In a seminar on the film one student showed his frustration with Gertrud when he demanded – echoing Freud and Lacan – to know what it was that she wanted. Such a frustration arises perhaps because her desire is for an ideal, of absolute love, and hence not for any particular man in his imperfect individuality, and when Gertrud ceases to be a subject of desire with the loss of Erland our identification with her is undermined, for while she retains an ideal of love (hence her rejection of Lidman and of her husband) she withdraws any demand for love in the world. She gives up her desire. But it cannot be said that the lost object of her desire is then set up internally, on the model of a regressive identification, for Gertrud's new world in Paris follows the model of her friend – not lover – Axel Nygren. Dreyer reaffirms this by the inclusion of the postscript in the film, which was not in the original play. As an ideal, Gertrud finally desires what no man, or woman, has, and thus it does not involve a mise en scène of desire, for there is no longer an other to whom the demand for love is addressed; Gertrud burns the 'warm and friendly' letters of her friend, and only now in the film does Dreyer allow a shot-reverse-shot with point-of-view. In terms of my arguments in the chapter on identification, Gertrud appears here as the figure of an identification with or internalisation of the super-ego, where Freud says 'Every such identification [of the super-ego] is in the nature of a de-sexualisation or even of a sublimation.'[114] In taking up Gertrud's position here, if we do at all, we take up such an identification. But, insofar as there is no object of her desire the spectator cannot take up Gertrud's position and identify with her as subject of desire. Such an identification would be not a question of wanting what she wants and thus identifying, but of identifying with Gertrud as a subject who *wants*.

To ask the very question 'what does Gertrud want?', is to open the way to another question, of how one might come into position as the place of her desire, to be what she wants. For if identification is with the scenario of desire it is also a play between the positions of object of desire and subject of desire (and also onlooker). As a result, although displaced from an identification with Gertrud as subject of desire, we may instead take up the position of object of her desire. This is not Erland, a poor stand-in and revealed early on as such, but is the *ideal* place of her desire. This is also distinct from identifying with the position of the subject who desires Gertrud – here doubled in Kanning and Lidman – which the spectator may also do. Here, too, however, this is not to desire Gertrud necessarily, but to identify with their desiring, made poignant in their loss of Gertrud. Their predicament may arouse our sympathy, and though each has lost Gertrud by their own actions, nevertheless we may be moved by the pathos of that loss – seen in Lidman's realisation of what he has lost and that he can never be, or be again, that place, that cause of her desire. For Gertrud, he is cold, cold as stone. But what kind of narrative offers us as place of identification such a series of failures? Perhaps classical tragedy, rare in cinema which has adopted the romantic tragedy and melodrama of nineteenth-century drama. Or rather, what is in play here maybe close to something which a very different director, Howard Hawks, has described. Trying to explain why men go on in impossible and dangerous situations, in battle or whatever (and the stuff of his own films), he said that it was because the next Joe always thinks he's better, that he'll live, he'll make it. But, of course, Hawks says, he doesn't.[115] In a parallel way and undermining the tragedy of inevitability is the possibility for the spectator to insert his or her own fantasy of 'if only it had been me, it would have been different'. If such a fantasy is possible, it is because the narrative drive, the 'desire' of the *film*, finds us such a place. In *Gertrud*, it is the place of sufficency to her desire. What is the difference in this from saying that we desire Gertrud? All the difference between the active and the passive tense, for we do not desire Gertrud simply, but to be the desire of Gertrud, to come into place as that which is sufficient, an ideal of love. Thus the question 'what does Gertrud want?' can be answered: she wants the phallus.

Gertrud, in seeking to present woman's desire, has done so by posing it as elsewhere, outside of the film, and to which men such as Kanning, Lidman and Jansson are inadequate. Identification here is thus threefold: with Gertrud's point of view in finding these men inadequate to her ideal; as inadequate, they fail and lose Gertrud and we may identify with their position as lacking, as having lost what they desire; and we may identify with the place of sufficency to her desire – the phallus – even though, or especially because, it has no representation in the film, but is traced as an absence by the film's very narrating. However, by taking Gertrud's point, of, view, the film also presents a critique of these men's desire for her. For what, after all, is their desire but for Gertrud to *be* the phallus, a fetishisation which thereby secures their own possession of the phallus? Their desire is to 'have' Gertrud, to possess her like a toy (as Gertrud accuses Kanning, with shades of Ibsen's Nora). The mirror in Kanning's drawing room, which is constantly used to such visual effect in the film, exemplifies this critique (see the cover of this book). It is a mirror which had been given to Gertrud by Lidman so that on awakening she might see herself, beautiful, in something beautiful; now she is married to Kanning, it hangs in his room, displaced – since he now 'owns' her – by his gift of a less ornate mirror which we never see but are told hangs in her room. Both men thus celebrate her image, and their desire for the narcissistic woman. But Gertrud does not seem to participate in this celebration and, for example, tidying her hair in front of the mirror in the opening scene, when her husband remarks on her beauty she appears absentminded, in contrast to his visible desire, while the poem she wrote at sixteen, and which she has chosen for her epitaph, has the line 'Am I beautiful, no, but I have loved'. This is not simple modesty but rather a displacement from her construction as subject *to* the image of the other's desire, that is, a displacement from her fetishisation as beautiful to a position as subject *of* desire. A shift from passive wish to be loved, to be what the other finds loveable – namely, being beautiful – to an active wish and possession of desire: I have loved, found others loveable.

From this there emerges a strong feminist statement of opposition to the fetishisation of the woman's image. But there is also something more, for if the film is drawing upon a discourse of feminist rights and self-determination in order to put the woman's desire outside of, as different from that place in which these men seek to hold her, then by identifying with Gertrud's point-of-view we are brought to reject that fetishisation of her and thus also identify as those who do not fetishise (her). And what kind of address does this constitute but that of a son to the phallic mother? It evokes the pre-Oedipal relation, for what other place is there that will be sufficient to her desire? By identifying with the place or cause of Gertrud's desire, that is, with the place of sufficiency of her desire, I am loved (or 'had') by Gertrud, and thus I know I am the phallus which she wants. This in contrast to the formulation: by loving Gertrud I have her, that is, I have the phallus which she is. And it is a position which a woman, too, might occupy since to be the desire of the phallic mother is to be the phallus oneself. Therefore, to say that we come to take up a passive position in identifying with the place of Gertrude's desire is not to designate it as either a masculine or a feminine identification.

There is, moreover, another position, namely that by loving Gertrud I have her, that is, I have the phallus which she is, and which is the position of the father in relation to the mother, and the position which Kanning and Lidman both seek, though unsuccessfully, in relation to Gertrud. The phallic fraud, however, is for Gertrud exposed, for the other also lacks. Each man shows that Gertrud is not sufficient to his desire. Kanning says, 'But Gertrud, dear, love can't fill a man's life. It would be ridiculous, for a man', while Lidman had earlier written, pencilled beside his sketch of her profiled face, 'woman's love and man's work – enemies from the start'. Nevertheless the unfilled place of address of Gertrud's demand remains, a place orchestrated by the film, by 'Dreyer'.

There emerges in *Gertrud*, therefore, an organisation of desire which exceeds the conventional but does so not in terms of a deconstruction, or a simple pluralism, but by producing a play between the categories of sexual difference which are now not merely the conventional two but at least four – active masculinity and passive masculinity together with active femininity and passive femininity. These are not mere inversions of each other, however, for what is at stake in each case is a different positioning in relation to castration, to having and being the phallus, and to desiring the other and desiring to be the desire of the other. The *aporia* that lies in the question 'what does she – Gertrud or the woman – want?' is the hesitation between a being and a having in which the one position excludes the other. Which is not at all what anyone wants.

7

Figuring the Fetish

It is so generally and widely accepted that works of representation may be fetishistic that it may seem surprising to question what this means. Psychoanalysis itself has pointed to fetishistic imagery in painting and literature as well as in dreams,[1] and it has become a term widely used in criticism. But in fact the assumption that the psychoanalytic concept of fetishism refers to a singular and clearcut psychical process which can also be found in the cinema has obscured the very complex nature of fetishism for the psychical subject and for the subject of cinema. In the discussion of the drives earlier, fetishism was shown to arise as the result of a process of disavowal which was related to fantasy, to the subject's remodelling of reality, and thus to be a psychical process central to both women and men. Fetishism, as a specific disavowal arising in relation to sexual difference within sexual practices, emerged as having a double form. It is the implications of this view of fetishism in relation to forms of representation with which I will now be concerned. The use of the concept of fetishism in theories of representation and as an account of ideology and the spectator's relation to forms of representation, including cinema, will be explored in the concluding chapter. Here it is the fetishism of representation and the psychoanalytic account of the formation of the fetish which will be examined in relation to Joseph von Sternberg's film *Morocco*.

A number of questions and problems arise in considering fetishism in representation. Firstly, how can we determine objects as fetish-objects within a work where the 'text' is not the patient's discourse but a painting, a film or a novel? As a corollary the question arises: for whom is this a fetish-object, and thus, who is the subject who fetishes? In a narrative work the subject may be a character within the fiction or representation, but it may also be the author/producer, as well as the viewer or the critic, who finds his or her own fetish within the work. The author may have presented – unconsciously or quite self-consciously – her own fetishistic obsessions in the work, but while we may recognise and understand the artist's view and representation of her experience in relation to the fetish-object, we are not necessarily expected or able to have the *same* relation to the object-as-fetish. What is represented here is the fetishism of a character, or of the 'author', but not necessarily of the film or painting as signifying system.[2] It may be asked, in fact, whether the object can be represented as a fetish for anyone other than the fetishist, and whether for the fetishist it can be represented (does a photograph of a fetish function as the fetish?). There is the question, too, of the relation of fetishism to narrative itself, for fetishism implies a refusal or halting of the unfolding of narrative as a logic of cause and effect in favour of a fixed knowledge, and it requires repetition without difference.

It would seem that as a general form in representation, as a kind of aesthetic or rhetoric, fetishism in film must involve something more than simply reproducing images of fetishes, or fetish images, as if there could be an archive of fetishes. The move from the specific pathology of the fetishist to the cinema cannot consist in a generalising of fetish objects as universal (and hard to imagine given the idiosyncracy Freud affirms in relation to the formation of the fetish) but rather must arise from the generality of the pleasure afforded by a fetishised representation of objects. As a result it cannot be particular objects – or images – in themselves which guarantee the fetishistic form of representation; rather, what is involved must be a general structure of representation and hence of the subject-position of the spectator for the representation.

Fetishism, for psychoanalysis, is a form of re-writing reality, a personal language of substitution and a form of representation. How then does this function? In *Three Essays on the Theory of Sexuality* Freud described fetishism as arising when 'the normal sexual object is replaced by another which bears some relation to it, but is entirely unsuited to serve the normal sexual aim'.[3] The shoe *replaces* the vagina, and all the overvaluation normally invested in the loved object is now given over to its replacement. Freud also distinguishes transitional cases in which the sexual object is required to fulfil a fetishistic condition 'such as the possession of some particular hair-colouring or clothing, or even some bodily defect – if the sexual aim is to be attained'.[4] It is not until his 1927 paper 'Fetishism' that Freud connects disavowal with fetishism which he now sees as a defence against the castration anxiety which the boy's Oedipal complex gives rise to and which he may resolve by disavowing the mother's lack of a penis and thereby disavow the danger to himself by constructing a fetish-substitute for the missing penis. Through the fetish he preserves the belief in the mother's penis, so that the shoe no longer replaces the vagina but the mother's missing penis. Of course, the very fact that the fetish is required affirms the knowledge of the absence of the mother's penis. Three elements emerge, therefore: a process of dis-avowal; an overinvestment in the object which, displaced from its 'proper' use, now appears to have 'magical' properties and which in a sense it does; and a process of substitution by which some 'original' object is replaced by another to constitute the fetish.

In 'Fetishism' Freud gave two contrasting accounts of the forma-tion of the fetish. On the one hand he restates his earlier view that the fetish is founded upon 'the last impression before the uncanny and traumatic one', again citing the example of the foot.[5] This sug-gests a metonymical structure for the fetish, based on contiguity, in which a part of the body or an object which has a contiguous rela-tion to the mother's genitals constitutes the fetish and then, metaphorically, stands *for* the mother's penis. On the other hand Freud concludes the essay with the assertion that 'the normal pro-totype of fetishes is a man's penis'.[6] This introduces the notion of a model, and of the fetish being like an absent – but actual – original, functioning as a simile or metaphor. However the role of the man's penis as a model lies in the structure of disavowal, not in the con-struction of the substitute; after all, it stands for the mother's missing penis, not the father's. What characterises the fetish is not that it is penis-like – it often isn't – but that it figures disavowal in a process of metamorphising displacement. The fetish is not genital imagery. That the fetish is not straightforwardly a symbol of the penis was shown by Freud in his example of a man whose fetish was an athletic support-belt which could also be worn as bathing drawers. This piece of clothing covered up the genitals entirely and concealed the distinction between them. Freud called this a 'very subtle instance' in which both the disavowal *and* affirmation of cas-tration have found their way into the construction of the fetish itself.[7]

What Freud is describing therefore is a metonymic displacement and not just a metaphorical substitution. This is shown in another of Freud's examples, of a young man who

had exalted a certain sort of 'shine on the nose' into a fetishistic precondition. The surprising explanation of this was that the patient had been brought up in an English nursery but had later come to Germany, where he forgot his mother-tongue almost completely. The fetish, which originated from his earliest child-hood, had to be understood in English, not German. The 'shine on the nose' [in German *Glanz auf der Nase*] – was in reality a '*glance* at the nose'.[8]

Freud concludes that the nose was thus the fetish, as a metaphorical substitution. At the same time and perhaps more importantly there has been a metonymical displacement, for the nose itself is not enough, it must have a 'luminous shine' which Freud says the young man endowed at will and which was not perceptible to others. This shine is also, in English – which was the young man's nursery language – the glance; thus the displacement is not between objects, but between signifiers. Case-studies show that it is not simply the object itself but also the way in which it is deployed in a scenario which is important. For Kohon's patient, the magical properties of an apron were only mobilised within an enactment: his wife would berate him for not wearing the apron, then when, despite his resistance, she finally forced him to wear it – very tightly tied around his waist – he would now be able to achieve an erection and penetrate his wife (but not to reach orgasm). In Abrahams's study it was the too-tight shoe, so that the central element is the *enclosed* object which is all the more palpable insofar as it is pinched and constrained by its enclosure – in the shoe, the corset or whatever. The fetish is therefore not only the shoe, but also the enclosed foot, as well as the signified 'too tight' which thereby affirms the presence of something enclosed – the phallus.[9] The fetish is a *symptom* in fact, which must be read, or deciphered, involving a search for meaning in language 'rather than in that of vague analogies in the visual field'.[10]

The fetishism described in case studies is a quite specific – and personal – production; it is what has earlier been considered as 'perverse' fetishism. Fetishism, however, involves not only an array – more or less limited – of 'magical' objects, but also a disavowal, and the object, the fetish, is the monument to that disavowal. The disavowal may take one of two forms. It may wholly arrest the knowledge the subject wishes to refuse, setting up the fetish as the truth and evidence for the refusal; but while castration anxiety is fully allayed, desire is also displaced. Or the disavowal is accom-panied by an avowal, there is anxiety, but the fetish secures desire nevertheless. This fetish object which causes desire Lacan called the *objet petit a*. As a result, something of disavowal is involved in general in representation – including the cinema – and it operates for both women and men. Through the fetish the subject disavows lackingness, thus while both the fetish and the *objet petit a* stand in for another object, the fetish does so in order to disavow the lack, whereas the *objet petit a* signifies lackingness. Clavreul argues that the pervert 'brings his disavowal to bear' on the knowledge that 'only the *lack* can be the *cause* of desire' so that 'it is not the *lack* that causes [his] desire, but a *presence* (the fetish)'.[11] On the one hand, therefore, where lack is fully disavowed fetishism supplants representation by overturning the play of absence/presence in favour of one only of those terms, presence. On the other hand, and where lack is not fully disavowed, the same signifying process which gives rise to the fetish is in play in representation. Given this distinction it might seem that we should now speak not of the fetish but of the *objet a*. However, not only does this have the practical disavantage that the Lacanian term cannot be used as a verb or to describe an action, but more importantly Lacan emphasises the role of the *objet a* as the element which disturbs meaning, a little bit of the real erupting in the symbolic operations of signification. As argued earlier, the *objet a* is two-faced, arising on the cusp of the real and symbolisation. Fetishising seems appropriate to name a first moment, when the *objet a* is separated out from the real by the subject as a presence – the child's cotton reel about to become the stake in a game of *fort-da* – before it immediately also signifies its lostness. Causing desire, it cannot satisfy the drive.

It is such a fetishising which I want to propose is at work in cinematic representation, involving disavowal, displacement and substitution. Firstly, through the film's mise en scène objects can become foregrounded whether by repetition or by visual emphasis such as a close-up, and hence producing a narrative expectation – that the gun will later be fired. If such an expectation is not fulfilled the object appears *displaced* from its proper function while nevertheless seeming specially significant by this foregrounding. In sum, the object appears overvalued within the narration. Secondly, a certain disavowal is involved in cinema, for as a linear form given in time and space films make present what will become again absent, in the next scene, at the end of the film. At the same time, as a form of story-telling, the film holds off knowledge, and its narrative strategies of delay effect a blocking of coming to know.

Thirdly, the metonymic sliding and metaphoric substitution in the construction of the fetish are themselves paradigmatic process of representation which can cause us to hover between two meanings – of course we know, in *Now, Voyager*, that Charlotte and Jerry are just smoking cigarettes, but all the same it is also something more, something else. This 'fetishising' produces a doubling of meaning, both an obvious and a hidden signified – it is both smoking, and sex. Fetishism 'eroticises' representation, for through it any and every object can become a sexual signifier. As a result it also produces sexuality as a signification, a text. The 'perverse' fetishist would meet such an oscillation of signification with a blank stare – her or his disavowal does not allow for such contamination of meaning.

In representation, therefore, the fetish is the signfier of an excess of meaning, becoming thereby a signifier of excess. It functions like the joke so that the 'improper' use of the object, just as the improper use of language in the pun or wordplay, opens us to another chain of meaning, of sexual desire as excessive, as transgressive of borders and conventional codes, and as exceeding ordinary language – knowing no bounds. The fetish also signifies that the 'proper' object – the object in its proper use – is not the 'real' object, which is indeed the case, for it is only through fantasy, if at all, that a man or a woman can come to be brought to stand in the place of the object that will satisfy.

A film, therefore, does not produce a fetish object, or even a series of objects in some sort of hierarchy which may be taken up by (male) viewing subjects already psychically constructed to fetishise.[12] There is no such simple meeting of fetishist and fetish in the cinema. Rather, insofar as it presents to us objects in a relation of substitution and displacement, cinema fetishises them. Of course, too, something of disavowal as such is involved in representation in its making present of what is absent, but insofar as absence is also always thereby presented, what is figured for the subject is its relation to its *objets a*, not its fetishes. I shall continue to call the processes of substitution and displacement, as well as the narrative blocking and deferrment, a process of fetishising in film, for only when a figuring of lack enters the scene are the terms of the play fully in place.

The following analysis of *Morocco* attempts to show the processes of fetishising at work in the film, involving its narrative form, its structuring fantasy, and its mise en scène. At the same time the film is not without its *objets petit a,* those elements which re-mark absence – lack, causing desire; indeed it centres a narrative of coming to have and then losing the object of desire reminiscent of the cotton-reel game of Freud's young grandson. *Morocco* is a film which has already been established as paradigmatic of filmic fetishism by Laura Mulvey in 'Visual Pleasure and Narrative Cinema', as well as in the analysis of the film by the editors of *Cahiers du Cinéma.* The discussion here both follows and diverges from these two accounts in order to give a different place to the woman and to feminine desire in the film.

MOROCCO

> For all its frenzied fabulousness, *Morocco* succeeded in its
> time as illusionism for the general public. The proof of this
> success is the long-remembered disbelief in the final image
> of Marlene Dietrich setting out into the desert sands on
> spike heels in search of Gary Cooper. C.A.Lejeune of the
> London *Observer* has described this finale as one of the
> most absurd of all time. Yet to single out any one detail of
> a film for disbelief is to believe in the rest, and to believe in
> *Morocco*'s California desert is to believe in Sternberg's
> dream decor.[13]

The issues of belief and dream, knowledge and disavowal, fantasy and desire, which have been central for this book, are found nowhere more clearly than in Sternberg's *Morocco.*[14] A disavowal, the problem of two knowledges, one which cancels the other, is the central narrative enigma – 'She loves me, she loves me not' and 'He loves me, he loves me not' – while throughout the film a strategy of exchange and equivalence, of this object for that, this character or action for that, together with the insistent impression of *display* in the mise en scène, marks out a process of fetishistic substitution. As a result the very drive of the film is a certain fetishism. A corollary of this is that the foregrounding of the fetishistic desire also names it as such, in a flagrant display of impossibility. This fetishism is no longer a matter of fetish-objects, but of a fetishising, of the becoming substituted. Representation typically veils this process, and is added to the disavowal which is the very condition of representation – that I know it isn't real but all the same. *Morocco* relentlessly re-states its fetishistic desire, replaying a scenario of avowal/ disavowal, displacement and substitution.[15]

Within the fantasy structure constituted in the film the mise en scène functions not only as fore-pleasure supporting the fantasy, but also as a display and a play which fetishises. It is through this mise en scène and fantasy scenario that a series of 'figures' are produced involving a structure or code of repetitions, of oppositions, of exchanges and equivalences, of looks at and between characters, and of blocking or delay.

The fetishism of the mise en scène arises in two ways – from the use of objects and characters in a circulation of substitution and exchange, and in the palpable overinvestment in or excessive value on the visual within the image. Freud had characterised fetishism as just such an 'overvaluation' in an object such that it takes on 'magical' qualities, and this is also central to forms of representation; the spectator is made aware that the object is there for some 'other' reason than its usefulness or its function for the narrative. However this is not an allegorical or symbolic use because no signified emerges; rather, objects appear significant because our attention has been drawn to them in some way. At the same time this meaningfulness is not part of the unfolding of the story; the significance is not there to motivate the next event; it is not a question of 'plot' in the traditional sense. On the contrary, it produces an excess, a redundancy and a delay, so that the form of imaging can produce an effect of a disavowal of lack, the lack of 'anything more', displacing and blocking the narrative and the inexorable chain of its events, halting the unfolding of the 'next image' which will tell more of the narrative. Instead there is a lack of this 'more' outside of the image as such, its moment. Here, then, is the process of disavowal and substitution which Freud later posited as arising from the fear of castration to produce the fetish object, which therefore remains as its monument. The film, too, effects a displacement on to its objects which fill up the image, constituting moments which are complete, rather than pregnant with the expectation of the *next* image.

In *Morocco* Sternberg fills up the frame, and clutters it, pushing out narrative concerns and plot motivation in favour of the scene as seen; images are shown for their own sake and not as mere elements in the larger narrative drive of the film. The multiple and complex connotations of the mise en scène produce a 'richness' of visual scene which at times seems to be there in and for itself – for example, the opening of the film which introduces the 'orient' of Mogador, the donkey, the narrow streets, the Mullah calling the faithful to prayer, the 'Arab' girls, one barebreasted, another clasping a human skull impaled on a stake behind her, images of eroticism and death combined, which are now revealed, now hidden by the figures of the passing Legionnaires in foreground. Sternberg also frames within the frame, filling it with with drapes or architectural features which traverse the filmic space, marking it out but also cutting it up as a space – for example in Amy's dressing room at Lo Tinto's an electric cable criss-crosses Amy Jolly's actions like a spider's web (see still from shot 50, plate 4) and at the beginning of the film the narrow streets of Mogador are shown beneath suspended nets which cast shadowy webs ensnaring the figures below. Light and shade are manipulated to change or enhance spatial relations: space is foreshortened, the screen becoming one-dimensional; or lengthened, as in the opening of *Morocco* where the troops march forward toward a mule stubbornly stopped in the middle of the roadway. The deferment of narrative is seen clearly as well in this sequence, which is on the one hand an elaborate and lengthy establishing of time and place as well as verisimilitude – its images of the Foreign Legion soldiers and of the indigenous people are what we expect Morocco to be like, while this also creates a realism, since the time given to the scene is longer than necessary for the narrative. On the other hand the sequence constitutes a vast and immediate displacement of the narrative action, for nothing yet has happened which constitutes a *fabula* event.

Sternberg subordinates character and theme to setting; he has something to show, and thus to say, so that actions become motivated through the mise en scène rather than through character. Andrew Sarris commented, 'Every bit of bric-a-brac, every shadowed shutter, every fluttering fabric conveys the characters inexorably toward an emotional decision they would resist if they could.'[16] Thus he points to the way that the elaboration of mise en scène appears to substitute for plot motivation. Laura Mulvey referred to Sternberg's quip that he would welcome his films being projected upside down so that the story and the character involvement would not interfere with the spectator's appreciation of the screen image. As she notes, of course the film must remain identifiable, but the comment is 'revealing in that it emphasises the fact that for him the pictorial space enclosed by the frame is paramount rather than narrative or identification processes'.[17] Sternberg is interested in cutting out a space, creating a view, *framing* – in a literalisation of Barthes's definition of fetishism in his essay 'Diderot, Brecht, Eisenstein'.[18]

In contrast to this fixing within the frame there are a multitude of objects circulated and exchanged, set working to produce signification through repetition and reversal. There is the dough-nut and the bangle Tom steals from the street stall, the rendezvous hour signalled by the girl's fingers echoed in confirmation by Tom (see still from shot 13, plate 4). La Bessiere's card, given to Amy on the boat but immediately discarded by her is a blocked exchange, tossed in tiny pieces into the ocean. Later there are fans passed from one character to another, a rose taken from a woman, as well as a kiss, by Amy, who then throws the rose (but not a kiss) to Tom who also wears it – as the woman had done – 'in his hair', behind his ear; Amy sells Tom an apple and passes him her key as his 'change' – Tom bites into the apple as, in the next shot in big close-up, Tom clenches the key in his fist, rubbing the tip with his thumb (see stills from shots 52, 83, 86, 87, 101, 118, 121, 122: plate 4). Later there is the expensive bracelet La Bessiere has given Amy, care-lessly put aside by her amongst her make-up. After Tom and Amy have agreed to leave together that night, Tom remains in her room while she performs on stage; he idly picks the bracelet up, replaces it, then picks it up again, as if registering its implications – the wealth La Bessiere can give Amy in contrast to himself – then picks up items of her make-up, including her lipstick which he looks at before turning to her mirror where he uses it to write his message 'I changed my mind. Goodluck'. La Bessiere's second gift, the string of pearls, is spilt by Amy as she rises in agitation from their engage-ment banquet, not at the news of the Legionnaires return – which she has already learnt of – but at the sounds, the bugle, which metonymically convey their presence – off-screen . There is the knife Tom returns to retrieve, after which Amy sees the carving he has etched on the table; and finally there are the shoes she aban-dons in the sand. While these objects are clearly functional for the narration, this is not in terms of their direct use-value, but in a dis-placed manner, through the signified or 'figure' they come to con-stitute.[19] The objects appear 'fetishised', while their displacement and exchange also constitutes a form of blocked communication, in which the possibility opened by the object, La Bessiere's card etc., is closed off. As a result a loss is also inscribed.

A certain fetishism also characterises *Morocco's* narrative strategy, exemplified in the repeated scene of a possible consummation of desire, and its delay, deferment, blocking. The film is thus highly circular, *en*closed, but thereby without effective closure. Of course there is nothing perverse in the content of the scenes, but the obsessive staging of the same scene – of a meeting and a separation – is the kind of blocked scenario Joyce McDougall described in relation to the pervert's fantasies; nothing will happen – because nothing ever did happen – between mummy and daddy. At the same time the film embeds an Oedipal scenario, of the older man rejected (La Bessiere) in favour of the younger (son) Tom Brown. The film sets up the possibility of a couple only to defer its consummation, disavowing its realisation, while the impossibility of the Oedipal desire is reinscribed by the same invariable blocking of any outcome to this scenario. The fantasy is directly fetishistic, for it proposes the pleasure of disavowal – the woman wants nothing from the father (because she has it) – and avowal – I have what she desires.

In *Morocco*, as in most Sternberg films, the seen is foregrounded within the scene, thus foregrounding too the spectator's look, as well as providing us with a privileged point-of-view onto the film's protagonists, Amy Jolly and Tom Brown. How far are the characters thereby fetishised – as Mulvey has suggested of Dietrich – in being held for our view – and does this replace identification? Laura Mulvey suggested that 'the powerful look of the male protagonist (characteristic of traditional narrative film) is broken in favour of the image in direct erotic rapport with the spectator' thus enabling the fetishistic relation to the image.[20] The replacement of identification with a character's look by a direct pleasure in looking does afford the spectator a direct scopophilic pleasure. However, such a looking becomes a fetishism not because of the image and any eroticism of the image itself, but when, as Mulvey says, the film freezes the look, holding the spectator's look to the image as sufficient in itself. It is the imaging which is the fetish, the 'seeing', not the seen. In this the image of Dietrich produced by the film is central, but it is not itself the fetish. The 'flawlessness' of the image of Dietrich marks its function not as the 'ultimate fetish'[21] but as the image which completes oneself – the phallic mother of the mirror phase – which thus affirms the subject's own, imaginary, unity. The very flawlessness pointing to its function as an idealisation of the mother, of the other, as perfect, complete and whole, in a much more archaic gesture than fetishism, radically pre-Oedipal, and in play for women as well as men. What is involved here is not so much the eradication of a flaw – castration – as the production of an ideal-ego, an ideal image which has not yet had to undergo dismemberment and repair. Yet the very cinematicity of the flawlessnes of Dietrich's beauty – filmed in soft-focus, filtred through gauze, marks a constructedness in her image as idealised – and it is an idealisation which is also found in the image of Gary Cooper in the film.

The image as made, or re-made, already marks as lost what the imaging seeks to make present, so that castration and lack have entered the scene, together with an oscillation between being and having the phallus. This is not yet fetishism, however, for while there is an overvaluation of the object, there has been no substitution. For fetishism something must fall away from the image or displace it, just as our first look at Dietrich in the film is interrupted and displaced – her suitcase falls opens and her clothes and objects tumble out, so many fetish objects, to be collected, replaced and returned to her by La Bessiere. Fetishism's disavowal of lack is realised through a process of substitution, which is the role of the circulating objects in *Morocco*.

In its fetishising displaying *Morocco* presents an omniscient narration marking a separation of spectator-look and character-look. This is not, however, the whole story, for not only has the play of wishes which the film embeds, together with their Oedipal references, opened us to identification with the narrative drive, but intercharacter looks and pov (point-of-view) shots are also central to the film's narration. Nor is it only the male characters who hold the look: women too are the agents of a look, notably but not only Amy Jolly; and to the extent that Amy Jolly looks back at other characters within the film, and we as spectators are positioned with her pov look, then she is not always and not only an object of the camera's look. Equally Tom appears as the object as well as the subject of a look.[22] *Morocco* makes particular use of two distinct strategies in relation to characters' looks. On the one hand we see characters watching other characters, often themselves unseen, for example La Bessiere, but also Madame Caesar and Adjutant Caesar. On the other hand characters find themselves being looked at, as is the case for both Amy and Tom, in an inversion of the usual point-of-view shot structure.[23] In the scene which introduces Tom (see stills from shots 8, 9, 13, 14, plate 4), he is shown standing at a street stall, half-hidden behind the vertical strands of the hanging goods (which produces a further visual gridding of the fame). The camera cuts 45° to a frontal shot of Tom who looks around to his left and right, then upwards; the camera cuts to low angle shot of two women on the roof of a house – one is looking down, we may infer, at Tom, for she opens her veil to show her face, and the other woman then turns to look down at Tom as well. The low angle marks the shot as Tom's pov, however, by showing Tom finding himself looked at; the film implies the look of the women *before* it shows Tom seeing them. This is immediately repeated in Tom's encounter with the girl at the stall in the following shots. Tom looks around, takes a doughnut from the stall, begins to eat it, looks around again, which motivates the cut. The next shot shows a girl watching him; she's seated obliquely, so that she has to turn her body to look round at him; she nods slightly at him, then the camera cuts back to Tom who looks around again, puts down his doughnut, toys with bangles on the stall, takes one and quickly throws it in the direction of the woman. This structure of the character finding herself or himself looked at is repeated in the introduction of Amy Jolly on board the ship bringing her to Mogador. We see firstly La Bessiere in medium-shot, then in long-shot, and now Amy enters into frame right past him, then when her suitcase falls open, Amy looks around left, away from La Bessiere who is now walking towards her, then right to find his gaze. Amy, however, blocks his gaze, for she looks away as she bends down to pick up her possessions, and then, in the next shot, she stands up, out of frame, while La Bessiere finishes collecting her things. When Tom arrives at Lo Tinto's he is shown again finding himself seen. Entering left of frame, striking in his dress uniform with white trousers, he looks around, then walks forward past the expensive tables to the pit, lights a cigarette, arrives at a table in the pit, sits down, looks around, then, seeing something off, left, he stands up and waves. In the next shot Adjutant Caesar, his wife and La Bessiere, are looking off frame right in the direction of Tom. When Madame Caesar glances behind, her husband turns to look as well, while she quickly looks back and waves in Tom's direction, wryly observed – we may infer – by La Bessiere. The next shot shows Tom as before. He sits down. He has, again, found himself being looked at.

In finding himself looked at Tom Brown is thus first an object of desire before he is a subject of desire, while through the film's emphasis on Gary Cooper as a seen object the figure of Tom comes to

connote to-be-looked-at-ness just as much as does Amy.[24] Cooper's
lanky tallness, marked out when he stoops to enter and leave
Amy's room, and again as he leaves the army cell, which while re-
marking his masculinity also makes him appears displayed, thus
also calling it into question since such parade, as Lacan noted,
appears feminine.

The film's narrative functions through a series of exchanges at-
tempted, a circuit of desire set in motion and then blocked.
Emblematically, this is also the first image of the film – a donkey
blocks the roadway but is pushed aside by the Legionnaires. Amy
is the initial narrative agent of this blocking, throwing away La
Bessiere's card and his offer of help on the ship, refusing Lo Tinto's
advice, brushing off the advances of a man in the audience, and rejecting La Bessiere's invitation to finish her evening with him. The
circuit of exchange she opens with Tom is then blocked by Amy
when she says she could become fond of him and sends him away,
then reopened when she runs after Tom, then blocked again when
he is attacked by Madame Caesar's hired men. It is reopened when
Tom visits her again at Lo Tinto's, but now he blocks it: he
'becomes decent' – as he later describes it to the sergeant – and
leaves her to a more wealthy fate with La Bessiere.

The figures of exchange, equivalence, opposition and repetition,
of looks, and of blocking, 'repercuss' across the film,[25] giving rise to
implications, significations exceeding the actions and events. This
can be seen in the sequence in Amy's dressing room, immediately
after Tom has arrived at Lo Tinto's (see stills from shots 49, 50, 51,
52, 62, plate 4).[26] The first shot of this sequence appears as a transition shot, for the space is initially unplaced, and it shows in
medium close-shot two dolls, one Chinese, one African, placed on a
window ledge, facing straight to camera, while a woman's voice
singing off-screen can be heard. The next shot shows Amy Jolly in
medium-shot in her dressing room, Amy's singing revealing her as
the voice in the previous shot. She is wearing a man's dress shirt
and evening trousers, one hand in her trouser pocket, the other
holding a small mirror. She looks frame left, then right to her image
in the mirror, then she picks up a fan in her other hand, looks at it
(it therefore doubles the mirror), and begins to fan herself. The following shot is an oblique medium long-shot, heavily shadowed,
showing two women – one seated – in the rear of the shot, framed
in mid-ground by two pillars. The women cool themselves slowly
with large palm fans. A man, later shown to be Lo Tinto, walks past

them, watched by the women as he approaches a door frame left. Next, in medium shot, we see Amy's dressing room again, but from a different angle as the camera has moved around to the right revealing an electricity cable strung across the room in mid-foreground. Lo Tinto walks through the door frame right, while Amy moves frame left to stand in a bright pool of light while he is in semi-darkness. She lights a cigarette, passes her fan to him, he replies thank you, interrupting the flow of his advice; he fans himself briefly then throws it down, continuing his advice. Amy picks up a folded top-hat, flicks it out – the noise stops Lo Tinto momentarily – puts it on, and looks at herself in the mirror she still holds, barely glancing at Lo Tinto. She picks up the coat tails which he helps her into, and she places a folded handkerchief in her breast pocket, then looks in the mirror again. Lo Tinto exits right as she adjusts her bow tie, stretching her neck as a man might when a starched collar scratches a newly-shaved neck.

Exchanges   Amy gives Lo Tinto her fan, while he gives her advice; just as he throws away the fan, so Amy will ignore his advice.

Oppositions   (i) Masculine versus feminine – the dolls juxtaposed in the next shot with Amy in masculine attire, just as the women are juxtaposed with Lo Tinto, but in each case the masculine term is 'mixed'. (ii) The large fans of the two women versus the small fan Amy holds and then passes to Lo Tinto – again feminine versus masculine but ironically inverting the conventional distinction of, respectively, large and small. (iii) Opposition between Amy and Lo Tinto – Amy's carefully groomed appearance in coat and tails, her cool nonchalance, her very controlled image, contrasts with his agitation as he mops his brow of sweat and fusses anxiously, an image of lack of control. He presents a mixture, of western evening dress and eastern in the huge hoop earrings he wears, and of sexual difference – this man appearing more feminine than masculine. While in contrast Amy is this woman appearing more masculine than a man.

Connotations   The dolls are marked out for our view, but are not used, or referred to, in the following shots, hence they appear unreadable, enigmatic, a quality which extends to Amy as their owner. They connote the 'exotic', and the artificial, a doubled sign of the feminine presented as masquerade. They reappear later, to be placed in La Bessiere's arms as he 'carries off' Amy after Tom's departure. 'Standing in' for Amy, they represent a critique of La Bessiere's very desire for her.

Repetitions   Fans recur later, used as a veil by the woman in the audience whom Amy kisses, and again by Tom when he kisses Amy in her room. The fan and mirror, one in each of Amy's hands, repeat and mirror each other. The foregrounding of the fan in this scene, passed to Lo Tinto, is repeated in Tom's visit, when he enters and grasps for the fan by the door, implying that he knows the apartment well, but not finding it immediately (i.e. in its 'usual' place). His fumbling undoes his bravado. This sequence is repeated at the end of the scene, when he goes to leave and nonchalantly tosses the fan on to a table, but it misses and he has to stoop to pick it up.

Looks   Tom's look off-screen at the end of the sequence of his arrival at Lo Tinto's is 'answered' by the dolls in the next shot, but this is clearly a blocking. The women outside Amy's room look at Lo Tinto, who looks at Amy, who looks at herself or off-screen away from Lo Tinto. There is no exchange of looks, and no pov looks.

The following sequence shows Lo Tinto introducing his new star. His comic role is emphasised when he stumbles as he pulls the stage curtains across, while his earnest remarks of introduction are treated humorously by the audience.[27] In contrast Amy walks on stage coolly smoking, to be greeted by the boos of the audience (including those of Tom's girlfriend) but receiving an appreciative look from Tom, who attempts to quieten those booing. Amy, walking off-stage around to the expensive tables, begins to sing; she shrugs off the hand of a male bystander. Finishing, she bows, then leaps the rail and accepts a glass of champagne offered her. She turns to go, then turns back to take a flower from a woman guest at the table, and then kisses her (see stills from shots 83, 86, 87 and 101, plate 5). Turning around again towards the pit, she bows to the applause, then throws the flower to Tom. The sequence repeats the opposition established between Lo Tinto and Amy of feminine masculinity and masculine femininity. It presents a sexual advance refused – the man whose hand Amy shrugs off – and one accepted – the kiss Amy gives the woman. Amy swings herself over the balcony rail and swigs back the glass of champagne offered her just like any man, then asks for the flower, which is given by a woman to another woman dressed as a man who gives it to a man who wears it like a woman. This overturns the relations proper to the conventions of sexual difference, but which are thereby confirmed. It is a scene above all else of a performance, of

Dietrich as cabaret star, of sexual difference performed, presented in the exquisite imitation offered by Amy, which constitutes a repudiation of the masquerade by which the woman denies her difference and covers this disavowal by the paraphernalia of femininity. The kiss completes Amy's performance as a man, and thus confirms sexual difference rather than introducing its negation, while also producing it as a guise, a show. Of course the fact that we know Amy to be a woman makes the performance no deception; and Tom really is a man. This allows Amy's kissing of the woman to reverberate as scandalous, as titillating in a highly conventional heterosexual way. The tension of the audience's hostility and opposition to Amy dressed as a man is overturned in their seduction by her performance, the performance of a man.

The looks in this sequence involve first of all Amy as the 'star', looking to find herself looked at. She appears on stage in shot 63; shot 64 is a close-up of Tom looking appreciatively at Amy; in shot 65 Amy walks forward, surveying the audience left and right. The following shot (66) is a high-angle oblique shot from the stage on to the audience, with Tom in centre foreground, the high angle suggesting it is Amy's pov, whereas the previous shots of Amy have not been low-angle, i.e. motivated as the audience's, or Tom's, pov. Shot 67 is a reverse angle of 66 with Amy looking down at the audience, shot 68 shows Tom trying silence the boos, and shot 69 is of Amy impassively watching as she draws on her cigarette – she is looking in the same direction as shot 66. In shot 70 Tom pushes his girlfriend to make her sit down and turns back to look at Amy. In shot 71, Amy gets up from the chair against which she was perching and walks across stage left and leans against the rail between the pit and the expensive tables; shot 72 is a medium-close shot of Tom watching, implying a reverse-shot of 71. Shot 73 is as shot 71 but closer in, and Amy begins to sing, turning her head as the camera cuts. La Bessiere now enters the sequence of looks, but never receives a look – shot 74 is a close-up of La Bessiere looking out of frame right towards – we may assume – Amy. Shot 75 is Amy singing; a man grasps her arm, propositioning her, but she pulls away from him. Shot 76, as 72, Tom watching Amy; shot 77, Amy in close-up turns her head to look screen left, i.e. in the direction of Tom. Shot 78, as 74, La Bessiere looking towards Amy offscreen. Shot 79, as 77, Amy singing. Shot 80, Tom turns his head to look around him, as he has often before but this time the context suggests he is looking to see not who is looking at him, but to see who is looking at Amy, and it ends with him looking back at her. Shot 81, a close-up of Amy singing; she turns her head, then tips back her top hat. Shot 82, Tom tips his Legionnaire's cap back – as a responding salute – and behind him in frame his girlfriend watches him. Shot 83, Amy finishes her song, looks around her for the applause, leaps the rail and takes the glass of champagne. After kissing the woman Amy again tips her hat; turning and walking away she removes her hat and bows to acknowledge the applause. Shot 84 is a reverse angle of 83, Amy walking back to the stage past Tom in the pit; he stands up to clap her. Shot 85 is from a similar angle but a close-up of Tom, now perched on a table, looking in what we understand to be Amy's direction and appeciatively clapping her perfomance. Shot 86, from the side, shows both Amy and Tom; Amy smells the flower, then looks down towards Tom. Shot 87, medium shot of Tom clapping, and smiling, off-screen, Amy throws the flower to him, he catches it, his face falls and his smile disappears; his girlfriend angrily watching stands up. Shot 88, Amy walks off looking right down at Tom. Shot 89 is of Tom again, from a new angle, close up, the flower in his hand, pensive; he then smells it, pressing his lips together in an enigmatic expression (he will later be seen wearing it behind his ear).

Within the segment, though every shot of Tom can be read as containing a look at Amy, not all of Amy's looks are at Tom. The series of exchanges between Amy and Tom are interrupted by La Bessiere; however, Amy does not look at La Bessiere. After shot 63 the sequence alternates between Tom looking at Amy and Amy who sometimes looks at Tom. The sequence establishes the erotic relation of the couple, but the exchange of looks is unequal, while Tom is primarily the object of Amy's actions. Moreover the cinema audience is shown that the scene is *over-looked*, by La Bessiere, who is who singled out as observer of the scene by the cutaway to him, and by the audience within the film.

The next sequence replays these figures. It is a second performance, but with differences.[28] It opens backstage again but now outside Amy's room. Lo Tinto is seen wearing a tray of apples like a cigarette-girl, baskets on his arms, when Amy enters frame left, now dressed 'femininely', wearing a tight bodice and satin shorts, with a long feather boa slung around her shoulders; she too carries a basket of apples (see still from shot 90, plate 4). Lo Tinto again urges her to make money, to sell the apples, as earlier he had advised her to find a rich patron. She will again reject his advice.

The opposition of the two figures is repeated, but now the masculine woman vs the feminine male is replaced by the feminine woman, replete with the trappings of the masquerade, contrasting with Lo Tinto's feminine male. There is a careful separation of the two, however, achieved by means of a the pillar between them, a phallic object cutting through the space, so that Lo Tinto's 'femininity' does not contaminate Amy's masquerade. Throughout the segment Amy exquisitely displays femininity by her gestures, as well as by her appearance, primping her boa on stage; selling fruit she leans across the balcony rail – which she had earlier leapt over – in a delicate ballet-like pose. When the same man who earlier had placed his hand on her arm now catches hold of her feather boa, Amy pulls it back through his hands in a movement which appears sexual. The boa held by the man again signifies a sexual proposition, but while Amy's response is also again a blocking, it is now as a passive – feminine – withdrawal.

Her performance as a woman is thus as studied as her performance as a man had been. Masculinity and femininity are paraded in each performance, implying something else, another femininity and another masculinity. There are thus not two but at least four 'sexualities' in *Morocco*. The division male and female is doubled but not overlaid by the division phallic/non-phallic or castrated, so that Tom and Amy line up on the side of the phallic, while La Bessiere, Adjutant Caesar as well as Madam Caesar appear on the side of the non-phallic or castrated.

The segment also repeats the previous one; Amy rejects one advance, and makes her own, to Tom once more. Two exchanges are blocked, the third is accepted. Tom's girl demands the flower, but when he refuses she angrily walks off. Amy sells an apple to La Bessiere, who proffers a note of large denomination and for which she has no change; he says keep it, and invites her to join him for the rest of the evening but she refuses. Amy sells Tom an apple, and as his 'change' gives him the key to her room. His appreciative munching of the apple metaphorises his appreciation of what the key means (see stills from shots 118, 121, 122, 123, plate 5). However, this scene also includes a blocking by Amy – one which will be repeated on Tom's visit to her apartment – when, after paying for his apple, Tom pulls her down to sit with him, and she gets up immediately saying 'You're pretty brave' (pause) 'with women', to laughter from the audience. However, this has immediately followed a blocking by Tom when he rejects Amy's offer of the apple 'for nothing' saying 'Nothing doing. I always pay for what I get', thus putting Amy in the place of a prostitute.

The structure of looks confirms the figure of overlooking, Madame Caesar is shown in close-up looking off frame right in the direction of Tom, hence overlooking his argument with his girl-friend about the flower, and underlining its meaning, for the flower now stands as a symbol of the sexual desire between Tom and Amy. Amy's look is again not marked as being directed at Tom; there is no reverse-shot structure, and instead her gaze is usually straight ahead to the audience in general. In contrast Tom's look at Amy is marked; he tips his cap at her when she first arrives on stage but this is not acknowledged by Amy. Only after she walks over to him in the pit do they exchange looks, but this is within the frame. The shot in which Amy turns to go to the pit could motivate her look as directed at Tom, but it is followed by a cutaway to the conductor and orchestra. The flirtation between the couple is there-fore delayed, but kept on the boil by the cutaways to Tom looking at Amy,[29] and these are paralleled by cutaways to the conductor who also turns to look at Amy, while the conductor's comic figure is rhymed in Tom, still with the flower behind his ear. However there is no cutaway to Tom during Amy's encounter with La Bessiere[30] so that Tom is not shown to overlook this scene, just as Amy does not overlook the scene of Tom and his girlfriend (al-though this could be inferred from the direction of his look it is not clearly marked as are the other 'overlookings').

In contrast, the cutaways to Madame Caesar and later to La Bessiere, who overlooks as Tom buys an apple and receives Amy's key (see still from shot 119, plate 5), produce an equivalence between these two characters, narratively confirmed when both are shown to be unrequited in their love for Tom and Amy respect-ively. (This also puts La Bessiere and Adjutant Caesar in the same position, losing the woman they love to Tom, but the film does not draw upon this possibility; Adjutant Caesar appears tragic and is killed, La Bessiere stays on to overlook Amy's departure.) Strikingly, in both shots the character looks, then looks away, then back again, producing a re-marking of their gaze, drawn back as if against their better judgement, or after thoughtful consideration, to the object of their desire. Such a gesture of looking, so familiar as 'Dietrichian' is thus also characteristic of many of the characters in *Morocco*, including Tom (and we may conclude therefore that it is an aspect of the Sternbergian authorial sub-code). In the final shot of the segment showing Tom simply smiling in close-up, the direction of his look is not motivated as a look at something, but rather refers metaphorically to a potential future realisation of the couple. This is repeated but inverted at the end of the film, when Amy sets off with the camp followers unknown to Tom.

The sequence presents in microcosm all the encounters between Amy and Tom, and Amy and La Bessiere during the film, of desire acknowledged then disavowed, then resumed just at the moment when consummation is made impossible – here by the public situation of the cabaret, later by Madame Caesar's hired thugs who attack Tom, at the end by Tom's departure (to manoeuvres, or a possible battle), but kept in play by Amy's decision to follow him, joining the band of forgotten women. However, this structure is mediated by objects: the flower, apple and key which are here enabling; the bracelet, the lipstick with which Tom writes 'I've changed my mind' which block; the knife, and carving – another sign – are once more enabling. The repetitions and reversal displayed are simply the basis for the subsequent encounters which repeat and reverse the figures established. La Bessiere succeeds Lo Tinto (as the similarity in the names suggests) as the feminine masculine insofar as his unrequited love for Amy places him as passive, wishing to be loved even when she makes him appear ridiculous at the engagement dinner. As he confesses to his dumbfounded guests, 'You see...I love her, I'd do anything to make her happy.'

Here happiness is not what anyone gets. Instead we have the future chance of happiness, safely preserved in the continued possibility of a consummation on condition that it is endlessly deferred. Amy, having kissed La Bessiere goodbye, departs through the city gates, casting her shoes off as if tossing aside the accoutrements of the feminine masquerade. But which masquerade? That of the phallic woman masquerading as castrated or of a castrated woman masquerading as phallic? The very ambiguity no doubt ensured the film's box-office success, the film's pleasure arising in its avowal/disavowal of the two knowledges involved. But to produce this pleasure, the film must also foreground this oscillation of knowledge, flaunting its very conditions. On the one hand it thereby constitutes a critique of fetishism, and of fantasy, but on the other hand it leaves open the possibility of a more radical disavowal, for while fantasy in general is disavowed, just here, this little bit, is sustained as reality.

8

The Fetish of Ideology

The view of fetishism which has been developed over the last few chapters has placed it at the centre of representation and as a process for women as well as men. What are the implications of the arguments presented here for theories of ideology which have drawn upon the psychoanalytic concept of fetishism?

For Roland Barthes, in his essay 'Diderot, Brecht, Eisenstein', the fetishism of representation is the cutting out of the scene from the seen, an act of *découpage* which thereby affirms the unity of the subject of that action as well as reciprocally affirming the truth – the realism – of the representation thus formed. It *is* the meaning. Thus the scene, the picture, the shot, the cut-out rectangle of cinema, all these are the very condition of theatre, painting, literature and cinema as arts:

> Here we have the geometrical foundation of representation: a fetishist subject is required to cut out the tableau. This point of meaning is always the Law: law of society, law of struggle, law of meaning.[1]

Barthes is concerned to show how in both Brecht's theatre and Eisenstein's cinema of montage this centering of the subject as a subject of knowledge is overturned. Stephen Heath, in his essay 'Lessons from Brecht', develops this argument:

> Separation is the mode of the classic – 'Aristotelian' – theatre which Brecht seeks to oppose, as it is also of classic cinema; the very mode of representation. The structure of representation is a structure of fetishism: the subject is produced in a position of separation from which he is confirmed in an imaginary coherence (the representation is the guarantee of his self-coherence) the condition of which is the ignorance of the structure of his production, of his setting in position.[2]

282

Drawing on Freud's account of fetishism, he argues:

> All this is to say that fetishism is a structure – popular accounts
> of fetishism with reference simply to objects are thus extremely
> misleading – and that this structure focusses a centre, the subject
> it represents, which derives its unity, its untroubled centrality,
> from the split it operates between knowledge and belief, between
> knowledge which disperses the stability of the subject, opens a
> production of desire in which the subject has everything to lose,
> and belief in which the subject positions himself in his structural
> plenitude.[3]

The fetishism of representation is aligned with the cinema as imaginary[4] and mainstream cinema is seen as a machine of the imaginary:

> Our hypothesis, therefore, is that a crucial – determining – part of
> the functioning of ideological systems is the establishment of a
> series of machines (institutions) which move – placing of desire –
> the subject ('sender' and 'receiver') in an appropriation of the
> symbolic into the imaginary (the definition of miscognition).[5]

And this fetishism of representation is allied with the realism of the classical cinema[6] which covers over the nature of film as illusion. As a result Ben Brewster and Colin MacCabe argued for a struggle 'against the fetishistic position of the spectator – fixed in his position securely by the reality of the image'.[7] Fetishism is here central to the subject-position of the spectator in cinema.[8]

Two kinds of cinema are implied by such a position. One is a cinema which re-makes the subject as imaginary, a full, centred subject of the misrecognition of the mirror phase; hence cinema, too, as imaginary. The other is a cinema in which the spectator-subject is posed as split, aware of the work of representation – Brechtian. Good cinema is didactic: it refuses imaginary identification to the spectator, and it presents itself as a construction through self-reflexive devices. Bad cinema is illusory: it centres narrative, fantasy and identification in a way which produces a fixed subject-spectator – disavowing its real conditions of production. It is also pleasurable, however, so that narrative cinema becomes a vice which we can't quite give up. A problem arises here, namely that fetishism is held to be, clinically, a male perver-

sion, and that the structure thus described would seem to be a masculine structure in so far as fetishism is the attempt to deal with the
reality of castration by producing a substitute for the penis missing
on the woman's, the mother's body. This is only part of the larger
problem presented by the use of psychoanalytic theory discussed in
the introduction to this book. Psychoanalysis places sexual difference as a central mechanism – and problem – for the human subject
but it does so by also placing the penis-as-phallus as the signifier of
difference. Moreover, for Lacan, accession to the symbolic is
through the acceptance of the law prohibiting incest, the Name-of-
the-Father as Lacan designates it, a law of the fathers, a patriarchal
law. Psychoanalysis can therefore be represented as itself supporting the dominant culture, patriarchy, and it now becomes a means
to demonstrate the ways in which cinema, too, is patriarchal, in its
fetishistic and hence oppressive representation of women.

The arguments throughout this book have sought to displace this
conflation of cinema, psychoanalysis and patriarchy, and the inter-
minable circularity it has brought forth. The reading of psychoanalysis as a theory of patriarchy had an important role for political
arguments at a certain conjuncture, but we were always thereby in
danger of throwing out the baby with the bathwater, of having to
reject psychoanalysis itself because certain of its tenets support,
indeed entrench, a masculinist view of the human psyche. The
concept of fetishism was paradigmatic for this critique. I have
argued, however, that it is disavowal that is the central psychic
structure, of which fetishism is a specific instance. The disavowal of
the mother's difference at the heart of castration is a fantasy both
the boy and the girl may subscribe to, as a result fetishism is a
symptom of women as well as men. The woman, too, must find
something more in the man than his anatomical distinction, for she
seeks the phallus which she can thereby have. In this way I have
proposed a rather different appropriation of Freud, and of Lacan, in
which women can also find an account of ourselves psychically. Of
course, at the same time psychoanalysis thereby ceases to be a
theory of our oppression as women. As a result, instead of the cer-
tainty of patriarchal psychoanalysis which we can deconstruct, we
must encounter the uncertainty of the contingent, of a cultural and
historical specificity which we must understand. And, while it is
clear that 'woman as lacking', or 'castrated' is also a socially constructed fantasy, we can no longer assume that it is equivalent to or
a mirror image of the psychological fantasy.[9]

The paradoxical theoretical role of psychoanalysis has arisen in part at least as a result of Althusser's appropriation of psychoanalysis for a theory of ideology which remains in effect a theory of misrecognition that assumes a true knowledge available to the subject – a non-ideological, a non-patriarchal knowledge. The imaginary, Althusser argued, provided the form of the subject's lived relation to society. Through this relation the subject was brought to accept as its own, to recognise itself in, the representations of the social order. The subject is thus 'interpellated'.[10] One implication of ideology as an imaginary relation has been to sustain at some level the presumption of ideology as a misrepresentation, as if the misrecognition by the subject in the mirror phase involved an identification with a false image and thus that it produces a false unified subjectivity, implying that such a mistaken identification can be rectified and an alternative, true subjectivity emerge in its stead. For Lacan, on the contrary, the subject who misrecognises is not a dupe; rather, misrecognition 'represents a certain organisation of affirmations and negations, to which the subject is attached'[11] and it is therefore a form of disavowal. Insofar as the subject takes the image as a unified image, by identifying with this unity, it thereby avows its knowledge of its own disunity, and in this very process precipitates an ideal ego as a forever lost, unified self. Misrecognition, like disavowal, produces the subject as a split subject. However, the divided subject is no more a truth, or lie, than the unified subject, and certainly cannot be the aim of a radical politics. Rather it is necessary to accept the impossibility constitutive of desire, although this can hardly be the goal of a new post-modern puritanism since it cannot be achieved through a simple and singular act of will but only through a relation of transference, of translation and internalisation and hence through a relation to the other, and too, it is never fully and finally achieved.

Lacan's concept of the imaginary cannot be used to support a theory of ideology as misrepresentation and as mask, covering and hiding a truth and reality lying elsewhere, behind the (mis)representation, a reality which could be revealed by peeling away the distorting mask of ideology. Nevertheless it is correct that ideology is mask, Slavoj Žižek has argued, but he does so now taking acount of the paradox of Lacan's imaginary misrecognition and hence inverting the usual relation: of course, the ideological discourse is distorting the reality, but this reality cannot sustain itself without this distortion; of course there is reality hidden behind the ideological mask, but if we take off the mask, we lose at the same time the reality hidden behind the mask, far from being able, finally, to grasp the naked reality in itself.[12]

At the same time it is clear that the subject struggles to find a place, to be fixed in its subjectivity as unified, as centred, a struggle exemplified by the *fort-da* game as a game of mastery but which Freud also used to show the work of the death drive in repetition, while for Lacan it reveals as well the role of the *objet petit a*. The stake of representation for this struggle is the way in which it addresses and hence fixes us as subjects for its discourse.

Representation is a process of discourse, of the symbolic in Lacan's terms, through which the subject is produced as such, is given its place. In the classical accounts of the spectator-subject provided by writers such as Metz, Baudry, and Bellour, the concept of fetishism provides a partial understanding of this process of fixing, but then introduces the issue of sexual difference for representation as an unaddressed, absent, but structuring question, leading Constance Penley to dub these accounts 'bachelor machines'.[13] Moreover such 'apparatus' theories, or, more properly, theories of the *dispositif* of the subject, explain only the fixing of the subject, and hence apppear to posit a passive spectator. But representation is also a relation of desire, including the desire to find one's place, to be placed by the text; the spectator is not a passive victim but an eager consumer. Moreover the process of representation, and the production of the subject in representation, is a process of fixing and unfixing, a play of identity and non-identity. This is not to propose, however, that one pole may be privileged over the other, in a projected aesthetics of the before-fixing.[14]

It is also such a fixing that produces the subject in Lacan's schema of identification, namely the retrospective action of the signifier in and for the subject. But this is not an imaginary relation, it is the work of the symbolic, of signification and language. In the floating chain of signifiers which surround the child, something intervenes to penetrate the child as meaning, reorganising the chain of signifiers as a sequence of signifieds. Lacan called this element the *point de capiton* which hooks down the not-yet meaningful signifiers just as the button or thread fixes the layers of material to quilt the chesterfield sofa or down bedcover.[15] Žižek argues that, in a similar way,

Ideological space is made of non-bound, non-tied elements, 'floating signifiers', whose very identity is 'open', overdetermined by their articulation in a chain with other elements – that is, their 'literal' signification depends on their metaphorical surplus-signification... The 'quilting' performs the totalisation by means of which this free floating of ideological elements is halted, fixed – that is to say, by means of which they become parts of the structured network of meaning.[16]

Žižek does not, however, argue that ideology is the same as the construction of the subject – as Althusser suggested.[17] Instead his point is that in both there is something which disturbs, something which makes incomplete the totalisation of the buttoning down of meaning, and of the subject, so that there is something missing, a lack is also inscribed and something is always left over as a residue – the *objet petit a*. The *objet petit a* has a paradoxical role here, a kind of borderline function which confounds any simple division of representation into a fixing and unfixing of the subject. The emergence of the *objet a* frames reality for the child, enabling the child to represent itself and its losses and thus to cross from the realm of the real to the domain of the imaginary. Subsequently it is the element which secures the subject as subject, but it does so insofar as the *objet a* is what falls away from the subject – and the narrative – unused and unusable. The *objet a* itself becomes a little piece of the real – hence Lacan terms it the blot or stain which 'spoils' the picture – it is unsymbolisable, and as a result, Žižek says, the *objet a* is 'an inert, nontransparent object which must drop out or sink before any symbolic reality can emerge'.[18]

Lacan's own privileged instance of the *objet petit a* was the gaze, which is apt in this discussion of cinema, and hence it is through this example that I will try to relate the issues of fetishism, fantasy and ideology.

THE GAZE

It was in relation to the scopic drive that Lacan explored the function for the subject of the *objet a*. What better luck could the film theorist have hoped for, since surely what characterises cinematic pleasure must be first and foremost its relation to the scopic drive? The gaze as *objet a* might then offer a theory of cinematic visual pleasure. That this has not been the case is hardly difficult to explain, for Lacan's discussion in 'Of the Gaze as *objet petit a*' in *The Four Fundamental Concepts of Psycho-analysis* fails at every point to provide any general theory of visual pleasure, including pleasure in the cinema. Instead it undermines any possibility of such a general theory by showing the opposing functions for the subject of the eye and the gaze.

The gaze is not the look, for to look is merely to see whereas the gaze is to be posed by oneself in a field of vision. The pleasure of the scopic drive is first and foremost passive – the wish to be seen (in one's sex, finally). In order to solicit the gaze of the Other, of the mother, the child comes to posit itself as an object for the Other's gaze – precisely in the same way that the child's look at and identification with its own image in the mirror produces a structure whereby the child sees from a place which is other than the place (the mirror) where it sees itself. The child's look is essentially alienated and hence is constituted as the 'gaze' in Lacan's terms. It is something from which the subject has separated itself off, but which was once part of the subject; it is thus an *objet petit*. The gaze is therefore not a seen gaze; after all, it isn't anybody's look, nevertheless it presents to the subject the reality (*tuché*, the contingent real) of its own alienation. It is a looking *imagined* by me from the place of the other. It has little to do with any particular thing that is looked at, it is not specularisable but, on the contrary, depends on the structure of vision, namely, a structure which poses the subject as looking on, which presents to the subject the realisation of its place as wishing to see and wishing to be seen. This opposes the narcissistic satisfaction of the all-seeing subject, the plenitude of a consciousness which believes itself the author of its own look. The gaze is the inverse of the omnipotent look, which is the imperial function of the eye.

But how does this gaze support desire? Desire here is not the wish to see some particular thing, or even just to *see*, but to see what is being shown, what I cannot yet see but know is there to see. It is when seeing brings us something more, an elsewhere but which at the same moment marks that 'more' as absent, lacking. The gaze surprises the subject in its desiring. Lacan's example is the famous anamorphosis in Holbein's painting *The Ambassadors* in which a manipulation of devices for giving an illusion of perspective allows an object in the painting to be seen as a shadow, an oblique object noticeable yet unrecognisable but, with the next few steps as one passes along it (perhaps to its neighbour), the realisation dawns – the object is a skull, and what had been seen but not known is suddenly recognised, and intrudes as a symbol of mortality. Here is the 'something more' but in relation to which the subject is always revealed to itself as lacking, castrated.

The function of the anamorphic ghost is not the production of a symbol, of death or the phallus, but of the gaze as such, for it is not a question of what is seen but of being held in a field of vision. This Lacan says, contrasts with most painting. The painting certainly solicits the spectator – it is offered to be seen; nevertheless though our look may be more or less orchestrated, in the end the painting by and large eludes and elides the gaze (though Lacan allows one exception, Expressionism). The painter sets the spectator up but not with a lure, a trap for the gaze – as Holbein's painting was – rather it is as if the painter addresses the spectator thus:

> *You want to see? Well, take a look at this!* He gives something for the eye to feed on, but he invites the person to whom this picture is presented to lay down his gaze there as one lays down one's weapons. This is the pacifying, Apollonian effect of painting. Something is given not so much to the gaze as to the eye, something that involves the abandonment, the *laying down*, of the gaze.[19]

Lacan is not concerned here to develop an aesthetic theory; however, two models in relation to visual representation can be deduced: one, the painterly, seems close to Barthes's notion of the readerly, where the reader lays himself down before the author, 'plunged into a kind of idleness – he is intransitive' so that the reader is a consumer not a producer of the text:

> instead of functioning himself, instead of gaining access to the magic of the signifier, to the pleasure of writing, he is left with no more than the poor freedom either to accept or reject the text: reading is nothing more than a *referendum*.[20]

The other model, a visual representation which 'satisfies' the gaze, is less clear, and it perhaps hardly qualifies as a model at all. It evokes but also diverges from Barthes's concept of the writerly where the reader is the producer of the text (in contrast to the readerly text). Barthes describes the writerly text as a perpetual present, upon which no *consequent* language (which would inevitably make it past) can be superimposed; the writerly text is *ourselves writing*, before the infinite play of the world (the world as function) is traversed, intersected, stopped, plasticised by some singular system (Ideology, Genus, Criticism) which reduces the plurality of entrances, the opening of networks, the infinity of languages.[21]

Barthes centres the role of the reader – and therefore of the subject – as a site of '*interpretation* (in the Nietzschean sense of the word). To interpret a text is not to give it a (more or less justified, more or less free) meaning, but on the contrary to appreciate what *plural* constitutes it.'[22] Here it seems it is the text which is split, multiple. For Lacan, however, it is the subject which is split, and it is the gaze as *objet petit a* which, while it secures desire, also introduces an openness or play in the representation in contrast to the painterly. But this is not in the control of the subject. On the contrary, it necessarily *escapes* the subject. Thus while the anamorphic object in Holbein's *The Ambassadors* opens us to desire, it also sets the terms for this – here death. However Barthes's emphasis on the writerly 'as a perpetual present' points to this very aspect of the gaze, in that the gaze surprises the subject in its desiring. Rather than the already-made, the completed, the representation engages the subject-spectator in the present tense, as a making – of desire, of the subject, and hence of its unmaking.

This other mode of visual representation arises when the look becomes the gaze and it does so when it begins 'to show'.[23] Grammatically this doesn't make much sense for 'it' does not refer to any subject, which is Lacan's point, and he illustrates this through the example of that other realm of non-sense, the dream:

> in the final resort, our position in the dream is profoundly that of someone who does not see. The subject does not see where it is leading, he follows. He may even on occasion detatch himself, tell himself that it is a dream, but in no case will he be able to apprehend himself in the dream in the way in which, in the Cartesian *cogito*, he apprehends himself as thought. He may say to himself, *It's only a dream*. But he does not apprehend himself as someone who says to himself – *After all, I am the consciousness of this dream*.[24]

The dreamer, though after all the author of her dream, nevertheless dreams it as if it were being shown to her, and as if seeing it for the first time. It is here that cinema finds its parallel with dreams; however, this has nothing to do with film being dream-like, that is, something taken to be an illusion, nor is it that cinema gives us the same experience as dreaming. What is involved is not an analogy, as Metz suggested,[25] but a homology. In contrast to the 'painterly' in which the viewer finds respite from the gaze, the 'dream-like' film draws the viewer's eye as it sets out a structure of showing which thereby posits a gaze in front of the viewer. In this latter, the system of representation must introduce a demand for a 'something more', the *objet a*. It is not enough to be visual, to solicit a look, to provide objects of desire. There must be something more. Lacan illustrated this through the classical tale of Zeuxis and Parrhasios, suggesting that the stake of the competition between them is not the success of verisimilitude but of a deceit, of putting over an illusion, which in each case is a *lure*.[26] While Zeuxis has the advantage, for he has painted grapes which fooled the birds who swooped to eat them, his friend Parrhasios nevertheless triumphs over him, for the veil he has painted on the wall is so life-like that Zeuxis turns to him and asks to see what Parrhasios has painted behind it. He is lured to discover what he imagines is there to be seen, and hence he imagines a gaze but which is objectless.[27]

The stake is not the deception as such but the lure, and thus the desire, it sets in play. The Pasha of Marrakesh, on a visit to Hollywood shortly after the making of Sternberg's film *Morocco*, will ask the director when he had been in his country to photograph the movie, such was the success of its verisimilitudinous deception. The lure, however, for which this so-called deceit sets us up, leads us rather to ask how Amy Jolly and Tom Brown will ever meet up again in the desert, the absurdity and impossibility of which is acknowledged at the same time that it is presumed. For to question the believability of Amy Jolly joining the camp followers in her high heels, which she then abandons to walk barefoot, is to betray our belief in the love story as a whole, as well, perhaps, our wish that the two lovers will meet again.

There is a paradox here in that the *objet a* lures the spectator – it is the secret to be revealed – while at the same time making the spectator aware of itself *as* a spectator, in a look which cannot simply be returned in an exchange, or subsumed in a metadiscourse. As a result there is a kind of 'self-reflexivity' in the gaze, and in the *objet a.* However this cannot be appropriated to a radical politics as if everything self-reflexive is also progressive, nor can it been seen as a gesture of the postmodern, although our understanding of this process may only be possible in the discourses we are now calling postmodern. And of course, to pin this process down as reflexivity itself produces a fixing of the subject and the text. Moreover in the desire to reveal the secret, to know what it means – which is also the drive of representation – there is a move from the gaze to the look and hence to an emplacement, while equally this is a drive for repetition, a re-presentation of the knowledge and its lack, that is, the death drive.

Julia Kristeva has also pointed to this opposed function of the specular in her contrast between the terror and dread of the specular and its seduction. The specular seduction brings identity, meaning, and symbolisation so that 'The glance by which I identify an object, a face, my own, another's, delivers my identity which reassures me: for it delivers me from *frayages*, nameless dread, noises preceding the name...Intellectual speculation derives from this identifying, labelling glance.'[28] But the specular is the point of origin not only of signs, and of narcissistic identifications, but also for 'the phantasmatic terror one speaking identity holds for another'.[29] Once that terror, which is the incursion of the other, 'erupts into the seer, that seen stops being simply reassuring, *trompe-l'oeil*, or invitation to speculation, and becomes the fascinating specular. Cinema seizes us precisely in that place.'[30] The specular, in Kristeva's sense, marks that which is beyond identification, unverbalised, unrepresented, namely, the drive, It represents the unrepresented because it 'includes an excess of visual traces', useless for signification, but insistingly there and naming the before of symbolisation.[31] It thus also bears the trace of the aggressivity in the drive within the visible, the look which returns to devour or attack.

The paradoxical role of the *objet a* for Lacan and the specular in Kristeva is paralleled in Barthes's later essay *The Pleasure of the Text*, where fetishism now functions to break open, to disturb, the closed Oedipal structure of narrative through its very different strategies of narrative delay, and the halting of narrative in favour of the word – or image. 'We can imagine a typology of the pleasures of reading – or of the readers of pleasure...The fetishist would be matched with the divided-up text, the singling out of quotations, formulae, turns of phrase, with the pleasure of the word.'[32] And he points to the pleasures of readings which are perverse:

Many readings are perverse, implying a split, a cleavage. Just as the child knows its mother has no penis and simultaneously believes she has one (an economy whose benefits [validity] Freud has demonstrated) so the reader can keep saying: *I know these are only words, but all the same*...(I am moved as though these words were uttering a reality). Of all readings, that of tragedy is the most perverse: I take pleasure in hearing myself told [tell] a story *whose end I know*: I know and I don't know, I act toward myself as though I did not know: I know perfectly well Oedipus will be unmasked, that Danton will be guillotined, *but all the same* .... Compared to a dramatic story, which is one whose outcome is unknown, there is here an effacement of pleasure and a progression of bliss (today, in mass culture, there is an enormous consumption of 'dramatics' and little bliss).[33]

Here is Barthes's central distinction between pleasure and the bliss or *jouissance* of the text.[34] But disavowal is now on the side of bliss, and contrasted to the classical text, the 'dramatic story' and to mass culture and a pursuit of stories 'whose outcome is unknown'. (Though Barthes ignores the extent to which popular fiction is predominantly a fiction of genres, and therefore the outcome of such narratives is also always in some sense already known.) Barthes points to the way in which fetishism in the representation may be disruptive of the illusion of the centred subject.[35] The *jouissance* of the text he posits is the 'bliss' of the edge, of an always between, an against; not because of what it is against, of what it opposes, but by the mere fact of opposition. 'Another bliss (other edges): it consists in de-politicising what is apparently political, and in politicising what apparently is not.'[36] It is also the bliss of loss – because it narrates a having-been-present; and bliss not in the union of the couple, but 'wherever a disturbance occurs in amatory adjustment'.[37] This *jouissance* is also the work of the death drive, and Barthes sets the pleasure of the text against the bliss of the text as parallel structures which can never interact in a kind of mutual support. Citing his own 'taste for works of the past' and his 'advocacy of modern works' he declares that these pleasures can never be combined – as a kind of pacification of the irregularity, of the scandal of bliss – 'in a fine dialectical movment of synthesis – this subject is never anything but a "living contradiction": a split subject, who simultaneously enjoys, through the text, the consistency of his selfhood and its collapse, its fall'.[38]

Barthes opposes this bliss to the pleasure of the text, which is an Oedipal pleasure. Contrasting it to the pleasure of the 'corporeal striptease or of narrative suspense':

> Paradoxically (since it is mass-consumed), this is a far more intellectual pleasure than the other: an Oedipal pleasure (to denude, to know, to learn the origin and the end), if it is true that every narrative (every unveiling of the truth) is a staging of the (absent, hidden, or hypostatised) father – which would explain the solidarity of narrative forms, of family structures, and of prohibitions of nudity, all collected in our culture in the myth of Noah's sons covering his nakedness.[39]

Where earlier fetishism had been placed on the side of Oedipus, as the cutting out of a space, a unity of identity, Barthes now sees it as the disavowal of that knowledge, the refusal to follow the path of this pleasure. A utopia of fetishism emerges as Barthes figures a new economy of textual desire, mobile, plural and freed from the fixed structure of Oedipus. Fetishism therefore now lies on both sides of Barthes's binary division *plaisir/jouissance*.

The possibility of that element or strategy of representation which will be the very death of representation as symbolic and thus as ideology has nevertheless remained a lure for many critical theorists. Julia Kristeva's concepts of the semiotic and of the abject have posited a moment before the imposition of symbolic law which has appeared as a positive and positivised field of creative production. For Kristeva, however, this is neither simply undermining of the symbolic, nor necessarily a 'good thing'.[40] Jean François Lyotard has appealed to the 'Utopia behind the Scenes of the Phantasy'. Fantasy, he argues, is figural, not discursive, and thus it does not partake of the structuring of language, of the law. It is a matrix, not a structure, it is not based on rules, nor is it instituted through structural oppositions, but instead 'its capacity to contain several places in one place, to form a bloc out of what cannot possibly co-exist – is the secret of the figural, which transgresses the intervals that constitute discourse and the distances that constitute representation'.[41] Re-examining Freud's study 'A Child Is Being Beaten' Lyotard concludes that in fantasy 'By a series of displacements that are highly irregular, the singular becomes plural, the feminine masculine, the subject becomes object, the determinate indeterminate and here becomes elsewhere.'[42] As a result, he argues, 'Now we understand that the principle of figurality which is also the principle of unbinding ... is the death drive: "the absolute of anti-synthesis": Utopia.'[43]

In the figural, as an aesthetic, the primary process 'erupts' into secondary processes, opposing the subordination of the image to the dictates of narrative meaning or representation, to language-like, rule-bound formalisms. A dualist opposition seems to be reasserted here, of the disrupting, nonrule-bound primary process on the one hand, and the fixity, structure and structuring, the emplacement and binding of the secondary process on the other hand. The primary process appears as the realm of a free – creative and unhindered – cathexis of energy, of the drives, in contrast to the control of the secondary process with its subordination of desire and the drives. But fantasy cannot be the 'good' place of plurality, polyvalency and mobility outside the law, outside of the binarism of signification. The paradoxical relation here cannot be resolved into a binary opposition between an imaginary or pre-imaginary flux, flow, and polyvalency on the one hand, and a domain of symbols, of structure and of a fixed placing of the subject – and therefore of 'ideology' – on the other hand, an opposition where one replaces or displaces the other. Such a dualist opposition is itself a fantasy, for the subject always remains exactly that – a subject, who imagines its own dissolution, entering into a plurality of de-differentiation – for the place from which this division seems possible, from which it is desired, is the place of the subject who knows itself as subject, a centred ego. What else but a 'subject' can appeal to the primary process over the secondary? Lyotard's argument – while pitting the figural against the discursive – in fact emphasises in the figural not an essence or a given domain, not the death drive as such, but a process, for, as David Rodowick says, 'if phantasy [for Lyotard] is a machine for producing *jouissance* its utopian potential derives from the fact that *jouissance* is neither representation nor death, but something that oscillates between them'.[44] Nevertheless Rodowick posits fantasy as a process of the subject outside of and against the identities and identifications of discourse, which Rodowick places as simply Oedipal, and as a result there remains the problem of the constitution of the subject as such and its identifications. The utopia of unbinding is however a rearguard action, of the primary process against an already-in place secondary process. Fantasy as the production of an oscillation between representation and death is a player in a game already established.

For Lacan, therefore, fantasy is part of the problem, and not its solution. Fantasy is constituted in the human subject insofar as it is a subject of lack, that is, a subject divided between a present lack and an imagined presence. Fantasy is what fills out a certain lack, a kernel of non-sense in the subject, and, more importantly, in the other, and it is at the level of fantasy that the subject continues to enjoy, which constitutes its *jouissance*. This *jouissance* binds the subject to the death drive, and the excess of signification and of the subject which arises is not free or freeing but loops the subject back to self-enclosed repetition. Fantasy here may escape or even oppose the constructions of the discursive, but it is not a point of release for it also enthralls the subject. Lacan therefore posits a beyond of fantasy as the resolution of psychoanalysis where the analysand 'goes through the fantasy' which sustains its desire and produces the irreducible symptom which is the neurotic's bain and pleasure. It is necessary, Lacan says, to identify with the symptom – one's own particular organisation of enjoyment – thus producing an identification with what Lacan terms the *sinthome*, a neologism for the synthesis between symptom and fantasy. This constitutes an identification in that the subject recognises in the *sinthome* the particular way in which its *jouissance* is bound to a certain signifying formation; it is a fantasy which, as signifying, is also within social, symbolic, relations. This thereby supports the subject's consistency of being in the world. Lacan abandons his earlier utopian expectation that the symptom, and its fantasy, can be dissolved through interpretation, offering instead only the encounter and embrace by the subject of its own condition of *jouissance* and hence its *sinthome*. It is an encounter which, being within discourse – indeed a psychoanlytical discursive relationship, the transference – is also in the symbolic as the field not only of lack (that is, of the imaginary) but of a symbolised and symbolisable lack (castration).

This positing of a beyond of fantasy – and thus too of the Oedipal identifications and of narcissistic desire – is questioned by Borch-Jacobsen in *Lacan, The Absolute Master*. He argues that Lacan, in his approach to the contradictory identifications instituted in the Oedipal scenario,

> continued to believe that there was a solution, beyond its 'failures'. Whereas Freud – in this respect, very modern indeed – went stubbornly on butting up against the paradox of an identification that was normative and neurotic, socialising and

desocialising, Lacan no less stubbornly sought to resolve it: by cutting through Freud's ambiguity ...by separating the good, normalising identification from the bad, rivalrous identification.[45]

And indeed Lacan sees this solution in the law of castration whereby

> Providing it oscillates alternately between $\mathcal{S}$ and o in the phantasy, castration turns phantasy into that supple, yet inextensible chain by which the arrest of the object-investment, which can hardly go beyond certain natural limits, takes on the transcendental function of ensuring the *jouissance* of the Other, which passes this chain on to me in the Law...Castration means that *jouissance* must be refused, so that it can be reached on the inverted ladder [*l'échelle renversée*] of the Law of desire.[46]

Lacan continues to imagine, it seems, a 'good' place of identity and identification, but this is not only not straightforwardly a 'place', and certainly not one we can come into possession of, but the proviso 'Providing...' which prefaces this categoric pronouncement undoes not a little the sense of determinacy and determination of the main clause. Everything hangs on a movement, an oscillation, not on a placing. Castration, the signifier of lack, is not given a fixed place. The metaphor – castration – produces the subject as a subject in process. Moreover a further identification is required, an identification with the Other marked by desire and hence lacking, and it is this which enables the subject to 'go beyond' fantasy. For, Žižek argues, the only way out of the impasse of fantasy is 'by fully assuming the impossibility constitutive of desire'.[47] This cannot, however, be undertaken as a moral imperative or conscious prescription on the part of the individual; rather, it must be a psychical relation to the lack in the other, or else the subject will feel only the impossibility of its own desire, and continue to posit full enjoyment in the other as non-lacking, an other who witholds enjoyment from the subject itself.

Fantasy, Freud said, is the means by which the subject 'attempts to replace a disagreeable reality by one which is more in keeping with the subject's wishes'.[48] It is difference which provides the most disagreeable reality, insofar as it presents to the subject its own lack in being; this reality of difference Lacan has re-termed the real. Social relations as well as parental fantasies and family structures determine the context for this negotiation of difference embarked upon by the small child, and thus too, the context for the production of all those fantasies which are part of this negotiation. In this sexual difference, just as much as racial difference, is not the problem but the solution. The problem of the *jouissance* of the subject and of the other of desire requires an acceptance of and placing of oneself within sexual difference. At stake, as a result, is not anatomical difference but an issue of the subject's relation to desire. This poses to it a problem of otherness resolved as difference and it is through this difference that desire is now organised. Racism similarly arises from and is justified by racial specificity produced as a difference, but it is not an equivalent issue of otherness and difference. The constitution of sexual difference in and for the human being thereby also constitues it as a subject in discourse and in the symbolic as a subject of lack. Sexual difference is not thus determining of other relations of difference, but it is determining of the subject.[49] It is therefore the fantasies – of women as well as men – which arise as a result of the difficulties of difference and the symbolisation of the lack in the other which must be addressed. And it is those fantasies that translate the difficulty of difference and its psychical and social organisation into a solution of subordination which must be challenged. Fantasy cannot, however, be divided up as either social or psychical. To borrow Saussure's metaphor for the relationship of the signifier and signified, fantasy is like a piece of paper: on the one side is the psychical, on the other the social, each distinct, but neither possible without the other, yet, and unlike Saussure's piece of paper, each penetrates the other. The social determines our psychical relations – for the family itself is a social form – but is also itself formed by psychical relations, of which fantasy is pre-eminent.

The apparent disjuncture between the social and the psychical disappears when we understand that the social relations of contingent reality, as well as the frames of understanding which we give to reality – our 'ideologies', are themselves formed through fantasy. Žižek argues that:

> Ideology is not a dream-like illusion that we build to escape insupportable reality, in its basic dimension it is a fantasy-construction which serves as a support of our 'reality' itself: an 'illusion' which structures our effective, real social relations and thereby masks some insupportable, real-impossible kernel.[50]

And, in a back-to-front way, elements of contingent, external and material reality are used to form the fantasy of social reality.[51] Nowhere is this seen more clearly than in racism where a contingent reality, a racial – or cultural or religious – specificity is reconstructed as a difference. In marking an otherness this difference is also signified as a danger: of the other as a threat, as potentially contaminating, but also as one's own inverse, a 'doppelganger', a screen on to which we project everything we wish to disavow and reject in ourselves. This other is both the other who is our feared rival and a reviled and denigrated other. At the same time – and this is the racist's dilemma – the fantasy is the support of the racist's desire and consistency of being. The potency of racism, as with sexism, lies in the fantasy-structure it supports, and this is distinct from the economic, political and social subordination which racism, and sexism, may also produce.[52] Of course the fantasy here is also a social discourse, not simply an individual's symptom, so that the fantasy secures the group, the community – on the model of Freud's account of identification between members of a group – in its relations of desire towards other groups.

Fantasy, as 'social reality', sets out a story of how things are – or could be – whereby the subject, or the group, can enjoy (live, work, play) without loss, in a state of plenitude. It thus covers over – more or less – the impossibility of the real. But only so far, for the traumatic-real kernel is itself constituted around a fantasy by which the subject sustains itself in its *jouissance*, an enjoyment without loss and hence outside symbolic relations. The fantasy attempts to sustain or repair this enjoyment, an effort made necessary because it is already jeopardised, penetrated by the symbolic. The impossibility of this *jouissance* – the real of lack – is covered over in fantasy not by denying lack (as in an hallucination) but by attributing it to a cause in social reality (rather than the real) whereby others act or have acted to deprive the subject or the group of its enjoyment.[53] Fantasy, in imagining enjoyment without loss, always posits a loss already enacted to which it answers. It therefore always inscribes loss in the very moment it seeks to annihilate it.

It has often been women who have been aligned with this 'traumatic-real kernel' of fantasy. This has involved two aspects. On the one hand it produces woman as the idealised but unreachable other, which is a particular fantasy of 'woman', producing the symptom 'woman' as the condition or guarantee of an enjoyment without loss. On the other hand the demands and desires of women pose back to the man the very impossibility of such enjoyment, provoking a wrath without equal, and producing another fantasy and discourse of woman, now denigrated and reviled. Both impose an impossible identity for women. A response to the impossibility of this discursive fantasy or definition has arisen in the competing arguments and discourses of feminism which seek to 'quilt' – to use Žižek's term introduced earlier – differently the ideological space. Žižek argues that the 'floating signifiers' of social discourse are quilted into what thereby becomes an ideological space, a structured network of meaning:

> If we 'quilt' the floating signifiers through 'Communism', for example, 'class-struggle' confers a precise and fixed signification to all other elements: to democracy (so-called 'real democracy' as opposed to 'bourgeois formal democracy' as a legal form of exploitation), to feminism (the exploitation of women as resulting from the class-conditioned division of labour) ... What is at stake in the ideological struggle is precisely which of the 'nodal points' [of the quilting] will totalise, include in its series of equivalances, these free-floating elements.[54]

Rather than Communism, of course, the meanings can be quilted through feminism, producing a competing discourse which 'pins down' the subject differently, which organises a different buttoning of the couch through which the subject, and the woman, is stitched into the chain of signification and of desire. But a left-over will still be produced as a residue tracing the failure of the discourse to wholly contain the 'floating signifiers' – the *objet petit a*. Alongside the feminist arguments for equality and social justice – themselves socially constructed concepts though which we organise our desire – there arises as well a discourse of 'discontent', a fantasy in which it is the Other, men, who enjoy – to women's cost – while the woman is excluded from access to this *jouissance*. All that is worthwhile and good, all that ensures enjoyment, rests in the hands of the other – of men. Of course, since women have been excluded from areas of social activity and from the scope for sexual activity men have enjoyed, this 'discontent' is founded on a reality; it is quite justified. Yet the 'enjoyment' of men here is also a fantasy; it is not secured or constituted through denying women *something*, which we could get, or get back. This 'enjoyment' is the *jouissance* of the other which we can never obtain, though the other too will enviously fantasise our 'enjoyment' from which he is excluded.[55]

The 'family' has also been a central object of fantasy. In our modern period it has come to be seen by many as the structure which opposes *jouissance*. For feminists and theorists of the left it imprisons the woman, subjecting her to patriarchal law and to the capitalist imperative to reproduce the labour force. This contrasts with earlier struggles, especially within the working classes, for the right to family life, that is, for a family wage which would enable the couple to afford to give the time and labour of one of them to the care and upbringing of the other members of the family. Here, the family represents a possible 'quilting' of desire, but also a *jouissance* which the middle classes enjoy. Of course it will be the woman who is the carer, but then, for the father, the mother's enjoyment of her children, and of childbearing, may appear to be at the cost of his own satisfaction; while the woman, excluded from the man's social world of work, of learning and social achievement, may see there the *jouissance* which she feels she is denied. For the child too it may be the family – as mother or father or the parental couple – which suborns its *jouissance*, which reserves to itself enjoyment and entails the child in the service of that enjoyment.[56] While the form and structure of the family can be a matter of social debate and ideological construction, for the child it is, firstly, a contingent reality, and it is the network of relations of desire in which she first encounters the question of the *jouissance* of the other.[57] This 'social reality' is both formed and deformed by the fantasies produced as a result of the difficulties of assuming a subject-position which requires the acceptance of difference, of otherness.

Fantasy can neither be abolished nor simply given a good, proper content. The real of lack, the kernel of nonsense which disturbs fantasy and undoes ideology, is not a resource of resistance to fantasy and to the discourses of social reality, but a part of the problem they pose. We may, however – by allowing in the excluded, impossible residue which continues to press upon our ideological 'quilting' as an eruption, a disturbance – open a space to re-quilt, to stitch over again and in another way the fixings of fantasy and their implications for our social relation; nevertheless this quilting itself will be rent by the real of lack it cannot contain or cover over. While fantasy is a way of imagining things otherwise, so long as it posits a possible enjoyment it remains a closed loop, returning us to a problem of lack it promised to abolish, and offering no way out. The path is not simply forward to castration as a given state, as the acceptance of lack, however, for at the end of that road would lie the annihilation of desire itself. What is needed is not the abolition of desire but the refusal of *jouissance* and its investment instead in the symbolic other from which it can return as desire, that is, as something unsatisfiable (via Lacan's supple but limited chain of fantasy). It is only then that we can imagine things otherwise while also acknowledging that there can be no, utopian, solution – that is, no full and sufficient satisfaction.

NEGOTIATING FANTASY, REALITY AND THE REAL IN REPRESENTATION

Works of imagination, fictional stories in literature and film, are part of our negotiation of 'sour reality', the real in Lacan's schema, while they also trace the very domain of that 'real'. Our fantasies, as public and published forms, are scenarios which will both evade and remark the problem of a desire which is always other. In presenting such scenarios feminine cinema, to paraphrase Sandy Flitterman-Lewis, does not speak a different desire, but rather it addresses the issue of desiring in difference.[58] It may resolve the difficulties of difference in a fantasy of a centred feminine subject of desire, or it may figure these difficulties as a structuring element of its narration which the narrative cannot wholly resolve. The following discussion considers the issues of desire and difference raised by three recent American films, each directed by a women, and each of which centres a female protagonist.[59]

Desperately Seeking Susan (Susan Seidelman, 1985) presents a delightful 'screw-ball' comedy whose central fantasy is of an idealised figure who is both identified with and displaced by the heroine who thereby escapes her oppressive marriage, for the plot contrives to swap the women's partners. Roberta becomes romantically involved with Susan's erstwhile lover, thereby becoming the sexual and sexually fulfilled woman she always could be. Meanwhile Susan encounters – and sexually dominates – Roberta's husband, producing not only a role exchange with Roberta, but also a role reversal for Roberta's husband. As a comedy the film can draw on generic expectations to motivate the extravagant wishfulfilment of the narrative. Everyone gets what they want, or their just deserts, and the problem of wanting, of desire, is successfully resolved. The

film affirms that things can be otherwise if we pursue our desires –
just as Roberta's fantasy obsession with Susan leads her to a new
relationship – and it centres women as subjects of desire. The fantasies here are not specific to women, however, and instead
Desperately Seeking Susan asserts itself as a 'woman's story' by its
deployment of the conventions of sexual difference, creating a
verisimilitudinous world of women – the film, for example, opens
in a beauty parlour, emphatically placing its heroine in a mise en
scène of conventionally coded femininity. It is the conviction of the
film's verisimilitude which marks it as a women's film – and which
might also prevent men identifying with the heroine Roberta – not
any essential feminineness of the fantasy.

Fantasies, however, it was argued earlier, are also subject to defensive processes, notably in the repression of the wish, for
example the Oedipal wish for the mother or for the father, but
which returns in a displaced form, or which may be turned around,
from active to passive. This is the process in which adult sado-
masochistic fantasy scenarios can be located, producing a pleasure
not so much in being beaten as in what this represents, and thus
what it makes present, namely the forbidden wish. This may
involve wishes and positions which, logically, would cancel each
other out – the wish to have something and not to have it – or
having a wish in order to be punished for one's wish. And fantasy
may also involve aggressive wishes which have been projected on
to others, producing a fear of attack from outside. Fantasy is therefore not only the realm of pleasurable wishes, but also a domain of
anxiety, of fear of punishment by others for one's forbidden wishes
(though this itself may be a wish). Public forms of fantasy too
involve the representation of such fears, and the wishes and projections which gave rise to them.

Smooth Talk (Joyce Chopra, 1985) and *Blue Steel* (Kathryn
Bigelow, 1990) each present a fantasy-scenario which brings about
the opposite of the wished-for outcome. In the following I want to
consider the kind of positions of identity and identification which
these films produce through their presentation of fantasy scenarios
which are negative and defensive, which do not produce a eupho-
ria of positive identification and pleasure.

Smooth Talk is about a girl's – Connie's – adolescence, and about a
summer holiday hanging around with her girlfriends at the beach
and at the shopping mall. It is very much Connie's story, of her
growing wish to be involved with boys, a wish to be wanted by

boys and hence, though not directly voiced, to enter into sexual awareness, and this is the central fantasy scenario of the film: Connie's wish to love and to be loved sexually. However she is also presented as a brat, selfish and thoughtless. She is narcissistically self-absorbed – she forgets the painting and decorating materials her mother asked her to purchase, then later she is shown trying out different poses in front of her mirror as she practises lines for chatting to boys with. Her mother focalises this negative view of Connie, saying 'I look into your eyes and all I see are trashy day-dreams'. We may identify with Connie and her self-absorption as something we have also done, a recognition of having been the same, once – relating to our earlier self with the same narcissistic investment that Connie applies to herself (such recognition, arising from the film's realism and verisimilitude, also functions as fore-pleasure, enabling an identification because of similarity which opens the spectator to also having the same *wish*[60]). We may also identify with her mother as the point of an enunciation which is critical of Connie. At the same time her mother's critical view proposes another Connie, the Connie she should be in order to conform to the demands of reality, to the symbolic – hence our identification here may be with the voice of the super-ego. We may also, however, identify with the mother's wish for Connie to be the daughter she wants her to be, and to be this for her – identifying therefore with the place of enunciation of what is for Connie's mother an ideal-ego – her daughter as ideal, but which she fails to be. For Connie it is the place of an ego-ideal, of what she must be in order to be what her mother wants. Connie's mother, however, wants her to be, or to remain, her little daughter of earlier times – but Connie must grow up and grow away, a separation figured in still 1, plate 8. And again the next day when, working together painting the house, although they present an image of harmony Connie nevertheless must hide her thoughts from her mother. The film also focalises Connie's older sister June, and her friend Jill, each of whom is shown to experience a sense of sexual lack in themselves in comparison to Connie. Jill is scared of the sexuality Connie and their friend Laura are exploring in their secret meetings with boys at a diner, while June is the plain sister who has failed to have such experiences. Our place 'with' or 'as' Connie is therefore qualified by the way the narration also places us with the desire of other characters.

The scene of Connie with her boyfriend in his car offers a similarly complex scenario for identification. While centrally focalised through Connie's words before she flees from the ardour of their kisses – she says 'Stop...I'm...not used to feeling this excited' – we do not necessarily wish to flee, or wish her to flee – as Connie does. For her boyfriend appears here as the ideal first lover, older but only slightly, who offers a tender and gentle but nonetheless erotic introduction to sexual relations as he sensuously massages her shoulders and back, no doubt foreplay prior to unfastening her bra. He is the lover we might wish to have or to have had, or to be. Connie however is frightened and runs off, for while we are shown that she is excited and aroused, that she wants Eddie's lovemaking, she cannot actively choose this experience. All this takes place in an underground car-park, the mise en scène introducing connotations of tackiness, of something out of place and nasty. The coarse and theatening side of male sexuality is realised in the next sequence when Connie has to walk home, to whistles and calls and then jeers from men in passing cars. (Laura and her father, who was to be their lift home, aren't there to meet her as arranged – Laura has been found out and is back at home; Connie's mother, too, will discover what, or what she thinks, Connie has been doing.) This both sustains the films's realism while it figures the terms of the question Connie confronts regarding her sexual desire, namely, whether her feelings are good or bad, and whether the object of her feelings – men – are sexually good or bad. That this is the conflict is confirmed the next day when her mother accuses Connie of having slept around, yet it was just because Connie felt that she was a 'good girl' that she fled from Eddie. Her mother's accusation is false, Connie didn't do anything. But insofar as she wanted to, her mother's words reduce Connie's feelings to something dirty and shaming. Here the narrative is once more focalised through Connie.

The film, in its displaying of Connie for our view, as it watches her and 'discovers' her secrets, also narrates a position of desire for Connie as sexual object, for her nubile and innocent sexuality. It is a voyeuristic desire which is then given a narrative representative within the film in the figure of Arnold Friend, yet this no doubt impedes as much as it reinforces identification with that position of desire, for it is now a character's desire, and no longer merely and more safely the narrative's desire. Now given a character's look, the voyeurism is 'shown', that is, 'seen' by the film, and by us as spectactors, but it is shown without any sanctioning motivation, so that it may now seem unacceptably – unpleasurably – voyeuristic, and

Arnold's marked look at Connie outside the diner appears as a portent of a future threat (see stills 2, 3, and 4, plate 8).

It is through the figure of Arnold Friend that *Smooth Talk* presents a fantasy-scenario which brings about the opposite of the desired event. Connie's longed-for but also feared sexual experience is realised in her encounter with Arnold Friend who, while he claims to occupy the place of her desire, to be able to give her what she wants, is also presented by the film connotatively – in his clothes, his car, his manner – as an abject though menacing caricature. Arnold, having learnt about Connie from Jill, arrives at Connie's home after, we may infer, seeing her family drive off leaving Connie alone – she has refused to go with them to a neighbour's barbecue following her row with her mother. Arnold's appearance as well as his car (the series of crosses on the wing marking his sexual successes) seem extravagant and are the occasion of humour at first, for Connie as well as the spectator, until his verbal ploys betray a threatening insistence and he appears monstrous and abject.

Connie tries to escape; withdrawing inside her home she shuts the door on Arnold, but she cannot still his voice, which now articulates the veiled threats already apparent while continuing to speak her desire for sexual knowledge. As he says, he knows what she wants, and he can give it to her. Connie's attempt to phone her mother is anticipated by Arnold, who tells her he'll cut the line, but nevertheless the film has her leave with Arnold without provoking him to enact the violence his words and body language threaten (see stills 5–9, plate 8).

After Arnold's long scene of 'seduction' the film elides the sexual event itself, only showing Connie returning to her home in his car so that we don't 'really know' what happened – we cannot tell if Connie was pleasured or not, we do not know if he 'fulfilled' her or not. Unrepresented in the film, it is markedly 'repressed', refused to the spectator, thereby also signifying the encounter as unrepresentable, as the 'real'. As a result, too, it becomes ambiguous, uncertain, and perhaps nothing happened, perhaps it was just Connie's imagination on a hot afternoon. Yet at no time does the film mark the action as fantasy, while the meaning of Arnold's intentions is made absolutely clear – he offers himself as her first lover, as the fantasy-man who can give her all she wants, and what she has always wanted. So the question remains – was Connie raped or was she willing? Connie resists, but not to the end. She leaves the house voluntarily, as Arnold demanded, but, once back home, Connie's warning to Arnold not to come near her again makes it certain that it is not something she wants to repeat with him. So, just as a judge and jury in our courts of law, we may question whether after all she did really want it. In any case given her behaviour – brattish and shallow, she's pretty and flirtatious but can't make up her mind what she wants – we may think that it is no more than she deserves. Or does she – as Joyce Carol Oates suggests – sacrifice herself for the sake of her family to prevent Arnold and his sidekick carrying out their threats to destroy her home? If so this is not confirmed and hence motivated in the film so that Connie does not appear a properly heroic victim. The scene is undoubtedly a 'downer' to spectators sympathetic to Connie, for the film, and Connie, fail to give us a proper image of resistance; Connie is neither properly a victim, nor does the film reassure us that we can, or a woman can, resist successfully. The film fails to offer us a positive image. Connie is not already a heroine, able to act – or submit – heroically, nor does she become the heroine of her own story through her experiences. Instead she is confronted with something like the demand 'Your money or your life!' which Lacan used to illustrate the fundamental alienation of the subject in its acceding to the symbolic, for a price must be paid, something must be given up – 'If I choose money, I lose both. If I choose life, I have life without money, namely a life deprived of something.'[61] Whether she resists or submits, Connie loses. If she resists Arnold, he will almost certainly violently rape her, as well as causing damage to her home and, by extension, to her family, while her parents will find out, and she will become for them sexually sullied, 'damaged goods'. But more, she will be revealed as the slut her mother has already accused her of being, for, after all, Arnold would not have followed her if she had not paraded herself, put herself forward for men at the diner. What is happening to her is certainly 'her own fault'. Better, then, to submit to Arnold Friend. Of course in doing so she takes up the position of sexual knowledge which her mother had forbidden her, accepting along with it a punishment. It is as if in order to become a subject of sexual desire Connie must enact a scenario of punishment, just as Freud's patients did in their fantasy 'A Child is Being Beaten'.

The ambiguity produced around the events of this hot afternoon foregrounds Connie's subjective experience, as if the scene were her dream – or nightmare. But while the focalisation here is centred on

Connie, identification does not necessarily follow. The filmic narration fails to show us how to understand what she 'really' wants, or to tell us what we should want for her, and hence enable us to enter into the scene. It has ceased to narrate a fantasy position for the spectator-subject. Things are no longer properly 'buttoned-down' for us. As a result the film does not confirm Connie as the subject of its 'punishing fantasy', it does not confirm it as her desire although it narrates it as a possible scenario – for her and the spectator, and it thereby *displays* this fantasy as such.

The self-censorship or guilt which produces this punishing scenario in the film and in Connie is the internalisation of the parental – here the mother's – probibition of sexual desire on pain of being a slut, dirty, and the film suggests that this is just how she feels as she leaves Arnold's car. The difficulty for Connie of achieving an active feminine desire is not only the result of a patriarchal discourse which condemns her desires, but also the problem of a parental discourse – represented by her mother – which defines sexuality as transgressive because it places her outside the family, because it realigns her relation to both her mother and father as an adult, as it must. And this is indeed what happens; her parents remain ignorant of the afternoon's events, but Connie's knowledge places her forever beyond childhood.

Ruby Rich, reviewing the film in *The Village Voice*,[62] pointed to the role of parental prohibition and placed this with the film's director, Joyce Chopra, 'the 48-year-old mother of a teenage daughter. And she's made a movie with a message for teenage daughters everywhere, keep a lid on your sexuality, don't you dare express it, don't you ever act out those "trashy daydreams" (as Connie's mother puts it) or you'll get it. Like a grownup bogeyman, Arnold Friend will come and get you.' That Arnold is like a figure from a fairytale is no doubt correct. Oates's original story drew on a case from the 1960s of a man – dubbed 'The Pied Piper of Tucson' – who seduced and occasionally murdered teenage girls, which Oates initially sought to cast as a realistic 'allegory of the fatal attractions of death (or the devil). An innocent young girl is seduced by way of her own vanity; she mistakes death for erotic romance of a particularly American trashy sort.' The conservatism of this moral view is clear, but it is not the story Oates wrote, or the one which was filmed. Instead, as Oates says, the focus of the story shifted from the 'charismatic mass murderer' to the teenage girl – still vain and foolish (like Oates herself may have been, she said) but no longer simply duped, and, too, capable of heroism. The story now articulates the contradictions between the *jouissance* of the drive and desire in the symbolic for the woman – as, perhaps, did the original folk or fairy stories.[63]

Connie is subject to fantasy, both its scenarios of wishfulfilment and its scenarios of punishment. What emerges is not a unified feminine identity – whether punished or triumphant – but a femininity, in the sense of being a subject of sexual difference, forged on these contradictions, for in the gap opened up is figured the real of desire and the impossibility of its representation. The reconciliation between Connie and her mother at the close of the film signifies Connie's rite of passage because it figures an irreparable separation between mother and daughter (see still 10, plate 8). Connie is playing out the role of the good daughter she can now never be, for she cannot be the ideal her mother demands, and which would resolve the lack in both Connie and her mother. Connie now knows this, though her mother doesn't. In this knowledge Connie accepts lack in the Other, and passes from childhood to an adult sexuality organised through the terms of lack in the symbolic order. When Connie begins to tell her sister June what happened to her that afternoon June's look – of horror or disbelief – stops her and she goes on to deny that anything happened after all. What is unspeakable here is not, however, the horror of the afternoon's events, but the ambivalence, the contamination of desire in abjection. It is in this unspeakable and its repression that Connie's womanliness is forged by the narration.

Smooth Talk's narrative strategies are important in producing its radical undermotivation of character, narrative and action. *Smooth Talk* becomes 'plotless' while its most plotted action – Arnold's seduction/rape of Connie, made possible just because she stayed at home after her row with her mother – is narratively enigmatic. Drawing both on Italian neo-realist cinema and on American 'observational' documentary films, *Smooth Talk*'s eviction of conventional narrative motivation pares the story down to an obscene cinematic realism, foregrounding the arbitrary and contingent, refusing proper sense-making.[64] It appears to confirm patriarchy and the punishment of the women's sexuality, justifying Ruby Rich's claim that 'the lure of *Smooth Talk* is a simple one: the spectacle of lust delivered unto the audience and then the punishment of its female embodiment, again for audience pleasure'.[65] But such a version of the film denies Connie's very desire, and the abject in femininity. There is something in Arnold that Connie wants – the real of her desire, its *jouissance*. We need to acknowledge this in femininity, together with its symptoms and fantasies, in order to unhook this enjoyment from its apparent support – male figures such as Arnold and their sexual exploitation of women.

Arnold is the *objet a*, the little bit of the real which must drop out before symbolisation can occur. Arnold is not thereby Connie's real object of desire; on the contrary he stands in as the cause of her desire. In Holbein's painting what was only a shadow until – from a new position of view – it takes up the shape of a skull functions as *objet a* not because all the many signifiers of the wealth and power of the Ambassadors suddenly appear null and void in the face of the force and reality of death, but because the real of desire – enjoyment – cannot be found in these objects, so many substitutes, and appears instead at the place of loss – death. Arnold is a caricature as well as a incarnation of stereotypical masculine attitudes to women, hence his character is both verisimilitudinous–he fits a socially real persona – and he is a joke. This ambiguity about Arnold motivates his coming to figure as *objet a* within the filmic narration for he precisely cannot be the idealised figure of fantasy, a proper, worthwhile love object. An obscene element, he is all one would want to turn away from in a sexual relation, but to do so one must also embrace and identify with this cause of one's desire in order to pass by *jouissance* and enter desire. The film is not a moral tale, as Rich supposes, which seeks to warn us that men like Arnold are waiting to deflower us – or our daughters. Rather it is a fairy tale which figures the issue of our desire, and appropriately, at least for the modern fairy tale, it has a happy ending, but – being a fairy tale, that is, fantastic – the ending reveals that it cannot cover over or resolve what has gone before. Desire and *jouissance* are incommensurable.

Chopra's film does not present a positive image or utopia of feminine desire, instead it explores the junctures between fantasy, reality and the contingent real of desire, and hence the way in which the identity of 'woman' is constructed on the contradictions and difficulties for humans of being desiring subjects within the discourses of social relations. It is, therefore, feminine cinema. The difficulties the film addresses show why, too, feminism remains a political necessity.

A different story is told by *Blue Steel*. It is identifiably a genre film, a police action movie, which offers an active, powerful woman protagonist and one who, it seems, is not subject to her femininity. Interviewed in 1990 about her film Katherine Bigelow said:

> I wanted to do a 'woman's action film', putting a woman at the centre of a movie predominantly occupied by men. When women go to see *Lethal Weapon*, many of them will identify with Mel Gibson. I was interested in creating a person at the centre of an action film who repesents an Everyman that both women and men could identify with. At our initial screenings at the Berlin Film Festival, some men at the press conference commented that they found themselves for the first time in their lives identifying with a woman. I found this very interesting because finally the notion of self-preservation is universal. I wanted to create a very strong, capable person who just happens to be a woman, using the context of the police genre.[66]

Bigelow's comments here reprise the debate on *Coma* in the late 1970s in their appeal to a cross-gender identification, the basis of which she suggests is, in *Blue Steel*, the universality of the drive to self-preservation. But the film's protagonist Megan acts to preserve others, not herself, in her attempts to bring to an end the murdering career of a killer. Her desire is not for self-preservation but the desire, as a cop, for justice and for the sake of which she puts herself at risk. She is shown defending – or helplessly failing to defend – not herself but others. She is not the object of his attacks, but she is their cause. As a result Bigelow is disengenuous in her claim that the protagonist, as a police officer, 'just happens to be a woman', for the film's plot is formed precisely on this point – she is the *woman* cop, a representative of the law, who exacts the ultimate punishment, death, upon a male gunman, precipitating the psychotic fascination with the woman as law – the woman as phallus/gun – of a bystander, Eugene, who now himself enacts the phallic power of the gun and becomes the film's killer. Megan comes into place for Eugene as the *objet a*. She is thus not just a cop investigating a homicide. She is also – as a woman – the 'cause' of the murders. Sexual difference, just as in *Coma*, becomes determining of the plot – there is no simple role reversal.

Unlike Susan in *Coma*, Megan is not yet proven in her profession. She is a rooky cop, newly graduated, and her career as a cop is marked by her failures – in the training practice, which is part of the credit sequence, Megan has to deal with a marital dispute and although when the man turns a gun on her she successfully despatches him, she then fails to anticipate a further potential danger, and is 'killed' by the wife who has grabbed the man's gun and shot her in turn. The scene of Megan's graduation also introduces a lack – and here the film displays exemplary narrative economy: Megan celebrates with Tracy, her best friend, now married with children, so that Megan's career-woman is juxtaposed with the conventional woman as wife and mother while the importance of this friendship to Megan is underlined; at the same time the absence of her parents is angrily noted by Megan, opening a question about her relation to them. The subsequent answer – namely her father's hostility to her career as a 'cop' – also introduces the motivation for Megan's wish to be a police officer, for we learn that he is regularly violent to her mother.[67]

On her first day as a 'rooky cop' Megan intervenes to stop an armed robbery at a supermarket (see stills 11–15, plate 7). It is Megan's inexperience which motivates her exceeding police procedure when she confronts the supermarket robber – when he refuses to lower his weapon she fires not once but six times, literally blowing him through the plateglass window. This 'failure' is compounded when the man's gun isn't found, her account is not supported by witnesses (though of course we saw what happened) and Megan is suspended from normal duties. When a bullet engraved with her name is taken from an unexplained murder victim, she is attached to work with Nick Mann in the homicide squad. Leaving work in the rain, Megan bumps into Eugene, a wealthy finance dealer, they share a taxi and a love affair develops. But unknown to Megan, although already revealed to the spectator, Eugene is the killer; he was a customer at the supermarket when Megan shot the armed robber and it was he who took the man's gun and commenced a series of arbitrary killings of men and women. When she begins to suspect him, he immediately confesses to her, and she calls the police, but she has no supporting evidence, and he is able to accuse the police of harassment. Later, Megan is certain that it is Eugene who shoots her best friend, but the killer was holding her from behind so that she did not actually see him. When Megan and Nick follow Eugene to the park where they believe he may have buried the gun, Megan handcuffs Nick to his car to enable her to go after Eugene alone, but she loses him and Eugene is about to kill the now-helpless Nick until Megan arrives back just in time to shoot and wound, but not capture, Eugene. After making love with

Nick at her apartment she is raped by Eugene who, though wounded, has followed her there and, having overseen their love-making, shoots Nick as he enters the bathroom where he has been hiding, before then attacking Megan. In each of her dealings with Eugene she comes off the worst until their final encounter. At the hospital, once assured Nick will recover, Megan makes her escape and now successfully counter-attacks.

Blue Steel presents a fantasy-scenario which brings about the opposite of the desired event. Its heroine, Megan, is the film's active protagonist. She wishes to be on the side of the law, to partake of its powers, a wish which is realised at the beginning of the film when she graduates from training school as a policewoman. Megan's fantasy, to possess the power of the law, becomes a nightmare when the man she desires shows himself to be obsessed with her precisely as the woman with the gun/phallus, and which he desires as an absolute and pure violence, as the power of death rather than life. Moreover he has identified with her – they are two halves of one person he says, in a grotesque inversion of the romantic language of ideal union between lovers.

Megan's identification with the law is figured at the beginning of the film (see stills 1–7, plates 6–7): she is dressing, putting on with obvious pleasure her police uniform – here coded as masculine – donning the law's insignia as she tightens her necktie, adjusts her trousers, laces her shoes, and packs her gun in its holster, ready for her graduation ceremony. After she graduates we watch her confident swagger as she walks home. This display of her possession of the insignia of the law is given further emphasis in the film by the editing and shot composition of the dressing sequence (which is also part of the credits) but it is then subsequently parodied (stills 8–10, plates 6–7). This arises directly at the level of narrative motivation, for Eugene, as the killer, desires Megan precisely in terms of that insignia, but not as the symbolic law: rather he desires her as the image of law made impossible, transgressive, in the woman/phallus, a conjoining of femininity and the power of death, the phallic all-powerful mother. The symbolism of the insignia is travestied and turned inside-out by Eugene's desire, while he consistently wrongfoots her, mocking the power of the police as a legal institution, so that the narrative action also enacts a mockery of the power of the police – and Megan.[68]

The insignia of the law is then parodied visually in the mise en scène. Megan is in hospital recovering from her ordeal at the hands of Eugene, who has still not been captured; she asks the policeman who is guarding her to come into her room and chats to him before knocking him out in order to take his clothes. She now repeats all the stages of dressing presented in the earlier scene, but with a difference: the uniform is no longer the insignia of an authority which she dons, it is no longer a magical – and fetishistic – object bestowing power, but a disguise by which she escapes unnoticed from the hospital. The visual parody thus also constitutes a break with Megan's former identification with the law, and in contrast to her earlier misjudgements and mistimings, she now moves unerringly towards her quarry. Ironically Megan no longer acts 'within' the law, but as the arm of justice itself. She no longer identifies with the law as ego-ideal – she is no longer acting on behalf of the law but as the law. Despite his injury, Eugene appears to have superhuman powers, so that Megan's shoot-out with him involves a series of spectacularly staged encounters. Yet the final shot of Megan after her despatch of the killer is not triumphant: rather she sits immobile, as if in shock, her gun dropped beside her in the front seat of her car as she is lifted out by the helping arms of another uniformed police officer. It seems to be not an image of phallic power, but of castration.[69]

Blue Steel is not, however, merely an unfulfilled fantasy – whether Megan's or Eugene's. Megan does not fail to possess the power of the phallus, but rather she, as it were, goes through the fantasy of phallic power and her identification with the law. The film parades the myth both Megan and Eugene subscribed to – of a phallic power which can really be possessed – only to explode the myth. That the parodying of the gun is a deliberate project of the film is signalled by the credit-sequence which presents a montage of pans and close-ups of a Smith & Wesson being loaded, presenting it as a shiny, luminous object, a fetish and a sign conventionally read in cinema as signifying phallic power. These shots may be inferred, retrospectively, as Megan's point-of-view when she puts the gun in her holster as she dresses, and this is also the 'view' and fantasy of the filmic enunciation and it will subsequently also be Eugene's view of Megan, his point-of-view as he lies on the supermarket floor in terror, watching her 'blow away' the robber. For Eugene, however, this is also an encounter with the real of his desire, and what drops out of the scene – quite literally, the robber's gun – becomes an *objet petit a*. Appropriated by Eugene, it becomes the cause of his desire. At the close of the film, having brought about Eugene's death, Megan discards her gun. It ceases to embody her *jouissance*. This is clearly quite different to castration.

Blue Steel binds or 'quilts' a set of meanings while foregrounding their very non-sense. That is, the nonsense of phallic power. *Blue Steel* thereby also places us as spectators in its fantasy scenario, and we too go through the fantasy of phallic power and its negation. Megan can act powerfully but her fantasy of phallic power, which meets its mirroring reply in Eugene, is broken. Megan overturns Eugene's fantasy construction, his symptom. The gun metonymically stands in for Megan – in the scene which precipitates his confession he asks her to pull out her gun and pose with it for him – so that Megan's combat with Eugene is also a struggle against her emplacement as *objet a* for Eugene. Of course at the same time she is also confirmed as the very condition of his enjoyment, his *jouissance*, as cause of his death.

The fantasy in *Blue Steel* is not simply negated or shown to be unrealisable, it is also 'gone through'. This fantasy is that which sustains the subject in its *jouissance*, its enjoyment outside symbolic relations and by which the subject seeks to evade lack in the other and itself. It sustains the subject's symptom, in fact. Fantasy as such is not thereby abolished. It remains the necessary imaginary scenario which functions to fill out the subject's constitutive void, but in doing so the subject, and the spectator, is brought up against the aporia of its desire, the limits, and lack, of fantasy. Works of representation both stage fantasy and enact our separation from fantasy, posing to us the possibility of thinking otherwise and opening us to such a desire by its fantasy scenarios which figure a lack which could be otherwise. 'Lack' in the subject does not, though, quite have a content, but our fantasies do – pulling into a placing the floating signifiers of our social reality. Can we quilt them differently? Surely so, but we find in attempting this the paradox that what we aim and plan to achieve at the same time brings into play the lack, the gap, the remainder of the real which pulls apart again the buttoning down of meaning. It is necessary to recognise and accept this cost while all the same going forward as if things could be otherwise.

Notes and References

Introduction

1. Boccaccio's version of the story, which was probably drawn from Anastagio Degli Unesti, appears as 'The Eighth Story' of 'Day the Fifth' of *The Decameron*. He concludes his story saying 'Their marriage was by no means the only good effect to be produced by this horrible apparition, for from that day forth the ladies of Ravenna in general were so frightened by it that they became much more tractable to men's pleasures than they had ever been in the past': Penguin Classics, trans. G. H. McWilliam (Harmondsworth: Penguin, 1972), p. 462. My thanks to Alan Millen for pointing out to me this thematic reference.

   Erik Hedling has noted that the picture in Dreyer's film differs from that in the play by Hjalmar Söderberg on which it is based, and I am very grateful to him for the following information about the picture. In the play the scene instruction at the beginning of the second act states 'The walls between the doors are covered by tapestries: at the left the birth of Venus, at the right a red deer torn by dogs.' Sten Rein, however, in his *Hjalmar Söderberg's Gertrud* (Stockholm: Bonniers, 1962) p. 79, claims that Söderberg changed the word 'woman' in his original manuscript into 'red deer'. The tapestry was partly an illustration of Gertrud's dream that she would 'run the streets, chased by dogs' as well as an allusion to the myth of Actaeon, whom Artemis made into a deer and who was subsequently torn to death by his own dogs. It is known that Dreyer had read Söderberg's original manuscript, so that the change he makes – replacing the red deer by a woman – returns it to Söderberg's original instruction for the tapestry. The most careful study of Dreyer, Edvin Kau's *Dreyer's Filmkunst* (Copenhagen: Akademisk Forlag, 1989), does not discuss the picture as an already existing artwork, although it pays much attention to allusions to paintings by Hammershøi and Munch in the film. Sven Holm at Palladium Pictures has informed me that John Hilbard, the associate producer of *Gertrud*, has confirmed that the picture is neither a painting nor a tapestry, but a drawing made with black and white crayon on canvas.

2. Freud discusses the *fort-da* game and repetition in *Beyond the Pleasure Principle* (1920), *The Standard Edition of the Complete Works of Sigmund Freud*, vol. XVIII (London: Hogarth Press, 24 volumes 1953–74, hereafter cited as *SE*), pp. 14–17. Lacan reconsiders Freud's account in *Écrits, A Selection* (1966), trans. Alan Sheridan (London: Tavistock, 1977), p. 104, and it is discussed further in Chapter 5.

3. Jean-François Lyotard, *The Postmodern Condition: A Report on Knowledge* (1979), trans. G. Bennington and B. Massumi (Minneapolis: University of Minnesota Press, 1984), p. 74.

4. Rachel M. Brownstein, *Becoming a Heroine* (New York: Viking Press, 1984), p. xxi.
5. Ibid, p. xxiv.
6. Ibid, p. xxvi.
7. Lacan's work has also drawn upon – as well as contested – other major psychoanalytic theorists, in particular Melanie Klein and D. W. Winnicott.
8. Juliet Mitchell, *Psychoanalysis and Feminism* (London: Allen Lane, 1974).
9. These debates are summarised by Juliet Mitchell in her introduction to the selection of articles by Lacan and members of the *École Freudienne* co-edited with Jacqueline Rose. As Mitchell shows, Freud's view of femininity was strongly contested and defended by psychoanalysts in the 1920s and 1930s, including Ernest Jones, Melanie Klein, Karen Horney, Helene Deutsch, Jeanne Lampl de Groot, Ruth Mack Brunswick: 'Introduction – I', *Feminine Sexuality: Jacques Lacan and the École Freudienne*, ed. Juliet Mitchell and Jacqueline Rose (London: Macmillan, 1982), pp. 1–26.

    The later critique in 1949 by Simone de Beauvoir in *The Second Sex* (London: Jonathan Cape, 1969) again challenged much of Freud's theory on femininity, while others, such as Betty Friedan in *The Feminine Mystique* (Harmondsworth: Penguin Books, 1965 [1963]) and Shulamith Firestone in *The Dialectic of Sex* (London: Jonathan Cape, 1971 [1970]) rejected Freudian psychoanalysis as 'anti-women'. Mitchell took up these critiques in *Psychoanalysis and Feminism*.

    Lacan's 're-reading' of Freud gave rise to a number of important new discussions of female sexuality, notably by Michèle Montrelay in 'Inquiry into Femininity' in *m/f*, no. 1, 1978, trans. Parveen Adams, reprinted in *The Woman in Question*, ed. Parveen Adams and Elizabeth Cowie (Cambridge, MA: MIT Press, 1990); Luce Irigaray, *Speculum of the Other* (1974), trans. Gillian C. Gill (Ithaca: Cornell University Press, 1985); *This Sex Which Is Not One* (1977), trans. Catherine Porter (Ithaca: Cornell University Press, 1985); Eugénie Lemoine-Luccioni, *The Dividing of Women or Woman's Lot* (1976), trans. Marie-Laure Davenport and Marie-Christine Regis (London: Free Association Books, 1987); Monique David-Ménard, *Hysteria From Freud to Lacan* (1983) trans. Catherine Porter (Cornell: University Press 1989). Julia Kristeva has addressed the maternal and the feminine in a number of her books, in particular *Tales of Love* (1983), trans. Leon S. Roudiez (New York: Columbia University Press, 1987).

    The debate with Lacan and Freud has given rise to a large body of critical writing, including Sara Kofman's study of Freud's repression of femininity, not least his own, in *The Enigma of Woman. Woman in Freud's Writings*, trans. Catherine Porter (Ithaca: Cornell University Press, 1985) and Jane Gallop's two books, *Feminism and Psychoanalysis* (London: Macmillan, 1982), and *Reading Lacan* (Ithaca: Cornell University Press, 1985). Elizabeth Grosz's *Jacques Lacan, a Feminist Introduction* is a review of Lacan's work and the feminist writing on Freud and Lacan (London: Routledge, 1990).

10.   Mary Ann Doane, *Femmes Fatales: Feminism, Film Theory, Psycho-analysis* (London: Routledge, 1991), p. 8.

11.   At times Freud's own arguments on femininity seem to be normative rather than theoretical; nevertheless he also strongly opposed the reduction of the psychical to the biological, and in a letter to Müller-Braunschweig in 1935 he writes 'I object to all of you (Horney, Jones, Rado, etc.) to the extent that you do not distinguish more clearly and cleanly between what is psychic and what is biological, that you try to establish a neat parallelism between the two....'; cit. Mitchell, *Feminine Sexuality*, p. 21. Moreover while Helene Deutsch's view of the fundamentally masochistic nature of femininity appears to return women to a submission to biology, she presents a wholly psychological view of the process of the little girl becoming a woman in 'The Psychology of Women in Relation to the Functions of Reproduction' when she says 'A woman who succeeds in establishing this maternal function of the vagina by giving up the claim of the clitoris to represent the penis, has reached the goal of feminine development, [she] *has become a woman*': *The International Journal of Psycho-Analysis*, vol. 6, 1925, p. 411. The maternal function is not therefore given by anatomy but must be achieved by the woman.

12.   *m/f* no. 8, 1983, p. 8.

13.   Mitchell, *Feminine Sexuality*, p. 24.

14.   Ibid, p. 26.

15.   Christian Metz, *Psychoanalysis and Cinema: The Imaginary Signifier* (1977), trans. Celia Britton, Annwyl Williams, Ben Brewster and Alfred Guzzetti (London: Macmillan, 1982).

1   Feminist Arguments

1.   In Britain sexual relations between men over the age of 21 in private were formally decriminalised in 1967, but the definition of 'private' continued to be debated in the courts, and the Act gave police new powers in relation to homosexuality in public places. In 1994 the age was reduced to 18. Sexual relations between women had never been criminalised but were, of course, subject to social opprobrium.

2.   The debates on this in the women's movement have been very extensive. My arguments here draw on the work by Beverley Brown, 'Natural and Social Division of Labour: Engels and the Domestic Labour Debate', *m/f*, no. 1, 1978, and by Mark Cousins, 'Material Arguments and Feminism', *m/f*, no. 2, 1978, reprinted in *The Woman in Question*. More recently Judith Butler has summarised the problems with the concept of patriachy and commented that 'The very notion of "patriarchy" has threatened to become a universalising concept that overrides or reduces distinct articulations of gender asymmetry in different cultural contexts': *Gender Trouble* (New York: Routledge, 1990), p. 35.

3. Joan Copjec, 'The Anxiety of the Influencing Machine', *October*, no. 23, 1982, p. 58.

4. Ferdinand de Saussure, *Course in General Linguistics* (1915), trans. Wade Baskin (New York: McGraw-Hill, 1966).

5. Jacques Derrida, *Positions* (1972), trans. Alan Bass (London: Athlone Press, 1981), p. 23.

6. Jacques Derrida, *Of Grammatology* (1967), trans. Gayatri Chakravorty Spivak (Baltimore: The Johns Hopkins University Press, 1974), p. 13, my emphasis.

7. This point is made by Mark Cousins in 'The Logic of Deconstruction', *The Oxford Literary Review*, vol. 3, no. 2, 1978, p. 74.

8. Whereas in earlier societies the category 'woman' was perhaps less important than categories of kinship relations (mother, sister, daughter etc.) in many modern societies it is sexual difference alone – summed up by the universal category 'woman' – which is privileged, to the cost in fact of the social positions of mother or daughter.

9. Roland Barthes, 'Rhetoric of the Image', in *Image-Music-Text* (1964), trans. Stephen Heath (London: Fontana, 1977).

10. Mitchell, 'Patriarchy, Kinship and Women as Exchange Objects', *Psychoanalysis and Feminism*, pp. 370–416.

11. The Danish linguist Louis Hjelmslev used the term connotation to describe the way in which a sign can denote a referent, for example, 'cricket' refers to the field game of that name while at the same time producing an additional signified or connotation, 'Englishness'. In *Prolegomena to a Theory of Language* (1943), trans. Francis J Whitfield (Madison: University of Wisconsin Press, 1963). The sign in denotation becomes the signifier for another signified in connotation. The work of connotation in languages, as the appropriation of a signified as the signifier for another system, has been seen by Barthes as the function of myth, or ideology: 'myth is always a language-robbery': *Mythologies* (1957), trans. Annette Lavers (London: Paladin, 1972), p. 131. Myth or connotation deforms and effaces an original denoted signified which is thus put to another use. Myth is therefore seen as the corruption of a proper language-use which enables ideology to seduce us. Barthes's thesis on myth – which differs sharply from Lévi-Strauss here – has had a singular and rapid success, yet in fact it presents the same problem as Lévi-Strauss's 'woman as sign', namely the assumption of a true and original meaning or denotation *before* its fall to the clutches of connotation, or kinship exchange.

12. Lévi-Strauss had attended Jakobson's lectures in exile in New York in 1942/3 and his introduction to the publication of these lectures in 1976 acknowledges his debt, in Roman Jakobson, *Six Lectures on Sound and Meaning*, trans. John Mepham (Brighton: Harvester Press, 1978).

13. Lévi-Strauss, 'Introduction', in *Six Lectures on Sound and Meaning*, p. xviii.

14. Claude Lévi-Strauss, *Structural Anthropology* (1958), trans. C. Jacobson and B. G. Schoepf (Harmondsworth: Penguin, 1972), p. 61.

15. Lévi-Strauss affirms that exogomy or marriage outside the family group is fundamental to social life. It represents a social imperative imposed on the group whose inverse is the prohibition on marriage within the family or clan, i.e., the taboo on incest.

16. 'Now, there is an intermediary between images and concepts, namely signs. For signs can always be defined in the way introduced by Saussure in the case of the particular category of linguistic signs, that is, as a link between images and concepts': Lévi-Strauss, *The Savage Mind* (1962) (London: Weidenfeld & Nicolson, 1966), p. 18.

17. Lévi-Strauss, *Structural Anthropology*, p. 60.

18. In their essay on Walsh's film *The Revolt of Mamie Stover* (1956), Claire Johnston and Pam Cook write: 'In Walsh's oeuvre, woman is not only a sign in a system of exchange, but an empty sign', a sign by means of which 'men express their relationships with each other, the means by which they come to understand themselves and each other'; 'Woman in the Cinema of Raoul Walsh' (1974), in *Feminism and Film Theory*, ed. Constance Penley (New York: Routledge, 1988), p. 27. Signs cannot be empty; rather they are arguing that woman-as-sign is empty of the signified 'woman' and instead is the signified of men's relations to each other, and they show that the production of the narrative figure of the woman, Mamie, is a set of meanings in the service of the definition of the male character and of masculinity. There can be no 'full' signified 'woman', however, which the specific signifying system, *The Revolt of Mamie Stover*, fails to signify. Moreover, as Cook and Johnston also show, the film comes to foreground this very use of the figure of the woman, producing an internal criticism which cracks apart the ideology upon which it appears to be founded (here they are drawing upon the arguments of Jean-Louis Comolli and Jean Narboni in 'Cinema/Ideology/Criticism' (1969), trans. Susan Bennett, *Screen*, vol. 12, no. 1, 1971). As a result several different and competing meanings in relation to the figure of Mamie arise. I would suggest, too, that the film quite consciously embeds many of the ironies surrounding Mamie.

19. Lévi-Strauss, *The Elementary Structures of Kinship* (1949), trans. James Harle Bell and John Richard von Sturmer (Boston: Beacon Press, 1969), p. 482.

20. Lévi-Strauss cites A. R. Radcliffe-Brown's discussion in 'Three Tribes of Western Australia' (1913) where he argues that the commonest question put to a stranger is 'Who is your *maeli* (father's father)' in order to establish kinship relations: Lévi-Strauss, ibid, p. 482.

21. Saussure, *Course in General Linguistics*, p. 120.

22. Lévi-Strauss noted that there was no theoretical reason why only women should be exchanged, but he, and later kinship theorists, invariably read the anthropological evidence as always showing that this is the case, and that it is men who exchange women.

23. In the matrilineal and matrilocal Hopi Native American society the men were the hunters and conducted the religious ceremonies, while the women undertook agriculture, and though helped by the men it was the women who owned the land as well as the produce. See

Robin Fox, *Kinship and Marriage* (Harmondsworth: Penguin Books, 1967), p. 89.

24. Lévi-Strauss, *The Elementary Structures of Kinship*, p. 117.

25. What I have pointed to as a contradiction and confusion in Lévi-Strauss's logic here has been addressed by Judith Butler as an identitarian logic which 'distributes "identity" to male persons and a subordinate and a relational "negation" or "lack" to women' so that 'Clan members, invariably male, invoke the prerogative of identity through marriage, a repeated act of symbolic differentiation': *Gender Trouble*, p. 39. Her reading of Lévi-Strauss here is rather partial, however. Lévi-Strauss does not imply that woman in exchange 'reflects masculine identity precisely through being the site of its absence', ibid, p. 39. Nor does he suggest that the bride does not have an identity. He is not concerned with the issue of individual identity but is proposing a way in which what had hitherto appeared as diverse, arbitrary and contradictory features of kinship and lineage could be read as a structure, and as a founding social structure for human communities. Lévi-Strauss's concern to recognise that women are also valuables in their own right clearly marks as contradictory his notions of person and of social agent in *The Elementary Structures of Kinship*.

26. The example of the Tallensi given by Robin Fox illustrates the complexity involved, a complexity which defies a simple binarisation of power and kinship between men and women. The Tallensi, who live in closely packed settlements in northern Ghana, are patrilocal and divided into patrilineal clans. However, Fox writes, 'The Tallensi have a belief that women should not be deprived of lineage membership just because an accident of birth has made them the wrong sex and so deprived them of the power to contribute to the continuity of the lineage': *Kinship and Marriage*, p. 118. As a result the clanswomen are given specific privileges and roles in clan affairs, including important roles in religious rituals. Sisters, as clanswomen, are privileged over wives, as non-clanswomen, and daughters are not wholly replaced by daughters-in-law.

27. Jacques Lacan, *Écrits, A Selection*, trans. Alan Sheridan (London: Tavistock, 1977), p. 66.

28. Ibid, p. 67.

29. Ibid, p. 319.

30. Charles Henry Pradelles de Latour, in 'Marriage Payments, Debt and Fatherhood Among the Bangoua: A Lacanian Analysis of a Kinship System', *Africa*, vol. 64, no. 1, 1994, pp. 21–33, argues that for the Bangoua the paternal function is not carried out by the biological father, but by the 'father behind', the mother's father. The Bangua have a system of double payment for a bride by the husband in the matrimonial exchange, one to the biological father but which is marked ritually as 'insufficient', and another to the maternal grandfather, which is held to be a 'full' repayment of the debt in so far as it can be repaid in a material manner. It is this latter payment and the function of the mother's father which ensures the social exchange

and the symbolic law. A split between the idealised father and the symbolic father is demonstrated here by Pradelles de Latour; at the same time it is also shown that the exchange of women is not simply a matter between men, but between a suitor and the bride's 'two' fathers.

31. Ben Brewster, drawing on the work of Yuri Lotman, argues that 'reading' a film 'both utilises the codes it has in common with the producer of the text and produces new codes that may or may not have gone into the production of the text with the proviso that the "reading in" of codes is not arbitrary, because it is governed by a rule of pertinence established by the motivations, i.e. multiple codings, that the reading can establish in the text': 'Notes on the Text "Young Mr Lincoln" by the Editors of *Cahiers du Cinéma*', *Screen*, vol. 14, no. 3, 1973, pp. 41–2.

32. The relation and role of cinematic and filmic codes are set out and explored by Christian Metz in *Language and Cinema*, trans. Donna Jean Umiker-Sebeok (The Hague: Mouton, 1974).

33. Lévi-Strauss, 'Introduction', in *Six Lectures on Sound and Meaning*, p. xxii.

34. Molly Haskell, 'Howard Hawks: Masculine Feminine', *Film Comment*, vol. 10, no. 2, 1974, p. 39.

35. Geoffrey Nowell-Smith, *Visconti* (London: Secker & Warburg, 1967), pp. 9–12.

36. Peter Wollen, *Signs and Meaning in the Cinema*, revised third edition (London: Secker & Warburg, 1972), p. 93.

37. Ibid, pp. 93–4.

38. Ibid, p. 86.

39. Ibid, p. 86. For example the scene between Jean Arthur (Bonnie) and Thomas Mitchell (the Kid) in *Only Angels Have Wings* (1939).

40. The strength of male friendships in Hawks's films certainly raises the question of homosexual desire, but this cannot be seen as simply a latent or repressed and hence true but hidden aspect of his heroes which the heterosexual resolution betrays; the Hawksian text inscribes a dilemma for the man, rather than repressing a solution. Relations of desire within positions of sexual difference as feminine and masculine, lesbian or gay, are not easily, if at all, unilateral.

41. Claire Johnston, 'Women's Cinema as Counter-Cinema' (1973), in *Sexual Stratagems*, ed. Patricia Erens (New York: Horizon Press, 1979), p. 27. My argument here, however, is that the differentiation of sexual difference never involves positive terms or full signifieds as essential meanings outside the system of signification.

42. Robin Wood, *Howard Hawks* (London: Secker & Warburg, 1968, 1981), p. 182.

43. Molly Haskell, 'Howard Hawks: Masculine Feminine', p. 36.

44. Jean-Louis Comolli writes of the correlations between Hawks's films that 'instead of helping to explain, for example, what might be central in these very diverse films, they simply cross-multiply images of this elusive centrality that are sometimes the right way up and sometimes upside down; and you need real cunning to find that

centrality or to make sense of it – if women are men, that doesn't quite mean that men are women; both sexes flirt with the transsexual but both stop short of crossing over to the other side...': 'The Ironical Howard Hawks'(1964), in *Cahiers du Cinéma – the 1960's,* ed. Jim Hillier (London: Routledge, 1986), p. 181.

45. Jacques Rivette, 'The Genius of Howard Hawks' (1953), in *Cahiers du Cinéma – the 1950's,* ed. Jim Hillier (London: Routledge, 1985), p. 131.

46. Active and passive in relation to femininity and masculinity, as well as the points made here in relation to fetishism and the constitution of the heterosexual couple are developed further in later chapters on the drives, on fetishism, and on female sexuality.

47. The role of circulating objects and signs in establishing the heterosexual couple is confirmed in *Red River* (1948) and *The Big Sky* (1952), two films in which the narrative is centred primarily on the relation of rivalry and identification between the two male protagonists – an older professional and a new young professional. Whereas in *Red River* the woman reconciles the two men, in *The Big Sky* Boone, chosen by Teale Eye over Jim, who really loves her, stays with her only in order to keep the love and respect of his friend with Jim, but thereby nevertheless loses Jim.

2   Narrative Positions and the Placing of the Woman Protagonist in *Coma*

1. Penny Hallow, reviewing *Coma* in *Spare Rib*, no. 79, February 1979, p. 40. She goes on to say 'I do have vague misgivings about the ending: if *Coma* had been the conventional Hollywood melodrama, who would have rescued the hero? ... Despite these doubts, my initial response still stands; any film which features a woman in a role of such strength deserves a visit.'

2. *Coma* was directed and written by Michael Crichton from a novel by fellow-doctor Robin Cook. Made in panavision and metrocolor, it starred Genevieve Bujold as Dr Susan Wheeler, Michael Douglas as Dr Mark Bellows, and Richard Widmark as Dr Harris. It was released in Britain with an AA certificate.

When surgeon Susan Wheeler's best friend emerges comatose from a routine procedure – an abortion – she determines to find out why. Initially expecting a medical or scientific cause, she begins to suspect a more sinister reason when her enquiries are blocked by hospital management. Meanwhile her investigation is seen by her fellow-surgeon and boyfriend Mark, as well as by her colleagues and superiors, as an emotional response and her suspicions as paranoid. Susan, however, is right, people are being murdered – by supplying carbon monoxide instead of oxygen during operations – in order to supply an international market in donor organs . Having discovered how it's done, and how the organs are distributed, she fails to get the right villain and almost herself becomes a victim, until rescued by Mark. The film does not start with a criminal act, however, but with Susan, first in her professional role at work, then in her personal relationship with Mark at his flat after work, but this initial situation is disrupted when she leaves after their row.

3. The term 'protagonist', indicating the chief actor, character or combatant, is used here in preference to 'heroine' to describe Genevieve Bujold's role as Dr. Susan Wheeler in order to emphasise the narrative function of the hero; the 'heroine' is not normally the female equivalent of 'hero'.

4. Marjorie Bilbow, in the British film trade journal *Screen International*, no. 156, 16 September 1978, p. 25.

5. Bilbow, ibid. Margaret Hinxman in the *Daily Mail*, 10 November 1978, similarly pointed to the realism of Susan's character: 'Another intriguing aspect of the film is that Genevieve Bujold emerges as a real, complicated person, not just a frightened lady caught in a trap. She is scratchy, unreasonable and intractable. She wears hardly any make up and her hair is obviously in need of the next shampoo and set. There is a kind of stubborn fanaticism about everything she says and does. It is a superbly constructed performance which stiffens the backbone of what has to be the best thriller of 1978.'

    The plausibility of character is also emphasised by Alan Brien in the *Sunday Times*, 1 November 1978, writing of the stunts: 'these are only a few of the daring, athletic improbabilities we are conditioned to find commonplace when our star is Burt Reynolds or Paul Newman, but still likely to strain credulity when she is called Genevieve Bujold. Crichton defuses such sexist prejudices partly by the speed, dash and bravura of his story-telling, partly by the creation of a prickly, likeable, contemporary liberated woman.'

    The reviewer in *The Sunday Express*, 12 November 1978, reached the opposite conclusion however: 'Genevieve Bujold as Dr Wheeler, tries to get to the bottom of the mystery. In the process she makes life hell for the rest of the staff. Her lover, Dr Bellows, doesn't believe her theories... Miss Bujold is so tedious and hysterical that I don't blame Doc Bellows for disbelieving her.'

6. For a discussion of *Coma* as melodrama, see Christine Gledhill, 'Pleasurable Negotiations', in *Female Spectators*, ed. E. Deidre Pribram (London: Verso, 1988).

7. Susan is shown behind a glass shower screen moving sensuously under the water, then the camera cuts to include Mark in frame as well, in profile close-up to the camera, the film then cuts to a view from over his shoulder, now becoming his point-of-view, so that we have Mark's view of Susan, and our own. Later when Susan wakes suddenly from a nightmare following her escape from the Jefferson Institute she goes over to the window of her hotel room and the camera shows a reverse shot seen through the window of her standing naked. Another marked moment of voyeurism – when Susan climbs the maintenance ladder in the basement, following the route of the carbon monoxide line to the ventilation shaft to the operating room, OR8 – is also mixed, for while we are shown a view of Susan from below, we cannot see very much, and when she removes her

tights and shoes, while the image of a striptease is necessarily connoted, the action is fully motivated by her need to remove them as encumbrances as she steps across from the ladder to the ventilation shaft. Undoubtedly a spectacle, but signifying more than simply sexual spectacle.

8. Here and at other points in my discussion my original article referred to the women's movement which, at the time of writing the article in 1978, was still a focus of political activity and organisation by feminists. Subsequently, while feminist activity in a wide variety of areas has not abated, it has not been articulated in terms of a movement. In revising the article I have usually referred simply to feminism.

9. Rosalind Coward has defined 'recuperation' in terms of an incorporation, for example in relation to sexual liberation 'where some truly liberatory force which has no relation whatsoever with capitalism is re-absorbed back into the existing capitalist forms'. My discussion here has drawn upon her critique in 'Sexual Liberation and the Family', *m/f*, no. 1, 1978.

10. The chronicle, moreover, simply stops, rather than bringing its account to a conclusion, as a story or history does, that is, it fails to bring its account to a closure. Hayden White, challenging traditional views of narrative history, argues that 'The events [of historical writing] must be not only registered within the chronological framework of their original occurrence but narrated as well, that is to say, revealed as possessing a structure, an order of meaning, that they do not possess as mere sequence': *The Content of the Form* (Baltimore: The Johns Hopkins University Press, 1987), p. 5. White observes that 'Narrative becomes a problem only when we wish to give to *real* events the *form* of story. It is because real events do not offer themselves as stories that their narrativisation is so difficult', ibid, p. 4. Of course, 'proper' history as a discipline also accords with certain notions of evidence and particular modes of treatment of historical material.

11. From Boris Tomashevsky's account of Shklovsky's distinction: 'Thematics', in *Russian Formalist Criticism*, trans. and ed. Lee T. Lemon and Marion J. Reis (Lincoln: University of Nebraska Press, 1965), p. 67. French theorists have used the terms *histoire* and *récit*.

12. The *Oxford English Dictionary*, in the entry for 'plot', cites Lewis (1852) 'In every narrative there is a certain connection of events... which, in a work of fiction, is called a plot', and Gladstone (1878) 'In the plot of the *Odyssey*, symmetry is obvious at first sight; in the plot of the *Illiad*, it has to be sought out.' Here he is pointing to the stylistic role of plot contrivance. The plot or 'intrigue' was central to drama, and is exemplified in the melodrama's plotting to produce the reversal and moments of recognition which became features of the genre. Edmund Gosse's entry for the novel in the eleventh edition of the *Encyclopaedia Britannica* praises Fielding's *Tom Jones* (1749) as a great advance in the development of the novel because of 'the sustained skill with which the author conducted the plot, the interwoven series of the actions of his characters'.

13.   Peter Brooks, *Reading for the Plot* (New York: Vintage Books, 1985), p. 13.

14.   Tomashevsky, 'Thematics', *Russian Formalist Criticism*, p. 69.

15.   In using the term 'narrating' I wish to emphasis the present tense of storytelling in film with its visual showing of events and actions that are happening in front of us but which are nevertheless also being narrated. This follows Gérard Genette's distinction between narrative – the signifier or statement, the discourse or narrative text itself – and narrating, the production of the narrative action; see *Narrative Discourse, an essay in method* (1972), trans. Jane E. Lewin (Ithaca: Cornell University Press, 1980). Film rarely marks its narrating voice, however, so that we are not listening to a storyteller but making sense of what we overhear and see.

16.   The term 'focalisation' was introduced by Genette, ibid, to distinguish between the instance of the narrator who recounts the events of the fictional world, and the instance of a character who 'lives' in the story and who sees and experiences its events. Focalisation is therefore within the diegetic world, while narration is outside, though still part of the fiction. The concept has been widely developed and debated, notably by Mieke Bal in *Narratology: Introduction to the Theory of Narrative* (1980), trans. Christine van Boheemen (Toronto: University of Toronto Press, 1985), and by Shlomith Rimmon-Kenan in *Narrative Fiction: Contemporary Poetics* (London: Methuen, 1983). Sarah Kozloff has drawn on Genette's concept in her study of voice-over narration in films, *Invisible Storytellers* (Berkeley: University of California Press, 1988). Edward Branigan also draws on the term, though critically, in his wide-ranging study of film narration, *Narrative Comprehension and Film* (London: Routledge, 1992).

17.   Of course there is also a figure behind or beyond the narrating within the text, whose name is on the frontispiece as author, who receives royalties on the book, and who we infer has selected the ordering, the devices and the modes by which the events and characters, the signs and representations of the text become *narrative* information. The inferring of a narrating intention or instance and our identification with it as place of knowledge is considered further in the chapter on identification in relation to the notions of historic and discursive narration introduced by Emile Benveniste. The category 'author' has been radically transformed – though not abolished – by the critiques of authorship in the last twenty years inaugurated by Roland Barthes in 'The Death of the Author' (1968), *Image-Music-Text*, trans. Stephen Heath (London: Fontana, 1977), and Michel Foucault in 'What is an Author?' (1969), *Language, Counter-Memory, Practice: Selected Essays and Interviews*, trans. Donald Bouchard and Sherry Simon, ed. Donald Bouchard (Oxford: Basil Blackwell, 1977). Ben Brewster has, however, pointed to the importance of the code of the author – a code constructed by the viewer in her or his reading of the film – in 'Notes on the Text "Young Mr Lincoln" by the Editors of *Cahiers du Cinéma*', where he shows the role of the Fordian sub-code in relation to the film's generic code of historical bio-pic.

18. Boris Eichenbaum argues that the Formalists freed themselves 'from the traditional correlation of "form and content" and from the traditional idea of form as an envelope, a vessel into which one pours a liquid (the content)': 'The Theory of the Formal Method', in *Russian Formalist Criticism*, p. 112.

19. J. Tynjanov writes that what constitutes the difference between the literary and filmic story is 'Not only the material, but also the fact that the style and laws of construction in cinema transform all the elements – all those elements which, it seemed, were indivisible, applicable in the same way to all art forms and to all their genres': 'On the Foundations of Cinema' (1927), in *Russian Formalist Film Theory*, ed. Herbert Eagle (Michigan: University of Michigan Press, 1981), p. 95.

20. Brooks, *Reading for the Plot*, p. 13. Brooks draws on Paul Ricoeur's definition of plot as 'the intelligible whole that governs a succession of events in any story': 'Narrative Time', in *On Narrative*, ed. W. J. T. Mitchell (Chicago: University of Chicago Press, 1981), p. 167.

21. Ibid, p. 13.

22. Ibid, p. 37.

23. This hesitation in Brooks parallels a certain conflation in his study between narrative desire and desire for narrative, and begs the question as to how does the reader as a subject of desire become subject to any particular narrative's machine of desire.

24. David Bordwell, *Narration in the Fiction Film* (London: Methuen, 1985), p. 53.

25. Ibid, p. 52.

26. The use of the terms 'style' and 'technique' interchangeably by Bordwell underlines their place in his view of narrative, namely as material elements which produce perceptual events that are used by the *syuzhet* but do not themselves constitute part of the work of meaning-production in a text. Arguing that 'Cinematic style, the repetition and development of instantiations of film technique, may... become what Tynjanov calls the "dominant", the factor that is pushed forward at the expense of others, "deforming" them': ibid, p. 275. Bordwell develops the notion of 'parametric' cinema to discuss those narrative films where style becomes 'dominant' – in his sense here – and he analyses films by Jean-Luc Godard and Robert Bresson, both directors for whom the interrelation of form and content were central. This issue is taken up again in the discussion of *Gertrud* later in this book.

27. Victor Shklovsky, 'Sterne's *Tristram Shandy*: Stylistic Commentary', in *Russian Formalist Criticism*. Sterne's parodic fiction was constructed at the time of the emergence of the novel in English so that it lays bare conventions which are themselves in the process of being established. Sterne himself, however, did not use the term 'novel' to describe his works. On this, see Geoffrey Day, *From Fiction to the Novel* (London: Routledge, 1987).

   Bordwell sees the basis for his distinction between style and plot construction or narrative form in Shklovsky's essay 'On the

Connection Between Devices of Plot Construction and General Stylistic Devices', in *Theory of Prose* (1925), trans. Benjamin Sher (Elmwood Park, Illinois: Dalkey Archive Press, 1990). But in *Narration in the Fiction Film*, note 8, p. 345, he comments in relation to Tynjanov's references to 'plot linkage' as distinct from style that Tynjanov's meaning is 'cryptic' . The Formalists were not in fact concerned with making this distinction in the way that later theorists have been and, I suggest, its benefits in theoretical clarity are outweighed by the practical problems in maintaining such a distinction in film analyses.

28.   Shklovsky saw this 'defamiliarisation' as the purpose of art in order to 'impart the sensation of things as they are perceived and not as they are known. The technique of art is to make objects "unfamiliar", to make forms difficult, to increase the difficulty and length of perception because the process of perception is an aesthetic end in itself and must be prolonged': 'Art as Technique', in *Russian Formalist Criticism*, p. 12. Perception here is, I think, the process of coming to know rather than an issue of a knowledge known. This is not necessarily an evacuation of content in favour of form, 'aesthetic' becoming a degraded formalism. Rather, the aesthetic is also the way in which one is moved by a work, actively engaged, to see, or to see anew. See also 'Literature Without Plot', in *Theory of Prose*.

Shlovsky's claim here is not dissimilar to André Bazin's view that 'The aesthetic qualities of photography are to be sought in its power to lay bare the realities. It is not for me to separate off, in the complex fabric of the objective world, here a reflection on a damp sidewalk, there the gesture of a child. Only the impassive lens, stripping its object of all those ways of seeing it, those piled-up preconceptions, that spiritual dust and grime with which my eyes have covered it, is able to present it in all its virginal purity to my attention and consequently to my love': 'The Ontology of the Photographic Image' (1945), *What is Cinema?*, vol. 1, trans. Hugh Gray (Berkeley: University of California Press, 1967), p. 15. For Shklovsky, those 'piled-up preconceptions' are, in literature, the result of the plot motivations, of the manoeuvres whereby the narration has organised the reader's sense-construction within the text.

29.   Boris Eichenbaum argued that 'Plot construction became the natural subject of Formalist study, since plot constitutes the specific peculiarity of narrative art': 'The Theory of the "Formal Method"', in *Russian Formalist Criticism*, p. 112. 'Plot construction' here involves not simply the code of narrative, but all the devices of representation – in cinema, the devices of cinematography, mise en scène, etc. It is how we come to learn of the story, narration as a whole.

30.   Roland Barthes, *Image-Music-Text*, p. 87. The 'purloined letter' is a reference to Edgar Allan Poe's story of that name.

31.   A form of contract described very well by Gilles Deleuze in his discussion of Sacher-Masoch's *Venus in Furs*, in *Masochism: Coldness and Cruelty* (1967), trans. Jean McNeil (New York: Zone Books, 1989).

32. The issues raised by the terms active and passive are discussed in Chapter 5.

33. The 'whodunnit' has been the subject of many definitions. Charles Derry summarises the genre as 'works which may or may not include a classical detective, but whose narrative is organised around the movement towards a final revelation which rationally attributes criminal culpability to at least one among a group of more or less equally treated characters': 'Towards a Categorisation of Film Narrative', *Film Reader*, no. 1, 1977, p. 111; see also his book *The Suspense Thriller* (Jefferson: McFarland Inc, 1988). The detective narrative must play fair with its readers, or audience, and allow them to make a calculated guess as to the solution. Introducing the murderer on the last page is not 'fair', so the 'clues' must be present but disguised in a number of ways.

34. The problem of a too-obvious exclusion from the place of knowledge of the detective is often resolved by the device of the detective's sidekick, such as Dr Watson in the *Sherlock Holmes* stories, from whose position of relative lack of knowledge the story is narrated.

35. Roland Barthes, *S/Z* (1970), trans. Richard Miller (London: Jonathan Cape, 1974), p. 79.

36. Roland Barthes, 'Introduction to the Structural Analysis of Narratives' (1966), *Image-Music-Text*, pp. 117–18. These two times are the *fabula*'s time and the *syuzhet*'s time.

37. Todorov, 'The Typology of Detective Fiction', in *The Poetics of Prose* (1971), trans. Richard Howard (Oxford: Basil Blackwell, 1977), p. 47. Todorov suggests that the suspense-thriller is a sub-genre within detective fiction arising just before and after the Second World War, but it is a much older form than Todorov allows: not only is it a device of nineteenth-century melodrama, but Conan Doyle's eponymous detective, Sherlock Holmes, succumbs in later stories to the suspense form, as he engages in struggle with his arch-enemy, Moriarty, to his cost.

38. Barthes, *Image-Music-Text*, p. 119.

39. Barthes, *S/Z*, p. 76.

40. Alfred Hitchcock interviewed by François Truffaut, *Hitchcock* (New York: Simon & Schuster, 1967), p. 80.

41. Hitchcock, ibid, pp. 78–9.

42. This was the statement on the promotional material and posters made available to newspapers and exhibitors by the film's distributor.

43. Thornhill's place as one of knowledge is explicitly undermined at the beginning of the film, to be 'refound' at the end. For a discussion of this Oedipal journey, see Raymond Bellour's analysis of *North by Northwest*, 'Le blocage symbolique', *Communications*, no. 23, 1975.

44. They window-shop in a quaint old fishing town, and play on the beach!

45. The point-of-view [pov] shot is elaborated by Edward Branigan as 'a shot in which the camera assumes the position of a subject in order to show us what the subject sees. More precisely, the pov shot is

composed of five elements usually distributed in *two* shots.' This is organised as shot A, one, the establishment of a point in space; two, the establishment of an off-camera object by a glance from that point. There is then, three, a transition between shots A and B which will involve temporal continuity. Shot B is then the reverse view of A, in which element four is the location of the camera at the point of or very close to the point in space defined by element one above; five, the object of element two, the source of glance, is revealed. Edward Branigan, 'Formal Permutations of the Point-of-view Shot', *Screen*, vol. 16, no. 3, 1975, p. 55; see also his *Point of View in the Cinema: A Theory of Narration and Subjectivity in Classical Film* (The Hague: Mouton, 1984). My arguments here also draw upon Stephen Heath's discussion in 'Narrative Space', *Questions of Cinema* (London: Macmillan, 1981), which shows the role of point-of-view shots in relation to the construction of narrative space.

46.   *Hitchcock*, p. 78.
47.   This form of identification is explored further in Chapter 3.
48.   This sequence of looks thus exemplifies the process of suture described by Jean-Pierre Oudart, 'Cinema and Suture', *Screen*, vol. 18, no. 4, 1977/8, whereby the spectator becomes displaced from the narration in her or his look, prompting the question of from where do I look. The answer, here at least, is from the place of threat to Susan! Jacqueline Rose, discussing the role of the point-of-view shot in *The Birds* (Hitchcock, 1963), identifies this cinematic code with a production of paranoia in that this process 'mimes the dialectic of the imaginary relation, while demonstrating: that this relation is reversible (it is this which Lacan defines as the paranoiac alienation of the ego); that the subversion of the imaginary polarisation is not only a function of the fact that the subject is looked at from the point of its own projection, but that the look can in itself be externalised': 'Paranoia and the Film System'(1976), in *Feminism and Film Theory*, ed. Constance Penley, p. 147.
      Rose locates in the shot-reverse-shot structure the aggressivity of the imaginary dialectic since its presentation of two 'looks' mimes that within the imaginary dialectic and it also reveals its potential reversal in as much as the camera must alternate between the positions of each look, and further it thus exposes the presence of a third look (undermining the imaginary dialectic) of the camera in neither position which 'cancels the observer's centrality and subjects the observer and the observed to a gaze whose signified is attack': ibid, p. 147. She indicates that her use of paranoia is in terms of the aggressivity of the imaginary dialectic and that 'it is clear that, taken in this sense, the structure of paranoia is not sexually differentiated but refers to the reversibility of an ego-structure which is restricted to two terms': ibid, p. 155. The role and concept of suture is considered again in Chapter 3.
49.   Rose, ibid, p. 145.
50.   It might be argued that the position of the protagonist in suspense is nevertheless 'feminine' regardless of her or his actual gender or sex,

and such a view would also echo Freud's view that paranoia is characterised by a passive homosexual current, and hence produces a
'feminine' position in both man and woman (discussed by Freud in
his consideration of the case of Judge Schreber in 'Psycho-Analytic
Notes on an Autobiographical Account of a Case of Paranoia
(Dementia Paranoides)' (1911), *SE*, vol. XII). However, 'feminine'
here is no more than the 'passive position', the reversal of the drive,
and hence is redundant and tautological. This issue is considered
again in Chapter 5 and Chapter 6.

51. In *Vertigo* (Hitchcock, 1958) it is the fear of heights which makes
Scottie 'weak', but this is not only a device for suspense – will Scottie
reach the top of the tower to save Madeleine? – but also part of the
plot contrivance, for Elster is certain Scottie will not be able to climb
the stairs and see him toss his wife's body off the tower, while at the
same time it is an element in the narrative enigma about Scottie as a
character and a subject who desires, that is, about the source and
cause of his symptom, his vertigo.

52. *The Hollywood Reporter*, vol. 250, no. 3, 25 November 1978, p. 3 and
p. 24, welcomed the film saying 'If nothing else, MGM's *Coma*
reminds us just how long is has been since we saw a good mystery
thriller on the big screen', making no special mention of the gender
of the detective. Certainly if *Coma* succeeds for the most part as an
exciting and thrilling film it is not least because it successfully mixes
suspense and action. The film is based on the novel by Robin Cook,
himself a doctor, who wote it after studying dozens of stories to establish the elements necessary for best-selling popular novels, a route
director Michael Crichton took, too, his subsequent novels including
Jurassic Park, which he co-scripted with director Steven Spielberg for
the film version, released in 1993.

53. The *News of the World* review, 12 November 1978, seems to work in a
this way, given the considerable inaccuracy of its summary: 'A grue-
some little thriller set in a hospital where patients arrive with minor
illnesses and leave in coffins. Michael Douglas plays a doctor who
wants to know what's going on. So, too, does his mistress, Genevieve
Bujold. Both have some hair-raising moments with Richard
Widmark lurking sinisterly in the background. A super shocker.'

54. Laura Mulvey, 'Visual Pleasure and Narrative Cinema' (1975), in
Visual and Other Pleasures (London: Macmillan, 1989).

3   Identifying in the Cinema

1. Sigmund Freud, *Group Psychology and the Analysis of the Ego* (1921),
SE, vol. XVIII, p. 110, note 2.

2. Paul Ricoeur , *Time and Narrative*, 3 vols, trans. Kathleen McLaughlin
and David Pellauer (Chicago: University of Chicago Press, 1984–8),
vol. 3, p. 184.

3. Melanie Klein discusses introjective and projective identification in
'Notes on Some Schizoid Mechanisms' (1946/1952), in *The Selected*

Melanie Klein, ed. Juliet Mitchell (Harmondsworth: Penguin Books, 1986).

4. Freud, 'The Splitting of the Ego in Defence' (1940 [1938]), *SE*, vol. XXIII. Juliet Mitchell makes this point in her introduction to Klein's essay 'Notes on Some Schizoid Mechanisms', ibid, p. 175.

5. This has been suggested by Jean Laplanche, *Life and Death in Psychoanalysis* (1970), trans. Jeffrey Mehlman (Baltimore: The Johns Hopkins University Press, 1976), p. 80.

6. Jean Laplanche and J-B. Pontalis, *The Language of Psycho-Analysis* (1967), trans. Donald Nicholson-Smith (London: Hogarth Press, 1973), p. 205.

7. Metz, *Psychoanalysis and Cinema: The Imaginary Signifier*.

8. Freud, *The Interpretation of Dreams*, (1900), *SE*, vol. IV, p. 149. Parveen Adams has shown that there are two concepts of hysteria in Freud, one involving conversion symptoms, such as the paralysed arm of Elisabeth von R, and the other, hysterical identification, in which conversion symptoms play no part. It is the latter, she argues – following Lacan – which properly characterises hysteria. The hysteric may also display bodily symptoms (although conversion symptoms have become uncommon in diagnoses), but these alone do not characterise hysteria: 'Symptoms and Hysteria', *Oxford Literary Review*, vol. 8, 1986, p. 182. Moreover Adams shows that when Freud connects hysteria to femininity it is in relation to hysterical identification not to conversion symptoms and which, as she notes 'in Lacan's hands makes of hysteria the problem of sexual difference for the woman', that is, the problem of the hysteric's question 'Am I a man or a woman?' and the problem of the relation of desire between men and women. This unhooking of hysteria from the conversion symptom is important in understanding the part hysterical identification may play for the subject, as I shall try to show later in this chapter.

9. Freud, *The Interpretation of Dreams*, p. 150.

10. Laplanche and Pontalis, *The Language of Psycho-Analysis*, p. 206.

11. Freud saw identification in hysteria as typically used to express a common *sexual* element, for example *The Interpretation of Dreams*, p. 150, but in *Group Psychology* he develops this notion of identification in cases where there is no sexual cathexis, pp. 107–8.

12. The process of identification here is similar to that described by Freud in relation to the dream-work, where the function of identification is to circumvent censorship by using another figure as a stand-in for the ego: 'Thus my ego may be represented in a dream several times over, now directly and now through identification with extraneous persons': *The Interpretation of Dreams*, p. 323. Such stand-in figures are linked by common elements which embed a wish, so that the identification supports the figuring of a wish. It is not the identification which secures the wish, but a wish which prompts the identification.

13. Freud, *The Interpretation of Dreams*, p. 150.

14. Jaques Lacan, *The Four Fundamental Concepts of Psycho-Analysis* (1973), trans. Alan Sheridan (Harmondsworth, Penguin Books, 1977), p. 100.

15. Mikkel Borch-Jacobsen's careful reading and critique of Freud on identification has been important in pointing to many of the problems and inconsistencies in Freud's position, which undoubtedly are considerable. His countering emphasis on identification as essentially mimetic is not followed here, however. Through the answering concept of mimesis, which Freud had rejected, Borch-Jacobsen poses desire as mimetic and mimesis as desire, as a result desire, object choice and identification often seem interchangeable: *The Freudian Subject* (1982), trans. Catherine Porter (Stanford: University Press, 1988).

16. Freud, 'On Narcissism: An Introduction' (1914), in *SE*, vol. XIV, p. 74.

17. Ibid , pp. 76–7.

18. In the original German the term Freud used was *Trieb* or drive, but this has been translated in English in the *Standard Edition* of Freud's work as 'instinct'. Freud does use the German word *Instinkt* but only when directly referring to automatic responses matched to a physiological stimulus. *Trieb* or drive, however, is distinguished by being a pressure differentiated only by quantity and not by any particular quality or object. I shall follow the now established practice of using the term drive rather than instinct, although instinct will be retained where it appears in quotations of Freud's work from the *Standard Edition*.

19. Laplanche points out that Freud also uses the notion of primary narcissism in a rather different way, to refer to the primary state of the human organism as a kind of monad, 'a kind of *hypothetical initial state in which the organism would form a closed unit* in relation to its surroundings': *Life and Death in Psychoanalysis*, p. 70. The primary narcissism to which I am referring would therefore be subsequent to this state.

20. Freud, *An Outline of Psycho-Analysis* (1940 [1938]), *SE*, vol. XXIII, p. 150. The concept of a reservoir of libido is problematic, however, and this issue is discussed further in Chapter 5.

21. Freud , 'On Narcissism', p. 90.

22. Ibid, p. 87. Freud had referred to the 'attachment' type of object choice, which he here calls anaclitic, in *Three Essays on Sexuality* (1905), *SE*, vol. VII, pp. 222–3 and note 1, p. 222. The role of anaclisis in the emergence of the sexual drive in relation to the self-preservation drive is discussed in detail in the chapter on the drive.

23. Freud, 'On Narcissism' , pp. 88–9.

24. This issue is taken up again in Chapter 6.

25. Laplanche, *Life and Death in Psychoanalysis*, p. 75.

26. Freud, 'On Narcissism', p. 88.

27. Laplanche, *Life and Death in Psychoanalysis*, p. 78. Borch-Jacobsen has developed the same point in his discussion in *The Freudian Subject*, p. 108.

28. Freud, 'On Narcissism', p. 93.

29. Ibid, p. 94.

30. Freud, 'Mourning and Melancholia' (1917[1915]), *SE*, vol. XIV, p. 246.

31. The reversal of libido in regressive identification suggests the process of the turning around of the drive on oneself which Freud describes

as one of the vicissitudes of the drive and which also involves a move from active to passive. This too may be said to involve an identification, while regressive identification itself implies that the ego, or a part of the ego, becomes the internalised love-object now set up within the subject. The vicissitudes of the drive are discussed in Chapter 5.

32. Freud writes 'we perceive that the self-reproaches are reproaches against a loved object which have been shifted away from it on to the patient's own ego. The woman who loudly pities her husband for being tied to such an incapable wife as herself is really accusing her *husband* of being incapable, in whatever sense she may mean this': 'Mourning and Melancholia', p. 248.

33. Ibid, p. 249.

34. Ibid, p. 249.

35. This is not fully elaborated in Freud's own writings, for Freud always retained a more biologistic model for the emergence of the ego. The view that primary narcissism is identical to the primary forms of narcissistic identification is put forward by Laplanche, *Life and Death in Psychoanalysis*, p. 79.

36. Freud, 'Mourning and Melancholia', p. 250.

37. Freud, *Group Psychology*, p. 107.

38. Ibid, p. 105.

39. Freud, *The Ego and the Id* (1923) , *SE*, vol. XIX, p. 3, and note l, p. 31.

40. Freud, *Group Psychology*, p. 106.

41. Ibid, p. 106.

42. Freud describes the difference between narcissistic or regressive identification and hysterical identification as follows: 'whereas in the former the object-cathexis is abandoned, in the latter it persists and manifests its influence, though this is usually confined to certain isolated actions and innervations. In any case, in the transference neuroses, too, identification is the expression of there being something in common, which may signify love. Narcissistic identification is the older of the two and it paves the way to an understanding of hysterical identification, which has been less thoroughly studied': 'Mourning and Melancholia', p. 250.

43. Freud, *Group Psychology,* p. l06. It may be asked whether in identifying with her mother's cough she is also identifying with her mother as feminine; this does not necessarily seem to be the case, for what is at stake is her mother's position *vis-à-vis* her father, and not her mother's femininity as such, though this may be adopted, just as the cough, in order to come into the mother's position in relation to the father. Whether this secures a feminine identity is not certain. Parveen Adams has argued that what characterises the production of masculinity and femininity in the Oedipal complex is hysterical identification, and that this always involves an oscillation between the reversible positions of desiring, and desiring to be, either the father or the mother: 'Per Os(scillation)', in *Psychoanalysis and Cultural Theory*, ed. James Donald (London: Macmillan, 1989), p. 86. All this may change, of course, with the intervention of castration.

44. Freud, *Group Psychology*, p. 107. Freud discusses his analysis of Dora in 'Fragment of a Case of Hysteria' (1905), *SE*, vol. VII.

45. In both examples Freud's analysis could be inverted, and the mother seen as the love object, so that the first involves an identification with the mother as love object, and the second an identification with the father in terms of his position in relation to the mother. Freud's assumption of the heterosexual object choice in his discussion of Dora's case has been criticised by a number of authors in the collection *In Dora's Case*, eds Charles Bernheimer and Claire Kahane (London: Virago, 1985) and especially in Jacqueline Rose's 'Dora, Fragment of an Analysis' (1978) in that collection. Drawing on Freud's own observations in his postscript to the case, it can be argued that Dora's cough is an hysterical identification in as much as she wishes to take her father's place in relation to Frau K – or indeed, in relation to her mother, that absent figure of the analysis. Freud emphasises the bisexual character of hysterical fantasies *and* their identifications in 'Hysterical Phantasies and their Relation to Bisexuality' (1908), *SE*, vol. IX. Bisexuality is considered further in Chapter 5.

46. Freud, *Group Psychology*, pp. 108–9.

47. Ibid, p. 107.

48. Hysterical identification ceases to be discussed by Freud, its last mention – as recorded in the index of the *Standard Edition* – is in volume XVI, and this refers to the discussion in 'Mourning and Melancholia'.

49. Freud, *Group Psychology*, p. 107, my emphasis.

50. Ibid, p. 107.

51. If this is the case Freud's example here can be aligned with his discussion of the fantasy scenario in '"A Child is Being Beaten" : A Contribution to the Study of the Origin of Sexual Perversions' (1919), *SE*, vol. XVII, in which 'beating' represents the forbidden and repressed wish for the father. This is considered further in Chapter 4.

52. Freud, *Group Psychology*, p. 108.

53. Borch-Jacobsen has also noted this relationship, though he draws a different conclusion. Associating it with suggestion and hypnotic suggestibility, he argues that Freud now returns to his starting point in his study of group psychology, to the theories of Le Bon etc., from whom he had sought to differentiate himself: 'That "identification" is never anything but another name for "suggestion" is confirmed once again in Chapter 11: the members of the group are "carried away.... by 'suggestion', that is to say, by means of identification".' *The Freudian Subject*, p. 234, note 70, the quotation is from Freud, *Group Psychology*, p. 130. Borch-Jacobsen concludes, 'Group psychology, in the form of hypnosis, invades everything, up to and including the relation of the ego to its ideal', p. 234. But Freud has posited *two* moments here, for the identification through 'suggestion' is with the other members of the group, not the leader. Freud's use of the term suggestion here is ambiguous, but he is quite categorical later: 'It is obvious that a soldier takes his superior, that is, in fact, the leader of

the army, as his ideal, while he identifies himself with his equals...':
Group Psychology, p. 134.

Hypnosis, and suggestion, for Freud are connected to the new role
of the ego-ideal which he is now concerned with. Freud sees hypnosis as resembling being in love, but where instead of the object of
love being put in the place of the ego it is put in the place of the ego-
ideal. It is here that its connection to transference arises. However in
transference the analyst is put in the place of a figure in the patient's
past, a figure of ambivalence, of love and hate. The patient acts out
her relations to the historic figure in relation to the analyst. Freud, of
course, saw hypnosis as more primitive, in which the erotic tie is
pre-eminent.

54. Freud, *Group Psychology*, p. 127.
55. Freud, *Totem and Taboo* (1912–13), *SE*, vol. XIII.
56. Freud, *Civilization and its Discontents* (1930[1929]), *SE*, vol. XXI,
    p. 132.
57. Freud, *Group Psychology*, p. 108.
58. Laplanche, *Life and Death in Psychoanalysis*, p. 81.
59. Freud, *The Ego and the Id*, p. 26. This is commented upon in a footnote
    in the first English translation and which is described as having been
    authorised by Freud: 'The ego is ultimately derived from bodily sen-
    sations, chiefly those springing from the surface of the body. It may
    thus be regarded as a mental projection of the surface of the body,
    besides, as we have seen above, representing the superficies of the
    mental apparatus', note 1, p. 26.
60. Lacan, *Écrits, A Selection*, p. 2.
61. Laplanche, *Life and Death in Psychoanalysis*, p. 81.
62. Lacan confirms the role of a certain disavowal in the misrecognition
    of the mirror phase and its identifications when he notes that
    'Misrecognition represents a certain organisation of affirmations and
    negations, to which the subject is attached': *The Seminar of Jacques
    Lacan – Book 1, Freud's Papers on Technique 1953–1954*, trans. John
    Forrester (Cambridge: University Press, 1988), p. 167.
63. This is made clear by Lacan, cit Jacqueline Rose, 'The Imaginary'
    (1975), in *Sexuality in the Field of Vision* (London: Verso, 1986), p. 186,
    from 'Remarque sur le rapport de Daniel Lagache: "Psychanalyse et
    structure de la personnalité"' (1960), *Écrits* (Paris: Éditions du Seuil,
    1966), p. 678.
64. Jacqueline Rose notes that 'As a result of identifying itself with a dis-
    crete image, the child will be able to postulate a series of equivalen-
    cies between the objects of the surrounding world, based on the
    conviction that each has a recognisable permanence': 'The
    Imaginary', p. 173.
65. Freud, 'Project for A Scientific Psychology '(1950a[1887–1902]), *SE*,
    vol. I.
66. Freud, *The Ego and the Id*, p. 48.
67. Lacan, *Écrits, A Selection*, p. 19.
68. Lacan, *The Seminar of Jacques Lacan – Book I*, p. 141.
69. Lacan, *Écrits, A Selection*, p. 22.

70. Lacan, *The Seminar of Jacques Lacan – Book I*, p. 170.
71. Ibid, p. 171.
72. It is here that the later concept of the *objet petit a* is placed. It, too, is something from which the subject has separated itself, a little other object, but it represents not a lost object, but the lostness of the object. Rose quotes from Jacques-Alain Miller's commentary in *Écrits*, 'the real image, henceforth designated as i(a), represents the specular image of the subject, whilst the real object *a* supports the function of the partial object, precipitating the formation of the body. We have here a phase prior to the mirror stage (according to an order of logical dependency) – a phase which presupposes the presence of the real Other': 'The Imaginary', pp 179-180, note 29.
73. Catherine Millot notes 'The superego and the ego ideal are both formations belonging to the symbolic register': 'The Feminine Superego'(1984), in *The Woman in Question*, p. 296.
74. Freud, *On Narcissism*, p. 94.
75. Millot, 'The Feminine Superego', p. 297.
76. Slavoj Žižek, *The Sublime Object of Ideology* (London: Verso, 1989), p. l06.
77. Freud referred to the 'double tie' of 'identification, and 'putting the object in the place of the ego-ideal': 'A Grade in the Ego', *Group Psychology*, p. 130.
78. Žižek, *The Sublime Object of Ideology*, p. ll0.
79. Louis Althusser, 'Ideology and Ideological State Apparatuses' (1969), in *Lenin and Philosophy and Other Essays*, trans. Ben Brewster (London: New Left Books, 1971), p. 160. The problems in attempting to map Lacan's real, imaginary and symbolic on to social forms and forces is taken up again in Chapter 8.
80. Freud, *On Narcissism*, p. 95.
81. Lacan, *The Four Fundamental Concepts of Psycho-Analysis*, p. 268.
82. Freud, *The Ego and the Id*, p. 34.
83. Millot, 'The Feminine Superego', p. 297.
84. Ibid, pp. 296–7.
85. Ibid, p. 297.
86. This is only one aspect of the Oedipus complex and castration, which involves not just the prohibition of the child's desire for the mother as the lack *of* the mother but also the confronting of the lack *in* the mother, the 'castration' of the mother which the small boy then fears for himself and the girl accepts or denies in herself. Thus the child will turn away from the mother to the father (*père-version* is Lacan's term for this) as the place of the other to which its demand is addressed. But the same relation of lack will be encountered in the father as in the mother, namely that the parent's desire lies elsewhere, and hence the father too is 'insufficient'. This is explored further in Chapter 6.
87. Millot, 'The Feminine Superego', p. 298.
88. Freud, *The Ego and the Id*, p. 54.
89. Lacan, *Écrits, A Selection*, p. 312.
90. Žižek, *The Sublime Object of Ideology*, p. 111.

91. Ibid, p. 113.
92. Metz, *Psychoanalysis and Cinema*, p. 45.
93. Constance Penley has addressed the problems of such 'visual apparatus' theories which draw on psychoanalytic theories of the gaze and voyeurism for the place of the woman's look: 'Feminism, Film Theory and the Bachelor Machines', in *The Future of an Illusion* (Minneapolis: Unversity of Minnesota Press, 1989). I have drawn upon her account here.
94. Metz, *Psychoanalysis and Cinema*, p. 49.
95. Ibid, p. 47.
96. Ibid, p. 46.
97. Ibid, p. 49.
98. Ibid, p. 49. Metz's thesis here parallels the work of Jean-Louis Baudry who argues 'Ultimately the forms of narrative adopted, the "contents" of the image are of little importance so long as an identification remains possible. What emerges here (in outline) is the specific function fulfilled by the cinema as support and instrument of ideology…. It is an apparatus destined to obtain a precise ideological effect, necessary to the dominant ideology: creating a phantasmatisation of the subject, it collaborates with a marked efficacy in the maintenance of idealism': 'Ideological Effects of the Basic Cinematographic Apparatus', trans. Alan Williams, in *Narrative, Apparatus, Ideology*, ed. Philip Rosen (New York: Columbia University Press, 1986), p. 295.
    Joan Copjec's discussion in 'The Orthopsychic Subject' critiques the epistemological foundations of this approach: *October*, no. 49, Summer 1989.
99. Metz, ibid, p. 49.
100. Jacqueline Rose, in 'The Imaginary', has shown that the structure of specularity in Lacan's account undermines the imaginary, for the relation of the subject who looks (at an object of desire) is not simply a relation of distance but also of externalisation and as a result the 'observing subject can become object of the look and hence elided as subject of its own representation', p. 96. My discussion here draws upon Rose's critique of Metz's account of a primary identification in cinema.
101. Sub-codes are part of the general cinematic code: for example lighting is a cinematic code whereas the kind of lighting which characterises American *film noir* movies of the 1940s is a sub-code; but the lighting system of any particular film is also a sub-code. The first is a cinematic sub-code because it occurs in more than one film, the second is a filmic code, that is, a sub-code specific to one film. The sub-code signifies insofar as it is part of the general code.
102. Geoffrey Nowell-Smith has also questioned the relation of primary and secondary identication in Metz's schema: 'To say something is primary is simply to locate it further back in the psychic apparatus. It does not, or should not, invite any conclusions about its efficacy. I would argue, therefore, that the so-called secondary identifications do tend to break down the pure specularity of the screen/spectator

relation in itself and to displace it onto relations which are more properly intra-textual – ie relations to the spectator posited from within the image and in the movement from shot to shot': 'A Note on History/Discourse', *Edinburgh '76 Magazine*, Edinburgh Film Festival, 1976, p. 31.

103. *Terminator 2, Judgement Day* (James Cameron, 1991), in presenting two terminators, sets up Arnold Schwarzenegger's re-programmed Terminator as the good ideal in opposition to the new model which is irredeemably programmed as a Terminator. This second Terminator literalises the mimetic desire – he physically takes over the appearance of his victims, visualised in the film through 'morphing', a computer-animation technique.

104. Constance Penley has pointed to the primal fantasy at the centre of this film, that is, the child's fantasy of being present at the scene of its parent's carnal relation, including the scene of its own conception; this is conjoined to the 'family romance' fantasy, for John Connor 'chooses' his father in sending Kyle back in time: 'Time Travel, Primal Scene, and the Critical Dystopia', in *The Future of An Illusion*.

105. Rose, 'The Imaginary', p. 58.

106. Roland Barthes, *Camera Lucida: Reflections on Photography* (1980), trans. Richard Howard (New York: Hill & Wang, 1981), p. 4.

107. Hence the emphasis on pov shots as a structure involving at least two shots, a character seen looking and, secondly, what they are looking at – as inferred by the juxtaposition of shots.

108. Janet Bergstrom, 'Alternation, Segmentation, Hypnosis: Interview with Raymond Bellour – An Excerpt', in *Feminism and Film Theory*, pp. 190–1. This, Bellour argues, involves a movement from the lawless adventurer to the husband and father which is achieved through 'the woman as the very image of castration, and the heroine who reverses the image, through whom the masculine subject will find, in constrast, the positivity of a regulated sexuality and a measured idealization, the woman who permits the fixation of his desire – in a word its symbolization – through the conjunction of his entry into the social order and the internalised, finally bearable image of his own castration', pp. 189–92.

109. This is therefore distinct from transference, where the subject identifies two other objects or people, one in the present – the analyst – and the other in her or his own past. The subject then relates to the present figure in the terms of her or his relation to the historic figure.

110. Discussed in 'John Ford's *Young Mr Lincoln* – a collective text by the editors of *Cahiers du Cinéma*' (1970), *Screen*, vol. 13, no. 3, 1972.

111. Roland Barthes, *A Lover's Discourse* (1977), trans. Richard Howard (New York: Hill & Wang, 1978), pp. 129–30.

112. Hugo Münsterberg, *The Film, A Psychological Study* (1916) (New York: Dover, 1970), p. 53.

113. Richard Wollheim, 'Imagination and Identification', in *On Art and the Mind* (London: Allen Lane, 1973), p. 67. Wollheim is concerned here to distinguish the role of imagination or imagining in identification, and posits two forms of imagination – central, where one imagines

the object, experience or process itself, that is, one sees it in one's mind's eye, or and by extension, one imagines oneself or someone else doing something. Wollheim further suggests that 'it is a mark of the character whom I centrally imagine that in imagining what he does I also imagine what he feels and thinks', p. 59. His second form of imagining arises where one imagines someone doing something but 'where no one is centrally imagined, I shall think of [these] as cases where I imagine that....', p. 59. This 'acentral' imagining is associated with the process of sympathy, while 'central' imagining is placed with empathy and related to the processes of identification described by Freud as regressive identification with the lost love object which Wollheim considers through Freud's account of Leonardo da Vinci. Wolheim also uses his category of central imagining to distinguish between projection and projective identification. As a result he sees as instances of central imagining situations where the individual imagines himself or herself as another without thereby being the person. For this he draws on the notion of a 'master thought' which functions here in a way which is similar to that which I will propose for fantasy in relation to identification in cinema. As a result while fantasy is an 'as if' relation of imagining it is nevertheless a form of central imagining, it is empathy, not sympathy.

114. *Fury*, made for MGM, was Fritz Lang's first American film after leaving Germany. Based on a story by Norman Krasna, the screenplay was co-written by Lang and Bartlett Cormack.

115. Münsterberg, *The Film, A Psychological Study*, pp. 53–4. He also pointed to the spectator's separation from the character which film affords – in contrast to the theatre – by the means of editing so that we see a character and we, but not the character, see what threatens them. Here then, as I argued in relation to *Coma*, we feel for and not as a character but it is not thereby sympathy, rather it is empathy, for we can imagine the terror – or joy – the character would feel if they had the knowledge we have been given.

116. Tomashevsky argues 'The emotions a work of art excites are its chief means of holding attention. It is not enough, for example, to state the phases of the revolutionary movement in the cold tones of a lecture; the listener must sympathise, must be indignant, joyful, disturbed. Only then does the work become *really* "real"; only then are the listener's emotions unprotestingly led in the desired direction': 'Thematics', in *Russian Formalist Criticism*, p. 65. He cites narrative devices such as the virtuous hero and evil villain through which feelings of hostility and sympathy are evoked and developed, but this also assumes a reader or spectator-subject who *wishes* to be moved by the work, and who can enter into the narration's appeal to feel for or against characters.

117. Smith proposes a tripartite structure, commencing with 'recognition', or the construction of characters on the basis of (1) a mimetic hypothesis – that the fictional figure is likely to be similar to 'real' persons, and (2) according to a 'person schema', a basic schema of what we

expect a person to be. It is clear that some process of this kind is involved in cultural interaction, whether in relation to fictional or to 'real' persons, but how we understand the human subject, or 'person' is much more controversial. Moreover the extent to which we 'recognise' a particular fictional character-array within a larger overall person schema may depend on the way in which the narrative text has organised knowledge of the character to enable certain connotative connections, so that the order and conjunction of information is important. Having established the spectator's engagement with a character, Smith distinguishes between empathy, which he sees as increasingly involuntary, and sympathy, within which the processes of alignment and allegiance arise, hence it is primarily a cognitive process and, as he demonstrates, is culturally determined. Murray Smith, *Engaging Characters: Fiction, Emotion and the Cinema* (Oxford: Oxford University Press, 1995).

118. In *Aesthetics of Film* the authors argue, dismissively, that many films 'particularly the most formulaic and stereotypical films (or even contemporary television series) – function largely according to a rather monolithic identification that is regulated by a phenomenon of recognition and by a stereotyped typology of characters: the good, the evil, the protagonist, the traitor, the victim, etc. We may say that in this case the identification with a character proceeds because of an identification of (and with) the character as *type*.... However this sort of typing effectively reactivates, in a tried and true manner that operates on a level that is both worn and deep, affects directly springing from identification with the roles of the Oedipal condition. There is, for instance, identification with the character faced with thwarted desire, admiration for the hero who represents the ego ideal, and fear before the paternal figure, etc.': *Aesthetics of Film* (1983), ed. Jacques Aumont, Alain Bergala, Michel Marie, Marc Vernet, trans Richard Neupert (Austin: University of Texas, 1992), p. 221. There is a conflation here of identification of and identification with; however I have argued that these constitute two distinct psychological processes, moreover the authors reproduce the fallacy that the Oedipal identifications are with *roles*, while their own examples go on to cite a judgemental position – admiration – and a placing in relation *to* the feared father, and not an identification *with* the father!

John Frow presents an overview of the debates on the consideration of character in 'Spectacle Binding – On Character', *Poetics Today*, vol. 7, no. 2, 1986.

119. For example, in D. W. Griffith's *True Heart Susie* (1919) we await William's recognition of Susie's 'true-heart'. In *Letter from an Unknown Woman* (Max Ophuls, 1948) we wish that Stefan recognise the love of Lisa for him.

120. The use of this term here is not, however, straightforward for it involves a move from a primarily Freudian and Lacanian terminology concerning identification to the incorporation of a Kleinian framework with its rather different perspective on object relations and on the Oedipal complex. Lacan himself both drew on and distanced

himself from Klein's concepts here. The fuller story of the role of projection remains to be told, or constructed.

121. Freud refers to transference or displacement of ideas in dreams, and later in *Studies on Hysteria* (1893–1895), *SE*, vol. II, describes – with reference to 'Dora' – the transference of unconscious ideas onto the person of the therapist or physician. With the discovery of the Oedipus complex transference comes to be viewed as involving the prototypes or imagos of the Oedipal figures; see here 'The Dynamics of Transference' (1912), *SE*, vol. XII.

122. Samuel Weber has drawn an analogy between the role of the anlayst as the one supposed to know in transference and Kant's transcendental principle of 'reflective judgement' in relation to aesthetic objects. For, Kant suggests, there are no universal principles on which to draw in order to judge the aesthetic; instead– as Weber puts it – 'In order to judge, the subject considers the particular thing that confronts it *as though* it were the product of an "understanding" like our own, and yet sufficiently different from ours to comprehend what we cannot. Faced with the singular unknown, what the subject does is to suppose a subject that knows, that comprehends what we do not, because it has produced it according to its knowledge': *Return to Freud – Jacques Lacan's Dislocation of Psychoanalysis* (1978, revised 1990), trans. Michael Levine (Cambridge: Cambridge University Press, 1991), p. 181. Metz's identification with the camera as omniscient is therefore transference in Weber's sense.

123. Emile Benveniste introduced the distinction between *énoncé*, the utterance itself, and *énonciation*, the act of uttering in order to distinguish between the subject who utters, and the subject who is 'uttered'. As a result he also distinguishes two modes of writing – *histoire* where the marks of enunciation, of a source of the speech – such as the pronoun 'I' – are absent; and *discours*, which is characterised as enunciation marked by the source or subject of the speech or stating: 'Correlations of Tense in French Verbs', in *Problems in General Linguistics*, trans. Mary Elizabeth Meek (Coral Gables: University of Miami Press, 1971), p. 206.

For example, in 'John said "I am going out"', John states his action, but John is also 'spoken' by the statement 'John said', producing a split between the subject spoken of – John, and a subject – unnamed – who tells us what John said. This splitting is, for Lacan, a splitting of subjectivity, illustrated whenever we speak about ourselves, and most notoriously in the grammatically possible statement 'I am lying' but which then raises the question: is the I who speaks lying or telling the truth in this statement? Benveniste's distinction is based on grammatical markers within written texts; however, film presents a visual scene in the present tense, with figures who speak – hence *discours* – but it does not mark the place or function of an 'enunciator', namely, that function of organisation of the scene for the camera etc., the 'directing', hence film is, in the main, 'historically' narrated.

124. Suture, he argues, acts like the number zero. Both are paradoxical, for zero, while founding the series of numbers is not a number. It is a

concept which states 'non-number' in distintion to 'one'. Zero does not exist in reality, but nor by extension, then, do the numbers one, two, etc., for the concept of numbers is contingent on the category not-one which founds the chain, making it possible as a series in which each element is fixed in relation to its predecessor and successor. Each number is characterised by being identical to itself, but zero is non-identical with itself since no thing can be nothing. However, in as much as it is a concept, it is something, the one of absence, and radically other to the chain of numbers it inaugurates: Jacques-Alain Miller, 'Suture (elements of the logic of the signfier)' (1966), *Screen*, vol. 18, no. 4, Winter 1977/8.

125. Miller, ibid, p. 34.
126. Serge Leclaire, cit Stephen Heath, 'Notes on Suture', *Screen*, vol. 18 no. 4, p. 55, from 'L'Analyste à sa place?', *Cahiers pour l'analyse*, no. 1, 1966.
127. Daniel Dayan, 'The Tutor-Code of Classical Cinema', *Film Quarterly*, vol. 28, no. 1, Fall 1974, p. 22. The 180-degree rule was a recognised norm within classical Hollywood cinema and a central convention of scene dissection or anlytical editing, itself a Hollywood norm of good film-making. It requires that, when cutting within a scene from one character to another character or an object, a line is posited between the characters – typically motivated as a character's glance , whether at another character or at an object – which the camera should not cross; instead the camera is moved only within the 180 degrees on one side of the line or eyeline. The rule is intended to ensure in the spectator a sense of continuity of space between shots, which can be disrupted if in a reverse-shot the camera crosses the implied eyeline, opening up previously unknown space behind a character. This emphasis on continuity and with it the avoidance of foregrounding the role of the camera or of editing has – wrongly – been made homologous to the 'seamless stitching' of the suturing of the subject.
128. Indeed the always-provisional and precarious closure opens the spectator-subject to the paranoia latent in the reverse-shot structure. This has been explored in the discussion of *Coma* in the scene of Susan's car breakdown. Here, where we should be 'sutured' by finally finding our place of look, we find ourselves as the villain, the very place of an aggressivity towards Susan.
129. Oudart, 'Cinema and Suture', p. 46. Stephen Heath describes this as producing a multiplication of the spectator-subject in the heterogeneity of the process of the film while at the same time involving a projection by the film of a unified subject-position, a narrative image, which secures the spectator. 'On Suture' (1977), in *Questions of Cinema*, p. 109.
130. Aumont *et al.*, *Aesthetics of Film*, p. 217.
131. Brooks, in his study *Reading for the Plot*, keeps in play a supple and complex sense of the desire for narrative: 'Desire as narrative thematic, desire as narrative motor, and desire as the very intention of narrative language and the act of telling all seem to stand in close interrelation', p. 54. He traces and excavates this desire across the texts

he considers. I have been concerned to clarify out the aspects to this desire in order to to ask questions of sexual difference.

132. Aumont *et al.*, *Aesthetics of Film*, p. 217.
133. Paul Ricoeur, 'History as Narrative and Practice', *Philosophy Today*, Fall 1985, p. 214. Anthony Paul Kerby develops this view in his analysis of the relation of language and persons: *Narrative and the Self* (Indiana: Indiana University Press, 1991). Peter Brooks similarly argues 'Our lives are ceaselessly intertwined with narrative, with the stories that we tell and hear told, those we dream or imagine or would like to tell, all of which are reworked in that story of our own lives that we narrate to ourselves in an episodic, sometimes semiconscious, but virtually uninterrupted monologue': *Reading for the Plot*, p. 3.
134. Roland Barthes, *The Pleasure of the Text* (1973), trans. Richard Miller, (New York: Hill & Wang, 1975), p. 47.
135. Barthes, *A Lover's Discourse* , p. 130.
136. Freud, *The Interpretation of Dreams*, p. 148.
137. Ibid, pp. 150–1.
138. Ibid, p. 148.
139. Ibid, p. 147.
140. Ibid, p. 149.
141. Lacan noted that the woman's has also identified with her husband, for having identified with her friend who was too thin she cannot satisfy her husband's desire for plump women – thus she gives her husband an unfulfilled desire as well, and hence she also identifies with him and this as the place that can satisfy for 'To be the phallus, if only a somewhat thin one. Was not that the ultimate identification with the signifier of desire': *Écrits, A Selection*, p. 262.
142. In hysterical neurosis the subject's identifications remain organised as 'hysterical', an identification with the other's place as the place of the Other's desire, while desire, too, is found in the place of the Other, who is thus also identified with. Apparently triangular, this structure is in fact dyadic, and it supposes a full enjoyment in the place of the Other.
143. Freud, *Group Psychology*, p. 107.
144. Freud, ibid, p. 108.

4 Fantasia

1. Hortense Powdermaker, *Hollywood the Dream Factory*: *An Anthropologist Looks at the Movie-makers* (London: Secker & Warburg, 1951).
2. *Heresies*, vol. 3, no. 4, 1981. The debate initiated by the writers in *Heresies* has continued to be a contentious issue for lesbians and feminists. Lesbian erotic literature subsequently began to appear, and in 1988 *A Restricted Country*, by the American lesbian writer Joan Nestle, was published by Sheba Feminist Publishers in Britain, followed by *Serious Pleasure* and *More Serious Pleasure*, also published

by Sheba. Sara Dunn has discussed the nature of this writing, and its desires, in 'Voyages of the Valkyries: Recent Lesbian Pornographic Writing', *Feminist Review*, no. 34, 1990. I have more directly considered the issue in 'Pornography and Fantasy: Psychoanalytic Perspectives', in *Sex Exposed*, eds Lynne Segal and Mary McIntosh (London: Virago, 1992).

3. Helle Thorning, 'The Mother–Daughter Relationship and Sexual Ambivalence', *Heresies*, vol. 3, no. 4, 1981, p. 3.

4. Pat Califia, 'Feminism and Sado-Masochism', *Heresies*, vol. 3, no. 4, 1981, p. 30.

5. Ibid, p. 32.

6. Ibid, p. 30.

7. Ibid, p. 31.

8. Lynne Segal addressed similar ground from a heterosexual feminist perspective while also arguing for a more positive view of fantasy: 'Perhaps we could touch upon, rather than ignore, women's actual sexual longings. We could explore how power is entangled with desire and pleasure in ways which may foster, disconnect from, or seek to redress more general relations of dominance and submission between men and women, one person and another': 'Sensual Uncertainty, or Why the Clitoris is Not Enough', in *Sex and Love*, ed. S. Cartledge and J. Ryan (London: The Women's Press, 1983). Segal reconsiders these issues in 'Sweet Sorrows, Painful Pleasures: Pornography and the Perils of Heterosexual Desire', in *Sex Exposed*.

9. This article follows the usual English spelling of the term, and it is the spelling adopted by Jean Laplanche and Jean-Bertrand Pontalis in 'Fantasy and the Origins of Sexuality', *The International Journal of Psycho-Analysis*, vol. 49, 1968, reprinted in *Formations of Fantasy*, eds Victor Burgin, James Donald and Cora Kaplan (London: Routledge, 1986). The 'ph' spelling for the psychoanalytic concept of fantasy was introduced in the English translation of Freud's works in the *Standard Edition* to mark the scientific nature of the term there, although no such distinction was made by Freud in the original German. It is also sometimes used to distinguish between conscious and unconscious fantasies. Laplanche and Pontalis make a cogent argument for rejecting both the use of this spelling and this distinction in the translation of Freud's work: 'It betrays little respect for the text to render words such as *Phantasie* or *Phantasieren*, which Freud invariably employed, by different terms according to the context.', p. 11, footnote 24. Quotations from the *Standard Edition* of Freud's work will retain the 'ph' spelling.

10. Laplanche and Pontalis, *The Language of Psycho-Analysis*, p. 317.

11. Laplanche and Pontalis , 'Fantasy and the Origin of Sexuality', p. 13.

12. *Chambers Twentieth Century English Dictionary*. The *Oxford English Dictionary* also refers to delusional imagining, because the fantasy has no basis in reality, and notes that the mental image of fantasy – as something not present – is now associated with fantastic and extravagant imaginings, that is, as having no basis in reality. It suggests that in modern use '*fantasy* and *phantasy*, in spite of their

identity in sound and in ultimate etymology, tend to be apprehended as separate words, the predominant sense of the former
being "caprice, whim, fanciful invention", while that of the latter is
"imagination, visionary notion".' A division, in fact, between proper,
serious imaginings, and the frivolous.

13. In his paper, 'Femininity', Freud writes 'In the period in which the
main interest was directed to discovering infantile sexual traumas,
almost all my women patients told me that they had been seduced
by their father. I was driven to recognise in the end that these reports
were untrue and so came to understand that hysterical symptoms
are derived from phantasies and not from real occurances': *New
Introductory Lectures On Psycho-Analysis* (1933 [1932]), Lecture XXXIII,
SE, vol. XXII, p. 120. For Freud the psychical importance of seduction, like the primal fantasy and castration, only arises because it is a
fantasy. This is not (or not primarily) because he wished to exculpate
his patients' fathers, but because for Freud it is only as a fantasy that
seduction is a psychical event.

There is, however, an ambiguity in Freud's treatment of the reality
or otherwise of the primal fantasy and castration – for example Freud
refers to the mother's castration as proof for the small boy of what
might happen to him. Laplanche has suggested that 'He was obsessed
by the notion of the real scene, but never managed to capture it. This
comes from the fact that Freud relates to only two categories: the real
and fantasy. If the seduction scene is just a fantasy, then it has no priority over other primal scenes, such as castration or return to the
mother's womb. For Freud, the problem then gets relayed to pre-
history, because if these primal scenes are not real, then real seduction
and castration must have taken place at some earlier point in human
evolution. So the problem becomes endless. Why endless? Because
Freud never conceived that there could be other categories than
factual reality and imagination, and he believed that imagination
must be founded on some pre-historical or biological reality. This is
where his seduction theory failed': 'Interview with Martin Stanton', in
Jean Laplanche – Seduction, Translation, Drives, eds Martin Stanton and
John Fletcher (London: Institute of Contemporary Arts, 1992), p. 9.
Laplanche argues instead that what is involved is not reality versus
fantasy: it is the issue of a message but one whose meaning is not immediately apparent to the child and hence Laplanche terms it an
'enigmatic signifier', ibid, p. 10, which comes to the child from its
parents or carers. This signifier – an unconscious message – is an
erotic signifier which penetrates the child with the parental fantasy.
As a result, and controversially, Laplanche places seduction as the
primary relation of the child.

14. Laplanche and Pontalis, 'Fantasy and the Origin of Sexuality', p. 3.
15. Freud, *The Interpretation of Dreams* (1900), *SE*, vol. V, p. 620.
16. Laplanche and Pontalis , 'Fantasy and the Origin of Sexuality', p. 12.
17. Ibid, p. 11.
18. Freud, 'A Case of Paranoia Running Counter to the Psychoanalytic
Theory of the Disease' (1915), *SE*, vol. XIV, p. 269.

19. Laplanche and Pontalis, 'Fantasy and the Origin of Sexuality', p. 10.
20. Ibid, p. 8.
21. The emergence of the drive and the role of fantasy is considered further in Chapter 5.
22. Lacan, *The Four Fundamental Concepts of Psycho-Analysis*, p. 185.
23. Moustafa Safouan, 'Men and Women: A Psychoanalytic Point of View', in *The Woman in Question*, p. 288.
24. Fantasy is therefore in a certain sense in conflict with narrative, in so far as this is defined as a structure of cause–effect relations. Lea Jacobs's discussion of Sternberg's *Blonde Venus* (1932) and the censorship wrangle with the Hays Office in Hollywood further illustrates the conflict, for Paramount studio rejected Sternberg's script which ended with the husband and wife united as unrealistic, for any woman would choose to stay with Cary Grant's millionaire. But the Hays Office objected to immorality being rewarded and Sternberg's ending was reinstated, with noticeable lack of motivation. Lea Jacobs, *The Wages of Sin* (Madison: University of Wisconsin Press, 1991), pp. 85–105.
25. Laplanche and Pontalis, 'Fantasy and the Origins of Sexuality', p. 17.
26. Freud, '"A Child is Beaten": A Contribution to the Study of the Origin of Sexual Perversions' (1919), *SE*, vol. XVII, p. 185 and p. 189.
27. Ibid, p. 191. In the male version the concious fantasy has the beating undertaken by the mother, or another woman, and the child is not the anonymous boy or boys of the girl's fantasy, but the subject himself, thus the fantasy 'I am being beaten by my mother'. Behind this Freud discerns the unconcious fantasy 'I am being beaten by my father', corresponding to the the second phase of the fantasy of the girl, and, while he does not discern here an initial sadistic phase equivalent to the girl's 'My father is beating a child' Freud anticipates that it might be found in certain cases. As a result he argues that for both the girl and boy 'the beating-phantasy has its origin in an incestuous attachment to the father', p. 198. The outcome for each in terms of sexual difference is complex. In the conscious fantasy the boy, Freud says, has repressed and remodelled his unconscious fantasy so that he occupies a passive, masochistic but still masculine position, that is, a feminine attitude (or aim) is combined with a heterosexual object-choice. The girl, however, who identifies with the father/male who beats as well as with the boys of the scenario, has turned 'herself in phantasy into a man, without herself becoming active in a masculine way', p. 199, and this, Freud suggests, leads the girl to escape from 'the demands of the erotic side of her life altogether'. Freud's conflation of femininity and passivity here (discussed further in Chapter 5) obscures the extent of the divergence between the active/passive aim of the drive, the sexual difference of the choice of love object, and identification on the model of a regressive identification with the lost love object – itself the basis for a homosexual object choice, Freud argued, for example in 'Mourning and Melancholia', as well as in 'The Psychogenesis of a Case of

Homosexuality in a Woman' (1920), *SE*, vol. XVIII. This issue is returned to in Chapter. 7.

28.   Laplanche and Pontalis, 'Fantasy and the Origin of Sexuality', p. 14.
29.   This emphasis on the atemporality of fantasy is taken up by Jean-François Lyotard. He argues moreover that this 'phantasmatic matrix', as he terms the scenario, is not a structure: 'The matrix does not consist in a series of fixed oppositions, and whatever "propositions" might be attributed to it that would combine the aim (to beat), the source (the anal zone) and the object (the father) of the drive in one sentence, are themselves condensed into a formula-product – "A child is being beaten" – whose apparent coherence conceals the fact that the the life of the psyche contains a multitude of "sentences" that are mutually exclusive, that cannot possibly coexist': Jean-François Lyotard, 'Fiscourse Digure: The Utopia Behind the Scenes of the Phantasy' (1974), trans. Mary Lydon, *Theatre Journal*, vol. 35, no. 3, 1983, p. 343.
30.   Paul Willemen's analysis of the role of fantasy and repression in *Pursued* (Raoul Walsh 1947) shows the way in which the trace of the prohibition of desire for the mother, and the marks of the repression of the scene of his father's killing which is misremembered by the hero, are present in the narrative as both cause and structure of the narrative while yet not acknowledged by the film as such. See Paul Willemen, 'The Fugitive Subject', in *Raoul Walsh*, Edinburgh Film Festival, 1974.
31.   Freud, 'Hysterical Phantasies and Their Relation to Bisexuality', p. 160.
32.   Ibid, p. 166.
33.   Nancy Friday, *My Secret Garden: Women's Sexual Fantasies* (New York: Pocket Books, Simon & Schuster, 1974).
34.   Laplanche and Pontalis, 'Fantasy and the Origin of Sexuality', p. 13.
35.   Barthes, *The Pleasure of the Text*, p. 47.
36.   Freud, 'Creative Writers and Day-dreaming' (1908), *SE*, vol. IX, p. 144.
37.   Ibid, p. 150.
38.   Ibid, p. 150.
39.   'What is realism as understood by the theoretician of art? It is an artistic trend which aims at conveying reality as closely as possible and strives for maximum verisimilitude. We call realistic those works which we feel accurately depict life by displaying verisimilitude': Roman Jakobson, 'On Realism in Art' (1921), in *Readings in Russian Poetics*, eds l. Matejka and K. Pomorska (Cambridge, MA: MIT Press, 1971), p. 38. Gerard Genette extends these points in 'Vraisemblance et motivation', in *Figures II* (Paris: Édition du Seuil, 1969).
40.   Freud, 'Creative Writers and Day-dreaming', p. 153.
41.   Sigmund Freud, *Three Essays on The Theory of Sexuality* (1905), *SE*, vol. VII, p. 210.
42.   Sigmund Freud, *Jokes and Their Relation to the Unconscious* (1905), *SE*, vol. VIII, p. 68.

43. In 'Family Romances' (1909 [1908]), *SE*, vol. IX, Freud outlined a common fantasy of children – that their parents are not their true father or mother and that their real parents or parent are more exalted persons, or simply different and better. The source of the fantasy is seen by Freud as multiple; enabled by the child's growing awareness of and comparison with other families, it arises from its anger with its parents for what it perceives as slights (the birth of a sibling, a sense of its parents' divided or insufficient love and attention) which are both explained and revenged by the child's fantasy of its adoption. Along with this may be found the wish to become independent of the parents, justified by the attribution of inferiority to the parents, but also fuelled by the Oedipal complex and its rivalries and hostilities towards the parents, with now just the father repudiated, while the mother is attributed secret infidelity through love affairs. Family romances clearly form an important material for public and published fantasy material. Freud also saw the 'family romance' as a key element in what he termed 'A Special Type of Choice of Object Made by Men' (1910), *SE*, vol. XI, pp. 171–2, where the man repeatedly falls in love with a woman who is attached to another man but whom he imagines he can rescue or reform – for she is often a prostitute. Here is found the central fantasy of the duplicitous woman in *film noir*.

44. Freud, *Jokes and Their Relation to the Unconscious*, p. 26.

45. Ibid, p. 27.

46. Such films have been described as film melodramas constituting a sub-genre of the 'woman's film' – as indeed Molly Haskell names them in her book *From Reverence to Rape* (New York: New English Library, 1974). The term 'melodrama' was not, however, used in Hollywood for such films; rather, reviewers in industry newspapers such as *Motion Picture Herald* used the term for adventure films, thrillers, and especially gangster films. It is modern debates in film theory and criticism which have designated the genre of melodrama. Insofar as the 'woman's film' was an industry category it was not directed solely at women, for it was largely an 'A' picture category. Steve Neale sets out new research and arguments on the definition of the category 'melodrama' in film in 'Melo Talk: On the Meaning and Use of the Term "Melodrama" in the American Trade Press', *The Velvet Light Trap*, no. 32, Fall 1993.

47. *Now, Voyager* was produced by Warner Brothers and released in 1943. It was directed by Irving Rapper from a script by Casey Robinson, based on the novel by Olive Higgins Prouty.

48. Molly Haskell, *From Reverence to Rape*, pp. 154–5.

49. By perverse here I mean a desire which is outside social norms. Charlotte's desire is only seemingly perverse – it may well be the most properly feminine desire.

50. The following discussion is indebted to Lea Jacobs's article on this film in '*Now, Voyager*: Some Problems of Enunciation and Sexual Difference', *Camera Obscura*, no. 7, 1981.

51. As Jacobs says, 'Even within *her* story, Charlotte's defiance of her mother is spoken through a man', ibid, p. 93.

52. Ibid, p. 99.
53. In her caring for Tina the film suggests that Charlotte shows a better understanding of Tina's needs than Dr Jacquith. Jerry's gift of a camelia, sent as a token of his love, is used by the film as a sign not only of the tragedy of their love, their separation and loss, but also and more importantly as an affirmation of Charlotte and her worthiness to be loved, freeing her of her mother as the place to which she addresses her demand for love, and enabling her to refuse her mother's demands to return to her previous role as daughter.
54. Jacobs, '*Now, Voyager*: Some Problems of Enunciation and Sexual Difference', p. 103.
55. In the original version of this article I suggested that this was also a homosexual desire. By this I had intended a feminine homosexual desire, but the ambiguity of my claim here has been pointed out, while my attempt to sum a sexual position of considerable complexity under this term is clearly inadequate. I have tried to contribute to this debate in Chapter 7. What I wished to note here, however, was that the woman's desire, Charlotte's desire, is not conventionally heterosexual, though it may be perfectly feminine.
56. Laplanche and Pontalis, 'Fantasy and the Origins of Sexuality', p. 17.
57. *The Reckless Moment* was produced by Columbia and released in 1949. It was directed by Max Ophuls, or Opuls as he was styled on his American films, from a screenplay by Henry Garson and Robert W. Sodeberg, based on a *Ladies Home Journal* story, 'The Blank Wall' by Elisabeth Sanxay Holding, adapted by Mel Dinelli and Robert E. Kent. It stars Joan Bennett as Lucia Harper, and James Mason as Donnelly.
58. Ophuls' film follows closely the events and structure of the novel – its fabula – but transforms the story in its narration. In the novel, too, Donnelly falls in love with Lucia but what is emphasised through the novel's focalising third-person narration is not Lucia's predicament but the tragedy of Donnelly's 'entrapment' by Lucia's helpless goodness. This leads him to betray his friend and benefactor, Nagle, only to be betrayed in turn by Lucia who, under pressure from the police and in order to protect her family's reputation, persuades him to come to her house where the police are waiting for him. Donnelly does not expose Lucia and Bea, but dies escaping from the police. The film's fantasy is quite different, not only because the element of Lucia's betrayal has disappeared, but because a different narrational focalisation is presented, so that Lucia appears less insincere and less weak.
59. As is the view of Andrew Britton, 'Reply to Paul Willemen', *Framework*, vol. 2, no. 4, 1976.
60. Jacques Lacan, 'The Meaning of the Phallus', in *Female Sexuality – Jaques Lacan and the École Freudienne*, p. 84 .
61. Freud, 'On the Universal Tendency to Debasement in the Sphere of Love' (1912), *SE*, vol. XI, p. 183.
62. Freud, 'The Taboo of Virginity' (1918 [1917]), *SE*, vol. XI, pp. 191–208.

63. Lacan, 'The Meaning of the Phallus', p. 85. Lacan continues 'except that in her case, the Other of love as such, that is to say, the Other as deprived of that which he gives, is hard to perceive in the withdrawal whereby it is substituted for the being of the man whose attributes she cherishes.'

64. Freud, 'A Special Type of Choice of Object Made by Men' (1910), pp. 166–7. Here, too, is embedded the 'family romance' structure discussed earlier.

65. One might, for example, take up the position of Tom Harper, the excluded and absent husband and father in *The Reckless Moment* who has done nothing to deserve his wife's implicit betrayal. The film, though, does not encourage us here – there's no picture of him, nor even a letter.

66. Penley, 'Feminism, Film Theory and the Bachelor Machines', p. 57.

67. Raymond Bellour, 'Hitchcock, the Enunciator', *Camera Obscura*, no. 2, 1977. Bellour has also explored the perverse fantasy arising in many of Hitchcock's films and the resulting shifting enunciative structures in 'Psychosis, Neurosis, Perversion', *Camera Obscura*, no. 3/4, 1979.

68. The duality in Hitchcock's filmic enunciation has been pointed to by Tania Modeleski in her wide-ranging study, *The Women Who Knew Too Much* (New York: Methuen, 1988).

5   The Partiality of the Drives and the Pleasures of the Look in Cinema's Voyeurism

1. Mary Ann Doane, '*Gilda*: Epistemology as Striptease' (1983), in *Femmes Fatales*, p. 101.

2. Mulvey's essay has been the focus of much subsequent debate, revision and critique, including in Mary Ann Doane's own work. The special issue of *Camera Obscura*, nos 20/21, 1989, 'The Spectatrix', presents the historical debates on and current views about the female spectator. David Rodowick has reviewed the work of Mulvey and Doane through a reconsideration of the theories of Freud and Lacan which they each draw upon; *The Difficulty of Difference* (London: Routledge, 1991).

3. Mulvey, 'Visual Pleasure and Narrative Cinema', p. 25.

4. Ibid, p. 14 .

5. Ibid, p. 19.

6. Ibid, p. 19. Mulvey's gaze here is thus not Lacan's concept.

7. Ibid, p. 19.

8. Ibid, p. 26.

9. It is the woman as subject of desire which is central to Bellour's analyses of Hitchcock's films *Marnie* and *The Birds* (1963), so that the desire which speaks in Marnie's or Melanie's look is, as Janet Bergstom says, 'the object of Mitch's [or Mark's] and Hitchcock's investigation, not primarily her body as scopic object or fetish. The woman's desire is crucial to the logic of the enunciation of Hitchcock's films, Bellour contends (this is possibly his most insidi-

ous point) and he extends this description to the classical American cinema generally': 'Enunciation and Sexual Difference', in *Feminism and Film Theory*, p. 180. Bellour's discussion of *The Birds*, 'Les Oiseaux: analyse d'une séquence', appeared in *Cahiers du Cinéma*, no. 219, 1969; his essay on *Marnie*, 'Hitchcock the Enunciator' was translated in *Camera Obscura*, no. 2, 1977.

10. This is the case even with the most the stereotyped pornographic image – say of the woman laying prone, her genitals exposed to the camera, her hand suggesting the gesture of masturbation – which nevertheless figures a scene of fantasy. This is not an image of simple denotation, with a corresponding automatic stimulus response. The image is already part of a complex system of signifying the sexual and of a complex process by which the woman's body for many men comes to be the sign of their desire. It is already a connotative system, signifying the possibility of sexual satisfaction for the man. The woman's naked body and the delineation of her genitals in part images present at the very least 'the object-which satisfies' or 'the object through which I am pleasured', just as the breast had done. (Such part-images are successors of the early part-objects, the breast etc., while also functioning as substitutes.) However the subject of the satisfaction – the spectator – is absent from the image, implying a scenario in which that subject would come to be present – a scene which might be variously imagined but no doubt would include the man putting his penis into the woman's sex thus displayed.

11. In her later article, 'Afterthoughts on "Visual Pleasure and Narrative Cinema" inspired by King Vidor's *Duel in the Sun* (1946)' (1981), in *Visual and Other Pleasures*, Mulvey takes up the issue of feminine pleasure in cinema through an exploration of the implications for the woman of her pre-Oedipal attachment to a masculine identification, or 'masculinity complex' in which the girl continues to believe that she has a penis, and takes an active, phallic role, whereas, Mulvey notes,

> the correct road, *femininity*, leads to increasing repression of the 'active' (the 'phallic phase' in Freud's terms). In this sense Hollywood genre films structured around masculine pleasure, offering an identification with the *active* point of view, allow a woman spectator to rediscover that lost aspect of her sexual identity, the never fully repressed bed-rock of feminine neurosis. (Ibid, p. 31)

Thus she sees three elements which begin to make possible the formulation of a female, if not a feminine, position of film spectatorship (not feminine, insofar as the woman remains fixed within her masculinity complex). These are (1) Freud's concept of 'masculinity' in women, together with (2) the identification triggered by the logic of narrative grammar, and finally (3) the ego's desire to fantasise itself in a certain, active manner. Mulvey calls this 'trans-sex identification'.

12. In 'Myth, Narrative and Historical Experience', Mulvey addresses the history and place of that essay:

There had been an enormous sense of excitement in exploring patriarchal myths, analysing images of sexual difference, trying to extract the meanings that lay behind the images of women in popular culture, revealing the 'taming and binding' that seemed to have organised representations of difference for nearly as long as our culture can remember. For all this, the binary mode of thought provided a necessary, dynamic analytic tool. (Ibid, p. 161)

She goes on to say:

The article wanted to provoke the question 'So what next, then?' Change seemed to be just around the corner in the mid-1970s, and an article written in a polemical spirit and above all, to precipitate change, loses significance outside historical context and integrated into the timeless body of film theory. To articulate the relationship between cultural forms and women's oppression, to use psychoanalysis in discussing and exposing this relationship, both of these must precipitate a next phase, that will shift the terms and connotations that cluster around representations of sexual difference. But the either/or binary pattern seemed to leave the argument trapped within its own conceptual frame of reference, unable to advance politically into a new terrain or suggest an alternative theory of spectatorship in the cinema. (Ibid, p. 162)

13. Freud writes 'in scopophilia and exhibitionism the eye corresponds to an erotogenic zone', *Three Essays on the Theory of Sexuality*, p. 169.
14. Ibid, p. 192, my italics.
15. Laplanche and Pontalis comment 'In psychoanalysis, all that can be affirmed is that there exists a sexual energy or libido; clinical experience, while it cannot help us define this energy, does show us its development and transformations': *The Language of Psycho-Analysis*, p. 420.
16. Freud, 'Instincts and Their Vicissitudes' (1915), *Papers on Metapsychology, SE*, vol. XIV, p. 120.
17. Ibid, p. 120. As pointed out earlier in Chapter 3, note 18, Freud's concept of the drive specifically excludes what might be conventionally understood by the term 'instinct'.
18. Freud, 'The Unconscious' (1915), *SE*, vol. XIV, p. 177.
19. Freud, 'Instincts and their Vicissitudes', p. 124.
20. Freud, 'The Theory of the Instincts', *An Outline of Psycho-Analysis*, p. 148.
21. Lacan, *Écrits, A Selection*, p. 102.
22. Freud discusses this in *Beyond the Pleasure Principle, SE*, vol. XVIII, pp. 14–17.
23. Lacan, *Écrits, A Selection*, p. 104.
24. Ibid, p. 28.
25. Freud, *Three Essays on the Theory of Sexuality*, pp. 181–2. The second sentence was added by Freud in 1915.
26. Freud, 'On Narcissism, An Introduction' (1914), *SE*, vol. XIV.
27. Freud, *The Ego and the Id*.
28. 'Every activity, modification of the organism, or perturbation is capable of becoming the source of a marginal effect, which is

precisely the sexual excitation at the point at which that perturbation is produced.' Jean Laplanche, *Life and Death in Psychoanalysis*, pp. 87–8.

29. Ibid, p. 8.
30. Laplanche's concept of 'leaning' or 'propping' and its implication for a theory of the woman's desire in relation to the body has been taken up by in relation to feminism and film theory by Mary Ann Doane in 'Misrecognition and Identity', *Cinetracts*, vol. 3, no. 3, Fall 1980, and in 'Woman's Stake: Filming the Female Body' (1981), in *Femmes Fatales*. Joan Copjec also draws on the concept in *'Thriller*: An Intrigue of Identification', *Cinetracts*, vol. 3, no. 3, Fall 1980, and in *'India Song/Son nom de Venise dans Calcutta Désert*: The Compulsion to Repeat', *October*, no. 17, 1981.
31. Jean Laplanche, *New Foundations for Psychoanalysis* (1987), trans. David Macey (Oxford: Basil Blackwell, 1989), p. 141.
32. Laplanche, *Life and Death in Psychoanalysis*, p. 22.
33. Ibid, p. 22.
34. Ibid, p. 24.
35. Laplanche, *New Foundations for Psychoanalysis*, p. 143.
36. Ibid, p. 141.
37. Laplanche has presented a summary of his views of the drive in 'The Drive and its Object Source', in *Jean Laplanche – Seduction, Translation and the Drives*, pp. 179–95.
38. Freud, 'Instincts and Their Vicissitudes', p. 122.
39. Ibid, pp. 122–3. Lacan's concept of the *objet petit a* can be seen in Freud's description here, for, as Freud says, 'The object is not necessarily something extraneous: it may equally well be a part of the subject's own body', ibid, p. 122.
40. Laplanche, *New Foundations for Psychoanalysis*, pp. 145–6.
41. Freud, 'Instincts and Their Vicissitudes', p. l26.
42. Freud, 'Repression' (1915), *Papers on Metapsychology, SE*, vol. XIV, p. 147.
43. This point is made by Otto Fenichel in his study 'The Scopophilic Instinct and Identification', *The International Journal of Psycho-Analysis*, vol. XVIII, 1937, p. l0. Fenichel emphasises the role of incorporation – seeing and taking in the seen – as a form of identification, and includes some vivid examples of feminine scopophilia and projective identification.
44. Described in James Gammils, 'Analytic Listening and the Dream Scene', *The International Journal of Psycho-Analysis*, vol. 61, 1980.
45. Freud, 'The Psycho-analytic View of Psychogenic Disturbance of Vision' (1910), *SE*, vol. XI, pp. 216–17.
46. Freud, 'Instincts and Their Vicissitudes', p. 127. Freud makes a distinction here between a change in aim, from activity to passivity, and a reversal in content, but which is found in only a single instance, in the reversal of love into hate; the latter distinction raises further conceptual issues in relation to the emergence of ambivalent feeling, but this does not bear on the arguments pursued here.
47. Ibid, p. 127.

48. Laplanche, *Life and Death in Psychoanalysis*, p. 88.

49. Freud, 'Instincts and Their Vicissitudes', p. 130.

50. In a note added to 'Instincts' in 1924 Freud acknowledges this new view: 'In later works (cf. 'The Economic Problem of Masochism', 1924) relating to problems of instinctual life I have expressed an opposite view': p. 128, note 2. In 'The Economic Problem of Masochism' (1924), *SE*, vol. XIX, Freud posits a 'destructive instinct, the instinct for mastery'. Where this is directed outwards it is sadism proper, but 'a portion does not share in this transposition outwards' instead forming an 'original, erotogenic masochism': pp. 163–4. If subsequently the sadistic drive outwards is once more introjected then, Freud argues 'a secondary masochism is produced, which is added to the original masochism', ibid. This new view was developed after 1920 following the theory of the death drive in *Beyond the Pleasure Principle*. The concept of a primary masochism however implies a more complex relation to sadism, involving a tripartite structure in which the initial stage is no longer sadism as an activity directed outwards to an external object, but the reflexive, masochistic moment: to make oneself suffer or to destroy oneself. It is this which is taken up by Laplanche in his revised schema for the drives.

51. Freud, 'Instincts and Their Vicissitudes', p. 128.

52. Ibid, p. 128.

53. Laplanche, *Life and Death in Psychoanalysis*, p. 89.

54. Freud, 'Instincts and Their Vicissitudes', p. 128.

55. Laplanche, *Life and Death in Psychoanalysis*, p. 92.

56. Mikkel Borch-Jacobsen has pointed out the importance of distinguishing the two senses of object invoked here, the first being the object of the drive, through which the drive reaches its goal, its *Ziel*, the second sense is used by Freud in a more specific, more classical sense, Borch-Jacobsen suggests, as 'Everything that is op-posed to the subject, everything that confronts it – in short, everything that is "not-ego" – is, then, an "object". It is in this second sense that auto-eroticism, for example, is said to be "deprived of an object" (even though this is not true in the first sense).' *The Freudian Subject*, p. 64.

57. Freud, 'Mourning and Melancholia'. This has been discussed in Chapter 3.

58. This is also the view put forward by Gilles Deleuze in *Masochism: Coldness and Cruelty*. But whereas for Deleuze the relation between sadism and masochism is now broken – and his interest in that essay is primarily with masochism – Laplanche shows the continuing interconnectedness of the two positions no longer as inversions of each other, but through the origin of each in a primary passivity.

59. Gaylyn Studlar has also drawn upon the arguments of Laplanche, as well as Deleuze, in her discussion of cinema and what she describes as its 'masochistic aesthetic': *In the Realm of Pleasure* (Urbana and Chicago: University of Ilinois Press, 1988), p. 27. In emphasising *masochism*, however, she loses sight of Laplanche's important distinction of *primary passivity* (or in Freud's terms, primary masochism) from which both sadism and masochism, activity and passivity, then

emerge. Studlar retains a certain conflation of masochism and passivity and as a result she maintains an opposition between sadism and masochism, placing them as two radically different and opposed routes to pleasure. Laplanche has shown that passivity and activity are a much more mixed affair.

60. Freud, 'Instincts and Their Vicissitudes', p. 30.
61. Laplanche, *Life and Death in Psychoanalysis*, p. 102.
62. Laplanche, *New Foundations for Psychoanalysis*, p. 126. Laplanche sharply differs from Lacan on the question of language and the unconscious, rejecting Lacan's view of the unsconscious as structured like a language. John Fletcher provides an extensive review of Laplanche's work in his essay, 'The Letter in the Unconscious: The enigmatic signifier in the work of Jean Laplanche', in *Jean Laplanche – Seduction, Translation, Drives*, pp. 93–120.
63. Helen Deutsch, *The Psychology of Women*, vol. 1 (New York: Grove Stratton, 1944), p. 240. Deutsch was an important contributor to the debate on female sexuality in the 1930s; on this see Mitchell, 'Introduction – I', in *Feminine Sexuality: Jacques Lacan and the École Freudienne*.
64. Freud, 'Femininity', p. 115.
65. Ibid, p. 115.
66. Ibid, p. 116.
67. Freud had introduced this correlation in his discussion of '"A Child is Being Beaten"': A Contribution to the Study of the Origin of Sexual Perversions' in 1919 and retains it in 'The Economic Problem of Masochism' in 1924. This feminine masochism is a secondary masochism, added to the original masochism. Its status as feminine seems to derive from its passive aim – the wish to be beaten, punished (though Freud acknowledges the infantile character of this too), its scenarios of castration and 'the situations of being copulated with and of giving birth, which are characteristic of femaleness', ibid, p. 165. The femininity of the masochism of the girl fantasyists in 'A Child is Being Beaten' is qualified by Freud, however, for he argues that the fact that it is boys who are beaten shows that the girl has given up her feminine role and identified as a boy so that, though the fantasy is still masochistic, 'She turns herself into a man without becoming active in a masculine way, and is no longer anything but a spectator of the event which takes the place of a sexual act', p. 199. In contrast, the boy's fantasy is heterosexual because the beater remains a woman. This, as Parveen Adams has argued, 'is a rather arbitrary division of difference between the boy and the girl's fantasy'; see 'Per Os(cillation)', in *Psychoanalysis and Cultural Theory*, p. 83. What arises here in fact is a divergence between the active/passive aim of the drive, the sexual difference of the choice of love object, and identification.

    Laplanche and Pontalis have argued that the fantasy must be viewed as a scenario, with multiple entries which may also be mutually exclusive positions, and these are taken up not sequentially – as in a narrative – but simultaneously or, rather, since the unconscious does not know time in this way, to take up any one position is also always to be implicated in the other(s). Freud here attributes to the girl a transformation of the drive comparable to that of the perverse voyeur – the sexual act is replaced by spectatorship.

68. Freud, 'Femininity', p. 126.

69. This accords with what Freud earlier describes as the bisexuality of the drive, ibid, pp. 116–17.

70. Laplanche has put forward a different view of repression. He sees it as the result of the inability of the infant to wholly transform passivity into activity, that is, to 'translate' the enigmatic signifiers penetrating it from its parental figures or carers. Activity, Laplanche says, is this effort of translation and the resulting integration. However a part of these enigmatic signifiers remains unintegrated, and is repressed, forming the unconscious so that, Laplanche says 'Towards this part the individual remains passive, that is the passivity towards the adult in the beginning becomes our passivity towards our unconscious. We are deeply passive in our relationships to the remainders of the adult messages': 'The Kent Seminar', in *Jean Laplanche – Seduction, Translation, Drives*, p. 25. The implications of this for retaining a notion of feminine passivity are not explored by Laplanche there.

71. Freud, 'Repression', p. 147.

72. Freud, 'Femininity', p. 128.

73. Ibid, p. 126.

74. It is in this final transformation, Freud says, with the substitution of a wish for a penis by a wish for a baby, that true femininity is arrived at. However he also notes that the archaic wish for a penis always lies behind the wish for motherhood. The nature of this psychical process of substitution is not explored by Freud here, but assumed. Sarah Kofman sums up Freud's views here as saying 'what is most specifically feminine in woman is in fact her masculine desire to possess the penis, her penis envy. This desire thus becomes at once the vestige of woman's "masculine" sexuality that *must* disappear in order to leave room for femininity and also what allows woman to bring her femininity to the best possible fruition': *The Enigma of Woman*, pp. 193–4. As a result Freud ends up defining femininity as the wish not to be a woman, since penis-envy remains behind every substitutive wish. Rachel Bowlby concludes that femininity is, therefore, the repudiation by the woman of her femininity: 'Still crazy after all these years', in *Between Feminism and Psychoanalysis*, ed. Teresa Brennan (London: Routledge, 1989), p. 50. The role of the woman's penis-envy is addressed in Chapter 6.

75. Freud, 'Femininity', p. 128.

76. Ibid, p. 130.

77. Ibid, p. 130.

78. Ibid, pp. 116–17.

79. Freud, *Civilization and Its Discontents*, p. 106.

80. Freud, *Three Essays on the Theory of Sexuality*, p. 219, note 1 (added in 1915).

81. Freud, *Civilization and its Discontents*, pp. 105–6, note 3.
82. I have drawn here on Jacqueline Rose's comment in an interview with her and Juliet Mitchell: 'It's that once construction has gone into place you can then shift places, but those places retain their identity. If those places don't retain their identity then psychoanalysis would not be able to offer us a theory of how masculinity and femininity come into being. It wouldn't have a theory of difference': *m/f*, no. 8, 1983, p. 13.
83. Lacan, *The Four Fundamental Concepts of Psycho-Analysis*, p. 192.
84. '...in the case of the speaking being the relation between the sexes does not take place': Lacan, God and the *Jouissance* of The Woman', *Feminine Sexuality*, p. 138.
85. Lacan, *The Four Fundamental Concepts of Psycho-Analysis*, p. 192. Lacan rejects here, therefore, the notion of 'feminine masochism', seeing it as a masculine fantasy – notwithstanding that is was put forward by women analysts such as Helene Deutsch.
86. Mitchell, *Psychoanalysis and Feminism*, p. 115.
87. Lacan, *The Four Fundamental Concepts of Psycho-Analysis*, p. 200.
88. Freud, *From the History of an Infantile Neurosis* (1918 [1914]), *SE*, vol. XVII.
89. Freud, *Introductory Lectures on Psycho-Analysis, Part II, Dreams, SE*, vol. XV, p. 124. Freud's discussion here is concerned with showing the relation between the manifest and latent dream content and the role of the analysis of thought associations arising in the secondary elaboration of the dream.
90. Ibid, p. 220. Freud returned to this dream in order to show the role of wishfulfilment. He argues that the latent content of the dream was her anger and dissatisfaction with her own early marriage, and hence with her husband, which the news of her friend's engagement had aroused. Where in reality she felt that she had been too hasty in marrying in comparison to her friend who was only now engaged, in her dream her early booking had secured good seats while her friend could not attend because only poor seats were left. Freud comments, however,

> But the anger in itself was not capable of creating a dream. A dream could not arise out of the thoughts that 'it was absurd to marry so early' until they had awakened the old wish to see at long last what happens in marriage. This wish then gave the dream-content its form by replacing marriage by going to the theatre, and the form was that of an earlier wish-fulfilment: 'There! now I may go to the theatre and look at everything that's forbidden, and you mayn't. I'm married and you must wait!' In this way the dreamer's present situation was transformed into its opposite, an old triumph was put in place of her recent defeat. And, incidentally, a satisfaction of her scopophilia was mixed with a satisfaction of her egoistic competitive sense. (Ibid, p. 225)

91. In contrast, as noted earlier, Deutsch argued that 'The mechanism of the turn from the active to the passive, moreover, pervades woman's entire instinctual life. As an illustration of this, one might cite the fact

that voyeurism has much more the character of passive-exhibitionistic being gazed at, while active gazing is more characteristic of men': *The Psychology of Women*, p. 240. Otto Fenichel does address women's scopophilia in 'The Scopophilic Instinct and Identification', however the main concern of his argument is with identification through projection, and he sees behind his women patients' scopophilia a castration anxiety.

92. Notably in the work of the photographers Grace Lau and Della Grace – for example in Grace Lau, 'Perversion Through the Camera', and Della Grace 'Xenomorphosis', both in *New Formations*, no. 19, 1993. A number of film-makers have similarly engaged the issue of the possession of the look and its pleasures, for example Jane Campion in her video-work *Almost Out* (1984), Betty Gordon in *Variety* (1987) and Chantal Akerman in *Toute une nuit* (1982).

93. Lacan, *The Four Fundamental Concepts of Psycho-Analysis*, p. 181.

94. Freud, 'On Narcissism', p. 73.

95. Michael Balint notes 'These people [fetishists] – as is generally known – are with few exceptions men. The actions that give them gratification consist nearly always in putting on the fetish, or in putting part of their body into the fetish', but he goes on to refer to a – rare – case of a woman fetishist, 'Thus, the perverse action of a patient treated by Dr Dubovits consisted in putting her nose into the handkerchief used as a fetish': 'A Contribution on Fetishism', *The International Journal of Psycho-Analysis*, vol. XVI, 1935, p. 482.

Such fetishism is not held to be characteristic of femininity, however, but of women who believe themselves to be men. See here Gregorio Kohon, 'Fetishism Revisited', *The International Journal of Psycho-Analysis*, vol. 68, 1987, p. 219. Kohon cites Juliet Hopkins's study of a six-year-old girl who developed a foot and shoe fetishism, 'The probable role of trauma in a case of foot and shoe fetishism: Aspects of the Psychotherapy of a six-year-old girl', *The International Review of Psychoanalysis*, vol. 11, 1984, pp. 79–91. The girl was, Hopkins says, psychotic and she believed herself to be a boy. Hopkins here draws on Phyllis Greenacre's view in 'Further Notes on Fetishism', *The Psychoanalytic Study of the Child*, vol. 15, 1960, pp. 191–207, that symptoms of fetishism only develop in females in whom the illusionary phallus gained such strength as to approach the delusional. As a result Kohon sees these cases as failing to demonstrate female fetishism! This seems linguistically perverted. Fetishism here is not characteristic of biological men, but of persons who disavow sexual difference, in which case it cannot be said that either the biologically male or female fetishist is a man or woman, psychologically. As described below, fetishism is a 'third way' and in this sense it is also a third form of sexual difference.

96. Freud, *Three Essays on the Theory of Sexuality*, p. 157.

97. Ibid, p. 157.

98. Ibid, p. 153. Freud continues 'Such substitutes are with some justice likened to the fetishes in which savages believe that their gods are embodied.' The use of the term in this way is not Freud's own but

had already been proposed by Alfred Binet in 1888 in 'Le Fétichisme dans l'amour', in *Etudes de psychologie experimentale* (Paris: Octave Doin, 1888) to describe the talisman-like role of particular objects in sexual relations. See Alasdair Pettinger, 'Why Fetish?', *New Formations*, no. 19, Spring 1993, pp. 83–93, for an account of the history of the term and its use to designate practices which were not simply different but also and more importantly the mark of inferior peoples.

Any anthropological reference in the term is now both inaccurate and offensive, and the use and selection of objects in rituals and social practices shown to be neither arbitrary nor foolish. One might consider however – in contrast and not without irony – the extraordinary success of the term 'fetish' in Western society as a result of Freud's adoption of it, though of course this success is not unrelated to the use of the same term by Marx in relation to commodity production. In each case the real role of the object or phenomenon is denied and another purpose given to the object – for Freud, in a new and inappropriate context of sexual relations. Or, in Marx's view, the relation of cause and effect are inverted so that what is the phenomenal form appears as the cause of the real relations of production. The concept of fetishism in Marx has itself been the subject of critique; see on this Ben Brewster, 'Fetishism in *Capital* and *Reading Capital*', and Jacques Rancière, 'The Concept of "Critique" and the "Critique of Political Economy" (from the 1844 *Manuscript* to *Capital*)', and his self-criticism 'How to Use *Lire "Le Capital"'*, *Economy and Society*, vol. 5 no. 3, 1976. The relationship of the Marxist and the Freudian notions of fetishism has been reconsidered by William Pietz, 'Fetishism and Materialism', in *Fetishism as Cultural Discourse*, eds Emily Apter and William Pietz (Ithaca: Cornell University Press, 1993).

While for both Freud and Marx a central element in their use of the term is the reference to a fictitious and fabricated entity together with a denial of the true and proper function of the object or phenomenon, the role and mechanism of this 'denial' for psychoanalysis and Marxism is quite different. The fetishist does not disavow the proper role of a shoe, or corset, he just uses the object to support his disavowal of castration. Moreover the capitalist knows very well the role of interest or land in wealth-creation, hence the demand for new financial laws to allow joint-stock companies etc. in the nineteenth century, while he or she also seeks to disavow the inequalities of inherited wealth or the exploitation of ursury in the claim for a 'natural right' to property. In both there is disavowal, but it is not the 'same' disavowal. Slavoj Žižek has proposed a rather different sense of disavowal in social relations, in *For They Know Not What They Do* (London: Verso, 1991), pp. 245–53.

99. Karl Abraham's study, 'A Case of Foot and Corset Fetishism' (1910), confirms Freud's claim: *Selected Papers of Karl Abraham*, trans. Douglas Bryan and Alix Strachey (London: The Hogarth Press and the Institute of Psycho-Analysis, 1927), pp. 127–8.

100. Freud, *Three Essays on the Theory of Sexuality*, p. 153.
101. Ibid, p. 154.
102. Ibid, p. 155, note 2 (added in 1910).
103. Freud, 'Fetishism', *SE*, vol. XXI, p. 152.
104. Ibid, p. 154.
105. Freud, in a note in *Three Essays on the Theory of Sexuality* added in 1920, p. 157, writes 'The compulsion to exhibit, for instance, is also closely dependent on the castration complex: it is a means of constantly insisting upon the integrity of the subject's own (male) genitals and it reiterates his infantile satisfaction at the absence of a penis in those of women.' Exhibitionism was for Freud but the passive inverse of active scopophilia or voyeurism.
106. Lacan, *The Four Fundamental Concepts of Psycho-Analysis*, p. 195.
107. Freud, 'Fetishism', p. 153. Freud first used the term in 'The Infantile Genital Organisation (An Interpolation into the Theory of Sexuality)' (1923), *SE*, vol. XIX, pp. 143–4, 'We know how children react to their first impressions of the absence of a penis. They disavow the fact and believe that they *do* see a penis, all the same.' Freud's use of this new term clearly distinguishes it from repression, and also from denial or negation. See on this the comment by the editors of the *Standard Edition*, ibid, note 1, p. 143.
108. Ibid, p. 154.
109. Freud, 'The Infantile Genital Organisation', pp. 143–4.
110. Freud, *Analysis of a Phobia in a Five-Year-Old Boy* (1909), ('Little Hans'), *SE*, vol. X, pp. 7–8.
111. Freud, 'Fetishism', p. 156.
112. Laplanche and Pontalis go on to note that 'It will be recalled in this connection that Freud constantly related the castration complex, or castration anxiety, not to the simple perception of a certain reality but rather to the coming together of two preconditions, namely, the discovery of the anatomical distinction between the sexes and the castration threat by the father': *The Language of Psycho-Analysis*, p. 120.

    Laplanche refers to the 'fantasy of castration' in *New Foundations for Psychoanalysis*, pp. 36–7, and to 'infantile sexual theories' in his essay 'The Drive and its Object Source: its fate in the transference', *Jean Laplanche – Seduction, Translation, Drives*, p. 194. Nevertheless Laplanche also makes it clear that by calling such theories fantasy this does not thereby disparage them as fictional or unreal. Fantasy is, as will be argued again later in this chapter, a form of reality.
113. Freud, 'The Dissolution of the Oedipus Complex' (1924), *SE*, vol. XIX, p. 176.
114. Freud, 'Some Psychical Consequences of the Anatomical Distinction Between the Sexes' (1925), *SE*, vol. XIX, p. 252. The denigration of the mother's sexuality, or even of any woman's sexuality, arises, Joyce McDougall suggests, when a child develops a 'neurotic avoidance of the unacceptable sex organ through reaction formation, phobia and so on, in which the female genital becomes dirty or dangerous, or in

which femininity in general is despised. In any case the mother's open sex is known and counterinvested; it is no longer an object of fascination but a place of disquiet which temporarily bars the gateway of desire': 'Primal Scene and Sexual Perversion', *The International Journal of Psycho-Analysis*, vol. 53, 1972, p. 380. This article appears in a revised form in *Plea for a Measure of Abnormality* (1978) (London: Free Association Books, 1990).

115. The emphasis here on the meaning of the parental relation for the child in the Oedipal complex is drawn from the work of Joyce McDougall, and in particular her discussion of disavowal and the castration complex in 'Primal Scene and Sexual Perversion', ibid.

116. McDougall, ibid, p. 381. A similar point is made by Vladimir Granoff and François Perrier as the basis for their conclusion that perversion is not found in women: 'To our way of thinking, we are inclined to say that apart from homosexuality, which is more a special path that female sexuality takes than it is a perverted course (if we take the specifically male perversion of fetishism as the structural model of sexual perversion), there are in women no sexual perversions strictly speaking': 'The Problem of Perversion in Women and Feminine Ideals' (1962), in *Psychoanalysis in France*, eds Serge Lebovici and Daniel Widlocher (New York: International Universities Press, 1980), p. 257.

117. I. Rosen, ed., *The Pathology and Treatment of Sexual Deviation* (London: Oxford University Press, 1979), p. 277.

118. Ibid, p. 278.

119. Freud, *Three Essays on the Theory of Sexuality*, p. 157.

120. McDougall, 'Primal Scene and Sexual Perversion', p. 377.

121. If we follow Lacan's view that in perversion the subject determinines itself as object so that there is a splitting of the subject, then we can say that this man also identified with the whip itself – the phallus – and with the marks or weals which appeared as a result: Lacan, *The Four Fundamental Concepts of Psycho-Analysis*, p. 185.

122. Rosen, ed., *The Pathology and Treatment of Sexual Deviation*, p. 278, cit Hirschfeld, 1944.

123. Voyeurism here becomes the repeated re-enactment of the original trauma, as Laura Mulvey noted in 'Visual Pleasure and Narrative Cinema', p. 21. However while the compulsion to repeat traumatic events is well recognised in psychoanalysis there is disagreement as to how to understand it. On the one hand it is seen as part of attempts by the ego to master and neutralise excessive tensions – as with repetitive dreams following mental traumas. On the other hand it is related in Freud's writings to the death drive, and to that tendency towards absolute discharge implied by this drive. For Lacan it is the encounter with the real or the *tuché* which the subject compulsively repeats: *The Four Fundamental Concepts of Psycho-Analysis*, pp. 53–64. If voyeurism is a compulsion to repeat the scene and seeing of castration, with, as a corollary, a sadistic component in the investigation of the woman and assertion of her 'guilt', it will also always fail to deliver the required 'mastery'.

124. Lacan, *The Four Fundamental Concepts of Psycho-Analysis*, p. 182.
125. The importance of excretory functions for voyeurs which Freud emphasised may thus be understood as arising from a theory of anal sex which continues the fantasy of the non-existence of a different female genital organ, the vagina, and of its function.
126. Lacan, *The Four Fundamental Concepts of Psycho-Analysis*, p. 182. Lacan's discussion here concerns the gaze as *objet petit a*, and which is considered more fully in Chapter 8.
127. Freud, 'Fetishism', p. 154.
128. Ibid, p. 156.
129. Freud considers but rejects the term 'scotomized' for the process he is conerned with here, instead using 'disavowal'. The term 'scotomize' had been suggested by the French analyst René Laforgue to describe the erasure of or avoidance of a perception, but Freud did not consider that it applied in the cases he was concerned with because it implied the complete erasure of the perception: ibid, p. 153, note 2. Subsequently the French grammarian Pichon, in an essay on the psychological significance of negation, isolated a grammatical instance which he called *forclusif*, and associated it with Laforgue's concept of scotomization as the motor mechanism of schizophrenia. It is this term which Lacan later used to develop the distinction between repudiation or foreclosure and repression: Édouard Pichon, 'Sur la signification psychologique de la négation en française', *Journal de psychologie normale et pathologique*, March 1928, p. 245. Pichon's influence on Lacan is discussed by Elisabeth Roudinesco in *La Bataille de cent ans*, vol. 1, p. 383 (Paris: Ramsay, 1982) and by Jeffrey Mehlman in his Translator's Foreword to Roudinesco's second volume (1986), *Jacques Lacan & Co*, p. xiv (Chicago: University of Chicago Press, 1990).
130. Lacan points to a certain disavowal in the misrecognition of the mirror phase and its identifications: *The Seminar of Jacques Lacan Book 1, Freud's Papers on Technique 1953–1954*, p. 167.
131. Freud, *An Outline of Psycho-Analysis*, p. 203.
132. Ibid, p. 203.
133. Freud, 'The Splitting of the Ego in Defence', *SE*, vol. XXIII, p. 277.
134. Freud, 'The Splitting of the Ego in Defence', p. 276.
135. Freud, *An Outline of Psycho-Analysis*, p. 203.
136. Ibid, p. 204.
137. Octave Mannoni, 'Je sais bien, mais quand même...'; in *Clefs pour l'Imaginaire ou l'autre scène* (Paris: Éditions du Seuil, 1969).
138. Freud, 'Formulations on the Two Principles of Mental Functioning' (1911), *SE*, vol. XII, p. 222.
139. Freud, 'The Loss of Reality in Neurosis and Psychosis' (1924), *SE*, vol. XIX, p. 185.
140. Freud, 'Fetishism', p. 156.
141. Freud, 'The Loss of Reality in Neurosis and Psychosis', p. 184.
142. Ibid, p. 184.
143. This is the case in fetishism as well where it is the wish for the mother which penetrates and disturbs the reality not of the mother's

lack of a penis, but its meaning, namely, of the role of the father's penis.

144. Freud, 'The Loss of Reality in Neurosis and Psychosis', p. 187.
145. Ibid, p. 187.
146. McDougall, 'Primal Scene and Sexual Perversion', p. 380.
147. Ibid, pp. 378–9. She gives as an example of this 'gap-in-knowing' the dream of a fetishist patient: 'I was lying beside a woman and was asked to look at her legs. I stared for some time but couldn't make out what I was supposed to reply. it seemed to be a problem of logic. Finally I said that I would never find the answer because I never had been good at mathematics', ibid, pp. 380–1.
148. Ibid, p. 379.
149. Laplanche, 'The ICA Seminar', in *Jean Laplanche – Seduction, Translation, Drives*, p. 83.
150. Lacan's view of perversion is considered below in relation to his notion of the *objet petit a*. McDougall's position here is very close to the Lacanian account of Jean Clavreul, 'The Perverse Couple' (1967), *Returning to Freud: Clinical Psychoanalysis in the School of Lacan*, edited and translated by Stuart Schneiderman (New Haven: Yale University Press, 1980), p. 225. Clavreul notes 'This fetishisation is marked by the fact that the activity, the knowledge, and the interests of the pervert must above all be *rigorously of no use*, to lead nowhere', ibid, p. 226.
151. McDougall, 'Primal Scene and Sexual Perversion', p. 371.
152. Sandor Lorand gives several examples of perverse fantasy where the sexual difference – the castration – of the woman is disavowed. In one dream the patient relates 'I am on the deck of a ship with girls. I want to convince one that I have an erection, but cannot. Then she tries to alight on top of me and says, "This is an erection" showing me her rigid penis. I want to seize it, but she runs away and I wake with an emission': 'Role of the Female Penis Phantasy in Male Character Formation', *The International Journal of Psycho-Analysis*, vol. XI, 1939, p. 177.
153. The disavowal in perversion for McDougall is a 'destruction of sexual truth' which therefore brings it close to psychotic foreclosure of knowledge. Crucial here, however, is the role of the substitute 'knowledge' which in fetishism takes the form of a magically invested object or activity, and as a result avoids the delusion through which the psychotic builds ever more complex structures to support the denied knowledge. Instead the 'perverse structuration is able to reduce the "influencing machine" (Tausk, 1919) of psychotic sexuality to a whip, a hank of hair, another man's penis. These tiny influencing machines are perhaps a miniature psychosis but they serve to protect the individual's sanity': McDougall, 'Primal Scene and Sexual Perversion', p. 382; Victor Tausk, 'On the origin of the "influencing machine" in schizophrenia', *Psychoanalytic Quarterly*, vol. 2, 1933, pp. 519–56.
154. As recounted in his interview with François Truffaut, in *Hitchcock*, p. 305. In *Vertigo*, Scottie (James Stewart) has resigned as a police de-

tective after causing a colleague's death as a result of his fear of heights. An old friend, Gavin Elster, asks him to follow his wife Madeleine, who he says has become obsessed with a figure in her family's past and who as a result may be suicidal. Scottie falls in love with Madeleine, resuing her from an apparent attempt to drown herself, but later is unable to prevent her death when she falls from the top of a church tower. Recovered from his subsequent nervous breakdown, an accidental meeting with Judy, who reminds him of Madeleine, leads him to pursue Judy and remodel her appearance to reproduce Madeleine. Judy, however, is the Madeleine he fell in love with and not Elster's wife, whom he has murdered.

155. Ibid, p. 304. Hitchcock continues 'In other words, we're back to our usual alternatives: Do we want suspense or surprise?' Hitchcock's two alternatives were considered earlier in Chapter 2.

156. Slavoj Žižek describes the *objet petit a* as the embodiment of surplus enjoyment, a surplus object, the leftover of the real eluding symbolisation: *The Sublime Object of Ideology*, p. 50.

157. Lacan, *The Four Fundamental Concepts of Psycho-Analysis*, p. 62. Lacan's concept of the *objet petit a* draws on Winnicott's account of the 'transitional object', an original 'not-me' possession which functions as a bridge between the child's internal psychical world and the external world. See D. W. Winnicott, 'Transitional Objects and Transitional Phenomena' (1951), *Playing and Reality* (London: Routledge, 1971). The role of the *objet petit a* in the structure of desire and the trajectory of the drive, as well as its 'doppelganger' aspect in being the trace of the real in the subject, marks a radical divergence from Winnicott's transitional object.

158. Ibid, p. 103. Lacan described this, punningly, as the *Hommelette*, arguing that you can't make an hommelette – man (homme) or omelette – without breaking eggs. It is also from the egg that something besides the child emerges, the placenta or afterbirth (or the caul) is separated out from the child but, Lacan argues, as the *objet petit a* it returns to 'coat' the child.

159. Smirnoff, however, sees the game of the cotton reel and string as fetishistic, but in its double-sided aspect of avowal and disavowal, for the fetish-object, he suggests, functions as a 'restoration of a lost continuity, broken when a rift or breach is experienced by the subject...the fetish-object is an attempt to fill that breach'. This is the function Lacan ascribes to the *objet petit a*. Victor N. Smirnoff, 'The Fetishistic Transaction', in *Psychoanalysis in France* (1963), p. 313. Smirnoff relates the notion of fetish in Freud to Winnicott's concept of the transitional object, a connection Winnicott also made, see *Playing and Reality*, p. 9.

160. Catherine Clément, *The Lives and Legends of Jacques Lacan* (1981), trans. Arthur Goldhammer (New York: Columbia University Press, 1983), p. 98.

161. Lacan, *The Four Fundamental Concepts of Psycho-Analysis*, p. 185. Lacan later adds that 'the pervert is he who, in short circuit, more directly than any other, succeeds in his aim, by integrating in the most

profound way his function as subject with his existence as desire', ibid, p. 206. But this is a pseudo-auteroeroticism, for the subject enacts this through a profound splitting in which, unable to proliferate the division and repair it through ego-ideals, it is caught in a dyadic dialectic of hopeless repetition.

162. Lacan comments that the woman will busy 'herself with other *objet a*, being children', *Feminine Sexuality*, p. 167.
163. Jean Clavreul notes that for the pervert 'it is not the *lack* that causes desire, but a *presence* (the fetish)': 'The Perverse Couple', p. 223.
164. Slavoj Žižek, *The Sublime Object of Ideology*, p. 74.
165. What characterises perverse fetishism is the displacement of the sexual act – including masturbation – by the fetish object or scenario. This was observed by Abraham in 'Remarks on the Psycho-Analysis of a Case of Foot and Corset Fetishism', and later featured in the case discussed by Sylvia Payne, 'Some Observations on the Ego Development of the Fetishist', *The International Journal of Psycho-Analysis*, vol. 20, 1939, pp. 161–70, as well as in Gregorio Kohon's account of 'Mr M', 'Fetishism Revisited', pp. 213–28. Mr M's fetish scenario involved his wearing an apron while making love. However, although the apron-fetish enabled him to obtain an erection, he remained unable to ejaculate and he failed to reach orgasm with his wife. The couple sought help because they wished to conceive a child, but Mr M resolutely refused to recognise the 'cause' of their 'infertility' and left analysis with Kohon to consult a fertility expert developing *in vitro* fertilisation.
166. Jacques Lacan, *Feminine Sexuality*, p. 159.
167. Granoff and Perrier explicitly argue that her children may be fetish objects for the mother:

> If, however, as a real object, he [the baby as signifer of the phallus] becomes the screen onto which is projected this lack that is the focus of his mother's interest beyond her love object, he will become the object in a perverse relationship analogous to fetishistic perversion. The distinguishing feature of such an object is that it is the central element in the workings of desire and, at the same time, lies outside the paths of the fulfillment of desire. 'The Problem of Perversion in Women and Feminine Ideals', p. 262.

Here, rather, is the function of the *objet petit a*. This may become perversion, but cannot typically be so.

6 Female Sexuality, Feminine Identification and the Masquerade

1. Freud, 'Some Psychical Consequences of the Anatomical Distinction Between the Sexes', p. 252.
2. Freud, 'Female Sexuality', p. 233.
3. Freud 'Some Psychical Consequences of the Anatomical Distinction Between the Sexes', p. 253.

4. Freud, discussing the strength and duration of the girl's attachment to her mother, notes that some women never achieve 'a true change-over towards men. This being so, the pre-Oedipus phase in women gains an importance which we have not attributed to it hitherto', 'Female Sexuality', p. 226. In 'Femininity' Freud refers to the work of Ruth Mack Brunswick in showing the importance of the girl's pre-Oedipal attachment: see Mack Brunswick, 'The Pre-Oedipal Phase of the Libido Development' (1940), in *The Psycho-Analytic Reader*, ed. Robert Fliess (London: The Hogarth Press, 1950), pp. 325–6. Mack Brunswick assumes that in 'the normal course of development the impossible is given up and the possible retained', ibid, p. 311, but she also argues that women rarely and only with difficulty give up their attachment to the mother. She sees the wish to have a baby as earlier and not replaced by the wish for a penis. The wish for a penis she sees as arising from the narcissistic wish to have what the boy has, and she sees this as connected to what the mother wants for 'An object root is formed when the little girl realises that without the penis she is unable to win the mother.' John Forrester and Lisa Appignanesi suggest that this is 'an argument that Jacques Lacan would take up and extend considerably', *Freud's Women* (London: Weidenfeld & Nicolson, 1992), p. 450.

5. Freud, 'Femininity', p. 124.

6. Ibid, p. 124.

7. Ibid, p. 126.

8. Freud elsewhere says that the girl has no need to fear the loss of the penis, but does have to deal with the fact of not having received one, and he sees envy as the logical response. He suggests that she sees her clitoris as a stunted penis and that if her masturbation proves un-satisfactory this is extended to her sense of inferiority in lacking a penis: *An Outline of Psycho-Analysis*, p. 193.

9. Freud, 'Femininity', p. 124.

10. Kristeva points to the role of the 'so-called pre-Oedipal mother, to the extent that she can indicate to her child that her desire is not limited to responding to her offspring's request (or simply turning it down)' by indicating her desire 'for the father's phallus': *Tales of Love* (1983), trans. Leon S. Roudiez (New York: Columbia University Press, 1987), p. 44. As she notes, this may be as easily her own father's as her child's father's phallus! What is thus indicated to the child is that 'the mother is not complete but that she wants... Who? What? The question has no answer other than the one that uncovers narcissistic emptiness: "At any rate, not I".', ibid, p. 45.

11. There also arises here the question of how the wish to be pleasured in her clitoris becomes, for the woman, a wish for the penis genitally, that is, to have the penis in her vagina. Such pleasure must no doubt be a psychically organised pleasure, since a woman does not at the level of neurology experience an orgasm in her vagina. (The extens-ive research of William H. Masters and Virginia E. Johnson, *Human Sexual Response* (Boston: Little, Brown, 1966) showed the singular role of the clitoris in female sexual pleasure.) This does not to make of it a

mental pleasure, however, but rather confirms that for both the man and the woman genital pleasure is a question of the structure of desire which each finds his or her place within, rather than of nerve endings.

12. Freud insisted that castration is distinct from all the other separations or the losses, such as the breast, which the child has already experienced: see, for example, *Analysis of a Phobia in a Five-year-old Boy* ('Little Hans'), p. 8, note 2 (added 1923).

13. Freud writes 'Her new relation to her father may start by having as its content a wish to have his penis at her disposal, but it culminates in another wish – to have a baby from him as a gift': *An Outline of Psycho-Analysis*, p. 127..

14. Examples of the importance of images of the body in parts can be found in the discussion by Otto Fenichel, 'The Scopophilic Instinct and Identification', pp. 6–34. Such images are also important, of course, in the work of Melanie Klein.

15. Catherine Millot, 'The Feminine Superego' (1984), trans. Ben Brewster, *The Woman in Question*, p. 300.

16. Ibid, p. 301.

17. Rachel Bowlby, 'Still crazy after all these years', p. 50.

18. Freud, 'Femininity', pp. 128–9.

19. Freud, 'Some Psychical Consequences of the Anatomical Distinction Between the Sexes', p. 253.

20. Fenichel, 'The Scopophilic Instinct and Identification', pp. 18–19.

21. These substitutes may include a child or children. Granoff and Perrier see this as a form of fetishism in women; however I suggested earlier that these are, as Lacan emphasises, *objets petit a*. The feminist artist Mary Kelly has both represented and interrogated this process in her work *Post-Partum Document* (completed 1979), which displays and plays the series of substitutive constructions enacted between mother and child, culminating in written language. The fetishism of this relation is discussed by Kelly in her introduction to her book *Post-Partum Document*, which reproduces the six-part work (London: Routledge & Kegan Paul, 1983), p. xv.

I would now place this 'fetishism' with the paradoxical function of the *objet petit a* rather than as perverse fetishism. Mary Kelly has developed this focus in her later work *Interim*, particularly in its first section, 'Corpus', while also addressing the issues of feminine masquerade and of womanly desire beyond motherhood. Her work is characterised by involving both a metadiscourse on fetishism, and, in the objects and representations themselves, an encounter with the pleasures of fetishism. Emily Apter's examination of literary fetishism similarly suggests the important role of a fetishism for women, as well as the possibility of a feminine fetishism: *Feminizing the Fetish* (Ithaca: Cornell, 1991). This is also the view of another recent discussion, *Female Fetishism: A New Look* by Lorraine Gamman and Merja Makinen (London: Lawrence & Wishart, 1994).

22. Kaja Silverman, exploring the possibility of a female fetishism suggested by Freud's reference above to the woman's disavowal, cites

Sarah Kofman's claim in *The Enigma of Woman*, pp. 88–9, that the bi-sexuality of the hysteric resembles fetishism, in that each hinges upon a fundamental undecidability: Silverman, *Male Subjectivity at the Margins* (New York: Routledge, 1992), p. 119. But the fetishist does not ask a question, as the hysteric does, of whether I am a man or a woman; rather she or he holds both knowledges at once; she knows very well she has no penis, but all the same she does, and, again, it is sexual difference itself which is disavowed.

23. Smirnoff says that for the man, 'The fetishistic act represents masochistic identification with the *mater dolorosa* in her suffering and her unrecognised castration: a dual image of a phallic mother and a castrated mother, which echoes the splitting of the ego in the fetishist': 'The Fetishistic Transaction', p. 313. This characterises fetishism in general, I would suggest. W. H. Gillespie similarly states that 'the fetishistic act represented a passive feminine masochistic identification with the suffering mother, and the fetish was her phallus': 'A Contribution to the Study of Fetishism', *The International Journal of Psycho-Analysis*, vol. 21, 1940, pp. 401–15.

24. Kohon cites D. W. Winnicott's claim that, 'what the baby later knows to be a penis, he earlier senses as a quality of the mother': 'The Observation of Infants in a Set Situation' (1941), in *Through Paediatrics to Psycho-Analysis* (London: Hogarth Press, 1975). Kohon goes on to argue that 'This phallic mother is an intrapsychic structure present for the little boy as well as for the little girl. She will always be there', 'Fetishism Revisited', p. 219.

25. George Zavitzianos sees the woman's fetish as representing 'the paternal phallus, which is the woman's ideal ego. She wishes to possess her father's penis in order to disavow the feeling of being castrated': 'The Perversion of Fetishism in Women', *Psychoanalytic Quarterly*, vol. 11, 1982, p. 424. Whether this circulating penis is the paternal phallus is not clear for what is at stake for the perverse fetishist is a disavowal of sexual difference, of the role of the father's penis for the mother, in order to retain the phallic mother.

26. Where for the boy who fetishises Smirnoff suggested an identification with the castrated mother, for the girl who is homosexual, McDougall argues, there arises an identification with the father but not as phallic, 'not as an object of libidinal investment but as a mutilated image possessed of disagreeable and dangerous (anal) qualities' and later she suggests 'The originally phallic father through identification was now an anal-erotic possession': 'Homosexuality in Women', in *Female Sexuality* (1964), ed. Janine Chasseguet-Smirgel (London: Virago, 1981), p. 187 and p. 189; this essay appears in a revised form in her book, *Plea for a Measure of Abnormality*. As a result the penis as such does not guarantee phallicism.

27. McDougall, describing the role of objects, including the thick leather wristband Olivia always wore, and the large knife she carried, sees this as an identification with her father, his supposedly menacing strength and readiness to kill, rather than as fetishes, ibid, p. 188. But

these are also 'magical' objects. Similarly McDougall rejects describing as fetishistic the fabricated penis one patient always wore when she went out, as well as the fabricated 'play penis' used in elaborate games by homosexual women, for, she argues, it has 'few of the qualities of the fetishistic object, the primary function of which is to enable sexual desire and sexual fulfilment', ibid, p. 197. However what characterises male perverse fetishism – as described by Abraham and Kohon – is the loss of sexual function and the replacement of sexual intercourse by 'play' involving the fetish. Moreover, just as for the man, the phallus at stake for the woman here is the maternal phallus, while the paternal phallus is disavowed.

McDougall's essay both marks the perverse fetishism of these particular patients who were also homosexual, while placing this in a more normative account of the woman's identification with her father; however this father is both castrated and not-castrated. That this perversion is distinct from the patients' homosexuality is shown by her account of one woman who was horrified when asked by her woman lover to place her fingers in her lover's vagina, ibid, p. 209. What would pleasure her lover exceeded the bounds of the patient's sexuality. A number of these patients, moreover, found satisfaction in heterosexual relations subsequently. What McDougall's account confirms is perversion as the disavowal of the meaning of sexual difference, of the primal scene, and its reconstruction in fantasy, which – for her women patients – was not without its costs, but homosexuality – whether female or male – is not in this sense equivalent to perversion, as McDougall argues.

28. Millot, 'The Feminine Superego', p. 303.
29. Ibid, p. 303. She refers here to the unpublished study by Lacan, 'Le Séminaire livre V: Les Formations de l'inconscient', 1957–58.
30. Freud, 'Some Psychical Consequences of the Anatomical Distinction Between the Sexes', p. 253.
31. Millot, 'The Feminine Superego', p. 303.
32. Freud, 'Femininity', p. 130.
33. Freud, *The Ego and the Id*, p. 32.
34. Eugénie Lemoine-Luccioni also shows the necessity for a division and separation involving an identification with the other as different, a symbolic identification.
35. Raquel Zak de Z. Goldstein, 'The Dark Continent and Its Enigmas', *The International Journal of Psycho-Analysis*, vol. 65, 1984, p. 179.
36. Freud, 'Femininity', p. 134.
37. Freud, *An Outline of Psycho-Analysis*, p. 193.
38. Freud, 'Femininity', p. 129.
39. Moustafa Safouan, 'Feminine Sexuality in Psychoanalytic Doctrine' (1975), in *Feminine Sexuality*, pp. 134–5.
40. Ibid, p. 134.
41. Safouan, 'Is the Oedipus Complex Universal', in *The Woman in Question*, p. 280.
42. Ibid, p. 280.
43. Ibid, p. 280.

44. Ibid, pp. 281–2.
45. Ibid, p. 282.
46. Lacan, 'Seminar of 21 January 1975', in *Feminine Sexuality*, p. 168.
47. Granoff and Perrier, 'The Problem of Perversion in Women and Feminine Ideals', p. 244. They also note that 'As it happens, this man, the father, can accept his sex only at the cost of castration', p. 252.
48. The so-called lack of a super-ego in the woman is in fact a theoretical assumption arising from the logical implications of Freud's concept of the girl's castration – implications which were also adopted by Lacan. Evidence of its presence or absence in the woman relies on an empirical and *social* description of the super-ego as an agency of judgement, of ethics. Of course, the clinical observation of its presence in women had early on led Freud and other analysts to acknowledge the formation of a super-ego in women, but this was seen as an aberration, a malfunction of femininity in the woman, which was then called the 'masculinity complex'; this 'false' super-ego was also, nevertheless, flawed in comparison to the man's, being more severe in its demands. However this is also a feature, and equally neurotic, in the man.
49. Freud says that 'It is in the woman's identification with her mother [her affectionate, pre-Oedipal identification] that she acquires her attractiveness to a man, whose Oedipus attachment to his mother it kindles into passion. How often it happens, however, that it is only his son who obtains what he himself aspired to! One gets an impression that a man's love and a woman's are a phase apart psychologically': 'Femininity', p. 134.
50. Judith Butler's discussion of being and having the phallus places the issue of desire in psychoanalysis as simply a question of law, a symbolic and paternal law which she is concerned to challenge. 'To *be* the Phallus is to be signified by the paternal law, to be both its object and its instrument and, in structuralist terms, the "sign" and promise of its power': *Gender Trouble*, p. 45. Woman-as phallus then produces an affirmation of, and a content to, the man's identity. Lacan, however, is far from proposing a law of identity. To be or to have the phallus is an attribution which arises in the sexual relation, a play of masks, and this is not equivalent to a fixed identity in the social. To have the phallus is to be sufficient to the desire of the other, but the symbolic law demands that the subject acknowledge the lack not in the woman but in the symbolic other – the phallus as signifier of lack – and hence acknowledge that the subject, man or woman, is a subject of lack.
51. Lacan, *The Four Fundamental Concepts of Psycho-Analysis*, p. 107.
52. Lacan, 'The Meaning of the Phallus', p. 84. Miran Božovič summarises this paradox or bond of love. The loved one does not know what he or she has which the lover wants so that 'The only way for the beloved to wriggle out of this impasse is by returning love, that is by assuming the position of the lover and thus becoming the desiring subject, the subject of lack.' This of course contrasts with the narcissistic response also elicited, namely that I love myself through the

other's love for me. In Miran Božovič, 'The Bond of Love – Lacan and Spinoza', *New Formations*, no. 23, Summer 1994 special issue 'Lacan and Love', p. 69.

53. Ibid, p. 85. This was the redoubling which it was suggested was at work in *The Reckless Moment*.
54. Lacan, 'A Love Letter', *Feminine Sexuality*, p. 151.
55. Ibid, p. 157. Lacan writes that 'In point of fact a woman is no more an *objet a* than is a man – as I said earlier, she has her own [being children], which she busies herself with, and this has nothing to do with the object by which she sustains herself in any desire whatsoever', p. 168. She has yet another *objet a*, the penis which 'takes on the value of a fetish': 'The Meaning of the Phallus', p. 84.
56. Lacan, 'Seminar of 21 January 1975', p. 168. The symptom for Lacan is both complementary to and opposed to fantasy. The symptom represents the way in which the subject organises its enjoyment, as a result while – as a message – it can be deciphered, interpreted, nothing of this enjoyment may be changed. Fantasy is that which supports the symptom. Woman is perhaps in this sense also a fantasy.
57. Lacan, 'A Love Letter', *Feminine Sexuality*, p. 151.
58. Granoff and Perrier, in a discussion which raises more questions than it answers, point to 'a man's constant surprise at the appearance of female sexual desire, which he sees emerge before his eyes at the very moment he is manifesting his own', posing to him the enigma of the cause of the desire: 'The Problem of Perversion in Women and Feminine Ideals', p. 227. But the 'eternal enigma of women' which they cite, and its question 'What does the woman want?' is a fantasy on the part of the man to cover over the knowledge that the woman has her own desire. Rhetorically the enigma is an *aporia* in the older usage of that term cited by the *Oxford English Dictionary*: '*Aporia*, or the Doubtfull. [So] called because oftentimes we will seeme to cast perils, and make doubt of things when by a plaine manner of speech wee might affirme or deny him. (1589)'. It is, therefore, also a form of disavowal, a refusal of the knowledge that the man does not cause the woman's desire and is thus confronted by the Other in her desire.
59. Lacan, *The Four Fundamental Concepts of Psycho-Analysis*, p. 268.
60. Lacan, 'God and the *Jouissance* of The Woman', *Feminine Sexuality*, pp. 144–5.
61. Rose, 'Introduction – II', *Feminine Sexuality*, p. 51.
62. Lacan, 'God and the *Jouissance* of The Woman', p. 147.
63. Lacan, 'A Love Letter', p. 157.
64. 'The Subjective Import of the Castration Complex', in *Feminine Sexuality*, p. 121 (anonymously authored).
65. Lacan, *The Four Fundamental Concepts of Psycho-Analysis*, p. 193.
66. Joan Riviere, 'Womanliness as a Masquerade', *The International Journal of Psycho-Analysis*, vol. X, 1929. Riviere had been in analysis with Ernest Jones, then later with Freud himself in Vienna, and in the 1920s she became associated with Melanie Klein and her work. For the context of her article, see Stephen Heath, 'Joan Riviere and

the Masquerade', in *Formations of Fantasy*, eds Victor Burgin, James Donald and Cora Kaplan (London: Routledge, 1986). Riviere's article is also reprinted in this collection. Appignanesi and Forrester give a general account Riviere's work and her place in the development of psychoanalysis in *Freud's Women*.

67. Riviere, ibid, p. 306.

68. Lacan, 'The Meaning of the Phallus', p. 84.

69. Moustafa Safouan, cit Heath, 'Joan Riviere and the Masquerade', p. 52, from *La Sexualité féminine dans la doctrine freudienne* (Paris: Editions du Seuil, 1976), pp. 136–7.

70. Lacan, *Écrits, A Selection*, p. 322.

71. Heath, 'Joan Riviere and the Masquerade', p. 52.

72. In fact Riviere posits femininity as founded 'as Helene Deutsch and Ernest Jones have stated, on the oral-sucking stage. The sole gratification of a primary order in it is that of receiving the nipple, milk, penis, semen, child from the father. For the rest it depends upon reaction-formations': 'Womanliness as a Masquerade', p. 313. The key reaction-formation being the emergence of penis-envy with castration.

73. Michèle Montrelay discusses Fellini's *Juliette and the Spirits* (1965) as an illustration of the masquerade – 'a film so baffling, no doubt, because it brings out the presence of the "dark continent" so well. The dimension of femininity that Lacan designates as masquerade, taking the term from Joan Riviere, takes shape in this piling up of crazy things, feathers, hats, and strange baroque constructions, which rise up like so many silent insignias. But what we must see is that the objective of such a masquerade is to say nothing. Absolutely nothing. And in order to produce this nothing the woman uses her own body as disguise': 'Inquiry into Femininity' (1977), trans. Parveen Adams, *The Woman in Question*, p. 264. However for Montrelay the woman's lack of a lack makes the woman's sexuality an effect of her body and its concentric organisation even though this must still be symbolised, and the difficulty of this symbolisation of lack when the woman lacks the signfier of lack, the phallus, leads, she argues, to this masquerade in which the woman attempts to signify her lack. Here she sees the masquerade as a defence, as does Riviere, but in a quite different way. Moreover Lacan sees the masquerade as saying alot, that the woman is the phallus. Parveen Adams has discussed the implications of Montrelay's position on female sexuality in her introduction to Montrelay's essay, 'Representation and Sexuality', *The Woman in Question*, pp. 233–52.

74. Riviere, 'Womanliness as a Masquerade', p. 303.

75. Riviere also sees her patient as one of a category of women of whom she says 'It is really a puzzle to know how to classify this type psychologically'. They are women in university life, scientific professions and in business 'who seem to fulfil every criterion of complete feminine development... At the same time they fulfil the duties of their profession at least as well as the average man', ibid, p. 304.

76. Ibid, p. 305.

77. Ibid, pp. 305–6.
78. Millot, 'The Feminine Superego', p. 303.
79. Ibid, p. 302, quoting Freud, *Jokes and Their Relation to the Unconscious*, p. 115.
80. Safouan, cit Heath, 'Joan Riviere and the Masquerade', p. 51, from 'Entrevue avec Moustafa Safouan', *Ornicar?*, no. 9, 1977, p. 10. Riviere, following Klein, connects castration to frustration against which the woman rebels by seeking to overcome what she lacks by obtaining it elsewhere, thus, failing to receive it from the mother, she seeks it from the father. On this see the discussion by Appignanesi and Forrester, *Freud's Women*, p. 364 For Lacan too what is central is a lackingness, the lack in being for the subject engendered around what is imagined to be the stake of the other's 'fullness of being'. But for Lacan the sense of 'frustration', the lack produced by non-fulfilment of a demand, characterises what he termed the imaginary – a demand which is refused, but thereby implying it could be met. In contrast castration symbolises a lacking which no thing can repair or resolve.
81. Riviere, 'Womanliness as a Masquerade', p. 310.
82. Ibid, p. 310. Ruth Mack Brunswick makes a similar point, arguing that while the original basis for penis-envy is narcissistic 'An object root is formed when the little girl realises that without the penis she is unable to win the mother': 'The Pre-Oedipal Phase of the Libido Development', p. 310.
83. The father too was castrated and 'reduced to nothingness, like the mother' and hence also required propitiation: Riviere, 'Womanliness as a Masquerade', p. 310.
84. Ibid, p. 311.
85. This is a similar dissimulation to that which Žižek ascribes to ideology, for the masquerade hides nothing, rather it produces something to hide, but if the veil is removed what it hides also disappears: *The Sublime Object of Ideology*, pp. 28–9. This is discussed further in Chapter 8. Heath also points to this problem of the mask in his reference to Nietzsche's account of women as actresses: 'Joan Riviere and the Masquerade', p. 51.
86. This is the woman whose 'penis-envy' Maria Torok discusses: 'The Significance of Penis-Envy in Women', in *Female Sexuality*, pp. 135–70.
87. Heath, 'Joan Riviere and the Masquerade', pp. 55–6, quoting Lemoine-Luccioni, *La Robe* (Paris: Editions du Seuil, 1983), p. 124.
88. Lacan, 'The Meaning of the Phallus', p. 85.
89. Rose, 'Introduction – II', *Feminine Sexuality*, p. 40.
90. Safouan, 'Feminine Sexuality in Psychoanalytic Doctrine', p. 134.
91. Safouan illustrates this by a story of a stamp which authenticates the antiquity of furniture and which is demanded even though it can be false, and even though not all antiques have one: ibid, pp. 133–4.
92. Lacan, 'A Love Letter', pp. 153–4.
93. Rose continues 'a division which produces the feminine as its negative term': 'Introduction – II', *Feminine Sexuality*, p. 55. This is not,

however, to pose the feminine negatively, that is, as not good enough or lacking, for in language Saussure says, meaning is only ever constituted by the negative value of a word.

94. Lacan, 'The Meaning of the Phallus', p. 84; Freud, 'On the Universal Tendency to Debasement in the Sphere of Love'.

95. The 'facts' of anatomical distinction are a social – scientific – discourse of biology, and hence form part of social reality as distinct from the real and the unrepresentability of sexual difference, while also being distinct from the psychical reality produced for each social subject in their personal social history

96. Teresa de Lauretis has suggested that just such a 'bisexuality' is in play for the female spectator, producing a double desire – active as well as passive, and also a double identification – with both the subject of the narrative, the active hero, and the space of the narrative movement, that is 'the feminine position as mythical obstacle'. But it seems to me that this is also in play for the male spectator as well, for 'Oedipal logic' is not only or always a masculine proposition; *Alice Doesn't – Feminism, Semiotics, Cinema* (London: Macmillan, 1984), p. 143. In her book, *The Practice of Love* (Bloomington and Indianapolis: Indiana University Press, 1994), de Lauretis presents an extensive exploration of psychoanalysis' account of lesbian sexuality and develops very suggestively a rather different approach the notion of the sexed – lesbian – spectator, as well as offerering a radically new view of the role of perverse desire for lesbianism.

97. For example, the wish of a man to be penetrated like a woman and thus the fantasy of taking up the position of woman does not require the man to have a vagina and may not even involve the rectum as a 'substitute' vagina (since the pleasures of anal sex may be separately organised). But for the subject who has taken the 'middle way' of perversion as McDougal describes it, this wish which forms the subject's sexual positioning may only be met by really having a vagina, ultimately through a surgical transformation. Transsexuality is considered by Catherine Milot is her book *Horsexe: Essay on Transsexuality* (1983), trans. Kenneth Hylton (New York: Autonomedia, 1990).

98. *Gertrud*, made in Denmark, released in 1964, directed by Carl Theodor Dreyer, script by Dreyer based on the play by Hjalmar Söderberg (1906), produced by Palladium Film, A/S, Denmark. Gertrud is played by Nina Pens Rode; Gustav Kanning by Bendt Rothe; Gabriel Lidman by Ebbe Rode; Erland Jansson by Baard Owe; Axel Nygren by Axel Strøbye.

Elsa Gress Wright, reviewing the film, suggested that Dreyer has made something much more significant out of this material. 'He has made Gertrud the unconditional heroine by removing all traces of contempt for her (or for woman as such) and emphasising her superiority of intelligence and character.... All this has been translated into a film of the usual majestic slowness of speech and movement and the usual Dreyer "purified realism" of milieu and the carefully composed frames of great beauty': 'Gertrud', *Film Quarterly*, 19, Spring 1966, pp. 36–40.

99. Dreyer in 'My Way of Working is In Relation to the Future: A Conversation with Carl Dreyer', Carl Lerner, *Film Comment*, no. 4, 1966, p. 62.

The film is set in the same period as the play. Söderberg was a successful playwright. His play has not been translated but a discussion in English of the play, and Söderberg's work as a writer overall, can be found in Sten Rein, *Hjalmar Söderberg's Gertrud* (Stockholm: Bonniers, 1962). Rein emphasises that Söderberg sought to move away from Ibsen, 'he prefers the bitter tragedy of having to go on living even though ideals and happiness have been destroyed. But the most important innovation lies in Söderberg's dialogue. Conflicts materialise out of apparently trivial conversations, his characters frequently fail to communicate, and mean different things with the same words. Söderberg loves understatement, and in contrast to Ibsen's heavily emphasised points he often consciously introduces a crucial psychological moment, through a quietly spoken line or even through a silence', p. 356. Dreyer's film is faithful to this approach, however – if Rein's account is correct – it does not reproduce the original, for Dreyer replaces loneliness with solitude, removing the sense of absolute tragedy in Söderberg, and by giving her a life after her loves – her work in Paris – Dreyer makes Gertrud a woman of her own choices and not, as Rein suggests, a woman who sacrifices herself to a fatalistic ideal in her doctrine of love.

100. Dreyer, 'My Way of Working is In Relation to the Future', p. 62.

101. Dreyer, 'A Little on Film Style' (1943), in *Dreyer in Double Reflection*, ed. Donald Skoller (New York: Da Capo Press, 1991), p. 134.

102. Noël Burch and George Dana, 'Propositions', *Afterimage*, no. 5, 1974, pp. 63–4.

103. David Bordwell, *The Films of Carl-Theodor Dreyer* (Berkeley: California University Press, 1981), p. 176.

104. Dreyer, 'My Way of Working is In Relation to the Future', p. 63.

105. Dreyer, interviewed by John H Winge, *Sight and Sound*, no. 18, 1950, pp. 16–17.

106. The issue I am trying to address here is not Dreyer's intended meaning but his approach to the construction of meaningfulness in film, an approach which foregrounds not form rather than content, but rather focusses the problem of the meaning of content, of the fixing of the 'sense' or import of the representation through an emphasis on formal methods of 'showing' in the film. The gap thereby opened up, the 'lack' introduced, may be filled – projectively – by a 'transcendental' meaning, or it may remain, as I suggest, as the 'problem of meaning', and hence, the problem of the real of desire.

107. Söderberg, *Dr Glas* (London: Chatto & Windus , 1963), p. 82.

108. Kirk Bond, 'The Basic Demand of Life for Love', *Film Comment*, no. 4, 1966, p. 68.

109. Ibid, p. 69.

110. Tom Milne, *The Cinema of Carl Dreyer* (London: Tantivy, 1971), p. 168.
111. Ibid, pp. 170–1.
112. Barthes, *S/Z*, p. 4. 'Readerliness' is taken up again in Chapter 8.
113. Hence the tendency to ascribe 'transcendental' meaning to Dreyer's films, as in Paul Schrader's *Transcendental Style in Film: Ozu, Bresson, Dreyer* (Berkeley: California University Press, 1972).
114. Freud, *The Ego and the Id*, p. 54.
115. From an interview with Howard Hawks, *Movie*, no. 5, 1962, p. 11.

7   Figuring the Fetish

1. Freud, *Delusions and Dreams in Jensen's* Gradiva, *SE*, vol. IX, pp. 45–6.
2. The films of Jayne Parker, non-narrative and independently produced in Britain, pose this issue very clearly, for example in *I Dish* (Jayne Parker, 1982), the mackerel which is washed, prepared, and cooked and eaten, appears symbolic, representing both the male penis as well as, cut open and displayed, the female vagina. The imagery of fish hooks drawn from the murky water by a young naked woman does not resolve so easily into metaphor. The associations of inside and outside are clear, but which is which, and what is the relation of the hooks to the penis-vagina? An excess of meaning without signified presses upon us here, pleasurably.
3. Freud, *Three Essays on the Theory of Sexuality*, p. 153.
4. Ibid, p. 153.
5. Freud, 'Fetishism', p. 155.
6. Ibid, p. 157.
7. Ibid, p. 156.
8. Ibid, p. 152.
9. Abraham, 'Remarks on the Psycho-Analysis of a Case of Foot and Corset Fetishism', pp. 126–7. Balint notes that 'The actions that give them [fetishists] gratification consist nearly always in putting on the fetish, or in putting part of their body into the fetish': 'A Contribution on Fetishism', p. 481. The object chosen as the fetish and which comes to have such a revered or pivotal role is rarely a valued object – its overvaluation arises only in the disavowal – instead it is often a cast-off, old and worn, nor is it the unique object – another apron or shoe might do as well: Balint, p. 482. The role of smell has also be shown to be important, and this has been connected to the pre-Oedipal equation penis-faeces in the choice of fetish-object.
      On the representation of the woman's penis, see also here Sandor Lorand 'Role of the Female Penis Phantasy in Male Character Formation'.
10. Jacques Lacan and Françoise Granoff, 'Fetishism: The Symbolic, the Imaginary and the Real', in *Perversions: Psychodynamics and Therapy*, ed. S. Lorand and M. Balint (New York: Random House, 1956), p. 267. The fetish is a signifier of another signifier, the phallus, but the phallus itself is an imaginary object.
11. Clavreul, 'The Perverse Couple', p. 223.

12. In 'Photography and Fetish', Christian Metz returned to the issue of fetishism, arguing that photography is more capable of becoming a fetish – 'pocketed' and held, talisman-like, while cinematography plays on fetishism:

    > Film is much more difficult to characterise as a fetish. It is too big, it lasts too long, and it addresses too many sensorial channels at the same time to offer a credible unconscious equivalent of a lacking part-object. It does *contain* many potential part-objects (the different shots, the sounds, and so forth), but each of them disappears quickly after a moment of presence, whereas a fetish has to be kept, mastered, held, like a photograph in the pocket. Film is, however, an extraordinary activator of fetishism. It endlessly mimes the primal displacement of the look between the seen absence and the presence nearby…cinema literally *plays* with the terror and pleasure of fetishism, with its combination of desire and fear. (*October*, no. 34, 1985, pp. 87–8)

13. Andrew Sarris, *The Films of Joseph von Sternberg* (New York: The Museum of Modern Art, 1966), p. 28.

14. Tom Brown, a womanising private with a 'past', now in the Foreign Legion, falls in love with Amy Jolly, a singer with her own 'past', down on her luck in Mogador. She returns his love, but is also pursued by La Bessiere, a wealthy local magnate. Amy and Tom agree to leave together, he deserting the army, but he changes his mind and leaves her to a wealthy marriage with La Bessiere. Sent on manoeuvres, his commander Adjutant Caesar orders Tom to accompany him on a dangerous mission when, as Caesar is about to shoot Tom in revenge for his adultery with his wife, Caesar is killed by a sniper. Back in Mogador Amy abandons her engagement party to look for Tom – accompanied by La Bessiere. Finally she finds him in a bar, with two girls; asking why he left, she gets no satisfactory answer, but when Tom leaves she finds his carving in the table, a heart and arrow enclosing their names. Certain now of his love, she sees him off the next day, then turns to rejoin La Bessiere, but changes her mind and walks out to accompany the women camp followers trudging behind the troops, waving goodbye to La Bessiere.

15. My discussion of *Morocco* is indebted to the analysis of the film undertaken by the editors of *Cahiers du Cinéma* in *Sternberg*, ed. Peter Baxter (London: British Film Institute, 1980). In particular I have drawn upon their account of the process of exchange and equivalence operating in the film which transgresses and re-forms the figures of opposition constructed by the film such as high/low, eastern/western. However I have not followed their conjoining of Freud's notion of fetishism and the Marxist theory of value and commodity fetishism by which they conflate the objects in the film, such as the pearls Amy spills, as fetishes in both these senses, arguing 'Thus in *Morocco*, the fetishes literally function simultaneously as *both* bourgeois value *and* erotic signifiers; they are therefore inscribed both as inalienable values, not capable of being squandered, *and* as signifiers of that squandering', pp. 91–2. This arises because, they

argue, 'Each time therefore that Sternberg wishes to show us Amy Jolly in a non-fetishist erotic situation [which they say is illusory] she begins to be "squandered"; she offers Brown an apple, she gives him her key, she breaks her pearl necklace, she throws off her shoes. The fetishist nature of this "critique" of fetishism is marked in the fact that Amy Jolly's rejection of her accessories immediately makes them rise retroactively to become fetish-objects in their turn', p. 92. These objects arise as fetishes because of their foregrounding by the mise en scène. The pearls, however, are also part of a blocking – spilt, they signify the blocking of the sexual union with La Bessiere, the father, for Amy breaks them in her panic at being reminded of Tom's danger, that is, that she loves Tom, not the father. This meaning has already been established by Tom, for the diamond bracelet given to Amy by La Bessiere, casually left on her dressing-room table, was earlier the spur to Tom's first abandonment of Amy, and another blocking of the narrative – although in so doing he prostitutes Amy by exchanging her love for him for her material comforts with La Bessiere. It is not clear, however, why as fetishes these objects are also signifiers of a squandering; the apple is eaten by Tom, and the key is used by him to enter Amy's room in the next scene.

Furthermore, what they describe as an effacement of sexual difference through the production of the woman as a fetish, a 'pseudo-centre' which exists to mirror and justify the centre, the author, the Man, itself ignores the role of the masquerade, virile display and inversion which they point to as the 'erotic paradigms' of *Morocco* by subsuming these to this monolithic argument. Sexual difference is, on the contrary, very much present and central to the film, and while drawing on the opposition castrated/not-castrated as the terms of avowal/disavowal, these are not contained by the gender definitions of characters as male or female, and thus invert conventional definitions of masculinity and femininity. As they point out, Lo Tinto displays 'mother-cum-brothel-keeper behaviour' towards Amy Jolly – he is a foolish figure of fun as he crashes down on the stage after tripping while pulling the stage curtains, and he rhymes with Amy, she as ultra-feminine in her tights and brief skirt, as they both carry baskets to sell apples.

16. Sarris, *The Films of Joseph von Sternberg*, p. 28.
17. Mulvey, 'Visual Pleasure and Narrative Cinema', p. 22. In her discussion *Morocco* is the example of fetishistic cinema, contrasting with Hitchcock's voyeurism in *Vertigo*, and she points to three ways in which fetishism operates in the film, firstly in the way that 'Sternberg plays down the illusion of screen depth; his screen tends to be one-dimensional, as light and shade, lace, steam, foliage, net, streamers and so on reduce the visual field.' Secondly, that 'There is little or no mediation of the look through the eyes of the main male protagonist.' Thirdly (though this is listed first by her), 'Sternberg produces the ultimate fetish... the beauty of the woman as object and the screen space coalesce; she is no longer the bearer of guilt but a perfect product', p. 22.

18.   Roland Barthes, 'Diderot, Brecht, Eisenstein', in *Image-Music-Text*, p. 70. Barthes's argument here is considered further in Chapter 8.

19.   Howard Hawks is an interesting comparison here, for, as shown in Chapter 1, he too uses objects circulated and exchanged – the double-headed coin in *Only Angels Have Wings*, and the ring returned to the wrong fiancé in *Ball of Fire*, the red bloomers in *Rio Bravo*, while Feather's black tights at the end of the film will signify not a public eroticism but a private sexuality. Hawks also uses reversals, especially sexual revesals, and indeed Hawks claimed to have suggested to Sternberg that Dietrich appear dressed as a man: interview with John Kobal, *Film*, no. 14, 1974, p. 5. Jules Furthman who wrote the screenplay for *Morocco* also scripted several of Hawks's films.

20.   Mulvey, 'Visual Pleasure and Narrative Cinema', p. 22. Mulvey describes this as preventing the spectator 'from achieving any distance from the image in front of him', p. 26. But the fetishist does indeed require the fetish-object to be out there in the scene, separated from him, in order to function as the 'fallen object'. The lack of separation from the image is found, rather, in the mirror phase and in the transitivist identification it gives rise to, as well as in the image of the phallic mother – Dietrich's flawless image.

21.   Mulvey, ibid, p. 22.

22.   The absence of a controlling male character is a correlate of the kind of film *Morocco* is, namely a vehicle for its female as well as its male star. Dietrich was being groomed by Paramount, if not Sternberg, as another Garbo. What is interesting is that the films of both stars centre them as figures who do as well as are done to, i.e. active protagonists, and involved romantic dramas which centre the woman character. It is a type of film which has been barely addressed as a genre, and not without reason, since while clearly part of melodrama it veers away from what has come to be seen as the central elements of that genre – women's issues, the family – while having the structure of heightened emotions, coincidence, and an 'if only' narrative structure. Obsessed with the problem of the 'fallen woman' these films often come up with much less sadistic resolutions than later melodrama – and the couple may be achieved or regained at the end. Examples here would include Garbo in *Flesh and the Devil* (Clarence Brown, 1927) where she dies, in contrast to *Susan Lenox: Her Fall and Rise* (Robert Z. Leonard, 1930); Dietrich in *Shanghai Express* (Sternberg, 1932) in which the couple is achieved at the end, as in *Blonde Venus* (Sternberg, 1932), in which she also 'falls' before rising again to reunite with her husband. Where the woman is 'punished' by death or abandonment, often for her exploitation of the man, the film's emphasis nevertheless is on the sexual desire of the woman.

23.   That is, the camera shows a character who then looks off-screen, while the next shot shows another character who is already looking off-screen in an eye-line direction matching the first shot, thus the first character is retrospectively placed as already the object of a pov look.

24. Mulvey suggested that, in dominant cinema, it is the woman's appearance in film which connotes 'to-be-looked-at-ness': 'Visual Pleasure and Narrative Cinema', p. 19.

25. In the sense given this term by Stephen Heath in his analysis of Orson Welles's *Touch of Evil* (1958): 'Film and System: Terms of an Analysis', *Screen*, vol. 16, no. 1, 1975 and vol. 16, no. 2, 1975.

26. The detailed analyses here are based on my own unpublished shot-breakdown of the first reel of the film. The sequence at Lo Tinto's is marked by fades at the beginning and end, and consists of two sub-segments also separated by a transition to a fade, shots 38–89 and 90–123. In addition there are two further sub-sections indicated only by cuts in the first sub-segment, marking the move between the cabaret space containing Tom, shots 38–48, Amy's dressing-room and the space outside this room, shots 49–52, the cabaret space, shots 53–89; the next sub-segment commences outside Amy's dressing room, shot 90, then cuts to Tom in the cabaret space, shot 91. The script of *Morocco* was published by Lorimar (London: 1970).

27. Shots 53–59. Tom is joined by the girl he'd earlier made an assignation with. Amy appears again in shot 62 with Lo Tinto backstage, she appears onstage in shot 63.

28. The transition is marked by a fade.

29. Shots 95, 101, 103, 106.

30. In shots 108–113.

8   The Fetish of Ideology

1. Barthes, 'Diderot, Brecht, Eisenstein', pp. 76–7.

2. Stephen Heath, 'Lessons From Brecht', *Screen*, vol. 15, no. 2, 1974, p. 106.

3. Ibid, pp. 106–7.

4. Metz sees fetishism and voyeurism as additional structures which are important but are not determining of cinema as imaginary: 'The Imaginary Signifier – Disavowal, Fetishism', in *Psychoanalysis and Cinema – the Imaginary Signifier*, pp. 69–78.

5. Ben Brewster, Colin MacCabe and Stephen Heath, 'Reply to Julia Lesage', *Screen*, vol. 16, no. 2, 1975, p. 87.

6. Classical realism was discussed by Colin MacCabe in his essay, 'Realism and the Cinema: Notes on some Brechtian theses' in the same special issue on Brecht, *Screen*, vol. 15, no. 2, 1974.

7. Ben Brewster and Colin MacCabe, editorial to *Screen*, vol. 15, no. 1, 1974, p. 19.

8. This approach contrasts with the positions taken by Bellour, Mulvey and Doane who, while differing in their approach, each takes fetishism more specifically as a defence, a particular mechanism in play for the spectator in cinema – for the male spectator – but not necessarily constitutive of the cinematic-relation as such.

9. The denigration of women is a complex and diverse affair historically. The case of kinship again provides interesting cases of contra-

dictory approaches. Robin Fox, in his primarily functionalist approach to kinship, says of the Chinese patrilineal and patrilocal system that 'It obtained brides from other lineages to bear up sons to its name. Thus, the Chinese illustrate with harsh clarity the point about the lineage not having any use for its "non-reproductive" members (its "rubbish"). A woman has no role as sister and daughter, but only as wife and mother': *Kinship and Marriage*, p. 117. But Fox also acknowledges that the Tallensi people of northern Ghana, who have a similar system of lineage in which the daughters and sisters have no part in relation to their biological kin, nevertheless accord these women a role in clan and lineage affairs not available to the wives and mothers; 'What is more, they say, the bridewealth obtained for the women is important, because it enables the men of the lineage to obtain wives in their turn', pp. 118–19. That the Tallensi value their sisters appears here an ideological 'choice', for it has no function, it is not required by their marriage system.

10. Louis Althusser, 'Ideology and Ideological State Apparatuses' (1969), *Lenin and Philosophy and Other Essays*, p. 160. See also here his 'Freud and Lacan' (1964/1969) in the same volume, pp. 178–9. The epistemological assumptions of Althusser's theory in relation to ideology and its relative autonomy have been questioned by Paul Hirst, *On Law and Ideology* (London: Macmillan, 1979), ch. 3. Althusser's invocation of psychoanalysis and the imaginary relation of ideology have been addressed by Mladen Dolar in 'Beyond Interpellation', where he presents succinctly the opposition between Althusser's and Lacan's subject: *Qui Parle*, vol. 6, no. 2, 1993, pp. 75–80.

11. Lacan continues 'Hence it cannot be conceived without correlative knowledge. If the subject is capable of misrecognising something, he surely must know what this function has operated upon. There must surely be, behind his misrecognitiion, a kind of knowledge of what there is to misrecognise': *The Seminar of Jacques Lacan Book 1, Freud's Papers on Technique 1953–1954*, p. 167. His illustration – 'Take someone who is deluded, who lives in a state of misrecognition of the death of someone close to him' – draws on Freud's reference to two cases of young men who 'scotomised', avowed and disavowed, knowledge of the father's death: Freud, 'The Splitting of the Ego in Defence', p. 276.

12. Žižek, *The Sublime Object of Ideology*, pp. 28–9.

13. After Marcel Duchamp. See Penley, 'Feminism, Film Theory and the Bachelor Machines', in *The Future of an Illusion*, p. 57.

14. This 'fixing' has also been termed the suturing of the subject in the text, and has been discussed in Chapter 3.

15. Another term for this is 'The Name of the Father', the ideal agency which regulates legal, symbolic exchange, insofar as it is the obverse to 'the desire of the mother'. It is not the real father, but the Other of the mother.

16. Žižek, *The Sublime Object of Ideology*, p. 87.

17. These two processes of ideology and the formation of the subject are not therefore identical, hence we do not need to 're-make' the subject in order to re-make ideology.

18. Žižek, 'Hitchcock', *October*, no. 38, Fall 1986, p. 108. Harry's dead body is just another example of the many objects in Hitchcock's films which must drop out, or be put (back) in place – microfilm, a ring, a tune, a glove.

19. Lacan, *The Four Fundamental Concepts of Psycho-Analysis*, p. 101.

20. Barthes, *S/Z*, p. 4.

21. Ibid, p. 5.

22. Ibid, p. 5.

23. Lacan, *The Four Fundamental Concepts of Psycho-Analysis*, p. 75.

24. Ibid, pp. 75–6.

25. Christian Metz, 'Film and Dream: The Knowledge of the Subject', in *Psychoanalysis and Cinema*.

26. For Lacan the lure, or decoy, is not necessarily thereby a deception: 'The function of the lure, in this instance, is something else, something before which we should suspend judgement before we have properly measured its effects': *The Four Fundamental Concepts of Psycho-Analysis*, p. 100.

27. Lacan, ibid, pp. 103 and 112. Kohon's account of fetishism in the case of Mr M offers an example of Lacan's point. His patient tells Kohon '"I know quite a bit about what I want, what I like, what my desires are. I think I know myself fairly well. At the same time, there is something in me that I do not know. It's like a curtain, a veil separating me from what I need to know." "No", he corrected himself, "it's worse than that: it's not only that I don't know what's behind the curtain, but that I don't even know whether there is anything behind the curtain in the first place. What could happen if the curtain is opened?" he asked. "Is it worth knowing what I might need to know? Maybe better a devil you know, than one you didn't know".' :'Fetishism Revisited', pp. 216–17.

28. Julia Kristeva, 'Ellipsis on Dread and the Specular Seduction' (1975), trans. Dolores Burdick, *Wide Angle*, vol. 3, no. 3, p. 42. *Frayage* is the French translation of Freud's term *Bahnung*, in English 'facilitation'. For Freud, facilitation is the pathway which enables the movement of excitation between neurones in his early neurological model of the functioning of the psychical apparatus: *Project for a Scientific Psychology* (1950 [1895]), *SE* vol. 1, p. 300. Kristeva juxtaposes the term with *frayeur* – terror, dread – to produce a similarity of meaning from their similarity in sound in French, a connection which is not present etymologically.

29. Kristeva, 'Ellipsis on Dread and the Specular Seduction', p. 45.

30. Ibid, p. 42.

31. That is, the drives or primary processes, and for Kristeva – the semiotic. But, seduced to speculate, Kristeva labels terror as 'to do with the dependency on the mother' while seduction lies with 'an appeal addressed to the father'. While she invites a dangerous homogenisation in the categories 'man' and 'woman' by arguing that 'In that which the specular proposes to man and woman as a node connecting terror and seduction... man and woman find themselves differently', she is nevertheless right when she goes on to say 'But if they enter the game, they will both be led to cross both zones and attempt both identifications –

maternal, paternal. Test of sexual difference – of homosexuality, that brush with psychosis – they never stop letting it be intimated, even when they don't let it be seen: Eisenstein, Hitchcock.', ibid, pp. 45–6.

32. Barthes, *The Pleasure of the Text*, p. 63.

33. Ibid, pp. 47–8. The text in square brackets is Miller's original and indicates a change in the translation to follow more closely the French original.

34. Stephen Heath has commented of Barthes's distinction *plaisir/ jouissance* that

> English lacks a word able to carry the range of meaning in the term *jouissance* which includes enjoyment in the sense of a legal or social possession (enjoy certain rights, enjoy a privilege), pleasure, and, crucially, the pleasure of sexual climax. The problem would be less acute were it not that *jouissance* is specifically contrasted to *plaisir* by Barthes in his *Le Plaisir du texte* on the one hand a pleasure *(plaisir)* linked to cultural enjoyment and identity, to the cultural enjoyment of identity, to a homogenising movement of the ego; on the other a radically violent pleasure *(jouissance* which shatters – dissipates, loses – that cultural identity, that ego. ('Translator's Note', *Image-Music-Text*, p. 9.)

35. Linda Williams points to this process in Surrealist film: 'It is perhaps the final paradox of Surrealist film that, although it gives a concrete form to the fetish within its narrative, it simultaneously ruptures the fetish function of the cinematic institution as a whole': *Figures of Desire* (Berkeley: University of California Press, 1981), p. 218.

36. Barthes, *The Pleasure of the Text*, p. 44.

37. Ibid, p. 25.

38. Ibid, p. 21.

39. Ibid, p. 10.

40. Rose suggests that in *Powers of Horror* (1980), trans. Leon S. Roudiez (New York: Colombia University Press, 1982), Kristeva – as a response to the idealisation latent in her own formulations – was 'replying that the semiotic is no "fun"': 'Julia Kristeva – Take Two', in *Sexuality in the Field of Vision*, p. 155. Rose goes on to argue that while Kristeva's work 'has, however, been attractive to feminism because of the way she exposes the complacent identities of psychosexual life' it cannot found an oppositional politics:

> But as soon as we try to draw out of that exposure an image of femininity which escapes the straitjacket of symbolic forms, we fall straight into that essentialism and primacy of the semiotic which is one of the most problematic aspects of her work. And as soon as we try to make of it the basis for a political identity, we turn the concept inside out, since it was as a critique of identity that it was originally advanced. No politics without identity, but no identity which takes itself at its word. (Ibid, p. 157.)

41. Lyotard, 'Fiscourse Digure: The Utopia behind the Scenes of the Phantasy', p. 344.

42. Lyotard's reading here follows closely the view developed by Laplanche and Pontalis in 'Fantasy and the Origins of Sexuality' discussed earlier in Chapter 4.

43. Lyotard, 'Fiscourse Digure: The Utopia behind the Scenes of the Phantasy', p. 357. Lyotard's reference here is to the essay by J-B. Pontalis, 'L'Utopie freudienne', *L'arc*, 34, 1968, p. 14.

44. Rodowick, *The Difficulty of Difference*, p. 93. Rodowick seeks to displace identification in film in favour of a process of reading whereby 'Reading encounters the text as a relation of difference not identity', p. 138.

45. Mikkel Borch-Jacobsen, *Lacan, The Absolute Master*, trans. Douglas Brick (Stanford: Stanford University Press, 1991), p. 41.

46. Lacan, *Écrits, A Selection*, pp. 323–4.

47. Žižek, *For They Know Not What They Do*, p. 267 .

48. Freud, 'Reality in Neurosis and Psychosis', p. 187.

49. The problem of racial difference is not thereby determined by the problem of sexual difference, and the problem of the group and its other is clearly entwined with the problem of the subject and its other. This is only one aspect in the issue of racism which itself is, of course, not a singular phenomenon either historically or in our own contemporary period.

50. Žižek, *The Sublime Object of Ideology*, p. 45.

51. *The Reckless Moment* uses contingent elements from its contemporary social context, and of course the traditional nuclear family is the centre of the film, as the opening male voice-over emphasises. On the one hand these elements are only a mise en scène functioning as another form of fore-pleasure. The film is not about this social context, it is not about women's entrapment in the home and family. On the other hand this context is necessary for the fantasy to be played out: Lucia must be contained by something in order to for the wish to break out of that containment to be figured.

52. Homi K. Bhabha gives a powerful account of fantasy and the colonial other in his discussion, 'The Other Question – the Stereotype and Colonial Discourse', in *The Location of Culture* (London: Routledge, 1994). On the conjoining of sexual and racial fantasy in a discourse of racial and sexual difference see Sander Gilman, 'Black Bodies/White Bodies: Toward an Iconography of Female Sexuality in Late Nineteenth-Century Art, Medicine and Literature', *Critical Inquiry*, vol. 12, Autumn 1985, pp. 205–42.

53. On the question of the group's, or the nation's 'enjoyment', see Slavoj Žižek, 'Eastern Europe's Republics of Gilead', *New Left Review*, no. 183, pp. 50–6; and Glenn Bowman, 'Xenophobia, Fantasy and the Nation', in *The Anthropology of Europe*, eds Victoria A. Goddard, Josep R. Llobera and Cris Shore (Oxford: Berg, 1995).

54. Žižek, *The Sublime Object of Ideology*, pp. 87–8.

55. The notion of 'womb-envy' has been put forward as an apparent equivalent to the woman's 'penis-envy'. If this is so, in each case what is really sought is not what one lacks oneself but what seems to secure the enjoyment of the other.

56. This is not a question of sexual abuse, but a refusal of the child's difference, its enjoyment, and as a result the child is, in its relation to desire, bound to its parents for whom it has its being.

57. It is here that the importance of Laplanche's work on seduction and the child discussed in the chapter on the drive is again demonstrated.

58. Sandy Flitterman-Lewis, *To Desire Differently* (Urbana: University of Illinois Press, 1990), p. 2.

59. *Desperately Seeking Susan* was released in 1985, scripted by Leora Barish, it starred Rosanna Arquette as Roberta who is seeking Susan, played by Madonna. *Smooth Talk*, also released in 1985, was adapted from a short story by Joyce Carol Oates, and scripted by Tom Cole, Joyce Chopra's husband. Laura Dern plays Connie. *Blue Steel* was released in 1990, co-scripted by Kathryn Bigelow and Eric Red; it stars Jamie Lee Curtis as Megan. My analysis of these films will place them within Teresa de Lauretis's definition of the role of women's cinema, 'to enact the contradiction of female desire, and of women as social subjects, in the terms of narrative; to perform its figures of movement and closure, image and gaze, with the constant awareness that spectators are historically engendered in social pratices, in the real world, and in cinema too': *Alice Doesn't – Feminism, Semiotics, Cinema* (London: Macmillan, 1984), p. 156.

60. Joyce Carol Oates has commented 'Connie is shallow, vain, silly, hopeful, doomed – perhaps as I saw, and still see, myself? – but capable nonetheless of an unexpected gesture of heroism at the story's end': *The New York Times*, 23 March 1986.

61. And, Lacan says, 'This alienating *or* is not an abitrary invention, nor is it a matter of how one sees things. It is a part of language itself': *The Four Fundamental Concepts of Psycho-Analysis*, p. 212.

62. Ruby Rich, 'Good Girls, Bad Girls', *The Village Voice*, 15 April 1986, p. 67.

63. In pointing to a shift or change I don't think an 'original' and radical function of the fairytale was lost or expelled in the cultural transposition of these tales as a result of their coming to be written and published stories from the late seventeenth century on. In their pre-modern form the tales emphasised the arbitrariness of fate and desire, without explanation – things were so and they were incommensurable. In the early modern era the assumption that, by God's grace, through human will and endeavour things may be different, replaces fate with the moral failure of the individual, while the late modern era of the twentieth century has substituted rationality for morality. Modern tales speak their time and culture no less than earlier tales. What we want is not a pre-modern notion of the contingent but a post-modern squaring of rationality and the impossible real.

64. 'Observational' documentary film has also been termed direct cinema or *cinéma vérité*, although this last term derives from a French documentary tradition which, while similarly seeking a direct observational filming of reality, nevertheless also includes self-reflectively an acknowledgement of the process of film-making and the presence

of the film-maker. Joyce Chopra began her career as a documentary film-maker working within the direct cinema tradition with, for example, Richard Leacock on *A Happy Mother's Day* (1965) and *The Fischer Quintuplets* (1965).

65. Rich, 'Good Girls, Bad Girls', p. 67.

66. *Monthly Film Bulletin*, vol. 57, November 1990. My discussion of *Blue Steel* draws on Pam Cook's review of the film in the same issue while trying to suggest a rather different role to the phallicism of the film.

67. Later Megan will exercise her new authority and obtain the wish behind it when she arrests her father after discovering he has again been hitting her mother. But this concludes in a reconciliation, for on their way to the police station Megan relents and accepts in good faith her father's promises to change. Here Megan gives up her *jouissance*, her enjoyment, as having the phallus. The answering real of her desire is, however, waiting at her parent's house, where, on their return they find Eugene, the mocking proof of her wish, but also failure, to be the law.

68. Eugene appears as a projection of Megan's worst fears, blocking her every attempt to act powerfully. The film also implies that Eugene is part of Megan's dream-world by showing her nightmare of falling from the helicopter, and Eugene's mocking refusal to help, after their earlier helicopter flight together over the New York skyline.

69. This image of the protagonist 'expended', exhausted, is also found at the end of *Predator* (John McTiernan, 1987), as Arnold Schwarzenegger – having despatched the alien hunter and now rescued by helicopter from the forest – sits huddled, grasping his arms around his legs. Such a scene is therefore available to a generic reading in relation to 1980s American action pictures.

Index